THE BOOK OF
BANNING

A Collection of Biographical Sketches of Bannings throughout the Centuries in Europe and the USA, Set in Their Genealogical and Historical Context

Includes Genealogies of the Netherlands, England, and Germany

Elisabeth van Schaick-Banning

HERITAGE BOOKS
2008

HERITAGE BOOKS

AN IMPRINT OF HERITAGE BOOKS, INC.

Books, CDs, and more—Worldwide

For our listing of thousands of titles see our website
at
www.HeritageBooks.com

Published 2008 by
HERITAGE BOOKS, INC.
Publishing Division
100 Railroad Ave. #104
Westminster, Maryland 21157

International Standard Book Numbers
Paperbound: 978-0-7884-3286-6
Clothbound: 978-0-7884-7280-0

TABLE OF CONTENTS

ACKNOWLEDGEMENTS

First and foremost, and in keeping with the traditions represented in this book, I dedicate this to my own family. To my father, who gave me the name. To my mother, who instilled in me the value of it. To my brothers, nieces and nephews, and those generations yet to follow: for whom the original translation of their lineage was a cherished duty I consider as their birthright, and which inspired this project. My beloved brother and my aunt have passed the way of those within the book, but they are close to mind and I dedicate this to their memory. Last but most certainly not least, to my husband, sons and daughter who, while they were inclined to flee when they so much as heard the name, congenially and more-or-less permanently surrendered the dining room table, circumvented piles of paper for years, eased my frustration with computer problems and accepted with total equanimity and humour my commitment to this quest as an inevitable matter of course.

I am indebted to those Bannings who assiduously recorded the data of the genealogies in the past, which formed the backbone of this book, and without which it would not exist: Mary Elizabeth, Pierson Worrall, Josephus Alphonsus Willibrordus, Jan and Leroy.

I am grateful to many others who took the time to contribute and assist in various ways: the learned participants of Germanic language groups at Yahoo.com, for keeping me in line (not always effectively), with a wealth of information and wit: Harry, Dirk, Ingemar, Fabio, Johnny, Kees, Lars, Rick, Kevin and others. I owe Alric van den Broek my special appreciation and thanks for his critical dissection of the first chapter, advice which I took to heart but did not always implement. Stubbornness is cited as a family trait. To Thomas Weyn Banningh and Jan Pieter Ouweltjes, for generously sharing their information and research, for their own pursuit of it, but above all for sharing my fervor. Carina and André, Jürgen, Knud, Jan and Michiel Banning, Jan Bennink, Saskia Barker, Frans van Heijningen, Carol Marston, Nicholas Barratt, Stephen Millar, Marjolein van Gessel, Paul Cavill, John Haines, Jarich Renema, Marianne Theunis, Karin Haverkamp, Margaret Rojas and Maike Brandes all kindly took time and effort to make this story more complete. Numerous others generously contributed photographic material and information, and there were organisations that, even though it is their line of work, responded to my queries 'above and beyond the call of duty'.
Thank you.

This did not start off as a book, nor does it end here. It grew from the translation of my own genealogy, that of Maurits Arnoldus Banning of Friesland, the Netherlands. Having encountered so many interesting people in the process, I researched their past and collected their stories. As more Bannings emerged from the anonymity of the archives, the story grew.

And yet, it's growth is not complete. New facts turn up every day. A Banning Foundation is a goal several people would like to realize in the near future, to collect all the available data and to preserve and protect all that exists so far. DNA research is now underway with a Banning Surname Project at www.dnaheritage.com, to discover more about the relation between the various branches throughout the world. Several European genealogies are avidly being researched and assimilated with an aim to publication, with inclusion of the DNA results.

In writing this book, I made a conscious choice to elaborate only on those Bannings of the past, and deliberately excluded those of the present. There are several reasons for not writing on those living now. Firstly, I do not know them all and would definitely overlook many who merit mention. Secondly, their contribution to history is still in the making and their story incomplete. Thirdly, much of this information is not in the public domain and fourthly, the text was voluminous and arduous enough without venturing into new frontiers! With a heritage such as this, I am confident that the Bannings of today will provide sufficient material for a sequel, should our descendants feel compelled to write one in the future.

As a tribute to Pierson Worrall Banning, author of The First Banning Genealogy, I feel compelled to quote the words here which he wrote in 1909 in capital letters, for emphasis: "It would be of the greatest value not only to the Banning genealogy as a whole, but to each and every branch so handled, if those having the time would investigate their own special lines as thoroughly as possible, making every effort to obtain all missing facts as shown in this book, and where possible to enlarge on the statements about the individuals who were of prominence or before the public." Although this was almost a century ago, I am sure he would have been gratified that his work is still read and valued, and that it has been enlarged on as he hoped. On his title page he writes: "So far as I know being an excellent foundation for further investigation," and this belief has most definitely proven well-founded. It is incomprehensible how he managed to complete his work in only ten months, with access to no more than a typewriter and carbon paper, postal services probably still by stage coach, and perhaps a primitive telephone.

7

In spite of the most conscientious research, proof-reading and editing of this book, I am sure that errors will come to light. New facts will be found that perhaps contradict some mentioned. The genealogists and researchers who provided much of the information made errors in their time, many of which I was able to rectify. They too, wrote in good faith and with the means and resources available in their day and age, and had it not been for their efforts, very little of our heritage would have been recorded at all. Their place in this history is well-deserved. Pierson Worrall Banning noted in 1909: "It is hoped that all persons finding errors or correction items of any nature which they can substantiate, or new facts not shown herein, will not only insert them where they belong, but at the same time be so kind as to communicate them to the compiler of this book." I, too, welcome efforts to rectify and substantiate any errors found in this text.

Pierson Worrall lamented the fact that almost nothing was known on the Bannings in the Netherlands and expressed the hope that this would some day be researched. It is regrettable that he was unaware that three centuries of the Amsterdam Banning genealogy had already been set out and published even before he embarked on his own monumental work. J. E. Elias, a Dutch historian and author in 1903, is mentioned by Pierson Worrall in passing but to whom he had no access. I hope, with this publication in English, to have set this to rights.

He goes on to say: "I trust that at some later date, with the aid of others who may know of facts that have been omitted, or corrections that should be made, to finally get a history complete enough to put into book form for distribution to those interested, and toward this end solicit the aid of any in position to co-operate with me in any manner whatsoever. I further trust that this information will be found of value to those desiring facts it contains, and that from time to time, as the generations come and go, revised works may be brought out, and thus the record be kept complete." Leroy Banning followed well in his footsteps, devoting years of research to produce The Banning Branches in 1997, a worthy American sequel to The First Banning Genealogy. In the Netherlands, Josephus Alphonsus Willibrordus Banning's equally monumental genealogical record was published in 1934, members of the family of Weyn Banningh compiled valuable records in subsequent years, as did Jan Banning in 1984.

The material for The Book of Banning accrued for many years before, like a storm gathering and breaking, it came to completion within two years to become what you now have before you, a largely European complement to the American publications. It represents a comprehensive perspective of what has been, for those who follow.

PREFACE
What's in a name?

While doing research for this book an intriguing point came up: who is a Banning and who is not? Is being a Banning, or anyone else for that matter, dependant on the name or on the actual biological connection? The following variations were encountered:

1) The most obvious is the issue of adoption. Jeremiah Banning, for example, adopted the three children of the widow Mary Gossage from her first marriage and gave them his name. Descendants of the two boys are known as Bannings, although their link to Jeremiah was a legal and not a biological one.

2) In the middle ages in the Netherlands it was not uncommon for a son to take the name of his mother: Jan Wuytiers Banning, Jan Banning Coeckebacker, Frans Banning Cocq. If the son of a Banning female qualifies as a Banning descendant, than why not a daughter? The mother of Barbara Villiers, mistress of King Charles II, was Mary Banning. Although Barbara carried the name of her father, she was as much Banning in terms of physical heredity as, for example, Frans Banning Cocq of the Nightwatch. Christina Banning retained her name upon marriage (now very common) and was included among the males in her genealogy, (Netherlands, 1745-1778) her offspring therefore also carry the Banning name.

3) Occasionally people acquired the name by other means: a former slave could have taken the name of its owner, tenants often took the name of the homestead on which they lived, such as the painter Jacob van Ruisdael, who lived on the estate Ruysdael belonging to Gerrit Banning's father-in-law Ruysch). The father of Knud Banning in Denmark purchased the name from a list at the request of his employer, who felt that his own name (Olesen) was too common.

4) The spelling of the name, particularly until the end of the middle ages, varied sometimes considerably, even within one family and on one legal document. If Banning was the father, is Banninck the son considered a descendant?

5) In Germany, for a time it was custom for a husband to take his wife's name, as was done at the homestead Banninghof near Wettringen (Germany), where Frau Julia Banning resided and whose husband surrendered his own family name, taking that of his wife.

6) Even if, after weeks of research, we jubilantly find verification that one was the son of another, who is to say that the proverbial travelling salesman was not the actual father and that for generations

9

after historians have been barking up the wrong family tree, so to speak?

With such variables, which occur in any genealogy, we might wonder which criteria are required as genuine qualifications to claim a specific heritage. If the facts are known they at least merit a footnote, which is perhaps, when in doubt, better than banning a Banning from any mention at all. In this light family names could at most be considered markers on a trail. This publication does not endeavour to follow that trail but to introduce the traveller to those we meet in passing.

1 BACK TO BAN
History of a name

A number of the current family names in Europe can testify to having a very ancient history, often having spread throughout the world. The family name BANNING is one of these, which is said to appear in records as early as the ninth century.

Strictly speaking, Banning is a word. A word is a (written) representation of a combination of sounds. The combination of sounds is intended to convey a specific meaning. The word Banning thus came, at one time, into use as a name to designate a specific individual and his people. In Western Europe surnames acquired systematic and widespread usage after the French Revolution. Before that time they were generally only held by families with a certain social status. Since the French Revolution it became mandatory to record births, marriages and deaths in public records, so that tracing a family ancestry back to this time is not all that arduous. Between the 17th and the 19th century, many churches began to record such events and often, with a bit of luck, the existence of an individual can be found in those records preserved, or on grave markers still in existence. Some churches kept records as early as the 16th century. Previous to this time, individual names can be found in charters, land transfers, prison records, etc., if for some juridical purpose there was reason to record them. For the genealogist, this is a matter of providence and perseverance. As a rule, only persons of social or political status, or historical significance, were recorded in other sources , thereby enabling a scant number of future generations to discover more about their heritage. In this respect the Banning name frequently found it's way into the annals of history and we therefore know without doubt that the name is old and respected.

Banning, as with any surname, can be viewed in a genealogical context, an etymological or historical context, genetic, cultural and geographic. Superimposing one discipline upon another is neither scholarly nor accurate. Possible sources of the origin of Banning as a name have been explored in this book, which is not to say that any one or more of these are an actual, proven source of ancestry of Bannings known, nor that one is related to another. The name may have originated from some place or time or person(s) unrecorded, but it may equally have originated from one or more of those mentioned. In any case, they serve as examples of what might have been.

A century ago, genealogists[1] said the name Banning was of Danish origin, originally in reference to a class of 'Hero Worshippers' and signifying a home or dwelling. References are said to be found in legends of the Crusades and in the Scot and Bard Songs, the earliest ballads on record, where we find 'Becca ruled the Banings'. Becca is alleged to have been the Hero or ruler of the Banning clan of Vikings. Where did this claim come from?

There are two types of Old English poetry: the heroic, the sources of which are pre-Christian Germanic myth, history, and custom; and the Christian. Although nearly all Old English poetry is preserved in only four manuscripts - indicating that what has survived is not necessarily the best or most representative - much of it is regarded as high literary quality. Moreover, Old English heroic poetry is among the earliest extant in all of Germanic literature. It is thus the nearest we can come to the oral pagan literature of Germanic culture, and is also of inestimable value as a source of knowledge about many aspects of Germanic society. The 7th-century work known as Widsith (143 lines) is one of the earliest Old English poems found in the Exeter Book, and is thus of particular historic and linguistic interest.

Widsith recounts his wanderings as a Germanic minstrel and relates several legends. However, Widsith (meaning 'wide journey') was primarily a tale, and intended as such. Widsith was a bard and not a historian. His poetic account contains many discrepancies in time and place, fact and fiction, and although numerous tribes and persons are well-known to history, others are mentioned for which no historic verification has been found to date.

The poem gives an excellent – if not always historically reliable - description of minstrel life in the Germanic heroic age, and it is here (on line 19) that we find one of the first references to Banning[2]:

"Widsith (verse indeterminate Saxon)

1   Widsið maðolade,   wordhord onleac,
         se þe monna mæst   mægþa ofer eorþan,
         folca geondferde;   oft he on flette geþah
         mynelicne maþþum.   Him from Myrgingum
5

         æþele onwocon.   He mid Ealhhilde,
         fælre freoþuwebban,   forman siþe
         Hreðcyninges   ham gesohte

---

[1] P.W. Banning, *The First Banning Genealogy*, Chicago, 1909; Banning, M.E., private letter dated 1 January 1897
[2] The Exeter Book, *Widsith, The Wanderer*, compiled +/- 975 AD

```
        eastan of Ongle,        Eormanrices,
        wraþes wærlogan.        Ongon þa worn sprecan:
10

        "Fela ic monna gefrægn      mægþum wealdan!
        Sceal þeodna gehwylc       þeawum lifgan,
        eorl æfter oþrum        eðle rædan,
        se þe his þeodenstol       geþeon wile.
        þara wæs Hwala         hwile selast,
15

        ond Alexandreas        ealra ricost
        monna cynnes,        ond he mæst geþah
        þara þe ic ofer foldan       gefrægen hæbbe.
        ætla weold Hunum,        Eormanric Gotum,
        Becca Baningum,        Burgendum Gifica.
20

        Casere weold Creacum       ond Cælic Finnum,
        Hagena Holmrygum       ond Heoden Glommum.
        Witta weold Swæfum,       Wada Hælsingum,
        Meaca Myrgingum,       Mearchealf Hundingum.
        þeodric weold Froncum,       þyle Rondingum,"
        etc.
```

Translation: (Douglas B. Killings)[3]

1   "Thus Widsith spoke, revealing a treasury of words,
        he to the greatest degree of the tribes over the Earth,
        and its peoples have travelled through; often he in the hall
            received,
        valuable treasures. He from the Myrgings

5   his noble blood sprang. He with Ealhhilde,
        the beloved peace-weaver, was on a journey,
        the Victory King's village they sought
        to the East of Angle, Eormanric,
        the angry and traitorous. Thus he spoke these many words:

10   "Many people have I talked to, rulers mighty in power!
        Obliged these people are in virtuous conduct to live,
        one earl after another their country to rule,
        he who his throne wishes it to prosper!
        There was Hwala for a while the most noble,

---

[3] Widsith, a verse translation by Douglas B. Killings;
http://www.georgetown.edu/faculty/ballc/oe/widsith-trans.html; accessed July 2004

15   and Alexander's entire kingdom
as well as his kin, and he was the most that thrived
which I have often on this Earth have heard reports of.
Attila ruled the Huns, Eormanric the Goths,
Becca the Banings, the Burgundians by Gifica.

20   Casere ruled the Creeks and Caelic the Finns,
Hagena the Holm-Riggs and Heoden the Gloms.
Witta ruled the Swaefe, Wada the Halsings,
Meaca the Myrgings, Mearchealf the Hundings.
Theodric ruled the Franks, Thyle the Rondings,"
etc.

Widsith's lyrical account of his wanderings has been subjected to exhaustive study, and scholars throughout the centuries have attempted to identify the various tribes mentioned by the roving Germanic minstrel. References in literature pertaining to the tribe or clan of the Banings, ruled by Becca, are scant, but do exist. Both Chambers and Malone, in their extensive studies of Widsith, mention the Banings and refer to the *Origo Gentis Langobardorum* which calls them the 'Bainaib'[4], which they assert is possibly to be identified with Ptolemy's 'Banochaemae' in the 1st century (although some authorities contend that 'Bainai/Banochaemae' refers to Bohemia). However, Ptolemy distinguishes between the 'Banochaemae' and the inhabitants of Bohemia. He places his 'Banochaemae' in the region of the Elbe River, to the east of the 'Cherusci' and 'Chamavi', i.e. around Torgau, Saxony, in east central Germany, a port on the Elbe [Albis] River. (In 1970 a large Saxon cemetery was discovered in Liebersee[5], near Torgau, with over 2000 graves. The cemetery was in use for a prolonged period of time, from about 1000 BC to the early middle ages. The region of Liebersee was characterised by many small and diverse cultural groups, a cultural diversity reflected in the archaeological finds.)

      Ptolemy's reference[6]: "Below the Semnones the Silingae have their abodes, and below the Burguntae are the Lugi Omani; below these are the Lugi Diduni extending as far as the Asciburgius mountains, and below the Silingae are the Calucones on both banks of the river Albis; below whom are the Chaerusci and the Camavi extending as far as Melibocus mountain, from whom toward the east along the Albis river are the Banochaemae; above whom are the Batini, and above these, but below

---

[4] *Origo Gentium Langobardum* , c. 650 AD
[5] http://www.archaeologie-online.de/magazin/fundpunkt/2004/04/liebersee_5.php; accessed June 2004
[6] C. Ptolemeus, *Geographia*, 150 AD; abridged, from Edward Luther Stevenson (1932) , Book 2, Chapter 10

the Asciburgius mountains are the Corconti and the Lugi Buri extending as far as the source of the Vistula river; first below these are the Sidones, then the Gotini, then the Visburgi above the Orcynium forest."

Malone[7] concludes that the Banings 'were a tribe of middle Germany', and also places them near the River Elbe in Germany, which was Saxon territory. The *Origo Gentis Langobardorum* (a brief account of Lombard history written ca. 650 AD) links the Banings/Bainaib with the Burgundians, also mentioned together in Widsith. The Origo reference[8] reads: "Et moverunt se exhinde langobardi, et venerunt in golaidam, et postea possiderunt aldonus anthaib et bainaib seu et burgundaib; et dicitur, quia fecerunt ...": " Then the Longobardians left their country and came to Golaida, and thereupon they occupied Aldonus, Anthaib, Bainaib, and Burgundaib....". Golaida was localized on the Elbe, in middle Germany. (T. and F. Meijer[9] note that it is very uncertain where Golaida was located; perhaps in Luenenburg Neder-Saxon on the left bank of the Elbe, Anthaib perhaps between the Oder and the Weichsel, Banaib perhaps to the north of Bohemia and Vurgundaib possibly on the left bank of the Elbe.)

The *Reallexikon der Germanische Altertumskunde*[10] (*The Encyclopaedia of Germanic Antiquity*) mentions the Baningas as follows: "The Baningas are mentioned together with the Burgendas in Wids. 19, a tribe in the east Germanic region called Bainaib, which is the name of a district of eastern Germany adjacent to Burgundaib, below the regions where the Langobardian migration occurred. The tribal name, in Goth Bainos, Bainjos is related to Bainiggos just as later Flanders was related to Fleming, and probably refers to the meaning 'just' and 'accommodating, hospitable'. See also Langobardians 6 and Helvecones."

Gudmund Schütte (1872-1958), an erudite Danish philologist and historian, studied the tribes mentioned by Widsith. In his book *Gotthiod und Utgard* he looks more closely at the Banings. The German translates as follows:

"A previously unexplained tribal name Báningas is mentioned in the old English account *Widsith*, next to Burgundern, prominent in the group of the 'European great powers'. Correspondingly, the *Origo Langobardorum* mentions the region of Baynaib adjacent to Burgundaib. And Ptolemy cites the names Böhmen in the more basterdised form of Bainochaimai. Until now, there was no background on this mysterious name and it remained unexplained; but this was in itself insignificant: a

---

[7] K.Malone, *Angelistica, Widsith*, Rosenkilde and Bagger, Copenhagen 1962, vol. VIII, p. 130
[8] *Origo Gentium Langobardum* c. 650 AD
[9] T. and M. Meijer,, Athenaeum Polak and van Gennep, Amsterdam, 1999
[10] J. Hoops, *Reallexikon der Germanische Altertumskunde*, Trübner, Strassburg, 1911, p. 165

people honoured with a major role among the European great powers cannot have been an insignificant people, they must have played a major role in Germanic heroic legends. Actually, a neighboring people, whose role in Germanic history is quite outstanding, has now been identified, whose Germanic name was previously unknown, i.e the Sarmatian Pannoniens. Since the beginning of our time calculation and until after the year 500 AD, the Sarmatians take an important political position and hold themselves next to the leading Germanic tribes in a more steady 'entente cordiale' with the Quadic Sweben. The last outstanding leader of the Sarmatians was Beuca, who in the year 469 AD, together with the Quaden (Sweben) unfortunately fought against the Ostgoths, cf. Jordanes LIV, 277. Now the sovereign of the Baninger in 'Widsith' is, in actual fact, named Becca, and the subsequent conclusion is that we have here no one other than the Sarmatian sovereign Beuca before us. The name Báningas, or the older Bainingóz, would signify 'Pannonier'. The Germanic form follows the phonetic written form, so that in a more recent development 'p' was changed to 'b', as in several south German derivations such as 'Blatten Sea' = Pelso, 'Bettau' = 'Poetovio', 'Barten' = 'Partanum'. (The present forms Platten, Pettau and Partenkirchen are influenced by the high German phonetic version, although the 't' is missing). See my article 'The Nationality of the Baninger' ('P. B. Beitrage' LVII, 230 ff.) and Bruinier, 'The Germanic Hero Legend', S. 114." [11]

G. Schütte includes a map[12] in his book of the tribal settlements, illustrating the location of the Baninger/Sarmatian tribe as he envisioned it.

[11] Gudmund Schütte, *Gotthiod und Utgard*; Altgermanische Sagengeographie in neuer Auffassung; republished under auspices of the Carlsbergfonds; Copenhagen: Aschehoug dansk forlag, G. M. Steffensen & Co. Jena: Frommannsche Buchhandlung, Walter Biedermann, 1935, p. 46-47.
[12] Gudmund Schütte, *Gotthiod und Utgard*; Altgermanische Sagengeographie in neuer Auffassung; republished under auspices of the Carlsbergfonds; Copenhagen: Aschehoug dansk forlag, G. M. Steffensen & Co. Jena: Frommannsche Buchhandlung, Walter Biedermann, 1935, p. 98

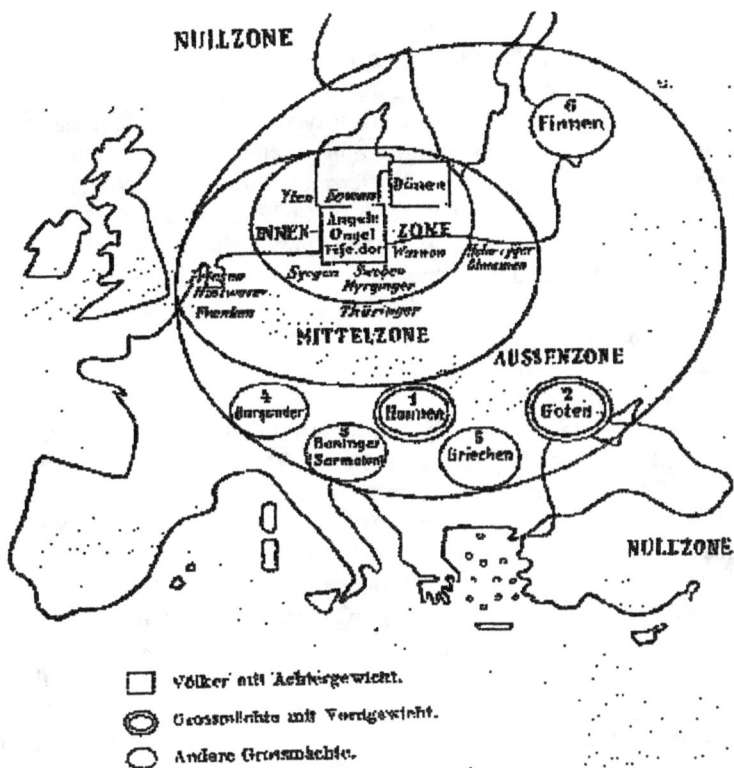

NULLZONE

INNEN-ZONE

MITTELZONE

AUSSENZONE

NULLZONE

NULLZONE

□ Völker mit Achsergewicht.

◎ Grossmächte mit Vorrgewicht.

○ Andere Grossmächte.

Fig. 3. Die Zonen in »Widsith I«.

Die Schweden sind in obiger Skizze nicht verzeichnet, weil es eine Streitfrage ist, wo die Handlungsszene des in W. I erwähnten Schwedenkönigs Ongendþeow liegt. — in Schweden oder in der Nachbarschaft der Angeln.
Vgl. § 39.

1. 'The Zones of Widsith' according to Gudmund Schütte, showing the 'Baninger' tribe in 3);

from Gotthiod und Utgard; Altgermanische Sagengeographie in neuer Auffassung; 1935

While some academics find Gudmund Schütte's theory quite plausible, others dismiss it as highly improbable. Soon after the publication of Schütte's Gotthiod und Utgard, Siegfried Gutenbrunner[13] wrote a lengthy article entitled 'The Origin of the Baininge', contesting Schütte's claim that the tribe was equated with the Sarmations, and Schütte's reasoning that the king, or chieftain, Becca, was none other than Bikki. His argument was basically that the linguistic parallels drawn by Schütte were

---

[13] Siegfried Gutenbrunner, Die Herkunft der Baininge, Beiträge zur Geschichte der Deutschen Sprache und Literatur, Max Niemeyer Verlag, Halle (Saale) 1936, vol. 60, p. 339-350

unrealistic, and that an assumption that Becca and Beuca were the same was neither well-founded nor a basis for identity of a tribe.

Gutenbrunner did not dispute the existence of a tribe called Baininge, he merely stated that their identity was not as Schütte claimed. He submitted references to Bainingus, a high-ranking civic official to the Frankish King Pipins II, (he actually referred to Pipins I, which must have been in error, as Pipins I reigned from 628-639 AD and Pipins II from 670-714 AD), who is mentioned in 700 AD in two charters in Echternach, Luxemburg; the first time the name was officially recorded. He states that the name otherwise only occurred a few times in southern Germany – Lorsch and Salzburg. He says that the names Bainus, Baino and Baynenchaim would have a common root, and that the oldest known Bainus was the Bishop of Terouanne in France, who reigned from 701-709 AD. Gutenbrunner justifiably had reason to believe that this Bishop Bainus and Bainingus were the same person. He suggested that perhaps Schütte had been misled by these references. Gutenbrunner emphasised the link with the Burgundians, mentioned by earlier historians, and was in agreement with the supposition put forth by others that the tribe would have been located in middle or northern Germany, on the Elbe.

Schütte reiterated with 'The Controversial Baininge'[14]. He conceded on several points to Gutenbrunner, but raised a few questions as well in his own defense. Both gentlemen, however, were basing their arguments largely (but not entirely) on Widsith, placing significance on the sequence of tribal names in the poem, and the premises that his was a historical and factual relaas, which in itself is soundly contested.

The subject was raised again in 1962. K. Malone, in *Anglistica: Widsith*, cites numerous historians who have debated the identity of the Banings. He concludes with a reference to R.W. Chambers:
"Chambers in his note on Widsith 19 (p. 191) called attention to the fact that in the Origo 'the land of the Bains is linked with that of the Burgundians, just as here [i.e. in Widsith 19] Banings and Burgundians are classed together.' The further connection with the Bainochaimai of Ptolemy makes it possible to say with some assurance that the Banings were a tribe of middle Germany, and to reject with finality such identifications as that of Schütte with the Sarmatians."[15] In view of the fact that the Sarmations were related to the Scythians, further south, this seems to be a reasonable argument.

(Malone[16] states that R. Much (1889) cited the Bainobaudes in reference to the Banings, saying that he reaffirmed this identification with

---

[14] Gudmund Schütte, *Die Umstrittenen Baininge, Beiträge zur Geschichte der Deutschen Sprache und Literatur*, Max Niemeyer Verlag, Halle (Saale) 1936, vol. 62, p. 460-463
[15] K. Malone, *Anglistica: Widsith*, Rosenkilde and Bagger, Copenhagen, 1962, vol. XIII, p. 130
[16] K. Malone, *Anglistica: Widsith*, Rosenkilde and Bagger, Copenhagen, 1962, vol. XIII,

the Banings in 1893, and in his description of the Banings in Hoops *Reallexikon der Germanische Altertumskunde*. However, there appears to be no such reaffirmation in this passage, nor is the relevance clear, as Bainobaudes was a military commander of the Roman Cornutii in a historic battle fought in 243 AD, described by the Greek soldier and historian Ammianus Marcellinus in his *Historiae Liber*.)

J. Marquart[17] (1912) specified the Germanic tribal name Banochaemae as mentioned by Ptolemy, although C. Müller took this name to be a corruption of the Bohemians. Müller's assertion (or assumption) was cast in doubt by O. Cuntz in his *Die Geographie des Ptolomeus* (1923). Malone assures the reader that Cuntz's doubts would have been verified, had he known of the Baningum of Widsith and the Bainaib of the Origo, name-forms which support the reading of Ptolemy, who differentiated quite clearly between the Banochaemae and the Bohemians.

Becca, as 'King' (chieftain) of the Banings, is mentioned in several sources, and identified with 'Beocca'. Price and Redin[18] (1826) identified Becca with the treacherous, Icelandic Bikki, or Bicca, as did Chambers[19] and Schütte[20]. Both Gutenbrunner[21] and Malone[22] however, are adamant in his dismissal of this conjecture. Both state that there is no etymological connection, neither is Bikki referred to anywhere as a Baning or in connection with the Baning tribe. Malone feels that Becca and Bikki have become confused because of the similarity of the names.

Many of the tribes which made up the Germanic migration to the continent are said to have had their origins in Scandinavia, although this is debated among scholars. Some time before the first century they became spread along the European coasts in parts of Germany, the

---

p. 129
[17] K. Malone, *Anglistica: Widsith*, Rosenkilde and Bagger, Copenhagen, 1962, vol. XIII,
p. 130
[18] K. Malone, *Anglistica: Widsith*, Rosenkilde and Bagger, Copenhagen, 1962, vol. XIII,
p. 131
[19] R.W. Chambers, *Widsith, A Study in Old English Heroic Legend*, Cambridge University Press, 1912, p. 191
[20] Gundmund Schütte, *Gotthiod und Utgard*; Altgermanische Sagengeographie in neuer Auffassung; republished under auspices of the Carlsbergfonds; Copenhagen: Aschehoug dansk forlag, G. M. Steffensen & Co. Jena: Frommannsche Buchhandlung, Walter Biedermann, 1935, p. 46-47.; and *Die Umstrittenen Baininge, Beiträge zur Geschichte der Deutschen Sprache und Literatur*, Max Niemeyer Verlag, Halle (Saale) 1936, vol. 62, p. 460-463
[21] Siegfried Gutenbrunner, *Die Herkunft der Baininge, Beiträge zur Geschichte der Deutschen Sprache und Literatur*, Max Niemeyer Verlag, Halle (Saale) 1936, vol. 60, p. 339-350
[22] K. Malone, *Anglistica: Widsith*, Rosenkilde and Bagger, Copenhagen, 1962, vol. XIII, p. 132

Netherlands and Denmark. Between 350 - 550 AD the tide of the Migration of Nations swept across western Europe, following on the heels of the collapse of the Roman Empire, thereby forming new colonies in the newly conquered areas. For the first time large organised Germanic states appeared.

The northern half of the Netherlands had been Germanic territory since the earliest settlement of Germanic peoples in the country between the Rhine and the Elbe (Germany), dating back to at least 500 BC.

In the Netherlands, the Saxons first established permanent settlements in the area now known as the province of Overijssel, around 500 AD. The Saxons lived communally and all lands were originally used in common. Over time, the residents had their own freehold areas to farm and each freehold farm was passed on from the previous generation to the next heir. The principle farmsteads in the area were called 'erven', or fiefs. These fiefs, or homesteads, included land for the vassal's personal use but the large grazing pastures, fields of heather, forests, and peat bogs were collectively managed and used by all. Dr. B.H. Slicher van Bath[23] mentions numerous fiefs in the Province of Overijssel with variations of the name Banning, between 933-1500 AD. These fiefs, as well as various persons bearing the name, can be found today in numerous charters and other documents in the archives. These are individually specified in context in the chapter on (Medieval) Homesteads.

The major Germanic states in Europe were the Jutish, Saxon, Anglo-Saxon, Frankish, Burgundian, West-Gothic, East-Gothic, Vandal, and Frisian. (Frisian is still spoken in the province of Friesland in the Netherlands and is the Germanic language most closely resembling modern English; the Saxon language was the predecessor of the Old English language. One key historical figure in Frisian history is King Finn Folcwalding (sixth century), who also makes an appearance in the Anglo-Saxon epics (*Widsith, Beowulf* and the *Finnsburgh* fragment.))

The most northerly border of Clovis's Frankish empire in the Netherlands of the sixth century was formed by the cities Utrecht and Dorestad, neighbouring the Frisian territory at the mouth of the Rhine. After the death of Clovis and the ensuing Frankish power struggle, the Frisians captured Utrecht and Dorestad. Both cities would stay Frisian for over a hundred years (511 – 628 AD). The capture of these cities was of very great importance to the Frisians, since they were the gateways of trade from the Saxon and Frankish hinterlands to the North Sea. In the sixth and the seventh centuries the Frisians were the major traders on the North Sea, which was called 'Mare Frisicum' during this period.

In the 10th century a number of feudal, semiautonomous vassal states emerged in this particular region, owing allegiance to the Holy

---

[23] Dr. B.H. Slicher van Bath, *Mensch en Land in de Middeleeuwen*, Van Gorcum & Comp. N.V., Assen, Utrecht, 1944

Roman Empire but enjoying many privileges. Among the more important of such states were the bishopric of Utrecht, the duchies of Brabant and Gelre, and the lands held by the counts of Zeeland and the increasingly powerful counts of Holland. Again, the name Banning, and variations thereof, are found both as place names and as a family name in numerous old archives and charters of East Frisia, the bishopric of Utrecht and the duchy of Gelre from the 10th century on. These, too, are listed in their historical context in the chapter on (Medieval) Homesteads.

Around 450 AD Angles, Saxons, Jutes and a Frisian fraction crossed the North Sea and established the Anglo-Saxon Empire, (currently known as England), settling around the River Thames in southern and eastern Britain. The fact that numerous place names in this region end with '-ing' attest to Saxon influence. Place names ending in 'ham', (meaning settlement, manor or homestead) are reckoned to belong to early Saxon place names, (as well as those ending in '-ley' and '-ing'). Many such villages were founded by leaders or chiefs, after whom the village was named[24]. The personal name (i.e. Ban, Banno) followed by '-ham' indicates so and so's village. Another source[25] states that place-names ending in '-ham', '-ingaham' and '-ingas' are indicative of Germanic settlement. 'Ham' means a settlement, '-ingaham' the settlement of a particular people (i.e.Banningham) and '-ingas' (i.e. Baningas) was a clan designation.

One peculiarity of the language was closely studied by Dr. Slicher van Bath[26] and described in his book Mensch en Leven in de Middeleeuwen (People and how they lived in the Middle Ages). Dr. Slicher van Bath's extensive research focuses on the Eastern provinces of the Netherlands.

He emphasises that there is one specific name suffix peculiar to this particular geographical area: the suffix '-ing', which is also particularly indigenous to Eastern England. In the Netherlands, these names only occur outside of the Eastern provinces in insignificant numbers. The author states that the origin of names comprising '-ing', as an entity, dates only from the 12th century, but the compound of a name (e.g. Bann, Benno) with the suffix '–ing' dates back to the 9th century or earlier. Significantly, these '–ing' names are found also to occur in England and especially in the east, the area most exposed to Saxon influence. Ekwall[27] therefore attributes these names specifically to Saxon

---

[24] Early Villages of the Marsh, http://www.saltfleetby.co.uk/east_lindsey_2.htm, accessed Feb. 2004
[25] William Bakken, The end of Roman Britain: Assessing the Anglo-Saxon Invasions of the Fifth Century, http://members.aol.com/bakken1/angsax/asinv.htm 1994, accessed Feb. 2004
[26] Dr. B.H. Slicher van Bath, Mensch en Land in de Middeleeuwen, Van Gorcum & Comp. N.V., Assen, Utrecht, 1944
[27] Eilert Ekwall, , English Place-names in – ing, Lund, Gleerop, 1962, p. 109

influence. He also attributes the fact that similar names occur on the continent and in Scandinavia to the Saxons, the names being very old. At the time of Slicher van Bath's publication in 1944, there were 49 names in the eastern Netherlands which corresponded with those in England. In Sussex there were 39 and in the eastern provinces of the Netherlands 50 compounds of a name with the suffix '–ing'. This parallel is unusual and therefore led researchers to conclude that the origin in both countries is related, and Saxon.

By 500 AD, Norfolk was under Anglo-Saxon control. The continental origins of the Anglo-Saxons were given a clear archaeological context for the first time in 1856. This was a break-through achieved by John Mitchell Kemble, a scholar of wide interests and competence. He noticed that cremation urns found at Stade in the Elbe valley were · identical with others found in 1650 in Norfolk, (East Anglia) and Lincolnshire, establishing a definite link between the Saxon groups of northern Germany and eastern Britain.[28]

Banningham, a market town in Norfolk, East Anglia, first mentioned in the *Domesday Book*[29] in the 11th century, means 'settlement of Baning's/Banning's people/tribe'. It most likely came into existence around the 5th or 6th centuries. Dr. Paul Cavill, (Research Fellow, English Place-Name Society, University of Nottingham) and a colleague from medieval language and literature at the University of Toronto, mentioned that Banningham might have acquired its name from the original settlers, a clan or tribe called Banning, that the Bannings/Banings were most likely continental and that it was conceivable that the Bannings in Norfolk were descended from those in Germany, but that there is no evidence to support this. The discovery of the Saxon cremation urns in both locations would, however, seem to lend credence to this supposition.

In addition, examples of Saxon pottery[30] with deep furrowed grooves on the shoulder were excavated from cemeteries in Norfolk; sharply angled pots with facets cut out, precisely like those from the Saxon regions of the Elbe Weser area in North West Germany. Pottery vessels with a characteristic Early Anglo-Saxon globular form, dating from between the early 5th -early 6th centuries AD, were found more to the north, in Lincolnshire, where the above-mentioned cremation urns mentioned by John Mitchell Kemble were also found. The unique incised arch decoration is of a well known type, often referred to by its German name 'Stehende Bogen': standing arch decoration. It was first recognised

---

[28] Matthew Todd, Anglo-Saxon Origins: The Reality of the Myth, www.intellectbooks.com/nation/html/anglos.htm; accessed Feb. 2004
[29] *The Domesday Book*, 1086
[30] Watching Brief, Great Hatfield; www.hullcc.gov.uk/archaeology/watch06.htm; accessed Feb. 2004

on pottery of late 4th - mid 5th century date from the North Sea coast of Germany and the Netherlands - hence the German name. This type of decoration on early Anglo-Saxon pottery in England has often been seen as indicating an affinity with or migration from northern Germany and Frisia during the 5th century.

Another interesting find, in the southernmost reaches of England, on the site of Chessel Down on the Isle of Wight, was a copiously decorated bronze pail, dated 520-570, discovered during the excavation of a rich woman's grave. It is said[31] that the pail may have been an import from the eastern Mediterranean. Runes are cut over the original decoration, the conclusion being that they were thus a later addition, although there is no clue as to when and where the runes were carved. Although some are damaged, the last are legible, interpreted to read: 'bekka, wekka, sekka,' three masculine personal names. J.H. Looijenga,[32] the author of this study, goes on to say that: "Two of the names are known from the Old English travelogue Widsith (line 115). Becca was the name of one of Eormanric's followers, ruler of the Banings. In Widsith, his full name was Þeodberht (Malone 1962:196). In legend, he was the evil counsellor who advised Eormanric to murder Sunilda. The Secca of Widsith is the hypocoristic form of Sigiwald (cf. Malone 1962:131f. and 196f.). Wecca is reminiscent of the name of Wehha, the father of Wuffa, king of East Anglia, who started his reign in 570 AD." The reference here to Becca as an 'evil counsellor' may perhaps be an example of the confusion between Becca and the villainous Bikki argued by Malone, who contends that neither the Becca of line 19 nor the Becca of line 115 are synonymous with Bikki.

Ms. Looijenga continues: "If the Becca and Secca on the pail are the same as the historical Becca and Secca, this might explain the exotic origin of the pail, since Secca had to flee and live in exile in Italy (Gregory of Tours, *Historia Francorum* iii, 13, 16, 23f.). The Runic form shows significant similarities with Danish inscriptions: a remarkable link between England and Denmark possibly illustrated by the use of the particular runic formula used to indicate bekka, wekka, sekka. This might imply that Becca, the tribal leader, was originally Danish."

"110   seeking I companions that were of the best variety;
such was the household of Eormanric.
Hethca sought I and Beadeca and the Herelings,
Emerca sought I and Fridla and the East Gotans,
wise and good, the father of Unwen.

---

[31] J.H. Looijenga, *Runes around the North Sea and on the Continent AD 150-700, Texts and Contexts*, SSG Uitgeverij Groningen, 1997, p. 165
[32] J.H. Looijenga, *Runes around the North Sea and on the Continent AD 150-700, Texts and Contexts*, SSG Uitgeverij Groningen, 1997, p. 165

115   Secca sought I and Becca, Seafola and Theodric,
      Heathoric and Sifeca Hlithe and Incgentheow.
      Eadwin sought I and Elsa, Aegelmund and Hungar,
      and that stately company of the With-Myrgings."[33]

And finally, new frontiers of research are being broached with DNA analysis, in determining migration and settlement. One study, entitled *Y chromosome evidence for Anglo-Saxon Mass Migration*[34] looked closely at DNA samples of 313 males in seven towns located along an east-west transect from East Anglia to North Wales. The towns were selected from the Domesday Book, because of their relatively small population. The Central English towns (Ashbourne, Southwell, Bourne, Fakenham and N. Walsham) were genetically very similar, whereas the two North Welsh towns differed significantly both from each other and from the Central English towns. When the data were compared with an additional 177 samples collected in Friesland (Netherlands) and Norway, the Central English and Frisian samples were found to be statistically indistinguishable. The authors propose that the best explanation for these findings is that the Anglo-Saxon cultural transition in Central England coincided with a mass immigration from the continent. Such an event would simultaneously explain both the high Central English-Frisian affinity and the low Central English-North Welsh affinity. The authors accept that their data do not prove conclusively that an Anglo-Saxon mass migration event took place, and that adoption of new cultures could occur through trade or by the influx of a small ruling elite. Other studies have questioned the evidence for large-scale immigration and continental emigration. The sudden change to an Anglo-Saxon culture has been attributed instead to rapid acculturation and indigenous developments, with only a small number of Germanic immigrants (perhaps a male military elite) settling in Britain.

The Anglo-Saxons not only used the Frisian islands as stepping stones in their migration to Britain, but also as areas in which they settled permanently. Archaeological artefacts found in Frisia have been labelled as 'Anglo-Frisian' and 'Jutish-Frisian' indicating the place of origin of the settlers: the Danish peninsula. Archaeological, historical, and linguistic evidence also confirms this fact.

Although DNA research is a new field and there is a great deal yet to be discovered, the study is mentioned here because Banningham (also included in the Domesday Book) lies only five miles from North

---

[33] The Exeter Book, *Widsith, 'The Wanderer'*, compiled +/- 975 AD
[34] M.E. Weale, D..A. Weiss, R.F. Jager, N. Bradman, M.G. Thomas, *Y chromosome evidence for Anglo-Saxon mass migration*, Molecular Biology & Evolution ,Oxford University Press, July 2002, 19(7): p. 1008 – 1021

Walsham, one of the sample sites on the east-west transect analysed in the first study. The logical conclusion would be that residents of Banningham therefore also have, by definition, the same DNA structure as it's near neighbours and are thus also statistically indistinguishable from the Frisian DNA - a strong argument for relation between the two.

The above findings are derived from various disciplines and should be viewed within their own context. Be that as it may, if parallels were drawn, a scenario might be envisioned in which a Saxon tribe called Baning settled on the Elbe River in middle Germany and migrated west at some time around the 5th century. In reaching the north-west of Germany and the north-east of the Netherlands, members of this tribe may have set up homesteads, some of these homesteads becoming known by the name of Banning, (or derivatives) which still exist today. A faction of this tribe could have migrated further around the same time to the southeast of England, settling in Norfolk, where their settlement was called Banningham, and throughout the southeast provinces of England.

This is, admittedly, idealistic conjecture, and there is no way at present of knowing how feasible or how far-fetched the scenario is. There is no evidence to verify the existence of a Baning tribe, Bannings in the various locations might have evolved independently of each other and be completely unrelated, and while some academics dismiss several of the above quotes as unfounded, others cite the information as plausible. They are not presented here as an argument for authenticity, but as a summary of contemplation and discourse in various fields which may have some bearing on the topic of this book.

DNA technology holds tremendous potential for future research and perhaps some day will tell us more about tribal origins and migration. However, the migrations of these groups of people in settling Europe throughout the centuries appear to coincide largely with the references to Bannings that have been found and verified, and still hold true today.

The first historically recorded person whose name is closely affiliated with Banning is Bainingus[35] (mentioned above), a high-ranking civic official to the Frankish King Pippins II and suggested by Gutenbrunner to have been perhaps been associated with *Widsith's* Banings. Bainingus is mentioned in 700 AD in two charters in Echternach, Luxemburg. Gutenbrunner mentions that the name only occurred a few times in southern Germany at the time, in Lorsch and Salzburg. Bainingus is identified with Saint Bainus, the Bishop of Thérouanne in France, who reigned from 701-709 AD. His *Vita Baini episcopi Taruansis (Life of*

---

[35] Siegfried Gutenbrunner, *Die Herkunft der Baininge, Beiträge zur Geschichte der Deutschen Sprache und Literatur*, Max Niemeyer Verlag, Halle (Saale) 1936, vol. 60, p. 339-350

Baini, Bishop of Terouanne) was published by Lohier et Laporte, 1936[36]. After twelve years he returned to Fontanelle, where he was abbot. He is the main patron saint of Calais.

The name Banning is said to mean 'son of, people of, possession of' (Saxon '-*ing*') Ban, Bann, Benno, Benne etc.. Banning would thus at one time have evolved from i.e. 'Bann's people' or 'Bann's son', and so we look more closely at examples of 'Ban(n)' in early history.

One of the major personages in the legends of King Arthur and the Knights of the Round table is King Ban of Benwick (Benoic; Brittany). Viewing our ancestors as knights in shining armour and wreathed in legend is, perhaps, rather romantic, but how valid is the information presented? Scribes or monks, such as the 6th century Gildar and 7th century Muirchu, were more inclined to give their views on the Roman way of life and politics, and how it affected them, rather than recording historical fact. Moreover, names of people and places were written according to the way they were spoken in numerous languages and dialects, and later subject to the interpretation of translators, making it difficult to trace who was who and to determine geographical areas.

One of the questions that has occupied those interested in King Arthur is whether or not he is a historical figure. The debate concerning The Enthroned Arthur has been ongoing since the Renaissance, when his historicity was vigorously defended, partly because the Tudor monarchs traced their lineage to Arthur and used the alleged connection as a justification for their reign. Modern scholarship has generally assumed that there was some actual person at the heart of the legends, but whether his name was Arthur and whether or not he was a monarch will probably never be resolved. Although the tales may be fanciful, it seems that many of the characters did, in actual fact, exist.

It is in the tales of King Arthur that one of the earliest precursors of the name Banning appears: King Ban of Benwick (Benoic/Brittany). The following few lines are from *King Ban: A Fragment*[37], written by Algernon Charles Swinburne (1837-1909):

"These three held flight upon the leaning lands
At undern, past the skirt of misty camps
Sewn thick from Benwick to the outer march--
King Ban, and, riding wrist by wrist, Ellayne,
And caught up with his coloured swathing-bands
Across her arm, a hindrance in the reins,
A bauble slipt between the bridle-ties,
The three months' trouble that was Launcelot.

[36] H. Halbertsma, *Frieslands Oudheid*, Matrijs, Utrecht, 2000, pp. 239-240
[37] A.C. Swinburne, King Ban: A Fragment; www. camelot.celtic-twilight.com/poetry/swinburne12.htm, accessed Feb. 2004

For Claudas leant upon the land, and smote
This way and that way, as a pestilence
Moves with vague patience in the unclean heat
This way and that way; so the Gaulish war
Smote, moving in the marches. Then **King Ban**
Shut in one girdled waist of narrow stones
His gold and all his men, and set on them
A name, the name of perfect men at need,"
etc.

      Swinburne based his writing on that of previous historians, such as those of the monk St. Gildas (500 AD); Bede, historian and doctor of the Church (672 AD); Nennius, a historian who wrote a collection of documents called *Historia Brittonum*, with the first specific reference to King Arthur (796 AD), and the historian Geoffrey of Monmouth (1139).

      King Ban appears again in the High History of the Holy Graal[38]; originally written in Old French sometime in the early half of the 13th Century A.D.:

"Fair Sir," saith the Hermit, "And you, who are you?"
"Sir," saith the knight, "I will tell you. I am the son of **King Ban** of Benoic."
"Ha, fair nephew," saith King Hermit to Perceval, "See here your cousin, for **King Ban** of Benoic was your father's cousin-german. Make him right great cheer!"

      King Ban is mentioned in a poem by Folgore da San Geminiano in 1260, a dedication to a series of twelve convivial sonnets. A translation of this, and of the sonnets, was published in Dante G. Rossetti's *Early Italian Poets* in 1861[39]:

"Whose praise in Siena springs from lip to lip.
Tingoccio, Atuin di Togno, and Ancaian,
Bartolo, and Mugaro, and Faenot,
Who well might pass for children of **King Ban**,
Courteous and valiant more than Lancelot,
To each, God speed! How worthy every man
To hold high tournament in Camelot."

      King Ban was the son of King Lancelot, who married the daughter of the King of Ireland. King Lancelot's father was Jonaans, who

---

[38] author unknown, translation Evans, Sebastian, The High History of the Holy Graal, Online Medieval and Classical Library Release #19, 1898,
www.sunsite.berkeley.edu/OMACL/Graal, accessed Feb. 2004
[39] Folfore da San Geminiano, translated by D.G.Rossetti, Early Italian Poets, Canto 29:125; www.worldwideschool.org/library/books/lit/poetry/TheDivineComedy1-Inferno/chap29.html; accessed Feb. 2004

went into Gaul and married the daughter of Maronex from whom he received the kingdom. Jonaans' father was Nascien, son of Celydoine, first Christian King of Scotland. Celydoine, in turn, was a son of Nascien, who took this name on conversion to Christianity and was previously known as Seraphe. Nascien was brother-in-law to the heathen King Evalach (once converted to Christianity he took the name Mordrain). Nascien and Mordrain were baptised by their friend (related through marriage), Joseph of Arimathea, a devoted follower of Jesus (New Testament, Matthew 27:57; Luke 23:51; John 19:38).

2. King Arthur and King Ban plan a tournament as Queen
Guinevere and courtiers watch, ca. 1300
Bibliothèque Nationale, Paris

In the famous legends, King Ban of Benwick was one of King Arthur's staunchest supporters.

Lancelot, (named after his grandfather), was born in 508 AD, the son of King Ban and Queen Elaine. (King Ban's godson was Banin). Lancelot was the First Knight of the Round Table, and it is written that he never failed in gentleness, courtesy, or courage and very willing to serve others, the greatest fighter and swordsman of all the knights of the Round Table. Lancelot was, in turn, father to Sir Galahad. Whether or not any of today's numerous Bannings (along with tens of thousand of others) can attribute their name or ancestry to King Ban, Lancelot and Sir Galahad seems most unlikely, but the point is that here we find testimony of how ancient the name actually is.

28

We return to Joseph of Arimathea. Joseph and his company fled from continued persecution by the Romans, travelling via France into Britain around 38-39 AD. "Joseph was accompanied by other Hebrews, companions and relations said to have intermarried with the families of the British kings or chieftains, and from them, by direct descent, in something like four hundred years, are said to have arisen the greater heroes of King Arthur's court - the Knights of the Round Table."[40] (including King Ban and his descendants)

Joseph and his companions built the first church in Lundy, (Isle of Avalon) which became the centre of early Christianity in Britain. Joseph died and was interred there in 76 AD, allegedly with the Holy Grail. In 1923 a stone was found at the ruined chapel of Lundy, inscribed 'igern', (labelled the 'Tigernus Stone') and ascribed to circa 500 AD as that of the mother of King Arthur, whose name was Ygern(a) / Igern(a)[41]. Another of two stones discovered a year later was inscribed with the letters 'POTIT' and is believed to be that of St. Patrick's grandfather, Potitus (+/- 340 AD)[42], a Christian Priest of the settlement *Bannavem Taburniae*.

St. Patrick was born between 385-390 AD, at the same *Bannavem Taburniae*, or *Banna Venta Berniae*. *Banna* occurs by itself, and in compounds, in Romano-British place-names; *venta*, apparently descriptive, is also found in compound names in Roman Britain to 500 AD. Many authorities assert that *BANNA* is a British word, and in place-names indicated a notable 'horn', 'spur' or promontory of rock. The word *Venta* was used by the Romans as a prefix for three civic capitals (Winchester was known as *Venta Belgarum*) . The exact meaning of *Venta* is disputed, it seems to be of Celtic or non-Latin origin. *Vendo* (Latin) means 'I sell' and the late Latin word *vendito* means 'market sale'. The general consensus seems to be that a meaning of 'local centre, market place, or meeting place' is close to the original use. *Berniae* is supposed, by most experts, to be related to the native population as in many other Roman - British place- names. Therefore St. Patrick lived in a villa at: *Banna* - promontory of rock, near, *Venta* - marketplace and local centre - of the *Berniae*. The exact location of *Bannavem Taburniae* has never been established, but it was presumably in Cumbria, South Wales or southwest England.

Ban features in numerous early European place names, noticeably those in Great Britain since the 3rd century AD or even earlier.

---

[40] J.W. Taylor, *The Coming of the Saints*, Covenant Pub., London, 1969, p.141
[41] Gravestones on Lundy, http://www.lundyisleofavalon.co.uk/lioa/ch11.htm, accessed Feb. 2004
[42] Gravestones on Lundy, http://www.lundyisleofavalon.co.uk/lioa/ch11.htm, accessed Feb. 2004

Although historically and etymologically the origin of the Bannings seems convincingly Saxon, the first genealogical essays hold that they descended from Vikings and Crusaders. This assumption is no more than legend and such a claim could never be supported, but further exploration revealed references to Bann which may or may not have provided some impetus to this belief.

Danish Vikings sailed up the Bann River, the longest river in Northern Ireland, in 830 AD and established colonies. Bann was one of the principal areas of 9th century Viking activity.

Bannavem Taburniae (*Banna Venta Burniae*) has already been mentioned. *Ban* in the Welsh and Gaelic etymology of place names, means 'hilltop[43]'. This corresponds with the above-mentioned interpretation of *Banna* being a (rock) promontory. A summary of place-names:

Bannaventa: Romano-British Fortified Town, (Roman burg) Whilton Lodge, Norton, Northamptonshire[44]

Material representing the remains of the Roman settlement of Bannaventa has been recovered from a the site. Occupation of the site, which may have begun before the Roman conquest, continued into the fourth century.

3. Celtic Coin (silver) found in topsoil at Bannaventa (Whilton Lodge) Northamptonshire , in 1971 (Northampton Museum)[45]
photo courtesy of Institute of Archaeology, University of Oxford

Banna: (suspected to be) the Roman name of Hadrian's Wall Fort and Settlement, Castlesteads, Cumbria. The Roman names of both the fort at Castlesteads and the one further east along the Wall at Birdoswald, have been the subject of intense debate for many years. The problem arises in the scarcity of geographical references of the period, and in those that do

[43] Etymology of British Place-Names, http://www.pbenyon.plus.com/Misc/Etymology.html accessed Feb. 2004
[44] Bannaventa, Romano-British fortified town; http://www.roman-britain.org/places/bannaventa.htm; accessed Feb. 2004
[45] The Celtic Coin Index; http://www.writer2001.com/cciwriter2001/coinrecords/71/710105.htm; accessed Feb. 2004

exist, there are a number of discrepancies. There are three main sources for the names of these forts, namely, the *Ravenna Cosmography*, the *Notitia Dignitatum* and the so-called *Rudge Cup*.

The Ravenna map places an entry named *Banna* between *Esica* (Great Chesters, Northumberland) and *Uxelludamo* (Stanwix, Cumbria)[46]. Archaeological evidence indicates that there were two large forts on the Wall between these sites, but unfortunately there is nothing in the *Cosmography* to indicate which of these two forts is to be identified with the *Banna* entry. The question seemed to have been settled with the discovery of an early 2nd century decorated bronze drinking-cup at Rudge in Wiltshire, in 1725, and another similar vessel at Amiens in France[47]. The inscription around the rim of this beautiful relic reads:

A.MAIS ABALLAVA VXELODVM CAMBOGLANS BANNA

These are the names of five forts in the Cumbrian group at the western end of the wall:
MAIS as the Roman fort at Bowness on Solway in Cumbria.
ABALLAVA as the Roman Fort at Burgh-by-Sands in Cumbria.
VXELODVM as the Roman fort at Stanwick in Cumbria.
CAMBOGLANS as the Roman fort at Castlesteads in Cumbria.
BANNA as the Roman fort at Birdoswald in Cumbria.

This indicated that the name of Castlesteads fort was *Camboglanna* and that of the Birdoswald fort, *Banna*, on the Hadrian Wall.

4. Birdoswald Fort/ Banna in Cumbria
photo courtesy of Britannia.com[48]

[46] Banna: Hadrian's Wall Fort and Settlement: http://www.roman-britain.org/places/banna.htm; accessed Feb. 2004
[47] The Holy Grail; www.newagedarkage.freeserve.co.uk/grail.htm - accessed Dec. 2002
[48] Britannia:http://www.britannia.com/tours/hadrianswall/birdoswald.html; accessed Feb. 2003

The lack of epigraphic evidence from either of these two sites meant that this view became firmly ingrained into the history books produced over much of the twentieth century. It was not until the latter part of the last century that extensive excavations were conducted at the Birdoswald site, and these unearthed evidence that the garrison was the First Aelian Cohort of Dacians, the unit associated with the name *Camboglanna*. This discovery has seemingly overturned the evidence from the Rudge and Amiens artifacts, and has once more opened the discussion over the naming of these two forts.

Adding further fuel to the *Banna/Camboglanna* argument outlined above, an altar to Silvanus the God of the Forest was uncovered at the Birdoswald fort, dedicated by a group calling themselves the *Venatores Bannienses*, or 'the Hunters of *Banna*'. It is possible that these men formed an irregular auxiliary cavalry unit, originally garrisoned at Castlesteads, and from which place their name is derived, who were later posted to the neighbouring Birdoswald or Banna fort sometime during the fourth century.

Banna as a personage appears in the Irish epic tale *The Destruction of Da Derga's Hostel (The Room of the Cupbearers)* from a text constructed on the basis of eight manuscripts, the oldest going back to about 1100 AD. The story itself is, without doubt, several centuries earlier, and belongs to the oldest group of extant Irish sagas[49].

"The Room of the Cupbearers, from the Destruction of Da Derga's Hostel"

"There I saw six men in front of the same room. Fair yellow manes upon them: green mantles about them: tin brooches at the opening of their mantles. Half-horses (centaurs) are they, like Conall Cernach. Each of them throws his mantle round another and is as swift as a mill-wheel. Thine eye can hardly follow them. Liken thou those, O Fer rogain!"

"This is easy for me. Those are the King of Tara's six cupbearers, namely Uan and Broen and *Banna*, Delt and Drucht and Dathen. That feat does not hinder them from their skinking, and it blunts not their intelligence thereat. Good are the warriors that are there! Thrice their number will fall by them. They will share prowess with any six in the Hostel, and they will escape from their foes, for they are out of the elfmounds. They are the best cupbearers in Erin. Woe to him that shall wreak the Destruction were it only because of them!"

---

[49] translated by W. Stoke, Medieval Sourcebook: *The Destruction of da Derga's Hostel*, ca. 1100, The Harvard Classics, New York, P.F. Collier & Son Company, 1909-14; vol. 49 part 3, 15.

We find Rabbi *Banna*[50] in the Talmud, a document said to have proven of great value archaeologically, as well as having preserved ancient laws and glinted light on history, forgotten forms in the classic tongues, and pictures of old civilisation.

"As Rabbi Banna went about to measure and to mark off the outward and inward dimensions of the different caves, when he came to the cave of Machpelah he found Eliezar, Abraham's servant, at the entrance, and asked him, "What is Abraham doing?" The answer he received was, "He is asleep in the arms of Sarah." *(Ibid., fol. 58, col. 1.)*

The Cave of Machpelah is the world's most ancient Jewish site and the second holiest place for the Jewish people, after Temple Mount in Jerusalem. The cave and the adjoining field were purchased - at full market price - by Abraham some 3700 years ago. Abraham, Isaac, Jacob, Rebecca and Leah were all later buried in the same Cave of Machpelah. These were considered the patriarchs and matriarchs of the Jewish people. The only one who is missing is Rachel, who was buried near Bethlehem where she died in childbirth[51].

King Donald *Ban* (Donalbain/Donaldbane) of Scotland reigned from 1093 AD, succeeding his brother Malcolm III on his death in that year until 1097 AD, with a brief interlude in 1094 AD when he was deposed by Duncan II. Unlike his brother Malcolm, he was raised in the Western Isles and Ireland, and remained 'an incorrigible old Celt'. Because of this he disapproved of most of Malcolm's Europeanising policies, and since the Anglicising of Scotland really only affected the Lowlands, he still had plenty of support in the still very Celtic Highlands.

He attacked Edinburgh Castle after Malcolm's death. His nephews fled with their mother's body, to England. With support from William II of England, Malcolm and Duncan marched north, deposed Donald Ban, and Duncan proclaimed himself king in May 1094. However, one of Malcolm and Margaret's sons, Edmund, made a deal with Donald Ban, and together they overthrew and murdered Duncan in November 1094, and became joint rulers, Donald Ban ruling north of the Forth-Clyde line and Edmund south of it. This lasted three years, until Malcolm's remaining sons (Edgar, Alexander, and David) marched north to stake their claims to the Scottish throne. Edmund was permitted to become a monk, but Donald Ban was captured in 1099, blinded, and imprisoned for the rest of his life. It is said that, as a final gesture of revenge, Donald Ban had sufficient strength left in his old age to throttle David's elder son Edmund. In their turn, Edgar, Alexander, and David all

---

[50]The Sacred Text Archive; III. *Ibid.*, fol. 58, col. 1; http://www.sacred-texts.com/jud/hl/hl06.htm; accessed Feb. 2004
[51] Jewish Virtual Library, The Cave of Machpelah, Tomb of the Patriarchs, http://www.us-israel.org/jsource/Judaism/machpelah.html, accessed Feb. 2004

became Kings of Scotland and continued the Europeanising policies started by their mother.

This turn of events formed the basis of Shakespeare's *Macbeth*[52]. (Macbeth was a grandson of Malcolm.) King Donald Ban is referred to as Donalbain in this historic drama.

Where is the name *Bann* found in geographical terms? The *River Bann* in Northern Ireland (the longest river in Northern Ireland), flows through the *Bann Valley*, and was travelled by the Danish Vikings in 830 AD; *Bann* was one of the principal areas of 9th century Viking activity.

The *River Bann* derives its name from the Goddess Banba.

The Pont map[53] (Timothy Pont was a renowned 16th century cartographer) shows two locations called *Bannagyith* and *Banaferry* (Scotland), derived from *Balnageith* and nearby *Balnaferry*. *Banna*-combined both with -geith (Gaelic gaoth, earlier gáeth, góith 'a marsh') and with -ferry would suggest that *Banna* is a water feature, as is, naturally, the *River Bann*.

Geographical coordinates for *Balnageith* *(Bannagyith* - the Gaelic gaoth, earlier gáeth, góith), in turn, were specified by Ptolemy[54], the 1st century Greek astronomer and geographer, on the Roman Map of Britain, which Ptolemy designated as *Bannatia*. Ptolemy places the tribe of Vacomagi at *Bannatia*.

In his book Picts and Ancient Britons, Paul Dunbavin[55] asserts that the Vacomagi Picts (Picts were Sythians, semi-nomadic Iranian-speakers who lived in Belarus or the Ukraine, who recently came to the world's attention through the discovery of frozen tattooed corpses in central Asia) had proto-Pict or Finnish origins. Dunbavin's proto-Picts were maritime peoples of the Baltic who spoke a Finno-Ugrian language. Dunbavin's evidence is the supposed Finnic origin of many of the tribal and place-names recorded by Ptolemy and other writers.

The first geographical reference to *Bann* would therefore seem to be Ptolemy's reference to *Bannatia* and would thus establish that the name was known in the 1st century or earlier.

A second location called *Bann* is an ancient town in south western Germany, in the province of Rheinland Pfalz. Archaeological

---

[52] Kings and Queens of Scotland; Celtic and Celtic-Norman Kings, http://www.legenca.freeserve.co.uk/monarchs/kings2.html, accessed Feb. 2004

[53] The Roman Map of Britain; Bannatia Balnageith?, Moray http://www.romanmap.com/htm/nomina/Bannatia.htm; accessed Feb. 2004

[54] The Roman Map of Britain, Ptolemy's Geography,II 3.8-9; http://www.romanmap.com/htm/ptolemy/pt3_8-9.htm, accessed Feb. 2004

[55] R. Samson, *Claiming Finnish Origins for Picts, review of P. Dunbavin's Picts and Ancient Britons in British Archeaology*, April 1999, issue no. 43

evidence[56] reveals that the first settlers lived here some time between 2000-3000 BC. Celtic stones mark a prehistoric path between *Bann* and Lanstuhl which the Romans expanded into a road between the 1st and 4th century AD; the ruins of a Roman fortress were found here. By the year 981 AD *Bann* and the surrounding area belonged to the cloister of Hornbach by order of Emperor Otto II. The first recorded mention of the German *Bann* was in the year 1182 AD, in a document from Pope Lucius III to the abbot Stephan and the convent of the cloister Rodenkirchen dated 14th March. However, this date does not mark the foundation of the town, which is estimated to have existed as such probably since the year 1100 AD. The origin of the name, in this case, is said to derive from the synonym for area or boundary (See Barnhart and Hekket, below). Besides the bann of Landstuhl, Oberarnbach, Kindsbach and Queidersbach, this bann was unsettled for a long period and thus remained nameless. Even after its settlement, it was known simply as *Bann*.

Banba, from which the *River Bann* and *Bann Valley* derive their names, is the goddess who represents the spirit of Ireland and the island is said to be named in her honour; *Banba* also being a poetic name for Ireland. Initially, she could have been a goddess of war as well as a fertility goddess.

(Roman) place names derived from Ban(n)[57] [58]:

Bana Insula: An island opposite the mouth of the River Taff, Glamorganshire.
Banatia: Bean Castle, Murray; Comrie, Perthshire; or near Inverness.
Bancornensis: Of Bangor (see below)
Banesinga Villa: Bensington, Oxfordshire.
Banna: River Ban, Ulster.
Banna: Cambeck, or Castlesteeds, Cumberland.
Bannauenna, Bannauentum, Bannouallum: Borough Hill, near Daventry; or Weedon, Northants; or Banbury, Oxfordshire.
Banneberia: Banbury, Oxfordshire.
Bannio: Abergavenny.
Bannochorus, Bangorium: Bangor, N. Wales.
Banua: Bannow, Ireland.
Banus Flu.: River Bain, Lincolnshire.
Bantia : site in Apulies (Italy)
Banata : site in Mesopotamia

---

[56] History: all about Bann; http://www.bann2000.de/e1-history.html, accessed Feb. 2004
[57] A.L.F. Rivet, & C. Smith, *The Place-Names of Roman Britain*, B.T. Batsford Ltd., London, 1979, p. 262
[58] Even—Kernivinenn, J.C., Encyclopédie Géographique et Historique du Monde Celtique, http://marikavel.net/lieux-accueil.htm, accessed Feb. 2004

Bandusia : well-known fountain near Horace

Bangor : historical community in the history of Brittany (Benwick/Benoic, where *King Ban* reigned); region/diocese of Vannes. Currently in the jurisdiction called '*de Bretagne*' (*Brittany*); province of Morbihan; district of Lorient; district of Belle-Ile-en-Mer (France).

Bangor : community in the region of Galles; county of Caernarvon

Bangor Is-Coed / Bangor-on-Dee: community in the region of Galles; county of Flintshire.

Banienses : people of Lusitania

Banna : Roman station in Great Britain : Birdoswald; Cumberland

Banna : currently called *Bannes*, in the Marne

Bannalec / Banaleg : community in the history of Brittany, in the diocese of Quimper. Currently in the jurisdiction of 'de Bretagne'; region of Finistère; district of Quimper

Bannatia. Banatia : most probably the Roman fort of Dalginros, in Perthshire, Scotland

Bannobriga : known today as *Banobre*, in the province of La Corogne, Spain

Bannovallium : name designated to a Roman fort, although this has not been verified, said to lie between Caistor and Horncastle, both in Lincolnshire;

Bannisdale: small remote valley in the North-East corner of the English Lake District, meaning ' The Valley of Banni' an old Norse nickname for one who curses (according to Barnhart, see below).

Banningham in Norfolk was recorded in the Domesday Book of the 11th century, as a landowners place name, which includes a detailed statement of lands held by the king and by his tenants and of the resources that went with those lands. It records which manors rightfully belonged to which estates, thus ending years of confusion resulting from the gradual and sometimes violent dispossession of the Anglo-Saxons by their Norman conquerors. It was moreover a 'feudal' statement, giving the identities of the tenants-in-chief (landholders) who held their lands directly from the Crown, and of their tenants and under tenants, commissioned by William the Conqueror. More on Banningham is related in the chapter on England.

*   *   *

Etymology

The Barnhart Dictionary of Etymology[59] states that *'ban'* means to forbid, prohibit. It was formed in Middle English in about 1378, appearing in a version of *Piers Plowman*[60] (14th century English poem) and is perhaps a fusion of a word of Scandinavian origin (compare Old Icelandic *banna* - curse, prohibit) + Old English *bannan* - summon, proclaim (prior to 800, in the poetry of Cynewulf, which is also preserved in the Book of Exeter). Old English *bannan* is cognate with Old Frisian *banna* (bonna) - command, proclaim; Old Dutch *bannen* - prohibit (modern Dutch, banish, exile); Old High German *bannan* - banish, expel, Gothic *bannan* - proclaim, command, forbid.

It also gives as a meaning 'edit, proclamation', from about 1300, earlier meaning 'a troop of warriors summoned by proclamation' (about 1250, in *The Owl and the Nightingale*, an old English poem in the Book of Exeter) and still earlier in the phrase *bane cruces*, crosses marking a boundary (1228). Formed in Middle English by fusion of Old English (1051-52) *ban*, earlier *geban*, *gebann* a summons, proclamation (before 800, in poetry of Cynewulf) + Old North French *ban*, a summoning of the king's vassals for military service, proclamation, from Frankish *ban*.

Hekket's dictionary on the etymology of eastern Dutch place-names[61] gives us the following meanings:

ban - territorial jurisdiction

Banning, Bannink: patronymic to the Christian name *Banne* or *Bane*. The Saxon *'-ink'* is equivalent to the Frankish (French) *'-ing'* and means 'son of, progeny, descendant' and in this case of *Bane*, still an existing Frisian Christian name. There are over 40 homesteads or properties based on the name Banning, Bannink. Benning in a study of the medieval eastern Netherlands between 933 AD and 1500 AD. Hekket mentions the following properties in the Netherlands:

1298-1304 *Banningehus* (Banninge house) in Uffelte

1321 *Banninghe* in Witten (Assen)

1356 *Banninc* in Lochem

1382 *Banninch* in Hengelo (Gelderland)

1385 that landholding *Banninck* in Essen near Deventer

1421 large landholding *Banninck* in Harfsen.

A list of the landholdings based on this name are specified in the chapter on (Medieval) Homesteads, specified in their original context.

[59] R.K.Barnhart, S. Steinmetz, *The Barnhart Dictionary of Etymology*, The H.W. Wilson Company, New York, 1988,

[60] W. Langland, *Piers Plowman*, Athlone, London, 1960

[61] B.J. Hekket, *Oost Nederlandse Familienamen, hun ontstaan an hun betekenis*, Witkam, Hengelo, 1983, p. 53

bant - area, 'gau'(specifying jurisdiction in the Frankish empire) or border (This would correspond with the above-mentioned *bane cruces*.

The Dutch Van Dale *Etymologisch Woordenboek*[62] *(Etymological Dictionary)* cites the following:

ban: medieval (middle) Dutch, official announcement, especially by government, legal consequence (fine or banishment), old Saxon, old Dutch, *ban*, old Frisian *bon*, old English *bonn*, old Norwegian *bann*, *ban*: landlord;

banal: originally 'belonging to the landlord', from *ban*: (proclamation of the landlord)

banus: Latin for *ban*

According to the French *Dictionnaire Etymologique de la Langue Latin*[63], *(Etymological Dictionary of the Latin Language)"banus/variant 'ban':* is without doubt Celtic in origin." *Banning* is known as a general Celtic male name meaning: blonde child, or fair and small.

Following the evolution of names, explanation for derivation of the name Banning is that it is patronymic and evolves from the old male Christian name *Banno*, followed by the prefix '-ing', which is said to mean 'descendent of', 'possession of' or 'son of'. It was not unusual for manor homes and farmsteads to be named after their owners. (See Hekket, above.) The spelling varies considerably - sometimes in one and the same document and for the same person - and we emphasise that the reader be aware of the fact that members of the same family are often known under various different spellings. To name a few common variations: Banninge, Benningh, Benninc(k), Bening(a), Bennynck, Bannyng(e) and Bayning(e).

A spontaneous - but erroneous - association, when hearing our kinship name, is that of 'being banned' and or 'banished'. It was unknown to the author of the 1934 Banning genealogy to which extent etymology was practiced in the 18th century, but he asserts that it must have been in a most primitive form if a learned man such as Notary Nicolaas Witsen (17th century Burgomaster of Amsterdam, related by marriage to the Amsterdam Bannings) laboured under such grave misconception as to say:

"...just as the Bannings, an olde lineage in this City, a family to which my forebears have often been wed and who bear that name because they were banned, or otherwise (so I have been informed) came from the married house of Van Velsen, who, after many years, and (after) the

---

[62] P.A.F. Veen, *Etymologisch Woordenboek*, Van Dale Lexicografie, Utrecht/Antwerp, 1993, p. 84

[63] A. Ernout, A. Meillet, *Dictionnaire Etymologique de la Langue Latine*, 4th Edition, Editions Klincksieck, Paris, 1979, p. 66

murder of Count Floris passed into obscurity, returned and have introduced this name (Banning.)[64]"

The author says that this does, however, indicate that the name Banning existed long before 27th June 1296, the day on which the aforementioned Count Floris V was murdered at Muiderberg in the Netherlands. It was originally plotted that the count would be kidnapped and brought to England. The villains of the conspiracy were Gijsbrecht van Aemstel, Herman van Woerden and Gerard van Velsen, who was wed to a daughter of Herman van Woerden. An Amsterdam Banning family was related through the maternal line to the Van Woerdens.

Besides Bainingus and Bishop Bainus of 700 AD who were mentioned earlier, the first 'Banning' (Benning) on record to date is of a family known by that name in 1238 in Coesfeld (Westphalia, Germany), whose members were aldermen. The *Oorkondeboek of Westphalen*[65] names the following in various charters:

1238: Gottfried (Godefrido) Benninc, father of Conrado
1238: Konrad (Conradus) Benning, alderman of Coesfeld from 1238-
1258)
1247: Heinricus de Benninghusen (Bennig-, Benninch)
1258: Conradus and Bernardo Benning
1275: Bernardo Benning (alderman of Coesfeld from 1258-1275)
1278: Ludolfo Benninc
1292: Thiderico Benynck
1295: Johannes de Benninchusen, Councillor of Geseke (to be read as Benninc-husen, meaning Benninc/Banning house)

Mary Elizabeth Banning (1822-1903/USA), said to be a woman of remarkable mind and a great student along scientific lines (she posthumously became a recognised mycologist), with an indomitable spirit, was a self-proclaimed etymologist who devoted considerable time to the study of the Banning name and family. Her prose is colourful and tends toward generalisation, and she upholds the Banning name with vehemence. A portion of a letter to her nephew Richard A. Banning in 1897 is included in this book. A quote from this letter:
"We are of very ancient date, our name is in the 'Scot and Bard songs', the first ballad on record, where it says 'Becca ruled the Banning'; each clan had it's ruler or hero. The Bannings were in the Crusades. Our blood was spilt in the Crusades, in the fight for the Holy Sepulchre. They were

---

[64] J.A.W. Banning, *Genealogie van het Geslacht Banning*, Uitgevers Ferd. Banning & Zonen, Groenlo, 1934, p. 85
[65] *Westfälisches Urkundenbuch*, vol. III, die Urkunden des Bisthums Munster, 1201-1300, Munster, 1871; no. 355, 637, 974 and 1160

Vikings, in other words, like all the early Norwegians and Danes, Piratical Chieftains, great fighters, warlike to the very teeth and I believe with all our modern civilisation there is fight in us yet." " Thus you have doubtless heard said a Banning is a strong friend but a bitter enemy. They have the spirit of old Hero Worship in them yet and you will find them clinging to those they love with lifelong affection." "I am only giving you information about your name and your ancestors who were the bravest, boldest fighting old Danes and Anglo-Saxons that ever figured in History; if you were to read 'Beowulf' and this would be hard for you to do as it is (without study) unreadable to us moderns. Nothing disgusts me more than this brand and beast about ancestry, but there is much in it that tells upon modern generations."

P.W. Banning renders a more modified description of the Banning characteristics in his genealogy in 1909, as follows:
"The Bannings have always taken an active part in the wars of countries in which they lived and an honourable record stands to the credit of many of them."
"There are certain characteristics or traits that have remained with the greater part of the Banning families. Among these might be mentioned the following, without pretending to include all. Determination and willpower almost to the point of stubbornness; loyalty to their friends and families to the last, with the greatest opposition but fairness to their enemies; clannishness, with strong feeling for those of their friends in need and ability for hard reliable work. In many cases the facial characteristics show a wonderful resemblance, especially in the firmness of the mouth. Dark hair and brown eyes are very common, although clear sharp blue eyes are often found. As a family they are healthy, probably from the hard active lives so many of them lived."[66]

This may or may not have been P.W. Banning's personal interpretation, and it too, is a generalisation. It is quoted here not only because P.W. Banning made such an invaluable contribution to the genealogical research of the family and its namesakes, but because both his view and that of Mary Elizabeth Banning concerning these characteristics have quite obviously been borne out and often cited concerning many of the Bannings who made a place for themselves in history.

*   *   *

---

[66] P.W. Banning, *The First Banning Genealogy*, Chicago, 1909

2 THE GENEALOGIES

The following genealogies form the basis of research for most of those described in this book. Information concerning their lineage was taken from the first six specified. Other existing genealogies, less frequently consulted, are listed further on.

1. *The First Banning Genealogy* (English, 1909)
The First Banning Genealogy was written in English by Pierson Worrall Banning in Chicago in 1909. Fifteen typewritten copies existed at the time, which were presented to:
U.S. Government Library, Washington D.C.
Königliche Bibliotheek, Berlin, Germany
Library of the College of Arms, London, England
Dr. Robert Joseph Banning, Shoeburyness, Essex, England
Felix Heinrich Wilhelm Banning, Duren, Rheinland, Germany
Mrs. Elisabeth Raymond Worton, Canton, Ohio, U.S.A., to be placed in the Public Library at Mount Vernon, Ohio
Pierson Worrall Banning, Chicago, Illinois (two copies)
Los Angeles Public Library, Los Angeles, California
Newsbury (?) Library, Chicago, Illinois
New England Historic Genealogical Society, Boston, Massachusetts
The State Historical Society of Wisconsin, Madison, Wis.
N.Y. Public Library (Astor Lenox and Tilden Foundation; Lenox Library), N.Y. City
Koninklijke Bibliotheek, The Hague, Holland

P.W. Banning's Genealogy covers 14 branches, primarily of American Bannings, although he includes valuable information on the history of the name, and on German, English and Canadian Bannings. It covers some 400 pages and includes 19 portraits.

2. *Genealogie van het Geslacht Banning (Genealogy of the Banning Family)* (Dutch, 1934)
The second known Banning genealogy was written in Dutch by Josephus Alphonsus Willibrordus Banning (born 31 July 1903), Utrecht, Netherlands and published in a limited, hardcover edition of 100 numbered copies by the publisher F.J.H. Banning (1895-1973) in Groenlo, the Netherlands, in 1934. The genealogy is available for reference at the 'Central Bureau of Genealogy' in The Hague. It covers five different branches: four in the Netherlands and one in Germany, the last of which P.W. Worrall also included in his work. This genealogy is extensively researched and contains a wealth of well-documented

information with references to numerous archives and records. A great deal of information on the Dutch Bannings is yet to be uncovered in the Dutch archives.

Following an introduction and a historical overview, the genealogies A, B and C outline three related lineages, which the writer describes as Roman Catholic, with the towns Gendringen and Ulft as their origin. Branch D follows, compiled by F.H.W. Banning, during life a manufacturer in Düren (Germany). Moreover, considerable attention is focused on the Amsterdam Bannings in a detailed genealogy E, included in this book. The Genealogy of the Banning Family also includes fragment genealogies of Bannings of the Hague (1512-1669) and eight generations of the family Van Banning (1757-1921).

Genealogy A counts eight generations. The eighth generation, including the aforementioned J.A.W. Banning and F.J.H. Banning, consists of nine male descendants, commencing with Everhardus Banning & Hendrina Hacvoor (married 12 Oct.1709 in Ulft).There are 22 principal male descendants in their ancestry, between 9 July 1710 and 31 July 1903. This genealogy was later revised and appended.

Genealogy B consists of five generations, with as ancestors Wessel Banning and Joanna Tychelhoven (married 10 May 1705 in Ulft). Eight principal male descendants are mentioned, with birth dates varying from 29 Sept. 1706 to 28 Nov.1917.

Genealogy C also summarizes five generations with nine principal descendants. The fifth generation comprises only two males, including Dr. Emile Th. J.H. Banning. The ancestors are Casparus Banning & Mechtilda Lamers (married 23 May 1703 in Ulft). The birth dates here vary from 26 June 1707 to 23 Oct. 1844. Wessel and Casparus Banning are assumed to be brothers.

Genealogy D, comprising eight generations, is presented as Protestant. The eighth generation consists of three sons of F.H.W. Banning (1861-1932), who compiled this information and did genealogical research during business trips throughout Europe and the United States. F.H.W. Banning was rendered access to an edition of the genealogy compiled by Pierson Worrall Banning. Thirteen principal male descendants followed the ancestors Adolf Friedrich Banning & Anna E. Detmeyers (married 11 May 1686), with birth dates varying from 24 May 1688 to 19 Oct. 1902.

Genealogy E of Amsterdam opens with the names Dirck Symonsz. Banning, bailiff 1388, Chief Officer 1393 and Jan Oude (Broeck) Banning, burgomaster 1420. Gerrit Banning, draper, is specified as ancestor. Seven generations are followed closely and extensively described, including 27 principal descendants with as extreme dates of birth 1370 and 1605. In the seventh generation we encounter Frans

Benningh (1544-1582), the father-in-law of Captain Frans Banninck Cocq, known from his central position in Rembrandt's Nightwatch.

For almost three centuries the Amsterdam Bannings held influential positions in public life. Their esteem declined in the seventeenth century, probably partly as a result of mutual differences of opinion. There were families who were considerably more tolerant toward their Roman Catholic fellow townsmen than the municipal council deemed desirable. It is possible that this provided impetus for emigration to Belgium, Germany or England.

Finally, the writer comes back to the families of the Gelderland province (Netherlands). It remains undecided whether their lineage stems from the Amsterdam and German Bannings, but this is currently being researched.

3. *Genealogy of Maurits Arnoldus Banning* (Dutch, 1984)

The third Banning genealogy was written in Dutch in 1984 by J.Banning of the Netherlands; entitled *Stamboom van Maurits Arnoldus Banning, Predikant te Oudemirdum 1687-1708 (Genealogy of Maurits Arnoldus Banning, minister in Oudemirdum)*. It comprises the family tree of the Frisian (province in the north of the Netherlands) Maurits Arnoldus Banning from 1687 and his descendants until 1984. J. Banning has focused primarily on the genealogical data but includes numerous references to P.W. Worrall 1909 and J.A.W. Banning 1934.

J. Banning introduces his findings with the following statement:

"It seems probable that one of the Gelderland (province of the Netherlands) Bannings settled in Workum around 1725. A certain Johannes Harmanus Banning - the ancestor of most of the Frisian Bannings now alive - came to Pingjum from there in 1778, to live here permanently." Since then, it has been established that these Bannings originated in Tecklenburg, Germany, as a branch of the German family specified as D in genealogy 2, above.

Eleven generations are listed in this genealogy, with a total of 113 genealogical codes.

In 1984 there were 17 Banning families known who resided in Friesland, of which 16 have been designated the following genealogical codes: VIIb1, VIIb2, VIIg1, VIIn2, VIIo2, VIIo7, VIIIa2, VIIi, VIIIa, VIIIg, VIIIh, VIIIk, VIIIl, IXm, IXo, IXp.

4. *Genealogy of Maurits Arnoldus Banning* (English, 2002)

The aforementioned genealogy evolved into a fourth: a translation into English of the genealogy of Maurits Arnoldus Banning, in 2002, by Elisabeth van Schaick-Banning, a descendent of this line and author of this book. Also included is a chapter in which historical and biographical information has been added.

5. *The Banning Branches* (English, 1997)

The fifth genealogy, entitled The Banning Branches, is written by Leroy Banning in the United States and published by Heritage Books Inc., Maryland, USA, in 1997. This extensively researched genealogy focuses on the American Bannings as a sequel to those set out (and included) by Pierson Worrall Banning, from the 18th century to 1997. It comprises primarily genealogical data, covering 3 to 9 generations depending on the branch. The book consists of 489 pages. About 200 copies were published.

6. *Genealogy Banning* of Ulft, Gendringen and Wehl (Dutch, 2001)

This is a detailed and updated genealogy based on the data in Genealogy 2.B (above). It was extensively researched by the family Weyn Banningh and consists of several adaptations, both published and private, in issues of the *Nederlands Patriciaat* (1950 and 1974), the *Annuaire des Familles Patriciennes de Belgique* (1940-45) and private research undertaken by E.H. Mijnssen in 1940. An excerpt from these data, with biographical information and illustrations added, was compiled by the brothers Michiel and Jan Banning, direct descendants of this line, in 2001 (unpublished). The most recent findings indicate that this genealogy commences with Hendrick Banninck, born around 1560 in or near the Castle Hackfort, Vorden, Hengelo. The genealogy covers some 14 generations, from around the turn of the 17th century to 1960.

Where an individual is mentioned in this book, the reference to his or her lineage, when known, is specified. 'G' is simply an abbreviation of 'Genealogy'. The number which follows e.g. G1, G2 etc., denotes in which of the above genealogical books the individual can be found. If an initial follows this, it refers to the fragment genealogy in that book, e.g. G2.E. The code, G2.E.VII, refers to the number which that individual has been designated in the genealogy and most often denotes the generation. If a small letter G2.E.VII.a is added, this person is mentioned as a descendant of G2.E.VII but not included in subsequent generations. G2.E.VII is therefore a seventh generation person (VII) in the Amsterdam line (E) of the second book G2 (*Genealogie van het Geslacht Banning, 1934*).

G1 *The First Banning Genealogy* (Pierson Worrall, 1909)

G2 *Genealogy of the Banning Family* (J.A.W. Banning, 1934)

G3 & G4 *Maurits Arnoldus Banning, minister of Oudemirdum (J. Banning,* 1984)

G5 *The Banning Branches* (Leroy Banning, 1997)

G6 *Banning* (Weyn Banningh, J. and M. Banning, 2001)

Several other Banning genealogies exist which were not specifically used as reference:

7. *De Vroedschap van Amsterdam 1578-1795*, J. E. Elias, 1903 (Dutch)

Johan E. Elias (1875-1959) was a historian born in Amsterdam. *The Vroedschap of Amsterdam 1578-1795 (The Amsterdam Town Council 1578-1795)* is among the most comprehensive histories of the town council of Amsterdam during that historic period and includes carefully researched genealogies of those holding influential positions in the Amsterdam town council, including that of the Bannings.

8. *Annuaire des Familles Patriciennes de Belgique*[67], 1940-45 (French)

The family lineage of which Dr. Emile Th. J.H. Banning of Belgium was a member, as outlined above in 2.C., as well as the family of Weyn Banningh is included in this French edition of *Yearbook of the Patrician families of Belgium, 1940-45*.

9. *Onderzoek Geslacht Banningh*, E.H. Mijnssen, 1940 (Dutch)

This privately commissioned report (*Banningh Family Research*) was commissioned by the family of Weyn Banningh and researches primarily the relations of Ulft and Gendringen and Wehl as set out in 2.A, B and C, above.

10. *Het Nederland's Patriciaat*, 1950, 1974 (Dutch)

Het Nederland's Patriciaat , (The Netherlands Aristocracy) has been published annually since 1910, by the Central Bureau of Genealogy in The Hague, Netherlands. Genealogies of some 1800 families have been published to date, including a Banning genealogy in 1950 and 1974.

11. Fragment genealogies

In addition to the above, several fragment genealogies have been compiled, the inter-relation of which has not yet been established. These are unpublished.

Where the name of an individual, in any of the records found, is spelled as Banning, it is consistently used throughout for the sake of simplicity and comprehensibility, as was done in the extensive genealogy of 1934. Very often a Banning was recorded by other spellings, but if Banning was included amongst those specified, it is adhered to here. Only when an individual was not referred to as Banning, then the spelling used for that person is maintained as found in the original source.

---

[67] Fortuné Koller, *Annuaire des Familles Patriciennes de Belgique*, vol 1-6, Edelweiss, Belgium, 1940-1945

Very few, if any, Bannings in France, Ireland or other countries are known to the author at this time. This does not mean they did not, or do not, exist, because they most certainly do, although not in significant number. However, the intent of this publication was not to research family connections, but to highlight persons already known in the lineage and to position them against the background of history. This story is thus more biographical and historical than genealogical. In a way, it will imbue many of the names in our family tree with distinctive character and colour and illustrate what a motley collection we are.

*   *   *

3   THE NETHERLANDS

Early settlement in the Netherlands

The earliest records of Bannings living in the Netherlands focus on the eastern provinces of Drenthe, Gelderland and Overijssel. To understand the significance of this, we will first look more closely at the history.

The first written source to cover the area of the modern Netherlands and Belgium is the book *De bello gallico* (*On the Gallic Wars*) by Julius Caesar. Caesar and the Romans invaded Gaul in 57 BC and then went on to conquer the provinces of the Netherlands. For some four or five centuries this region was an outpost of the Roman Empire; Caesar met mostly Celtic tribes here.

At the end of the Roman Empire, around 400 AD, chaos reigned in large parts of Europe. Tribal migrations increased and expanded into the great Wandering of the Nations. The Franks emigrated to the south in the direction of Gaul. The Frisians spread their area of influence to the north of the Rhine. The Alemanni left for south Germany, and the west Goths (Visigoths) for Spain, while the east Goths (Ostrogoths) settled in Italy. Many tribes of Angles and Saxons left for Britain; the Saxons that stayed behind made Westphalia, Germany, their home.

The Saxons were a large and powerful Germanic people and spread to what is now north-western Germany and the eastern Netherlands. They are first mentioned by the geographer Ptolemy[68] as a people of southern Jutland, Denmark and present-day Schleswig-Holstein, Germany, whence they appear subsequently to have expanded to the south and west.

Some Saxons, along with Angles, Jutes and Frisians, invaded Britain in the early Middle Ages, giving their names to the kingdoms of Essex, Sussex and Wessex (the lands respectively of the East, South and West Saxons), which with the shorter-lived Middlesex eventually became part of the kingdom of England.

The Saxon language was the predecessor of both the Old English language as well as to the modern Low Saxon language, and is most closely identified with Frisian in the north of the Netherlands.

One peculiarity of the language was closely studied by Dr. B.H. Slicher van Bath and described in his book *Mensch en Land in de Middeleeuwen*[69] (*People and property in the Middle Ages*). Dr. Slicher van Bath's extensive research focuses on the eastern provinces of the Netherlands.

---

[68] Wikipedia; Saxons: http://en.wikipedia.org/wiki/Saxons, accessed Feb. 2004
[69] Dr. B.H. Slicher van Bath, *Mensch en Land in de Middeleeuwen*, Assen-Utrecht, Van Gorcum & Comp. N.V., 1944

He emphasizes that there is one specific name suffix peculiar to this particular geographical area: the suffixes - '*-ing*' and '*-ink*' which are also particularly indigenous to Eastern England. In the Netherlands, names with these suffixes only occur outside of the Eastern provinces in insignificant numbers. The origin of names comprising '*-ing*', as an entity dates only from the 12th century, but the *compound* of a name (e.g. Bann, Benno) with the suffix '*-ing*' dates back to the 9th century. Significantly, these '*-ing*' names are found also to occur in England and especially in the east, the area most exposed to Saxon influence. Ekwall[70] therefore attributes these names specifically to Saxon influence. He also attributes the fact that similar names occur on the continent and in Scandinavia to the Saxons, the names being very old. In the eastern Netherlands there are 49 names which correspond with those in England. In Sussex there are 39 and in the eastern provinces of the Netherlands 50 compounds of a name with the suffix '*-ing*'. This parallel is unusual and therefore led researchers to conclude that the origin in both countries is Saxon.

Banning is one of these names - a compound of the Christian name 'Banno' or 'Benno' and '*-ing*'. Interestingly, the earliest 'Bennings' on record are a family known by that name in 1238 in Coesfeld, Westphalia (Germany), whose members were aldermen. Westphalia is also one of the original Saxon settlements on the continent.

Early records specify some 40 properties in the three eastern provinces of the Netherlands (and some in Westphalia, Germany) before 1500 which derived from the name Banning (Benning(h), Benninck, etc.), some of which still exist today. These are described further on.

The oldest mention of Banning on record in the Netherlands, to date, is that of Arnoldus Banning, Alderman in Zutphen in 1294. His son and grandson, both Arnoldus Banning, were aldermen, listed from 1343-1358. The Banning's belonged to the prominent Zutphen families in the 14th century, according to a list published in the *Nederlandse Leeuw* of 1935[71]: *Zutphen family names of prominence in 1390*. On the 13th line we find the specification "Reynoldum Banninc et eius uxorem". The second oldest mention is of a Banning(e) manor in the march of Uffelte[72], dated 1298-1304. There were also several Bannings in the area of Deventer, said to be the ancestors of the first Amsterdam Banning, Gerrit. Although Gerrit has not been found, to date, in the archives, the following persons are mentioned in Deventer:

---

[70] Eilert Ekwall , *English Place-names in – ing*, Lund, Gleerop, 1962, p. 109
[71] *De Nederlandse Leeuw*, Universiteit v. Amsterdam, Amsterdam, No. 1, LIIIe, Jan. 1935, column 11-14
[72] *Nomina Geographica Neerlandica*, Koninklijke Nederlandse Aardrijkskundige Genootschap, E.J. Brill, Leiden, 1899, volume V

1359: Alteti Banninge[73]
1385: Wyssa Banninx[74]
1403: Evert Banninek[75]
1443: Aleyt Banninek [76]
1451: Ludeken Bannynck [77]
1457: Lubbert Bannick[78]
1480: Griete Bannyngk [79]
1555: Albert Bannyng[80]

Amsterdam

Three Bannings are found as the earliest recorded in Amsterdam:
Jan Oude (Broeck) Banning, Symonsz., Alderman in 1419, 1420 and 1423, Burgomaster in 1420.
Dirck Symonszn. Banning, Bailiff from 13 December 1388 - 19 January 1390, 26 April - ....1393-1396, Chief Officer (or High Officer) 1393, died in 1405. Jan and Dirck were both sons of a Symon Banning and were presumably brothers. Dirck Symonsz. Banning, while featuring at the beginning of this genealogy, also ends here - coming to an abrupt, unfortunate and grisly demise. Together with the Bailiff Jan Nottard and Amel Janszn. Rijzer, he participated in one of the Kabeljauwsche uprisings which ensued when Count Willem VI was elected to government, occasioning the death of the priest Willem Bruinsz.. (The Kabeljauwsche conflicts broke out in the 14th and 15th centuries. When Count Willem IV was killed he had no legal successors; his closest relative was his sister Margaretha van Beieren, who succeeded him. Her son - who would later govern the Netherlands as Willem V - was also given a governing position. Differences arose between mother and son and when each developed their own factions these entered into a longstanding and historical conflict).

---

[73]Mr. J.I. van Doorninck, *Cameraars-rekeningen van Deventer, 1885*, part II, 1348-1360, p. 671
[74] Mr. J.I. van Doorninck, *Cameraars-rekeningen van Deventer, 1885*, part II, 1348-1360, p. 671
[75] Mr. J.I van Doorninck, *Cameraars-rekeningen van Deventer, 1885*, part II, 1348-1360, p. 671
[76] J.A.W. Banning, *Genealogie van Het Geslacht Banning*, Ferd. Banning & Zonen, Groenlo, 1934, p. 144-148
[77] Mr. J.I. van Doorninck, *Catalogus der archieven van het Groote- en Voorster Gasthuis te Deventer, 1879*, no. 476, p. 203-4
[78] Walther Stein, *Hansisches Urkundenbuch, 1451-1463*, Leipzig, Germany, Duncker & Humblot, 1899, p. 417-418
[79] Mr. J.I. van Doorninck, *Catalogus der archieven van het Groote- en Voorster Gasthuis te Deventer, 1879*, p. 292
[80] Mr. J.I. van Doorninck, *Catalogus der archieven van het Groote- en Voorster Gasthuis te Deventer, 1879*, no. 1043, p. 462, "Albert Bannynges-property on the Vorsterland, etc."

and when each developed their own factions these entered into a longstanding and historical conflict).

As a result of this uprising, Dirck Symonszn. Banning and his two compatriots were run out of town, captured in ambush and subsequently beheaded, and delivered as such to their friends.

Two other Bannings should be mentioned amongst the first known in Amsterdam, although neither have as yet found a place in the existing genealogy. **Johan Banninc**[81], priest, was mentioned as the owner of a house on the Damrak, adjacent to the Nieuwendijk, where the first Amsterdam Bannings are recorded as drapers in 1386, allegedly having come from Deventer. Although Johan Banninc's sale of the house was not until 1439, the original documents specified a lease of one Dutch pound per year. As this monetary unit was used in Amsterdam only until 1373, the historian's conclusion is that the owner had the house from 1373, or earlier. This is likely the same Johanne Banninc mentioned in a Latin entry in the archives: "Anno 1453 Prior Item a Domino Johanne Benninc iiii postolaet preter 1 stuver, ex paste cujusdam persone, que dubitat an tantum nobis debeat vel non, si non petit orationes nostras [Nota: wat zijn dit voor aalmissen, daar de gever twijffelt, an tantrum debeat? &e]" which translates as: " Anno 1453: the same for the lord Johanne Benninc, 4 postelaet (a guilder coinage of the time) 1 nickel, by a certain person, who doubts only whether he should give it or not, unless we offer a prayer for it. " This is interpreted as meaning that this Johanne Benninc was deceased, and that the alms were intended for prayers in his memory.

The other is **Jan Gerrit Bannincxz.**, mentioned in 1416 as owner of a house adjacent to the property mentioned above on the Nieuwendijk. Research is currently being done as to whether this Jan Gerrit Bannincxz. was a son of Gerrit Banning, who follows. (The chapter 'New Light on the Oldest Generations of Banning in Amsterdam – Ties to Assendelft' elaborates on this.)

Gerrit Banning, (*G2.*) is assumed to be the progenitor of the Banning families in the Netherlands, who governed the country to a greater or lesser extent for nearly three centuries, holding positions as aldermen, city councillors, burgomasters and numerous other leadership functions. Gerrit is said to be a descendant of the house of 'De Banninck' in Colmschate near Deventer, the Netherlands (1385), and settled in Amsterdam in 1386, where he established a textile trade on the Nieuwendijk in Amsterdam.

---

[81] *Gens Nostra*, Nederlandse Genealogische Vereniging, Amsterdam, no. 81, 1984, p. 126, 127

The textile industry became an extremely important and flourishing branch of industry in Europe for three centuries, and Amsterdam featured prominently as centre of trade. The following declaration from 1618 attests to this:

" Amongst all enterprise and trades, our city being blessed for this purpose by the Almighty God, the cloth industry has always been one of the most prominent, on which not only the dyers and drapers depend, but in particular the Drapery of all olde tymes has been associated."[82]

The 'drapery' referred to was generally a plain (as opposed to patterned), woollen fabric which, by means of a lengthy process, became closely woven and achieved a lustrous sheen. The best quality was to be found in Amsterdam. Membership to the draper's guild was an honorary function, and therefore the members had to be reasonably wealthy and prestigious citizens. Their task was to inspect the bolts of cloth, which they did three times a week. The members traditionally served office for the period of one year, from Good Friday to Good Friday.

Portraits of the members of guilds and trade organisations became popular following a fashionable trend for group portraits of the civic militia after 1580. These were prestigious commissions for portrait painters and represented a significant gauge of their status and success. The first of such group portraits was *Six Wardens of the Cloth*, painted by Pieter Pieterszn. in 1599, depicting a number of prominent representatives of this industry in Amsterdam.

Jacob Jansz. Banning, a descendant of the above mentioned Gerrit and an affluent cloth merchant in Amsterdam, is one of those portrayed. The painting is part of the collection of the Rijksmuseum in Amsterdam.

[82] J. Banning, *Stamboom van Maurits Arnoldus Banning*, 1984, p.II

5. Six Wardens of the Cloth Pieter Pietersz. 1599
Portrayed (left to right) are: Jacob Jansz Benningh, Lambert Pietersz, Hendrik Servaesz, Gijsbert Michielsz en Hendrik Boelensz.. The sixth person is unnamed and believed to be a servant.

collection: Rijksmuseum, Amsterdam

Rembrandt was later commissioned to portray wardens of the cloth in one of his most famous works, *Syndics of the Clothmaker's Guild* in 1662 (Rijksmuseum, Amsterdam), depicting members of the guild who held office from 1661 - 1662.

Jan Jacobsz. Banning (*G2.E.VI*)(born ca. 1500; descendant of Gerrit, above,) was a prosperous cloth merchant on the Nieuwe Langedijk 'on the south corner of the Jan Corten Lane', in an establishment called ''t Vliegende Varken' ('the Flying Pig') in Amsterdam. He died of the plague on 13 Apr. 1567, as did, within a month, two of his daughters (spinsters) and his wife.

His son **Jacob Jansz. Banning** (*G2.E.VII.a*) carried on family tradition and enjoyed a position among the most affluent cloth merchants in Amsterdam. He was elected to the town council in 1578 and held numerous influential positions in public life. Several years later, when consulted on the appointment of the Supreme Governor Prince William I, Banning was one of those most vehemently opposed to having His Serene Highness sworn in. He received a summons and a fine of 10,000 Leiden stones. (The fine actually constituted stones from the city of Leiden - the stones were used for purposes of building). He was also forbidden to leave the city. The Prince was exalted to Count, which met with considerable opposition especially in the provinces of Zeeland and Utrecht, which spread to Amsterdam, and he was ultimately assassinated (Delft, 10 July 1584). The fine of Leiden stones was thus cancelled. Jacob Janz. Banning is depicted above in the group portrait by Pieter Pietersz. *Six Wardens of the Cloth* in 1599.

Jacob Jacobsz. Banning (*G2.E.VII* / died 1581) was also a textile merchant on the Oude Zijds Voorburgwal in Amsterdam. He was 'Commissioner of the Grain Exchange ', from November 1565 to March 1566 , Tax Commissioner from May to July 1578, Councillor from 1578 until his death (elected by the representatives of the Civic Militia), Alderman in 1578, Commissioner of Orphanages 1579, Warden of the Cloth 1580. J. ter Gouw writes that November 1565 was "a time of excessive trepidation and famine," and that the populace faced an anxious winter. The Burgomasters wanted to know exactly how much grain there was in the city and permitted no action to be taken without their permission. They had all grain lofts and other grain storage depots inspected and took stock of all grain supplies. They appointed a supervisory commission, made up of Jacob Jacobsz. Banning and three others.

Jacob Banning was a staunch supporter of the Prince of the Netherlands during the 80 years War - he did not, at any rate, support the Spanish – a political position illustrated in a number of letters still to be found in the Amsterdam Municipal Archives. On 29 October 1583 Jacob Banning received an invitation from the exiled Arend Jansz. Coesvelt to meet him in the towns of Wormer or Westzaan, in order that he might reveal certain issues to Banning, largely in the interest of the city. Banning found this injudicious and forwarded the letter to the Burgomasters. Three days earlier, two copies of an anonymous letter had fallen into the hands of the Burgomasters, concerning an incitement to seek the Prince's protection. These letters were very unwelcome in view of the fact that the Duke of Alva had just arrived in Amsterdam. Jacob Banning was appointed by a majority of the Amsterdam citizens as commissary to carry a petition to Brussels. The historian J. ter Gouw describes the occasion:

"There was considerable unrest in Amsterdam, but the people restricted their action to petitions, without there being a direct uprising. This demonstrates that the leadership of the movement was in the hands of prominent citizens who, by means of filing complaints and appeals in Brussels, attempted to compel the governors to assume a different attitude in the case of the Satisfactie. 'Today, as we have been informed', (so wrote the Burgomasters on 17th June to their representatives), Jacob Banning has embarked to Brussels with a new petition, signed by a large number of citizens; we send you a copy which has been supplied to us by several good friends. Banning will wish to speak with you. If he seeks audience, ask to see his power of attorney, and observe carefully by whom it is signed; yes, take, if possible, a copy of the power of attorney, and scrutinise that which he undertakes in Brussels."[83]

They were later told that Banning had been to Delft to speak with the Prince about the 'new petition', and, informing the representatives of this fact, they added : "Be watchful, that such rebels, who oppose their governors, shall be reproved." Apparently it never came to this, since Jacob Banning was in 1578 a member of the new reformed government and behaved accordingly, in accord with the first Tax Commissioners following the Amsterdam Alteration. Although the last Tax Commissioner had closed office prior to this commotion on the 26th May 1578, on the 27th it was had been reopened, and the Tax Commissioners began after the Alteration to collect wine, brandy, beer and grain excises and they also received a salary as of this date. The Tax Commissioners in office following the Alteration - Jacob Banning Jacobsz., Hendrick Olfertsz Fuyck and Jan de Bisschop - were commissioned on 26th May 1578.

Jacob Banning was also a Warden of the Cloth; men required to have a thorough knowledge of every aspect of the textile industry. A treaty of 4th November 1411 determined that Aldermen and Councillors of Amsterdam in future had to meet every Good Friday, in the Town Hall, in order to select four or five prominent burghers as Wardens.

Amsterdam 1585-1672: the Golden Age
In February 1578 the *Satisfactie* marked Amsterdam history, when the city reluctantly agreed to join the revolt against Spanish rule. The famous *Alteratie* followed on its heels in May 1578. The Roman Catholic town council, supportive of Spain, was replaced by a Protestant Orangist council. This event represented a milestone in the history of the city. Initially, not much changed. The population of Amsterdam, some 30,000 inhabitants, stabilised. However, the fall of Antwerp in 1585 marked a turning point. The ensuing blockade of the Scheldt river (which was maintained even after the peace treaty of 1648) enabled Amsterdam to develop into the world's most important staple market.
Within only a few decades the city acquired an unprecedented wealth, established a colonial empire and exercised a political power with repercussions throughout the whole of Europe.

---

[83] J. ter Gouw, *Geschiedenis van Amsterdam*, Scheltema & Holkema, Amsterdam, 1880-1886, vol. VII. p. 205

The new patricians immediately started to work on plans to expand the city. However, after the fall of Antwerp in 1585 refugees started to overcrowd the city. Many of these new inhabitants of Amsterdam were forced to settle outside the city walls. Between 1580 and 1614 a suburb of alarming proportions developed west of the city. This situation gave rise to even more ambitious expansion plans. Following completion of Amsterdam's characteristic ring of canals, intersecting the city, in 1663, no further plans for expansion were undertaken until the 19th century.

The *Golden Age* had become a reality. It was a time characterized by large-scale immigration, the rapid growth of the corn trade and the absence of a feudal power structure. The rapid growth of the corn trade was caused by the European crisis of 1590, when there was a marked increase in wages to what were probably the highest in northern Europe. The wage increase led, in turn, to implementation of labour-saving technology, such as the windmill. Economic and financial innovations were introduced, and the VOC – The Dutch East India Company, was established in 1602, with Amsterdam securing a 50% ownership. New institutions such as the VOC, the Exchange Bank (1609), and also the Commodity Exchange in 1613 contributed significantly to Amsterdam's commercial success.

In 1600 Amsterdam was the most prosperous as well as the largest and most powerful city of the Dutch Republic. In the course of the 17th century the city gained control over the Republic's internal affairs as well as its foreign policy, even though technically Amsterdam did not hold a majority vote. The town council had become completely autonomous, the final stage in an ongoing development which had already become apparent in the late Middle Ages. This position allowed the city enormous freedom, i.e. freedom of trade but also freedom of thought and religion unparalleled by any other city in the Dutch Republic. With an phenomenal 700% increase of population within the course of a single century (1578-1675), Amsterdam had acquired a strongly cosmopolitan character and had become a commercial trade centre of international repute.

It was predominantly the freedom of the tradesman that prevailed in Amsterdam. Freedom of thought and religion developed as an inevitable consequence of the commercial climate. The burgomasters formed the only political power of significance even though they had to reckon with the city council, a powerful board of which the wealthiest and most influential citizens of the city were the members. However, as long as the burgomasters looked after the vested interests of the tradesmen, they enjoyed a considerable freedom of action.

In 1650 Stadtholder William III of Orange, who wished to bring the city more within the sphere of his own influence, came to establish his authority. The ruling oligarchy, led by the Bickers and De Graeffs, had become the uncrowned kings of the Republic; a thorn in William's side. The Bickers were forced to step down, but eventually regained their former power. The on-going power struggle between the House of Orange and the city of Amsterdam, indecision on the part of the republican government, took their toll. The country was left defenceless in the face of foreign threats. Wars and hostile action darkened the development of the second half of the 17th century. The first and second English Wars (1652-1654 and 1665-1667) were mainly fought at sea and had a very detrimental effect on trade. In 1672 the French attacked the Republic. There was a panic in Amsterdam, shares of the Dutch East India Company plummeted, men were called to fight, and the Golden Age came to a close.

Jacob Banning's daughter, **Agnieta Jacobsdr. Banning** *(G2.E.VII.1; 1561-...)* married (2 July 1596) the renowned surgeon and Professor of Anatomy, Dr. Sebastiaen Egbertsz., alias Dr. Sebastianus Egberti, who also fulfilled at various times the positions of councillor, alderman, burgomaster, treasurer, and regent of the orphanage, in Amsterdam. Dr. Sebastiaan Egberti is portrayed in numerous well-known paintings held in European museums today. His father had been Captain of the Civic Militia, and accused of having Lutheran sympathies. He was therefore taken prisoner on 1 March 1568, tortured, and sentenced to be beheaded. However, he died in prison on the night preceding his scheduled execution on 8 October 1568. The next day the executioner beheaded the lifeless body, carrying out the sentence as planned[84].

Gerrit Banning Jansz. *(G2.E.V;1460-1504)*; great-grandson of Gerrit, above) was Councillor of Amsterdam in 1498. His father-in-law, Dirck Heymansz. Ruysch, was Burgomaster of Amsterdam in 1483 and the first resident of Castle De Graft in the Dutch city of Naarden. The castle came to be known by his name, as 't Slot (Castle) Ruysdael, and was demolished around the beginning of the 18th century. Dirck Heymanszn. Ruysch died in 1509. His daughter Katrijn Heymanszn. Ruysch married Gerrit Banning in 1491 and they are assumed to have lived in Ruysdael Castle in 1526 (this does not tally with his date of death), after which their son Jan Gerritsz. Banning, and in turn his son Gerrit Jansz. Banning, also lived here.

Some time around 1590 a certain Jacob Jansz. van der Graft, an affluent furniture maker who renamed himself Goyen (the region where he lived is known as 'the Gooi'), moved onto the estate as a tenant, presumably in the farmhouse. Among his 6 sons were Salomon and Isaac.

---

[84] J. and M. Banning, *Genealogy of Ulft*, Netherlands, unpublished, 2001

Following the death of their father in 1616, Salomon and Isaac moved to Haarlem. The eldest son Jacob (1594-1656), also a furniture maker, remained on the estate Ruysdael. In 1619, at the age of 25, Jacob was eligible to vote and had also entered the Dutch Reformed Church. Both these qualifications made him eligible for municipal office, contrary to his father, who had been a Baptist. Registered as alderman of the city a year later, Jacob felt that his new status merited a new name and from then on he called himself Jacob van Ruysdael, after his residence. His brothers followed his example and also took the name of van Ruysdael. Salomon van Ruysdael is known as a celebrated landscape painter. Isaac, who painted as well, was a frame-maker and art dealer. His son Jacob van Ruisdael (1628-1682) (who for some reason was the only one to spell the name with an 'i') is now known as one of the most famous landscape painters of all time. Two of Jacob van Ruisdael's paintings represent 't Slot Ruysdael where the three generations of Bannings had once lived. The tower-like structure is believed to have been part of the Castle Ruysdael and the thatched farmhouse adjacent to this is believed to have been the Ruysdael's tenant home.[85]

6. Winter Landscape   Jacob van Ruisdael   1650-1682
collection: Rijksmuseum, Amsterdam

---

[85] Seymour Slive, H.R. Hoetink, *Jacob van Ruisdael*, Meulenhoff/Landshoff,Amsterdam 1981, p. 24,25

Jan Gerritsz. Banning (*G2.E.VI.a; ca.*1500-1557) son of the aforementioned Gerrit and Katrijn and resident of Castle Ruysdael, was also known as Young Jan Banning (Jan Banning Jr.). He was a Knight of Jerusalem in 1519, Alderman in 1531, Chairman of the Polder Board of Amstelland in 1537 and Captain of the Longbow Association in 1525. In the same year he was church warden of the Old Church. He travelled to Jerusalem in the company of a Dominican monk and two others, of which one, Jacob Heyn, was his cousin. This pilgrimage is illustrated in a painting called *The Church of the Nativity at Bethlehem*, rendered in 1519 (artist unknown). It currently belongs to the collection of the Museum Catherijneconvent in Utrecht. Jan Gerrtisz. Banning is on the extreme left, holding a palm branch. His coat-of-arms with the characteristic cross Moline is displayed behind him and above. The text on the wooden frame reads: "In the year of our Lord XVc. and XIX, brothers Wouter van Hoogesteyn, Jan Benninck, Jacop Heyn and Meyndert Willems together in Jerusalem; in praise of the Lord." Jacob Heyn, third from the left, is said to be a son of Frans Claes Heynenz. and Katrijn Banning, although this is not verified in the genealogy.

The *Church of the Nativity at Bethlehem* is said to be the oldest group family portrait in the Netherlands (although the panel of the Corsgen family is slightly older and is also mentioned as one of the oldest group portraits. In any case, there are only three such paintings still in existence). It originally hung in the Jerusalem Chapel, associated with the St. Olof's Chapel at the beginning of the Warmoestraat in Amsterdam. During the Alteration in 1578 it was rescued from the chapel by the family of Jan Gerritsz. Banning (portrayed).[86]

---

[86] Amsterdams Historisch Museum, *De Smaak van de Elite*, De Bataafsche Leeuw, Amsterdam, 1986, p. 20, 21, 22

7. The 'Church of the Nativity at Bethlehem'   1515-1524,   artist unknown
from left to right: Jan Banning, Wouter van Hoogesteyn, Jacop Heyn and Meyndert Willems
Collection: Museum Catherijneconvent, Utrecht, Netherlands

The portrait below has been identified as a Benningh (Banning) and dated approximately 1530. Although the identity of the subject was not unquestionably confirmed for a long time, it was recently established that he could be none other than the same Jan Gerritsz. Banning. Aside from the resemblance of the features as portrayed in the *Church of the Nativity at Bethlehem* – given artistic licence – a difference between 19 years of age and 30 or 31 years of age is plausible. The same cross Moline of the family coat-of-arms is illustrated, featuring a star (in the former painting), which signifies that the bearer is a third son. The figure holds a piece of paper and a carnation; the paper symbolises a badge of office, which Jan Gerritsz. Banning assumed (alderman) in 1531; people of status often had their portraits painted on assuming public office. The carnation symbolises devotion, and in the 16th century more specifically devotion of a religious nature. Testimony to Jan Gerritsz. Banning's devotion is found in the fact that he was a Knight of Jerusalem and church warden of the Old Church. Moreover, the painting belongs to a private collection of the Baron Heereman van Zuydtwijck, a direct descendant from the marriage between Katrijn Banning, (aunt of Jan Gerritsz. Banning) and Frans Claesz. Heynenz.. A member of the Heyn family and cousin of Jan Gerritsz. Banning, Jacob Heyn, is also portrayed in the Church of the Nativity at Bethelem, indicating that the two were close. Several Heyn family members are mentioned in the last will and testament of Jan Gerritsz. Banning.'s uncle (Jan Jansz. Banning *G2.E.VIa.2*) as partial heirs to his property, and numerous Banning documents are found in the Heereman van Zuydtwijck archives. The two families were mentioned together in several historical documents and a niece of Jan Jansz. Banning lived with and cared for him in his old age. These facts reinforce the conviction that the subject of the portrait is most likely Jan Gerritsz. Banning.

The most recent discovery (2004) of a line of text in a book on heraldry, dated 1873, and concerning the Banning (Benning(h)) coat-of arms, would seem to verify this identity:
"Jan Benning Gerritsz., married to Griet, Stans Claesdr., Alderman 1531, **cuius pictura apud Benningios** [whose portrait is in the possession of the Benning family]".[87]

---

[87] J.B. Rietstap, *Armoires des Familles*, ' Institutut Héraldique Universel, Paris, 1873, p. 215

8. Portrait of Jan Gerritsz. Benningh   ca. 1530   artist unknown
photo: Iconografisch Bureau, The Hague, Netherlands

Margriet Dircksdr. Banning (*G2.E.IIIa.1;*1430-12 January 1500) was not only a descendent of Gerrit but through the maternal line also of Herman van Woerden. Herman van Woerden was one of the assassins of Count Floris V in 1296[88]. She and her husband (Hendrick Coenenz. van der Schellingh.), who were extremely wealthy, were founders and benefactors of the new Minderbroeders Monastery in Amsterdam. Pope Pius II gave his approval for the founding of this monastery in 1464[89]. Until 1462 the monks had only a house in which to pursue their mission. After 1462 permission was granted to expand the house, and expand they did, because the Minderbroeders was one of the most extensive monasteries in the city.

There is a tombstone in the historic Old Church of Amsterdam bearing the inscription: "Here lies buried Hendrick Koenens van der Schellink, died in the year MCCCCXCV on the XIIJ day in September, thereafter died his wife Margriete Dirks in the year MCCCCC on the XIJ day in January. God grants all faithful souls peace[90]." This tombstone originally came from the old Minderbroeders Monastery. Apparently the church in the monastery was repeatedly plundered and robbed by Papists, so that the tombstones covering the graves of the Van der Schelling family were moved to the Old Church. However, there they were also damaged 'and greatly molested and broken."

The extent of their fortune became apparent when their estate was divided after they died. Records[91] in Amsterdam, dated 13 December 1503, specify that their assets came to 24 or 25 thousand guilders, which at the time was quite considerable.

Margriet Dircksdr. Banning and her husband had eight children. According to old Amsterdam archives: "The great wealth and the good connections of these 'Henrix' children resulted in a saying, common at the time, of his three daughters:

"Van Truy, Giert and Beert
Is de stadt af verveert"[92].

("The town is enhanced
by Truy, Giert and Beert")

One of these daughters, Geertruyt Hendr.dr.van der Schellingh, is portrayed on another painted panel and early group portrait, depicting also her husband, Corsgen Elbertsz. and their son Albert Corsgen.(Kors). The panel came from the St. Agnes Convent in Amsterdam and is now in

---

[88]K. Elhorst, *Floris V*, J.H. Kok, Kampen, 1982

[89] Dr. P. Scheltema, *Aemstel's Oudheid*, I, p. 47 and fol., J.H. Scheltema, Amsterdam, 1855

[90] J.A.W. Banning, *Genealogie van het Geslacht Banning*, Ferd. Banning & Zonen, Groenlo, 1934, p. 81

[91] J.A.W. Banning, *Genealogie van het Geslacht Banning*, Ferd. Banning & Zonen, Groenlo, 1934, p. 136

[92] J.A.W. Banning, *Genealogie van het Geslacht Banning*, Ferd. Banning & Zonen, Groenlo, 1934, p. 136

possession of the Amsterdam Historic Museum. Albert's son, Pieter Rodingh Albertsz, married a cousin, Brechtgen Banning Jansdr., a daughter of Jan Gerritsz. Banning depicted above in the *Church of the Nativity in Bethlehem*.

Margriet Dircksdr. Banning X Hendrick Coenenz. van der Schelling
from this marriage
(Old) Geertruyt Hendr.dr. v.d. Schelling X Corsgen Elbertsz.
from this marriage
Albert Kors X Brecht Pietersdr. Rodingh
from this marriage
Pieter Rodingh Albertz. X Brechtgen Banning Jansdr.

The painting was originally much larger, the focus being a crucifixion in the centre. The family was grouped on either side; the men on the left and the women on the right, as was frequently done at that time. The painting was donated to the St. Agnes Convent at the beginning of the 16th century by Margriet Corsgendr. to hang in the dining hall. She was a professed nun and after 1518 Mother Superior of the convent. Following the dissolution of the convent in 1585 the painting went to her niece (cousin?) Margriet Heijmansdr., and her descendants, the family Witsen (Notary Nicolas Witsen was a burgomaster of Amsterdam), probably sawed up the panel and removed its 'superstitious' subject at the centre. When it was auctioned in 1728 it was described as a family portrait with 15 kneeling figures. The two halves were later conjoined to represent one family group, and IHS painted in the middle to render the posture of prayer convincing. The remainder of the centre scene was repainted with a tile floor and drapery. Both sections are now displayed in a reconstruction at the Amsterdam Historic Museum.

9. Fragment of a Crucifixion with portraits of Corsgen Elbertsz. and his
family, ca. 1506, by Jacob Cornelisz. van Oostsanen
Amsterdams Historisch Museum, Amsterdam

Portrayed on the left are Korsgen Elbertsz. (foremost figure) and his sons
Dirck and Albert (background, both aldermen in Amsterdam) and (with
cap in hand) the son-in-law of Heyman Jacobz. van Ouder-Amstel,
Burgomaster of Amsterdam. On the left, foreground, Geertruyt Hendr. dr.
van der Schelling (daughter of Margriet Banning), her daughters Margriet
(prioress, in white) and Baerte, nun of the St. Agnes Convent. Also shown
is the wife of Heyman, Engeltje. The four children are said to represent
Geertruyt's children who died in childhood. The frame features a
dedication to Corsgen Elbertsz. and Geertruyt Hendr. dr. v.d. Schellingh,
by their daughter Margriet, when she presented the painting to the St.
Agnes Convent in 1518. A portion of the text is missing due to removal of
the central part.

Portraits in the early 16th century were not necessarily intended
to render a likeness of the subjects, who often posed as religious figures
in religious settings, and were secondary in size and importance to the
subject, a crucifixion or Madonna with child. After some years the
secondary figures were represented more prominently. It was common
practice for those who could afford the means to contribute generously
toward some aspect of religious practice, an effort to ensure their own
salvation through continued supplication and prayer by those of the
religious order. In an age with constant warfare, inquisition, famine and
plague, when many died in infancy and superstition and suffering were
rife, people depended on the clergy to intercede on their spiritual behalf -

in the pre-Reformation age nobody aspired to a personal relationship with God. This was the priest's or monk's duty and people paid their dues in order for them to fulfil their role of protection.

Several Banning families founded convents or monasteries in Amsterdam, or made significant contributions to religious orders. This too, was in keeping with the times, as numerous convents and monasteries were founded during the economic boon in the Netherlands in the fifteenth and sixteenth centuries. Around the turn of the century there were some 25 convents and monasteries in Amsterdam alone. However, the city began to suffer economic loss as a result. Large tracts of land used by religious orders were unavailable for expansion of the city, funds invested in convents and monasteries were exempt from taxes, and the manufacture and sale of products such as beer and linen by religious orders were also exempt from taxes. Moreover, religious orders were exempt from levies such as those imposed for waterways - dikes or canals. The religious orders supplemented their income by renting out premises for private citizens on the outer reaches of the convent or monastery grounds. In the second half of the 15th century the city began to discourage further establishment of convents and monasteries and imposed restrictions, such as the obligation that nuns provide care for 'fallen women', or medical care to the burghers, regardless of their financial position.

The new Minderbroeders Monastery, founded in 1462 by the very wealthy benefactors Margriet Dircksdr. Banning (1430-12 January 1500) and her husband Hendrick Coenenz. van der Schellingh, was one of these.

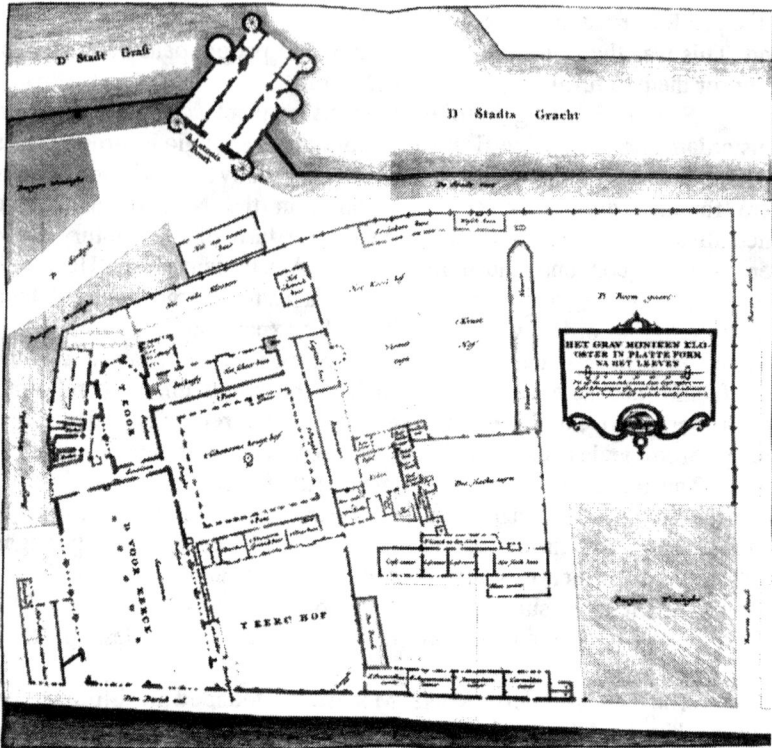

10. The Minderbroeders Monastery (or Gray Brothers Monastery) in
Amsterdam, ca. 1578. The spaciousness is apparent, showing many
gardens and an orchard.
Photo: Iconographisch Bureau/Rijksbureau voor Kunsthistorische Documentatie
(Netherlands Institute for Art History) The Hague

The traditional layout of the monastery is shown in detail, in a ground
plan dated about 1578. It illustrates the original designation of all areas
and outbuildings. The Minderbroeders Monastery was the largest in the
city. A supporting statue (telamon) of a Grey Monk, finely carved from
oak some time after 1462, is one of the only items salvaged from the
Minderbroeders Monastery that still exists today.

History reveals that the Minderbroeder monks in Amsterdam had
considerable influence and were held in high regard. They were favoured
in numerous ways, for example: the monks' beer was carried for them by
the beer carriers 'in God's service', the township presented them with a
new bell when required, yet they were absolved from many payments
imposed by the government on other religious orders, because they were
'only minor brothers (= minderbroeders)' and 'had to live in holy
poverty' from alms.

The Gemäldegalerie in Berlin has a record[93] that the daughter of Margriet Banning, Geertruyt Hendr. dr. v.d. Schellingh, acted as guarantor for the payment of a high altar in a chapel of the St. Agnes Convent (where her daughter became Mother Superior) in Amsterdam. Apparently the convent did not pay craftsman Jan Van Hout enough for his work, but it is said that he did not mind. The altar stone of the high altar has remained intact and today is displayed on a wall in the inner courtyard. A detailed description of the altar is available; it was said to be entirely financed by 'one woman' (presumably Geertruyt Hendr. dr. v.d. Schellingh) and quite costly.

During the 25 years that Margriet Corssendr[94]. was Mother Superior of the St. Agnes Convent, she donated (between 1516 and 1520) seven silver spoons and a silver cup for use in the convent hospital[95]. Silver was regarded as a significant gift; it was weighed and valued. She also donated a panel 'with the three Holy kings' , (which no longer exists) to the convent hospital. Jasper Corszoon donated a panel illustrating 'a figure of Magdalene' to the St. Agnes Convent in 1544, with the stipulation that they could retain it 'until his marriage or until he reclaimed it', this with consent of the orphanage patrons.

Gaeff Banning Gerritsz. (G2.E.IV) and his wife, Elisabeth Jansdr. (de Vlaming) van Oudtshoorn, who was of noble birth and whose father was Burgomaster of Amsterdam in 1452, were benefactors of 'the Barvoete Broedersclooster' ('Monastery of the Barefoot Brothers'), which was another name for the Minderbroeders Monastery mentioned above. Translation of a text from Gerrit Pietersz. Schaep in this regard reads roughly as follows:

"Founding of the Barvoete Broeders Monastery.

Having heard from my parents and friends during their various travels how the Barvoete Broeders Monastery was founded by their forefathers, and being unable to resist further enquiry; which was, in any case, for naught, since all writings and papers had been scattered and the monastery ransacked, we finally located one of the oldest monks, who replied to me that four widows named Lysbeth had been founders, of whom the most principal was Lysbeth van Outshoorn, who was called Lysbeth Gaeven nae Gaeff Benninck (her husband) and had funded the church, right up to the roof, for certain chantries there, also donating certain houses, one to the court (?)

However, these widows, in funding this cloister, were greatly troubled by certain rambunctious persons, who demolished in the night that which had

---

[93] Information provided by the Fotoarchiv Gemäldegalerie, Berlin, by e-mail, 4 Mar. 2003
[94] The name is spelled in various ways: Cors(g)en, Kors(g)en, Corssen, etc.
[95] Marian Schilder, *Amsterdamse Kloosters in de Middeleeuwen*, Vossiuspers, Amsterdam, 1997, p. 50, 51, 63

been repaired during the day, and had no support from the Council of Magistrates, so they, all four, together with all their labourers, went halfway to Haarlem to see the Count of Holland, and implored him to intervene, and he immediately recognised and appreciated the work begun in God's honour and the value of completing it, without hesitation enforcing his authorisation with dire threat to the troublemakers.[96]"

Gaeff Banning's wife Lijsbeth was also the founder of the 'Elisabeth Gaven Chapel' in the Old, or St. Nicholas Church in Amsterdam.

Following the death of Lijsbeth and her husband Gaeff Benninck their heirs, so authorised, funded 'an everlasting chantry in S. Lijsbeth's Chapel in the Town Hall of Amsterdam, now the infirmary, with six gold coins, for which the relevant documents are entrusted to the regents of the St. Pieter's infirmary'.

The heirs of Jan Banning Gerritsz. (*G2.E.IVa*) and his wife 'Elysabeth Jacob Heynrycxzoensdr.' funded a chantry in 1495 to the everlasting memory of their parents, on an altar in the New Church, appointing Claes Jansz. as vicar. This is recorded in the *Memorial Registers of the St. Agnes Chapel*: "The chantry for the parents of Jan Bannincx, Banninck his father and Elisabeth his mother with her children, from whom we have received XVIIJ Rhine guilders for their everlasting memory.[97]" A tombstone was placed in the nave of the Old Church in front of the organ, reading: "Anno MCCCCLXXXVII (1487) on the third day in March died Jan Benninck buried here. God rest his soul. Here lies buried Lysbeth van Banninck Amelisdaughter who was his wife who died in the year of our Lord MCCCCLXXXII (1482)[98]." ['Amelisdr.' is suspected to be confused with 'Auwelsdr.', or may be an error in the engraving.]

There is a record[99] of a certain Anna Banning, who has (to date) not been specifically identified in the genealogy. In 1567 Anna appointed the Priest Pieter Nicolaas as vicar for the chantry of Diderick Verkampen, for which the masses were read on the altar of H. John the Evangelist, in the New Church in Amsterdam at the chancel rail (north side of the church). Anna Banning was said to be wed to Dr. Jan Duyvensz., a nephew of Jan Duvensz. (jr.) and Hillegont Cornelisdr. Banning (daughter

---

[96] B.J.M. de Bont, *Bijdragen voor de Geschiedenis van het Bisdom van Haarlem; 'De Oude-of St. Nicolaaskerk te Amsterdam, hare kapellen, altaren en fundatiën*, volume XXIV, 1899, p. 12., no. 2

[97] B.J.M. de Bont, *Bijdragen voor de Geschiedenis van het Bisdom van Haarlem; Dr. J.F.M. van Sterck,, van kloosterkerk tot Athanaeum; uit de geschiedenis der S. Agneskapel te Amsterdam*, volume XL, 1921, pag. 236, 240, 258

[98] Mr. P.C. Bloys van Treslong, and Mr. J. Belonje, *Genealogische en Heraldische Gedenkwaardigheden in en uit de Kerken van N. Holland*, (1928), II, no. 399

[99] B.J.M. de Bont, *Bijdragen voor de Geschiedenis van het Bisdom van Haarlem; De O.L. Vrouwe- of Nieuwe Kerk te Amsterdam*, 1908, p. 250, enclosure II.

of Cornelis Banning Gerritsz (see *G2.E.VIb.2*) and brother-in-law to Cornelis Banning, although - not surprisingly - there is some confusion in this regard in the genealogy).

It took twenty years of resistance by municipal authorities before the Clarissen Convent could finally be founded in 1513, by **Jan Jansz. Banning** *(G2.E.IVa.2)* and his wife. It was apparent that the authorities felt that Amsterdam already had enough convents. The Clarissen Convent was subjected to strict regulations and not permitted ownership of any material goods. Taxes were imposed. The incomes of religious orders began to decline significantly.

The Clarissen Convent was more isolated than other convents and monasteries. The Court of Holland applied a restriction in 1513 that the ownership of property for convents could not exceed 60 square rods (225 m2). The buildings, possibly already existing at the time, were located on property to the south of the Heiligeweg and the Kalverstraat, which is today the busiest shopping street in Amsterdam. In 1595 the Clarissen Convent was designated as a bridewell or penitentiary institute.

Until 1578 Amsterdam was almost completely Roman Catholic. The Protestant reformers were particularly opposed to the 'idolatry' of the Host and the 'Roman Catholic concept' of the Holy Mass. In a historical episode called the Alteration, the Orangist Calvinists proved the superior force and on 26 May 1578, the Roman Catholics lost their position. In an bloodless revolution the Protestants in Amsterdam took over power and the Catholic magistrates were dismissed. Roman Catholics were strictly forbidden to openly profess their faith, which meant that all churches, monasteries and convents were confiscated by the authorities. The Protestant clergy were assiduous in denouncing every house used for Popish idolatry to the authorities, but the authorities exercised a degree of restraint in acting on these denouncements. The Catholics established churches in their houses so that they could continue to worship according to their faith.

After the Alteration in 1578 all buildings and properties belonging to convents and monasteries were confiscated by municipal authorities and used for various purposes such as hospitals or orphanages. Various pieces of art, artefacts and archaeological finds surviving events after the Alteration eventually found their way into modern museums.

11. Clarissen Convent in Amsterdam, founded in 1513 by Jan Jansz. Banning and his wife, Imme Reijers

Photo: Iconografisch Bureau/Rijksbureau voor Kunsthistorische Documentatie (Netherlands Institute for Art History) The Hague

The aforementioned Jan Janz. Banning was an example of the loquaciousness and leadership demonstrated by several of our ancestral namesakes. Jan Jansz. Banning, (master of law) was a well-known historic figure in the 16th century in land reclamation of Amstelland, shield-bearer (aide) of Emperor Maximilian of Austria and Archduke Charles, Councillor and Alderman, and Councillor of the Provincial Council of Holland. Amstelland (the environs of Amsterdam) was in perpetual threat of being flooded, which would have been disastrous for Amsterdam. Even worse, the surrounding polders were releasing their surplus surface water into Amstelland. "Among the prominent inland regions was a man of authority and influence, who was bold enough to address this issue - Jan Banning."[100] He called a meeting of the burgomasters of Amsterdam and members of the polder boards, which was held on 17 July 1520 in the city hall. During this meeting Jan Banning 'spoke effusively and at great length'. He was obviously convincing - "who else could the meeting appoint other than himself - that brisk, energetic and influential man?" Jan Banning was appointed for the task of protecting the lowlands. He proceeded with tremendous zeal.

The first result of his endeavours was a letter from the Emperor to the Viceroy and the Councils of Holland, written from Brussels on 3 September 1520, and the second was the instigation of the Polder Board of Newer Amstel on 31st Dec. 1520.

He travelled, had charts, maps and land surveys drawn, won lawsuits for damaged dikes and appeals for restoration, put labourers to work and ran up high bills, but in the end, he could say, "I have, with the help of God, the Emperor and Governess, managed affairs such that, at least in Amstelland, almost all threat of flooding has been eliminated."

Jan Beyguinck is mentioned in a description of the city of Gouda (no source or date specified) as having done land surveys along the Ijssel River in 1498[101]. He had been responsible for the design of a plan to improve the waterways around Utrecht. When the need arose for further surveys in 1520, this person was identified as Jan Banning or Benninck, regent of Amsterdam and councillor to the Court of Holland. He had exerted his influence in other projects concerning waterways, as member of the dike commission in 1510, restoration and maintenance of the Vriezendike in 1511 and founder of the Polder Board of Amstelland in 1525. Jan Banning was again consulted in 1527, but there was never sufficient agreement nor were there adequate funds to implement any of the five proposed reconstructive projects for the waterways of the Gouda/Utrecht regions.

---

[100] J.A.W. Banning, *Genealogie van het Geslacht Banning*, Ferd. Banning & Zonen, Groenlo, 1934, p. 95, 96
[101]http://www.waterstaatsgeschiedenis.nl/tijdschrift/tvw2001mei1/Ibelings.htm; accessed Mar. 2003

Jan Jansz. Banning was wealthy. His wife, Imme Reijers, was a farmer's daughter with substantial wealth of her own. In addition to founding the large Clarissen Convent in Amsterdam, they also had a country manor home (referred to as a castle) built on the outskirts of Amsterdam called 'Brillenburg' in 1492. It was known as the largest and most beautiful country estate on the Amstel River. Less than half a century later the manor was known as 'Kostverloren' and briefly as 'Ruiyschenstein'. As Jan Banning and his wife had no children, it was presumed that he willed his estate to his brother Gerrit wed to Katrijn Dircksdr. Heymanszn. Ruysch. The assertion was that this clarified the name of 'Ruyschenstein', just as the ancestral home Ruysdael Castle in Blaricum had acquired its name. However, Jan Banning's last will and testament[102], drawn up in 1534, clearly states that Kostverloren was willed to a son from his first marriage, Christoffel. A second son, Jasper, was also mentioned. (Jasper is mentioned only once in historic documents found to date: a payment was made to 'Jasper Banninck' in 1549 for 'painting' that he did for a large, specially constructed 'arch of triumph' for some municipal celebration.[103]) Until the will was deciphered in 2003 the existence of these two sons was unknown and for centuries it was believed that Jan Banning had no heirs. (Christoffel's name otherwise occurs only once, as 'Christoffel Banning Jansz.'; in relation to division of land on the Nieuwer Amstel which he owned on 2 June 1550[104].)

The estate is most well known throughout history as Kostverloren, a name still found today in the same area. Kostverloren Castle was a favourite subject for numerous famous artists, including Jacob Van Ruisdael, Rembrandt, S. Frisius, and A. Rademaker[105]. The manor was demolished in 1822 but came to light again during archaeological diggings in 1994, whereby a start was made to reconstruct the original building as faithfully as possible to the original. Intriguingly, preliminary findings indicate that the foundations were laid earlier than was once thought – not around 1500, but around 1420.[106]

[102] last will and testament of Jan. Jansz. Banning, *Het Archief van de Familie Heereman van Zuydtwijck 1360-1880*, Vol. I, J.A.M.Y. Bos-Rops, no. 372, 1987, National Archives of the Hague
[103] J. ter Gouw, *Geschiedenis van Amsterdam*, Scheltema & Holkema, Amsterdam, 1880-1886, p. 334
[104] *Ons Voorgeslacht*, Zuidhollandse Vereniging voor Genealogie, Rotterdam, 1984, p. 62
[105] Marius van Melle, *Huys Kostverloren Herrijst*, Ons Amsterdam, issue no. 4, p. 108-111
[106] Marius van Melle, *Huys Kostverloren Herrijst*, Ons Amsterdam, issue no. 4., p. 108

12. Kostverloren Castle on the Amstel River, built by Jan. Jansz. Banning in 1492
engraving by Simon Frisius, 1600-1610
Municipal Archives of Amsterdam

Jan Jansz. Banning left 100 guilders (a significant sum of money at the time) to the nuns of the Clarissen Convent, and an additonal sum of 100 guilders to the city of Amsterdam. Burgomaster Cornelis Banning accepted the bequest on behalf of The Muncipal Treasury in 1538. This is unusual in that it was the only legacy ever left to the city of Amsterdam. In comparison: in 1568 the floor of a hospital was laid with blue stones, for a sum of 13 guilders including material and labour, and in 1570 a sacristy with school were built for a total of 40 guilders and 85 cents. A cow for slaughter could be purchased for 30 guilders in 1573.

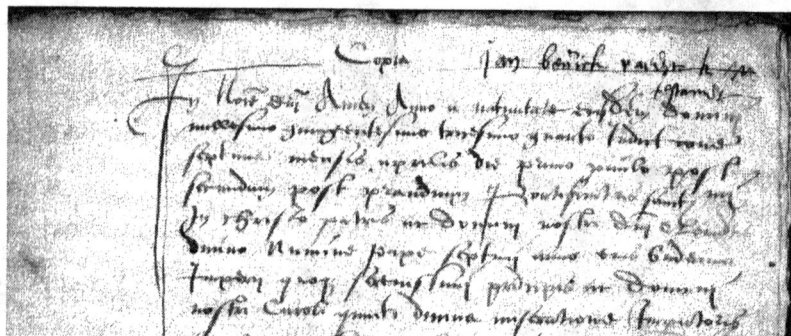

13. Fragment of the last will and testament of Jan Jansz. Banning, 1534
Nationaal Archief, the Hague, archives of the family Heereman van Zuydtwijck,
3.20.23, inv.nr. 372.

Jan Jansz. Banning's influence was apparent in the following incident in 1504: in a charter of 1400 it was stipulated that a Dike-grave could not vote in an election for Burgomaster. Even someone who had in the past served in the position of Burgomaster or Dike-grave, was not eligible to vote for Burgomaster. Dike-grave Banning, however, held a different view. He insisted on having a vote, and received a letter on 5th November 1507 from Emperor Maximilian, who granted him his wish. It is unknown whether he actually participated in the election.

Jan Jansz. Banning was influential in water management in the Netherlands, but another Banning also made a name for himself in this field. **Willem Jansz. Benningh,** (alias Ketel), born around 1569/70 in the town of Edam, is mentioned only in a fragment genealogy from the Banning branch of Edam/Alkmaar.

ONBEKENDE ALKMAARDERS

Willem Jansz. Benning

14. Article from the Alkmaarsche Courant, 5 Sept. 1933, concerning Willem Jansz. Benning as an 'Unknown Alkmaarder'

When Jacob Dirksz. de Graeff, distinguished magistrate, burgomaster and merchant in Amsterdam, was Chairman of the Polder Board of Zijpe, Netherlands in 1628, he approached the sluice masters of Amsterdam for advice concerning reconstruction of the old, wooden sluice in the dike near Oudesluis, which dated from 1564 and showed increasing deterioration. He was referred to sluice builder Willem Jansz. Benningh, who had constructed the Schuijers sluice in Dunkirk (French-Flanders) in 1619, laid the foundations for the Belgian harbour Oostende and from 1619 -1624 was actively involved in the construction of two sluices in Danzig, Poland). Willem Jansz. Benning was thus commissioned in 1629 to build one of the largest shipping sluices in Europe, in Zijpe, the Netherlands. The Zijpe was a polder created in the province of North Holland in 1597. The sluice was completed in 1632. Burgomaster of Amsterdam Jacob de Graeff (who owned an substantial country home on the Zijpe, as did two Banning families) laid the memorial stone for the opening, inscribed with the following verse:

75

"Als duysent en ses hondert yaer
En dartich een gekomen waar
Doen oceaen ons draygde fel
Layd Iacob van den Grave wel
Aen mijn den allereersten steen
Maer Benningh myn voltrock meteen" [107]

("When a thousand six hundred years
And thirty one had come
The ocean compelled us to dredge assiduously
And Jacob van de Grave layed
My very first stone
But Benningh brought me to completion")

After construction of the Groote Sluijs in Zijpe Willem Benningh is mentioned as having built the stone sluice in Nauerna, near the Dutch Assendelft, in 1633.

In a document dated 16 march 1620[108], Willem Jansz. Benningh (alias Ketel) is mentioned as being 50 years of age. (It is notable that the Bannings in Deventer were related by marriage to the noble family of Ketel in the 15th century, and that a Sir Thomas Ketel was mentioned as the brother of one John de Banyngham in 1328 in England). In the same year, only two days beforehand, his name occurs in a charter[109] in which a city carpenter and city mason made declarations on his behalf concerning construction design of sluices in Amsterdam. Willem Jansz. Benningh married Stijntgen Arisd. in 1619. Their signatures are found on this document (presumably a marriage settlement or division of property) dated 16 March 1620.[110]

15. Fragment of a marriage settlement dated 16 March 1620, bearing the signatures of Stijntgen Arisd. and Willem Jansz. Benningh
Regional Archives of Alkmaar

---

[107] P. Dekker, *Oude Boerderijen en Buitenverblijven langs de Zijper Grotesloot*, Pirola, Schoorl, 1988, p. 299
[108] Notarieel Archief Alkmaar, Regional Archives of Alkmaar, inventory no. 92, folio 46, dated 16 Mar. 1620
[109] Dr. J.G. van Dillen, *Bronnen tot de Geschiedenis van het Bedrijfsleven en het Gildewezen van Amsterdam*, Part II, 1612-1632, Martinus Nijhoff, The Hague, 1933, charter no. 605, p. 357
[110] Notarieel Archief Alkmaar, Regional Archives of Alkmaar, inventory no. 92, folio 46, dated 16 Mar. 1620

He embarked on his career as a hand for 8 years and then as lockkeeper for 16 years in Edam (Netherlands). In 1599 he was recorded as 'Master carpenter and lockkeeper in Edam.' In 1613 he was recorded as innkeeper and lockkeeper in Edam. Before that, he is recorded as having been a contractor for house building, in Schagen, amongst other places. In 1615 he was innkeeper of 'Het Vergulde Hoofd' (The Gilded Head) and from 1623 of 'De Oude Blinde Wereld' (The Olde Blind World) on the Lange Nieuwsloot in Alkmaar. It was around this time and afterward that he became involved in the construction of sluices and became known as one of the most important 17th century technicians in this field.

On 15 October 1635 there is a record of land[111] held in the name of Willem Jansz. Banning, in the polder of Schermeer. He owned 5 'morgens' in Polder K, which was equivalent to 5 hectare, 18,3 roods and 18,3 ells (somewhat over 10 acres). He had three sons from his first marriage: Augustijn Willemsz. Banning, (carver), Jan Willemsz. and Hendrik Willemsz..

Willem Jansz. Banning died after having suffered from gout, a common complaint among those who worked on the waterways, in all kinds of weather. He was buried on 29 February 1636 in the Grote Kerk of Alkmaar. His last will and testament was signed in Alkmaar on 7 June 1634 and witnessed by his son, Jan Willemsz. Benningh.[112]

16. signatures on the last will and testament of Willem Jansz.
Benningh, Alkmaar, 7 June 1634
Regional Archives of Alkmaar

Two families descending from Jacob Jansz. Banning also owned country homes in the Zijpe. Aeghje Wuytiers, a daughter of Dieuwertje (Debora) Jacobsdr. Banning, married Hendrick Barthoutsz. Cromhout (1581-1658);

---

[111] Gegevens rond eigenaars/bewoners vd kavels in de Schermeer http://de-wit.net/bronnen/kavel.txt, accessed Mar. 2003
[112] Notarieel Archief Alkmaar, Regional Archives of Alkmaar, inventory no. 65, folio 523, dated 7 June 1634

they owned the estate 'Ooijenbergh' in 1641[113]. Their son, Jacob Hendricksz. Cromhout, inherited 'Ooijenbergh' and added it to his enormous wealth; he married his cousin (6 Nov. 1635) Margaretha Wuytiers, (a daughter of Dirck Govertsz. Wuytiers and granddaughter of Dieuwertje Jacobsdr. Banning). The estate remained in the family until 1776.

17. Glass door panel from the interior
of the estate Ooijenbergh
photo courtesy of P. Dekker[114]

The dates 1671-1884 almost certainly refer to a specific phase in the history of the homestead. The engraving of sheep on a mountain refers to the name 'Ooijenbergh' (sheep/mountain) It is presumed that there were sheep on the estate which provided wool for the cloth trade in the 17th century, in which the Bannings and their relatives were involved.

Margaretha Wuytiers and Jacob Cromhout also owned the properties 'Zeenimf' (Sea Nymph), 'De Vos' (The Fox) and 'Hoop en Vlijt' (Hope and Diligence) in the Zijpe Polder[115], which still exist today.

---

[113] P. Dekker, *Oude Boerderijen en Buitenverblijven langs de Zijper Grotesloot*, Pirola, Schoorl, 1988, Part 2A, p. 191, 562-569

[114] P. Dekker, *Oude Boerderijen en Buitenverblijven langs de Zijper Grotesloot*, Pirola, Schoorl, 1988, Part 2A, p. 568

[115] P. Dekker, *Oude Boerderijen en Buitenverblijven langs de Zijper Grotesloot*, Pirola, Schoorl, 1988, Part 2A, p. 190, 191, 352, 353

18.   'Zeenimf'   1986
photo courtesy of P. Dekker[116]

19. 'Hoop en Vlijt'   1986
photo courtesy of P. Dekker[117]

20. 'De Vos'   1986
photo courtesy of P. Dekker[118]

These being country estates of Dieuwertje Banning's grandchildren, Margaretha and her (cousin) husband Jacob Cromhout, the couple also had a stately residence in Amsterdam; now a national monument. Four adjoining houses were built on the prestigious Herengracht in 1662, of which three were rented to others and the largest, number 366, for their own domicile.

---

[116] P. Dekker, *Oude Boerderijen en Buitenverblijven langs de Zijper Grotesloot*, Pirola, Schoorl, 1988, Part 2A, p. 111/113

[117] P. Dekker, *Oude Boerderijen en Buitenverblijven langs de Zijper Grotesloot*, Pirola, Schoorl, 1988, Part 2A, p. 353

[118] P. Dekker, *Oude Boerderijen en Buitenverblijven langs de Zijper Grotesloot*, Pirola, Schoorl, 1988, Part 2A, p. 190

21. Cromhout houses on the Herengracht in Amsterdam[119]
Municipal Archives of Amsterdam, Netherlands

A daughter of Christina Benningh (*G2.IX.1;1657-21 May 1703*) and Reijnier van Cuijck (Kuyck), Christina van Cuijck, was married to Michiel van Marselis (1684-1723: Honorary Captain of the Admiralty of Amsterdam); until 1714 they owned the homestead 'Sluiswijk' on the Slikkerdijk in Zijpe[120] with 50 'morgens' (hectares) of land in polder E.

22. 'Sluiswijk'   ca. 193
photo courtesy of P. Dekker[121]

---

[119]Monumenten en Archeologie in Amsterdam,
http://www.bmz.amsterdam.nl/adam/nl/huizen/h364.html, accessed Feb. 2004
[120] P. Dekker, *Oude Boerderijen en Buitenverblijven langs de Zijper Grotesloot*, Pirola, Schoorl, 1988, Part 2A, p.343
[121] P. Dekker, *Oude Boerderijen en Buitenverblijven langs de Zijper Grotesloot*, ,Pirola, Schoorl, 1988, Part 2A, p.343

Christina Benningh (*G2.IX.1;1657-...*)and Reijnier van Cuijck owned a gunpowder mill[122] in the environs of Amsterdam – Amstelveen. The map below shows this location, as well as several other properties owned by Bannings (and their direct descendants).

1) Gunpowder mill of Christina Benningh and Reinier van Cuijk.
2) Meerna
3) De Blauweverij
4) Welna
5) Vredenhof
6) Kostverloren

23. Detail of a map of Amstelveen showing the locations of the country estates G. Drogenham[123], 18th century

[122] J.A.W. Banning, *Genealogie van het Geslacht Banning*, Ferd. Banning & Zonen, Groenlo, 1934, p.71
[123] J.W. Groesbeek, *Amstelveen: Acht Eeuwen Geschiedenis*, De Lange, Amsterdam, 1966, p. 155, p. 191

Illustrated are the estates 'Kostverloren', 'Welna', 'Meerna' the gunpowder mill belonging to Christina Benningh and Reinier van Cuijk, 'Kostverloren' and 'Vredenhof', the first estate to the north of "'t Kalfje', first mentioned when Dirck Govertsz. Wuytiers purchased "the lands with house and property, measuring 17 morgens[124]", in 1643. It was in the family for a long time, until Aeghje Wuytiers (daughter of Dieuwertje Banning and Govert Dircksz. Wuytiers) and her husband willed it to her nephew, who sold it in 1738.

The estate 'Meerna', directly south of 'Amstelburg', was owned by Dirck Govertsz. Wuytiers in 1640, "an estate with outbuildings, flora, other appurtenances, consisting of 10 morgens 425 rods of land[125]". It remained in the family until 1659.

The estate 'De Blauwververij' (The Blue Dyer), adjacent to the estate 'Brandwijk' was a family possession until 1687. A record in 1777 clarifies the name and its function: "a cotton dying facility with homes and properties, boiler room, pressure mangle, warehouses, dye and 'ijzernat' (iron oxide?) sheds, loose and fixed tools, wagon shed, horse stable, and on the south side a newly constructed room or small dwelling[126]".

Dieuwertje (Debora) Jacobsdr. Banning *(G2.VII.1)* married Govert Dircksz. Wuytiers (10 Jan. 1580), a cloth merchant in "'t Vliegende Varcken', where the Bannings had pursued the textile trade for generations. Wuytiers came from a wealthy and influential family; he was Councillor of Amsterdam in 1579 and Alderman in 1581.

According to the genealogy, he lived on the homestead 'Welna' on the Amstel River, but Groesbeek in his chronology of Amstelveen[127] cites that the couple took ownership of the estate at a later date, in March 1626, whereupon it remained in the family until 1710.

The estate of 'Welna' served as a background to negations held between the governments of Amsterdam and Count Willem Fredrik of Nassau in 1650[128]. Count Willem Fredrik established his headquarters at 'Welna' when, after a period of relative peace in the Netherlands, there was a general uprising against spending on costly armies that had nothing to occupy them. The seat of unrest was in Amsterdam, where word had

---

[124] J.W. Groesbeek, *Amstelveen; Acht Eeuwen Geschiedenis*, De Lange, Amsterdam, 1966, p. 155,156

[125] J.W. Groesbeek, *Amstelveen; Acht Eeuwen Geschiedenis*, De Lange, Amsterdam, 1966, p. 190,191

[126] J.W. Groesbeek, *Amstelveen; Acht Eeuwen Geschiedenis*, De Lange, Amsterdam, 1966, p. 195

[127] J.W. Groesbeek, *Amstelveen; Acht Eeuwen Geschiedenis*, De Lange, Amsterdam, 1966, p. 163

[128] J.W. Groesbeek, *Amstelveen; Acht Eeuwen Geschiedenis*, De Lange, Amsterdam, 1966, p. 46,47

meanwhile been received of Count Willem Fredrik's impending visit. Amsterdam sent an armed delegation to 'Welna' to negotiate with the Count, urging him not to approach the city, in order to avert bloodshed. (This was represented in an engraving done by Is. Tirion after Simon Fokke in the 18th century.) When Prince William, in the Hague, received notice of the confrontation, he rode to 'Welna' in Amstelveen to intervene. The Prince signed a treaty with Amsterdam and peace prevailed.

24. The estate of Welna on the Amstel River, home of Dieuwertje Banning and her husband Govert Dircksz. Wuytiers around 1626
photo: Iconografisch Bureau/Rijksbureau voor Kunsthistorische Documentatie (Netherlands Institute for Art History), the Hague

'Welna' consisted of 20 morgens of land, houses, a horse stable, coach house, gardener's residence, stone cupola, orchards, streams, farmhouse, cow shed, hay shed, cart and wagon shed for the farmer. The gardens featured statues, vases, pedestals, park benches, bridges and greenhouses, and hothouses where peaches and grapes were cultivated[129].

Dieuwertje Jacobsdr. Banning and Govert Dircksz. Wuytiers had six children: Dirck Govertsz., Jan, Margaretha, Anna, Aeghje and Lieffge.

---

[129] J.W. Groesbeek, *Amstelveen; Acht Eeuwen Geschiedenis*, De Lange, Amsterdam, 1966, p.163,164

Jan Wuytiers Banning, *(G2.E.VII.1a)*, the second son, was born in Amsterdam in 1591. His was a wealthy and long established family of burgomasters which had fled the province of South Netherlands to the province of Holland in 1559 as a result of 'turmoil'. It would appear that Jan Wuytiers Banning was the only one of the six siblings who, perhaps from childish piety, took his mother's name Banning as well as that of his father. Initially he was the only one who returned to the 'old mother Church'. This did not satisfy his youthful ambition: he was invested as a Roman Catholic priest in 1619 and managed to reconvert most of his family and relations to Catholicism, the faith against which his father had striven so arduously. As Roman Catholics they became ineligible for government positions. The actual date and the reasons for Jan Wuytiers Banning's return to the Roman Catholic Church are unknown. A Latin verse under a portrait of the priest (Dives opum, vultu pulcher, etc.) reads: "Rich in treasures, pure in countenance, respected by his friends, poor and humbled through Christ; for many a living example and a genuine priest. What others accomplished by word, he accomplished by deed. He lives content in eternity and, enthroned in heaven, he radiates, he who was so accomplished[130]."

Jan Wuytiers Banning was widely acclaimed and lauded, amongst others by the renowned Dutch 17th century poet Joost (van den) Vondel[131] (1586-1679), who is still read and studied today. Vondel wrote the following eulogy as a tribute to Jan Wuytiers Banning after his death:

"The Lying-in-State of the late honourable Jan Banning Wuytiers, Priest

Who lies here, as though asleep?
Sir Jan has paid his death dues
Yet is not dead; he rests and seems to sleep
Till God's day will separate light from darkness
Unite bodies with souls,
(and) Raise him with the archangels' trumpet.
The worm the body may destroy, but not the soul
Wuytiers fell asleep, and went peacefully to bed
To rise joyfully in the other life
There his works follow him before the throne of God
And bear witness to the spirit that drove him
Who valued Christ's counsel, laws and commandments
More than temporal goods,

---

[130] Banning, J.A.W., *Genealogie van het Geslacht Banning*, Ferd. Banning & Zonen, Groenlo, 1934, p. 121

[131] Vondel, J., *De Werken van J. van den Vondel*, Mr. J. van Lennep, revised and edited by J.H.W. Unger, Leiden, A.W. Sijthoff, Part 1657-1660, pages 296-299

Who chose God's poverty before pleasure, honour and status
Sought to comfort and feed the poor,
Denied himself pomp and excess.
To assist benevolent God's needy.
God's altar was his domain day by day
The cross his staff, the body's pains and ills
The book of hours that lay open before him,
His clockwork mechanism for spiritual contemplation
A light ahead, like a beacon lit.
His scattered flock that wandered stubbornly further
From the truth, and found no pasture anywhere
He brought into the fold as a faithful shepherd.
Honour him and kiss his closed mouth.
Now rest, Wuytiers, you have fought the fight well
Remember us before God in your prayers."[132]

Vondel

Jan Vos, (1620-1667) another historically recognised poet, wrote the following verse:

"Thus art reveals Wuytiers, when the eye shall shine no more
But his piety cannot be contained in any frame
Virtue, that never dies, desires no narrow boundaries
He shows us by his teaching, the path to holiness
So he militias Peter's ship, full of souls, against the waves
Faithful teachers are God's upright pillars of the church [133] [134]."

---

[132] translation by dr. Saskia Barker, Cambridge, 2003
[133] J.A.W. Banning, *Genealogie van het Geslacht Banning*, Ferd. Banning & Zonen, Groenlo, 1934, p 121
[134] translated by dr. Saskia Barker, Cambridge, 2003

25. Etching of Jan Banning Wuytiers on his deathbed, Theodore Matham 1647
photo courtesy of Th. F. M. Weyn Banning

The last will and testament[135] of J. Wuytiers Banning was written on 22
March 1647 at 17:00 hours. It states that he was "ill in bed but coherent
and in full possession of his faculties, speculating on the fragility of life,
the certainty of death but uncertainty concerning the hour thereof"; he left
his worldly goods to his sister Anna, his brother Dirck Wuytiers, Jacob
Cromhout son of Aeghje Wuytiers (deceased), Jan Poppe and the children
of Elisabeth Poppe (deceased), the children and grandchildren of his sister
Aeffje Wuytiers.

There are several portraits of the priest, including a painted
portrait in the Roman Catholic Parish of Ankeveen, North Holland.
Portraits from the municipal archives were presented in an exhibition in
1925.

In Rotterdam in the autumn of 1597, a plan was conceived to sail a fleet
via the Strait of Magellan and the west coast of South America to Asia.
The two merchants who initiated this plan were **Jan Jacobsz. Banning
(Jan Banning Coeckebacker)** (*G2.E.V4a*) from Amsterdam and Gerrit
Huygensz. van der Buys from Rotterdam. Earlier that year, they had

---

[135] Municipal Archives, Amsterdam, last will and testament of Joan Wuytiers, PA 440, inv.
no. 321

invested in the sea voyage of a West-Indian fleet together with an experienced traveller and innkeeper named Olivier van Noort. To send out a fleet destined for the west coast of South America was a much riskier, but potentially more lucrative, venture.

While the captains organised practical affairs for the voyage, the ship owners were occupied with soliciting shareholders for the new Magellan Company, accruing capital, purchasing provisions and hiring a crew. Olivier van Noort was appointed captain of the fleet. Jan Banning Coeckebacker (who also took his mother's name of Banning) and his brother Claes Jacobsz. Coeckebacker, both merchants and ship owners in Amsterdam, outfitted two ships - the 'Mauritius' and the 'Hendrick Fredrick' to sail around the world. Together with the 'Hope' and the 'Eendracht' from Rotterdam, the fleet of four ships departed from Goedereede in the Netherlands on 2 July 1598 to sail through the 'Strait of Magellan to the Kingdom of Chili and the West-Indies'. The journey was wrought with hardship and adventure. Three of the four ships were lost and only the 'Mauritius' returned to port in Rotterdam on 27 August 1601, with 45 of the original crew of 248, subsisting on the last worm-infested bread and a meagre store of rice. These were thus the first Dutch ships to sail around the world.

26. The Eendracht, Mauritius, Hendrick Fredrick and the Hope
source: Om de Wereld 1601-1602, Olivier van Noort

The crew experienced hardship common to the age: mutiny, piracy, scurvy, adverse weather conditions and hunger. Many were murdered by the Spaniards and by hostile Indians. The 'Eendracht' leaked and sailed so poorly that it was finally abandoned in St. Clara, the captain taking command of the 'Hope' - (which was re-christened the 'Eendracht') the 'Hendrick Fredrick' became separated from the fleet when sailing out of the Strait of Magellan and did not return. The Spanish captured the re-christened 'Eendracht' at Manila and put the crew to death, after having them first converted to Catholicism.

Van Noort did not manage to acquire a valuable cargo, although he finally came into possession of a cargo of pepper in Borneo. He came home with nought more than leftovers of the original cargo, 200 pounds of mace and over a ton of pepper - by no means enough to cover costs of the original investment in the voyage.

After the 'Hendrick Fredrick' had became separated from the other ships, it sailed north along the coast of California and came at the end of 1601 to East India. It ran aground at the island of Ternate in the Moluccan islands and was too heavily damaged to continue. The Dutch were welcomed wholeheartedly by the natives and the king of Ternate was eager to purchase the grounded ship, including its cargo and canon, from the captain. He signed an acknowledgement of debt for a substantial load of cloves, which the Magellan company would receive as soon as the harvest came in. The crew returned to Holland throughout 1602 and 1603 on various other vessels that sporadically docked in the region.

On receipt of the acknowledgement of debt in exchange for the 'Hendrick Fredrick', the Magellan company was optimistic that they would be able to recoup some of their loss.

However, this proved more difficult than anticipated. The VOC (Dutch East India Company) which was founded in 1602 had been granted the sole rights to shipping and trade in the East Indies. It was not until 1635, after years of negotiations between the two companies, that the VOC finally paid 175,000 Dutch florins to the Magellan Company for all the cloves which had or had not been delivered from Ternate. After (partial) repayment of the investments, the company was dissolved.

Within a month of the return of the Mauritius, a concise account of the voyage appeared in print, illustrated by copper etchings made by an artist who had been on board. A more extensive account was published in 1602 and translated into French, German and Latin and in 1605 into English. Generations of readers, even today, thus became familiar with the historic sea venture.

Accounts of a historic sea voyage, in English and in Dutch
27. Rijksmuseum, Amsterdam   28. from *Om de Wereld*, Olivier van Noort

Margriet Banning (*G2.E.VII.7;1565-1641*) married (19 Apr. 1587) Pieter Dircksz. Hasselaer, an eminent merchant (brewer) and ship owner, known especially for his courage as an officer of the Haarlem Civic Militia during the siege of that city by the Spanish in 1572/73. He was City Councillor and Regent of Amsterdam from 1594 until his death in 1616, Alderman in 1595, Captain of the Civic Militia, Governor of the East India Company and Burgomaster of Amsterdam.

A reference to Margriet Banning is found in a letter from Maria Reigersberg, wife of the renowned Dutch jurist and politician Hugo de Groot (1583-1645), to her husband on 12th August 1624 where she mentions "tomorrow I am going to dine with Hasselaer's mother[136] ". The footnote specifies: "Margriet Benningh, mother of Pieter Hasselaer, governor of the East India Company, and of Major Nicholaas, who performed commendably during the uprisings of 1626 and 1629. Her husband Pieter Dircksz. Hasselaer had died in 1616. She died in 1641."

---

[136] Dr. P.C. Molhuysen, *Briefwisseling van Hugo Grotius*, Martinus Nijhoff, The Hague, 1936, Part 2 – 1618-1625, p. 394

29. Margriet Benningh   Nicolaes Eliaszn. Pickenoy   ca. 1610
Rijksmuseum Amsterdam

A sister of Margriet, **Sophia Banning** *(G2.E.VII.5; 1561-)* married (Dec. 1591) Claes Ment Cornelisz., who at the time of their marriage resided 'in the brewery Van den Arend'[137] ('of the Eagle') and it is thus concluded that he was probably employed by his brother-in-law brewer Pieter Dircksz. Hasselaer. A daughter of this marriage, Eva Ment (1606-1658), married (8 Apr. 1625) Jan Pietersz. Coen, who was Governor of the East

---

[137] J.A.W. Banning, *Genealogie van het Geslacht Banning*, Ferd. Banning & Zonen, Groenlo, 1934, p. 68

India Company. Jan Pietersz. Coen became one of the popular great men in Dutch history and he remained so until well into the twentieth century.

Few Dutch historians, however, would now agree with the words of esteem once used to describe the establishment of VOC power in the archipelago. No doubt Coen did establish the VOC monopoly in the Bandas and generally put Dutch power in the region on a strong footing, but the way in which he accomplished this was even in his own days not wholly uncriticised, his having applied means of excessive violence, execution and revolt which shocked and disgusted even seasoned men of the times. Coen was subsequently also known as Butcher of the Bandas. In spite of criticism of the extreme violence Coen exhorted in the Bandas, his actions were finally approved by his superiors and the States-General and until far into the twentieth century were looked upon as a token of Dutch enterprise and heroism in the east.

Hillebrand (Hildebrand) Benningh (Bennink) . It is unknown to which genealogy Hillebrand belonged, but a relation to the Amsterdam Bannings is deemed most probable, not in the least since specific mention is made of the Amsterdam magistrate's family of Banning in this source, and Bannings of the existing Amsterdam genealogy are all spelled 'Bennink' in the same source[138]. Hillebrand Benningh was a Burgomaster[139]. He is mentioned in 1577 when Amsterdam was occupied by Sonoy during the historical period of the 'Satisfaction'. Hillebrand Benningh wrote to Sonoy that he should ensure that those in his service should refrain from all violent action, which created a basis for negotiation, in keeping with the pacifist policy of the Prince. The commander Sonoy made good his promise with the following (somewhat incomprehensible) reply[140], from "Diderich Sonoy, Esq. to Hillebrand Benningh, my good friend of Amsterdam":

"My especial good friend,
V.L. (?) letter I ascertain with joy that those affairs indicate good hope, so that I pray to God to further give his blessing, on affairs wherein I fully hope that action can be avoided which may cause injury to anyone V.L. (?) could not only ensure of the established feudal lords as of all who live in the city or would wish to come to the city, even if they were to contribute funds to the court, and also toward a cause for which I came

[138] Jacobus Kok, *Vaderlandsch Woordenboek*, part VI, Johannes Allart, Amsterdam, 1787, p. 372-374
[139] Wispelwey, *Biographical Index of Benelux Countries*, K.G. Sauer, Munich, 2003, p. 135
[140] Jacobus Kok, *Vaderlandsch Woordenboek*, part VI, Johannes Allart, Amsterdam, 1787, p. 372-373

as with those in service of the people, herewith will I V.L. command the lord, expecting your arrival here in the Cathuiser Monastary. The end of December 1577.

Signed,

V.L. good friend,

Diderich Sonoy

to: Hillebrand Benningh"

Stans Banning (Benningh) *(G2.E.VII.ter)* was named after his maternal grandfather, Stans Claes Stansz., a prominent citizen of Amsterdam. As a fervent Reformed protestant[141], Stans Banning played a leading role in the iconoclastic fury in 1566, plundering the Minderbroeders Church in Amsterdam. He was a son to Jan Gerritsz. Banning who is portrayed in the *Church of the Nativity at Bethlehem*. His daughter Nelle (Aeltje) Banning is mentioned in a historical article in 1968[142] concerning the *Wedding Songs* of G.A. Bredero (1585-1618). G.A. Bredero was considered the greatest Dutch poet and dramatist of his generation and the first Dutch master of comedy. His work was collected in three volumes in 1890. His celebrated oeuvre included nine *Wedding Songs*, for which the third was written for the nuptials in 1607 of one 'Trijngen Stansen' and Wijnant Bartelson. According to the article, 'Trijngen Stansen' was in actual fact Nelletge Stanssen Banning, the widow of merchant Philip Adriaen Texel whom she had married in 1581. Nelletge Stanssen Banning was mentioned as a witness to the baptism of a Bredero child in 1596, presumably because the child, Jan, was named after her deceased brother or father. She had two children from her first marriage: Stans (jr.) and Lijsbeth, who both took their mother's name Banning. Stans jr. later became Bailiff of the city of Loosdrecht. The fact that there were several tracts of land and orchards outside of the Amsterdam city walls belonging to the Banning family at the time, including the Stans Benningh property, indicates that the family was one of standing and wealth.

Joan Bodecheer Banning *(G2.E.VII.1b.3aa)*, born in 1606 in the city of Loosdrecht where his uncle Stans Banning (Benningh) was Bailiff, Joan was the son of Lijsbeth Banning. She married dr. Nicholaas Bodecheer, a well-known and highly respected theologian in Loosdrecht and later in Alkmaar. Their son Joan (= Johannes =Janus) Bodecher Banning took his mother's surname Banning. Joan Bodecheer Banning was a Professor of Philosophy. He and his father were admitted (free of charge) to the University of Leiden in 1620 and Joan took his doctorate under Jacchaeus

---

[141] Jacobus Kok, *Vaderlandsch Woordenboek*, part VI, Johannes Allart, Amsterdam, 1787, p. 372

[142] *De Bruiloftszangen van Bredero*, Amstelodamum, Gemeente Amsterdam, 1968, p. 164

in 1624. The Curators named him Associate Professor of Ethics in 1629 and in 1635 Associate Professor of Physics, on which occasion he held two orations, *De Contagione* and *De Morte Contemnenda* (it was the fated year of the plague). In 1638 the Curators granted him leave for several years as political advisor to the West-India Company; he apparently did not make use of this leave. In 1640 his parents sought support for their son because, sadly, he had become insane. A satire by Joan Bodecheer Banning was published in 1631 shortly after his appointment as Professor, in which he denounced the morals of the students. This incited disorder in his lectures, such that the Senate was compelled to intervene. The Senate censured both the actions of the students and the contents of the publication. Joan Bodecheer Banning had numerous publications to his name, both as an exceedingly meritorious Latin and Low German poet and writer and as such, is still read today. He died, insane, in Leiden in 1642. His motto was 'quotidie morimur' ('we die daily')[143].

His writings include:

Leydsche oorlofdaghen: of Nederduytsche gedichten (1630)

Satyricon (1631)

Satyricon in corruptae juventutis mores corruptos (1631)

Dido, oft' Heylloose minnetocht. Treurspel (1634)

Compendium ethices (1635)

Orationes duae, de contagione, et morte contemnenda (1635)

Poemata (1637)

Jan Banningh, who is not specifically mentioned in the Amsterdam genealogy, was recorded in the address book of Dutch printers and booksellers[144]. He lived in Amsterdam from 1619-1659, and his position was that of printer for the Illustere School 1653-1659 and municipal printer 1654-1656. He lived on the 'Middeldam', on the corner by the Vispoort (later known as the Damsluys) from 1619-1629, on the Beurs (also Damsluys) from 1635-1653. The sign hanging on his shop front read 'In de Vergulde Bybel'('In the Gilded Bible'), 1619-1642. His name also occurs in the correspondence of the great philosopher and jurist Hugo de Groot[145] (1583-1645), in reference to a book he printed in 1941 of lectures by Caspar Barlaeus. (1584-1648: significant Dutch polymath, humanist, theologian, poet and historian).

---

[143] A.J. van der Aa, *Biografisch Woordenboek der Nederlanden*, J.J. van Brederode, Haarlem, 1852, p. 99

[144] J.A. Gruys, J. Bos, *Adresboek Nederlandse Drukkers en Boekverkopers tot 1700*, Koninklijke Bibliotheek, The Hague, 1999, p. 29

[145] *Briefwisseling van Hugo Grotius*, Rijks Geschiedkundige Publicatieën, The Hague, 1928-2001, Volume XII, p. 213

Jacob Pietersz. Banning(h) descended from the Bannings of the townships of Zaandam, Wormer and Jisp (quite likely related to the Amsterdam Bannings; this is as yet not verified). Only a fragment genealogy is available; date of birth unknown, died after 1698. Jacob was a miller in the (beam) sawmill 'Het Roode Hert' ('The Red Deer') in Zaandam in 1684 and miller in 'De Mol' ('The Mole') in Wormer, best known as a Baptist minister in the towns of Wormer and Jisp. Jacob Banningh was yet another of those Bannings of the cloth with an aptitude toward rendering troubled waters even more turbulent.

Biographical data on Jacob Banning are scant, even in the *Biographical Lexicon of the History of Dutch Protestantism* (J.H. Kok, Kampen 1978), where the following account is published.

"Jacob Banning had no academic education as a clergyman. In 1697 he was involved in a dispute with both of the townships of Wormer and Jisp because he advocated concepts which could, without doubt, be considered heresy. In a sermon concerning Psalm 139:8 he announced that the word 'heaven' should not be interpreted in a literal but in a figurative sense. Referring to Matthew 10:28 he further declared that the word 'hell' was nothing more than an erroneous translation for 'tomb'. Misgivings concerning Banning rapidly gained ground, although he stubbornly insisted that he never advocated heretical policies. Commotion ensued, especially when Banning dared to deny the existence of ghosts, devils and angels. It was finally decided to lay the matter before external arbitrators, including the clergymen E.A. van Dooregeest and H. Schijn. Although these gentlemen were not unsympathetic toward Banning, they eventually realised the need to propose that the municipalities of Wormer and Jisp discharge him of his duties. This transpired on 2nd April 1698, after which Banning had also claimed that he did not believe in the resurrection.

It was not, however, in Banning's nature to submit graciously to his accusers. He published a document with a scathing judgment of the procedures taken against him; it was reprinted in the same year. However, this measure of protest had no effect. After this, nothing more is known of Jacob Banning.[146]"

*   *   *

---

[146] J.H. Kok, *Biografisch Lexicon van de Geschiedenis van het Nederlandse Protestantisme*, Kampen, 1978, p 29,30

City Council in Amsterdam in the 15th-18th Century

Numerous of the Amsterdam Bannings mentioned held positions of public office: Burgomasters, Aldermen, Bailiffs or Dike-Graves, Treasurers, Reeves and Councillors. What did these offices entail? How was it possible that so many Bannings, as well as relatives, so frequently held the office of Burgomaster? In order to understand the positions held in municipal government, here is a closer look at that institution and what it constituted.

The City Council was known as the 'Vroedschap' of Amsterdam from the 15th - 18th century. Until the beginning of the 15th century tradition held, in most cities, that prominent burghers were called together by Dike-graves and aldermen to advise on affairs which could affect the citizens. The first known list of civil office of Amsterdam dates from 1333[147], although it is incomplete. The origin of the 'Vroedschap' lay in the fact that each burgher, according to his oath, was obligated to contribute, 'through counsel and deed and within the bounds of his ability', toward the welfare of the city. It was naturally more effective to discuss civil matters with a small, representative group than with the population in general. The burghers were thus requested to name their own representatives and this right was confirmed by charter in 1449, whereupon this form of government became more structured.

Until 1477 the City Council of Amsterdam had consisted of 24 members, but was increased on 1st February of that year to 36; this was the Council of Thirty-and-Six.

Burgomaster / Mayor

Where the term 'mayor' is used in this context; it connotes Burgomaster (a mayor of a Dutch or Flemish town). Four Burgomasters were appointed each year. The college of Burgomasters was the highest authority in the city, the highest under God and the Monarch, and it was considered a serious crime to offend them, even if this constituted only a few derogatory words in their absence. They were the reigning supreme governors, the heads of the Council of Thirty-and-Six, the ruling authorities on municipal property and finance, the upholders of municipal rights and privileges, the supreme regents of the churches and municipal organizations, and supreme guardians of widows and orphans. The office ensued from the original burgher organisation, the burgomasters being the successors of those who at one time would have been Captains of the

---

[147] J. ter Gouw, *Geschiedenis van Amsterdam*, Scheltema & Holkema, Amsterdam, Part I, 1879

Civic Militia Guilds. The burghers were still sworn guild brothers, this is evidenced by the burgher oath, without which no one could enjoy the rights and privileges of the burgher. The Burgomasters were still Captains of the guilds, because the burghers were appointed and sworn in by them and rights and obligations still prevailed which had their origins in the guild.

The Burgomasters were the heads of the council and decided when the Thirty-and-Six were to convene. The Thirty-and-Six were forbidden to enter the Council Chamber unless summoned 'by the bell' or by town messenger. Whoever absented himself was fined sixpence 'to the profit of those present'. The chairing burgomaster then had to advance the money and subsequently collect either the sum itself or collateral from the home of the absentee. No one was permitted to leave the assembly without permission from the Burgomasters.

Burgomasters were appointed annually on the 1st of February, in accordance with the charter of 16th January 1400, by a meeting of as many ex-Burgomasters and Bailiffs of Amsterdam as could be assembled, excepting those who held a position of Dike-grave or Reeve in Amstelland. A town messenger would make the rounds on 31st January to solicit as many as possible to attend the assembly on the following day. Election was held and three new Burgomasters were elected by a majority of votes. The candidates had to be 'good fellows' (that is, affluent and eminent), forty years of age, citizens or burghers of Amsterdam for a minimum of seven years, and could not have any familial relation to each other closer than 'direct after sister child'; that is, second cousin. The three new Burgomasters then, amongst themselves, appointed one of the three presiding Burgomasters from the previous year, and made their oath of office to this man.

The four Burgomasters, for three months each in turn - the Burgomaster from the preceding year first and then the new ones in order of seniority, acted as Chairman of the Municipal Board. One would think that candidates vied for the position of Burgomaster and covet it once they were named, but this was not always the case. In February 1484 Dirk Heymansz. Ruysch, (whose daughter Katrijn later married Gerrit Benningh), who had been burgomaster the year before, was re-elected by the newest three, but he opposed and rejected the appointment, even refusing to swear in the three newcomers. This was a very grave matter, as the charter could not be defied.

Counsel was held, consisting of the Law, the Thirty-and-Six and all ex-burgomasters and ex-aldermen, to whom Dirk Heymansz. Ruysch pleaded his case. "It is the custom in Amsterdam," he said, "to always re-elect someone who was once chosen. If it is a burgomaster, then he is re-elected every other or every three years, except that he sometimes has to serve for two consecutive years; and as soon as he leaves the office of burgomaster, a position as steward or some other office is open to him. This makes things all too difficult for the good people. I would prefer to say farewell to the city rather than be used in such a manner[148]."

After he left the meeting, it was decided that he was not entirely wrong and that the issue had to be addressed, but that they would not accept his refusal. The final verdict was: anyone who had held the office of burgomaster would be permitted three years of rest, "excepting the stipulation in our charter which specifies that one ex-burgomaster has to be re-elected.[149]" History in the making.

Dirk Heymansz. Ruysch complied with this and accepted the office of burgomaster, but the 'three years of rest' were obviously, if one peruses the lists of those who held office in subsequent years, taken with a grain of salt. This system clarifies why those appointed as burgomaster are frequently mentioned to have held office in so many different years.

The charter of 16 January 1400 also stipulated that a Dike-grave could not have a vote in the election of Burgomasters[150]. However, Dike-grave Jan Benningh Jansz. interpreted this differently. As an ex-Dike-grave, he did not wish to be refused a vote, and he petitioned the Emperor Maximilian who, on 5th November 1507, granted him this right. The letter would have had little effect. The burgomasters would have made it clear to Jan Benningh Jansz. that this was in opposition of the charter and therefore illegal. What we do know is that a settlement was reached and that he submitted his letter to the burgomasters, as it was recovered from 'the Iron Chapel' (a chamber on the second floor of the Old Church, which served as the municipal archives until 1892, and only accessible by means of two ladders) many years later. Jan Benningh Jansz., however, did not allow himself to be consigned to the back benches, as his names turns up again in a book on the history of Amsterdam almost four centuries later, concerning the position of Dike-grave.

Dike-grave

The office of Dike-Grave was traditionally held for six years from the 15th June, and seems to have involved money - more in terms of lending and borrowing, because it was not a very coveted position. The annual salary was 200 Dutch guilders, and a Dike-grave was not permitted to accept gifts, except for sundry items such as a hare or a brace of guinea-fowl. All revenue generated by the position of Dike-grave had to be

[148] J. ter Gouw, *Geschiedenis van Amsterdam*, Scheltema & Holkema, Amsterdam, 1879, p. 366,367
[149] J. ter Gouw, *Geschiedenis van Amsterdam*, Scheltema & Holkema, Amsterdam, 1879, p. 367
[150] J. ter Gouw, *Geschiedenis van Amsterdam*, Scheltema & Holkema, Amsterdam, 1879, p.367

credited to the municipal treasury, for which the Dike-grave was required to issue quarterly statements to the Treasurer. A great deal of money was borrowed in the second half of the 14th century; in 1354 there is a note that in the whole of Amstelland and Gooiland there were only six Dike-graves who did not borrow money. This was apparently still the case in the 15th century. In the list of Amsterdam Dike-graves from 1351 to 1413, which comprises 11 persons, we encounter Dirk Simonsz. Benningh from 1393-1396[151]. In the list from 1419-1517 we encounter 16 names, including that of 'Jan Benninck Jansz.' from 1st October 1495-15th June 1509. (The previous Dike-grave died in September 1495, one of six who died in office, two of whom survived in office only for a number of weeks). Jan Benningh Jansz. was paid 1063 pounds in repayment of a loan made by the city of Amsterdam to Emperor Maximilian. It seems that the city paid off this loan to divest themselves of Jan Benningh Jansz., because they were not eager to have him as Dike-grave, and apparently this suited him as he did not covet the position.

Alderman

Seven Aldermen were appointed annually on the 2nd of February. The appointment was traditionally effected by the Count or his bailiff. The Aldermen had to be selected from among the most reputable burghers, had to have been a burgher for a full seven years and thus at least 25 years of age, and the candidates could not – either amongst each other or in respect to the burgomaster - have a familial relation closer than 'direct after sister child' (second cousin). The Aldermen were sworn in by a Dike-grave.

Sometimes there were more than seven Alderman in a year, who substituted for each other. The wealth of Amsterdam was based on its merchant trade, and the most prominent burghers were the merchants who traded abroad and so most, if not all, of the Aldermen were chosen from these ranks. However, a merchant was often compelled to travel for his trade and it was therefore necessary for someone to serve office on his behalf.

The task of the aldermen was to judge all affairs which fell within the jurisdiction of Amsterdam, both criminal and civil. They also issued sealed letters on other issues: sales, rentals, leases and transfers of ownership, pardons, bail, conflicts, etc..

---

[151] J. ter Gouw, *Geschiedenis van Amsterdam*, Scheltema & Holkema, Amsterdam, 1879, p. 261

Councillor

Councillors 'of the port of Aemstelredamme' (Amsterdam), the predecessors of the burgomasters, were known only for a few years before 1413. (However, J. ter Gouw cites names of councillors from 1351-1413[152]). The oldest book of statutes stipulates that Councillors and Dike-graves were not permitted to rent out or to enter into long-term service during the time that they held office. Four primary offices are mentioned: those of schoolmaster, secretary, sexton and clerk. It would appear that the office of Councillor also required a certain degree of financial standing.

Treasurer

The treasurer held a position second in authority to the burgomasters, the office being established directly following that of the burgomasters, sometime between 1413 and 1444. They were not paid for their services but did receive two Flemish pounds and five sixpence each per year, for clothing. There were always two in office: often the burgomaster of the preceding year and a member of Council. 'Jakob Benninck' is mentioned in the list of treasurers for 1511[153].

Cornelis Banning Gerritsz. *(G2.VIb;1492-1547)* was a brewer in Amsterdam who held numerous prominent positions in local government: Alderman in 1518, 1522, 1523, 1525 and 1527, Councillor from 1519 until his death, Burgomaster in 1534 and 1536, Church Master of the New Church in 1513, 1516, 1519-1521, Commissioner of Orphanages 1523, Treasurer of the City Council 1525, 1526, 1528-1533, 1535, 1543 and 1544. He was a very accomplished diplomat, which was apparent through the various important national and international missions he undertook on behalf of 'Country and City'. His efforts in Hamburg and other places, particularly concerning disputes with the Hanseatic and Baltic Sea cities, are well-known in national history. His numerous negotiations with the imperial envoy Joris Schenk, Viceroy of Friesland, and the Danish King Christiaan II in the Dutch city of Beverwijk (1531) are most well-known.

Christiaan II had invaded the Netherlands with 3000 soldiers; especially the north of the country suffered at their hands. The army had meanwhile grown to 12,000 soldiers. This murdering and plundering horde met with no opposition, and the population was struck with terror.

---

[152] J. ter Gouw, *Geschiedenis van Amsterdam*, Scheltema & Holkema, Amsterdam, 1879, p.260
[153] J. ter Gouw, *Geschiedenis van Amsterdam*, Scheltema & Holkema, Amsterdam, 1879, p.25

Negotiations by Banning and Schenk had the desired effect, a promise of 50,000 Dutch florins plus 12 warships was the price demanded by the king to halt his attacks. On 26 Oct. 1531 the price was met and peace returned.

Most of Cornelis Banning's diplomatic travels are documented in J. ter Gouw's *History of Amsterdam*[154], but not in the genealogy. Dr. P. Scheltema describes his merits in *Aemstel's Oudheid. (Amstel's Antiquity)*: "Even greater tribute can be made to the Treasurer Cornelis Banning, who, not only then but also later as Burgomaster, accomplished so much to the credit of his nation and his home city. Until now, no especial public acclaim has been made in his memory, yet he deserved such distinction more than many others to whom memorials or commemorative obelisks have been erected, if only because they were wealthy or liberally titled. Banning shares in the misunderstanding of his memory with so many other noteworthy citizens of Amsterdam. However, our shortcoming may be yet corrected. There is enough space available in our city squares and churches, and sufficient financial means, to erect an authorized memorial. Would that there were one capable person to assume the task of describing Banning's political career and his social working environment. The labour itself cannot have been fruitless, because the long list of famous Dutchmen is increased with the name of a man who, to the honour of his country, has accomplished so much for the benefit of his fellow citizens and welfare of his compatriots, who has withstood so much in many a time of trial.[155]"

Cornelis Benningh Gerritsz. was a very wealthy landowner. The fact that extensive records remain concerning the history of development of his property in relation to the development of Amsterdam is doubtless due to the considerable fortune of this family, who inherited and enjoyed the properties until long after he died. The Banning landholdings were well-known because the northern moat, the 'Benninghsloot', served as a point of orientation for city surveys and development in 1585.

The Bannings also owned several tracts of land and orchards outside of the city walls, such as the Stans Benningh property, with the estate Benninghof on the Benninghpad (path) and a number of stately homes in the city center. The Cornelis Bennninghsteeg (Lane) ran past the houses along the south side to the water. The property with an estate and large orchard bordering on the Singel Canal is clearly recognizable on the map drawn by Cornelis Anthonisz. in 1544. This estate and the orchard in particular were occupied long after his death by his widow and children.

---

[154] J. ter Gouw, *Geschiedenis van Amsterdam*, Scheltema & Holkema, Amsterdam, 1879, Part I

[155] Dr. P. Scheltema, *Aemstel's Oudheid*, J.H. Scheltema, Amsterdam, 1855, Part I, p. 83, 84

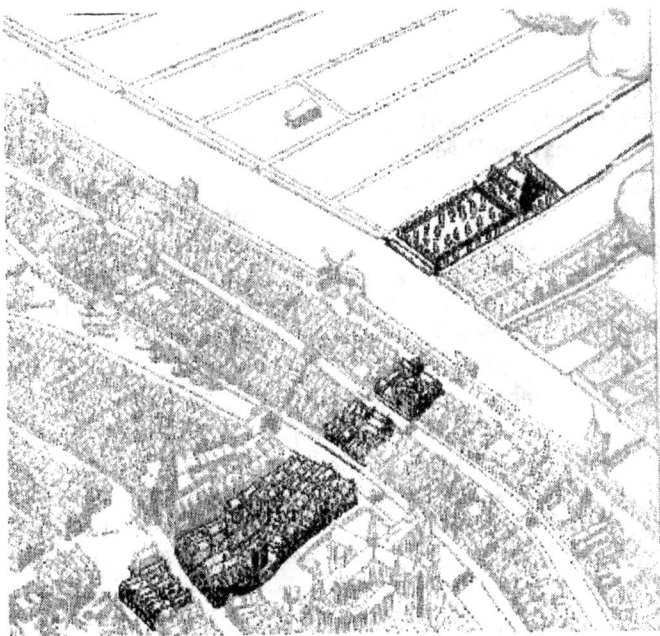

30. The Benninckweer. Detail of a map of Amsterdam by Cornelis Anthoniszn. 1544. The large estate with orchard outside of the Singel (canal) on the right belonged to Cornelis Benningh Gerritsz. (1492-1547). The estate on the left represents the Benninghhof on the Stans Benningh property. On the extreme right the Jan Roden gate with tower. The Cornelis Benningh property lies opposite the Gasthuis Mill, the home of Cornelis Benningh with the brewery near the city wall, to the right of the town hall the house 'the Bril' beside 'Brillenburgh' on the corner of the Kerksteeg, and in the lane opposite the church the 'house with the little tower' belonging to council member Jan Benningh Jansz. (d. 1536).

Municipal Archives of Amsterdam, Netherlands

When the garden is first mentioned in the assessment registers of 1557[156], Cornelis Benningh's widow Aeffgen Vrancken cultivated cabbage there to distribute amongst the poor. She was therefore exempt from land tax. Although the houses were let in subsequent years, Aeffgen maintained the use of the gardens. Directly within the city walls Cornelis Benningh owned - and very probably built - a brewery on the Nieuwezijds Achterburgwal (later Spuistraat), beside which his spacious home, 'the White Mill' (demolished in 1894), was located. There were also several orchards on the premises.

---

[156] S.A.C. Dudok van Heel, *Cornelis Benningh en het Benninghweer*, Amstelodamum 83, 1996, p. 4

More toward the medieval harbour on the Damrak, Cornelis Benningh is mentioned as owner of a house on the Nieuwendijk[157], as well as a house behind it. (This property had been in the family probably since before 1373, and the first Banning of Amsterdam, Gerrit, is recorded as having lived here.) On the south side the Cornelis Benninghsteeg ran toward the water. When other properties in the city centre were demolished in 1565 to build the Weighing-House and the Dam Square was enlarged, Benningh's houses became directly exposed to the Dam Square, and thus increased in value. The most important real estate owned by the family was on the opposite side of the Nieuwendijk on the south corner of the Kerksteeg (Church Lane). Cornelis' brother Jan Benningh (1495-1557) owned the house 'the Bril'. The neighbouring house, the 'Brillenburgh' on the corner was also owned by the family. The large house next door in the Kerksteeg with an intriguing little gabled tower was owned by his uncle, councillor of the Court of Holland, mr. Jan Jansz. Benningh (1455/1460-1536). Interestingly, the palatial country estate built outside of Amsterdam on the Amstel River by the same mr. Jan Jansz. Benningh in 1492 was initially also called Brillenburgh, later Kostverloren, as is described earlier in this narrative. (Jan Jansz. Benningh also used a coat-of-arms featuring a pair of eyeglasses – a 'bril'.)

As early as 1487 there was mention of "a howse and groundes located on the Plaats, residing therein Gaeff Banninex, with an orchard next to Bruyn the brewer's orchard.[158]" The house on the Dam Square and orchard directly outside of the Jan Rodenpad constituted part of a large family Banning inheritance in 1500.

Being located on the periphery of the Dam Square, the Benningh houses were very strategically positioned. An entire block of houses in the city centre was purchased by the city for construction of the new Town Hall. The houses were demolished in 1654. Their original foundations now lie under the cobblestones of the Dam Square, in the heart of Amsterdam. When the city was being expanded in 1585, the Benninghsloot was filled in. In exchange for the land where his home and orchard were located, a grandson, Cornelis Benningh Jansz. Duyvesz.(1550-1617), was offered 31 other properties. Cornelis Benningh Jansz. Duyvesz. had a large house built for himself on the Singel (no. 284), with a spacious garden running behind the neighbouring houses. His children, who entered into influential marriages outside of Amsterdam, sold the houses to the mayor in 1626. Cornelis Benningh's house still exists.

[157] S.A.C. Dudok van Heel, *Cornelis Benningh en het Benninghweer*, Amstelodamum 83, Amsterdam, 1996, p 1-11
[158] Amstelodamum, Municipal Archives, Amsterdam, 1951, p. 108

31. The Dam Square 'in about the year 1570', seen to the north, engraving circa 1610, by an unknown artist. To the right of the Weighing-House (center, square) the houses previously owned by Cornelis Benningh Gerritsz..
Municipal Archives of Amsterdam, Netherlands

Cornelis Banning Gerritsz., together with a few other Burgomasters, was one of those regarded as reformist. Although he was elected Burgomaster in 1536, accusations against him of Anabaptism increased and in 1538 those suspected of 'moderate' leanings or of heresy were excluded from government. Cornelis Banning Gerritsz. was considered one of the six 'heretic' Burgomasters. It was said that they were excluded from the regiment of the city because they had not prepared sufficiently and made no effort to prevent rebaptism, before the conflict occurred. The six Burgomasters did remain in the City Council, but were not again permitted a position as one of the governing council of four (Burgomasters).

Cornelis Banning Gerritsz. is recorded as having been Treasurer but apparently took ill afterward, suffering from bouts of 'insanity':

"On the XXVIIJ day in May anno XVCXLVIJ, the lords Bailiff Joost Buyck Zybrantsz. and Mr. Outger Clementsz, aldermen, witnessed the deceased Cornelis Banninck, once Burgomaster of this city, laid to rest in his howse, who had suffered an injurie to his cropper and also an injurie to his lower chest in the region of the heart, which injuries aforementioned Cornelis Banninck, as seen there, he had inflicted upon himself in a state of insanity on Monday fore of the crucifixion days.(Ascension Day)" . He died thereof on 16 May 1547, the sad end of a great man. "Sic transit Gloria mundi"![159]

---

[159] J.A.W. Banning, *Genealogie van het Geslacht Banning*, Ferd. Banning & Zonen, Groenlo, 1934, p. 105

Cornelis Banning Jansz. Duyvesz. *(G2.E VIb.2a)* was Burgomaster of Amsterdam in 1601, 1607, 1610, 1611, 1613 and 1616. He was the original owner of a historic home on the corner of the Gasthuismolensteeg 20, one of the premises acquired as compensation for that demolished to excavate the Herengracht (canal). Cornelis Banning sold the property in 1594.

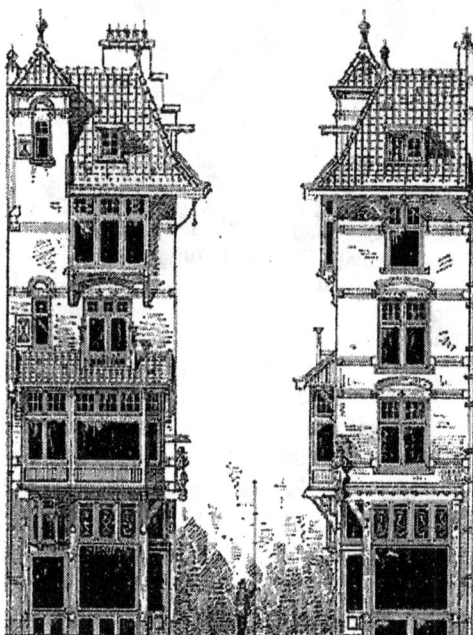

32. Gasthuismolensteeg 20, Amsterdam
Home of Cornelis Jan Benningh Duvensz.
(representing views from the front and the side)
Municipal Archives of Amsterdam, Netherlands

Cornelis held numerous other offices: Dike-Reeve of the Nieuwer Amstel 1580, City Councillor 1584 to his death; Alderman in 1584, 1586, 1588, 1590, 1596 and 1597, Dike-grave of the Nieuwer Amstel 1586, Commissioner of Marital Affairs 1600 and 1608, Commissioner of the Orphanage 1602 and 1609, Deputy Councillor in the States of Holland and West Friesland from 1 May 1603 to 30 April 1606, Auditor 1608, Commissioner of the Exchange Bank 1614 and 1615, Regent of the Civic Orphanage 1594 - 1596. He died on 30 March 1617.

He married Hillegont. Jansdr. and secondly Sophia Foet, who bore him two daughters: Lady Anna Banning and Emerentia Banning.

Lady Anna Banning *(G2.E.VI.2a.a;1584-1624)* married Joachim Cornelisz. van Cuyk van Mierop, from a very prestigious Dutch family. Their daughter Anna van Cuyk van Mierop married (5 Sept. 1649) Philippe Nicolas Count of d'Aumale and Margrave of Haucourt, a direct descendant of Charlemagne (King Charles the Great), who lived from the year 742 to 814 AD, also descending from King Louis of France, Charles V of France, Jean II King of France and Philip VI of Valois, King of France.

Emerentia Banning, *(G2.E.VIb.2a.b.b.)* was born in 1586. She married in The Hague in 1606 to Mr. Jacob van Brouckhoven (born 1577).

33. Page from a 3-volume handwritten genealogical record entitled 'Geslacht Register van Catherine van Hoogenhouck', written by Mr. Pieter Marcus et al; some time between 1700 and 1800. The text states particulars of the marriage between 'Emmerentia Bannings' and Jacob van Brouckhoven.

Photo courtesy of F. van Heijningen

J. van Brouckhoven held a number of prominent positions: in the Council of Forty to Leiden, 1610, Burgomaster of Leiden 1620, Deputy Councillor of the Dutch Parliament, Delegate of the States General, Dikegrave of Rijnland. He died on 16th June 1642 and is buried in Leiden in the St. Pieterskerk. There are numerous painted portraits of Mr. van Brouckhoven, and one of his wife Emerentia Banning in a painting rendered by Jan Anthonisz. van Ravesteyn in 1626. The painting was part of the collection of the Brouckhovenshof in Leiden and came into possession of Museum de Lakenhal in Leiden in 1892.

34. Portrait of Emerentia Banningh 1626 R. van Ravesteyn
Stedelijk Museum De Lakenhal, Leiden, Netherlands

Emerentia Banning founded the 'Small Sionshofje' in 1641, the smallest communal courtyard in Leiden. A 'hof' (or hofje = small hof) is an enclosed area of small homes facing onto an inner courtyard for communal use, generally with vegetable or flower gardens, walkways and a water pump or well. They often included a chapel or small church. Above the simple gateway of the 'Small Sionshofje' is an enormous memorial tablet with a - for some - mysterious text.

This text refers to the fact that the courtyard originally lay adjacent to the 'Sionshofje', founded in 1480 by Mr. and Mrs. Zwieten. This rules pertaining to this courtyard were stipulated in 1505 by two Leiden bakers, a legacy formulated by the words chiselled into the memorial tablet. One of the stipulations of the 'Sionshofje' was that women who became widows were obliged to relinquish their courtyard homes immediately. Emerentia Banning was obviously opposed to this medieval stipulation, which is apparent from the memorial tablet commemorating her 'hofje': 'tot de Weeuwen wee.[160], ('for the abandoned Widows')

She subsequently founded the 'Small Sionshofje', or 'Widow's courtyard', directly adjacent to the 'Sionshofje', consisting of four small houses specifically for widows banished from the 'Sionshofje'. If there were no widows, two houses could be let to others, but two had to remain available for the original purpose - housing for widows.

Emerentia Banning delegated four thousand guilders for, amongst other things, provision for the residents. Eight guilders per year per house were given to purchase butter and six guilders for the purchase of turf. The resident also received ten nickels per week in cash for other necessities, which was a generous gesture on behalf of the founder. However, the residents were expected to make some contribution toward the welfare of the citizens of Leiden in general, a most reasonable demand.

Burgomaster van Brouckhoven and his wife were respected citizens and both were socially committed to the welfare of other citizens endowed with fewer worldly goods. Burgomaster van Brouckhoven had founded another residential courtyard, built in 1640, also adjacent to the 'Sionshofje'. The 'Sionshofje' itself was moved in 1668 to the St. Josephsteeg behind the Haarlemerstraat, due to its dilapidated state. The courtyards founded by Emerentia Banning and her husband were still in existence over three hundred years after they were built, on their original sites. It seems most appropriate that a street in Leiden, the Emerentia Banning Straat, was named after her, which still exists today.

Emerentia Banning died in Leiden on 11 May 1667, where she is buried in the St. Pieterskerk. A description in the handwritten

---

[160] *Hofjes in Nederland*, J.H. Gottmer, Haarlem, 1977, p. 108

107

genealogical note illustrated above mentions that a fine marble sepulchre is erected to the memory of Emerentia and her husband, 'by the wall of the small organ of the chancel'. In January 1983 the city of Leiden named the street Emerentia Banningstraat in her honour.

*   *   *

The theme of the Civic Militia is central to several of the biographical sketches in this book, and it is therefore important to understand the concept of the Civic Militia and it's context in Dutch history and society at that time.

The Civic Militia

The Civic Militia evolved from the militia guilds and was instigated in 1580, on the order of William of Orange. The old militia guilds from the middle ages continued to exist, but they were eventually absorbed into the Civic Militia. The Civic Militia was organized according to city districts. Each district was assigned a company of militiamen, so that the number of districts in a city determined the number of squadrons in the Militia. Each squadron was, in turn, subdivided into corps under the authority of a corporal, who maintained contact with the various neighbourhoods of the city. A squadron, recognizable by the colour of its standard or banner, was led by a corps of officers: one captain, one lieutenant and standard-bearer - the head officers - and one or two sergeants. The commanding officers were delegated their own tasks, specified in the militia ordinance. Several squadrons were united in a department, under the authority of a colonel who maintained contact with the town council, and a provost who was responsible for imposing fines and meting out punishment

 In principle, every able-bodied male citizen between the ages of 18 and 60 was eligible for the Civic Militia and obliged to report, although there were numerous exceptions. Firstly, citizens who were unable to afford their own weapons were excluded and in some cities they were expected to be financially well off. Some were absolved from duty by the Burgomasters if they held other municipal positions or if other services were deemed of value, such as the painter Henrick Cornelisz. Vroom in Haarlem, who excelled in the rendition of naval battles and was permitted the freedom to pursue this art. Anabaptists were excused on religious grounds but compelled to pay an annual fee in exchange. Even then, the maximum number of members in the corps ensured that other citizens were absolved from duty, although they were obliged to pay a monthly fee in recompense. Ultimately, it was the captain or the corporal who decided who in a district would be appointed. Theoretically, the Captains had ultimate authority over the Civic Militia, but in practice they were given very little independence by the city council, from whom they had to request permission to meet and also had to submit the points on their meeting agendas for approval. In Amsterdam the military council was even chaired by the burgomasters who, in the words of a historical chronologist, "acted as their superiors."

The Civic Militia was often spoken of in denigrating terms. This ensued from the image they projected, a camaraderie carried over from the original guilds, its members frequently gathering for boisterous and lavish dinners, often charged with drunken and disorderly conduct, and for riotous practices such as 'parrot shooting' . The 'parrot' was a target of wood or clay, and the shooting matches were traditionally held every year at the beginning of July. It was a rowdy sport, a game: 'parrot shooting' strengthened the brotherly bond between the militiamen, and the winner became 'king'. In July 1514 one Militia Guild had 'shot their parrot', and three days later many affluent citizens lodged a complaint about considerable damage to their carefully tended gardens. The 'King's Hat' was the cause: the winner of the match was given a decorated hat, the higher the better, consisting of a tower of woven greenery and flowers which his companions had torn from the gardens they passed. The town council was subsequently compelled to outlaw the 'King's hat', issuing a fine of three pounds for whomever would accept one. Was this rule upheld? Not at all. No self-respecting militiaman felt that he could refuse this honour 'done the king', and that it would have been an insult to refuse the hat for a meagre penance of three pounds.

In more sober moments the Civic Militia was responsible for maintaining order, such as was called for when citizens rebelled vehemently against increased taxes on butter. Naturally, they could be called up in times of war to defend their country. A parade of inspection was a public spectacle, traditionally held on occasion of the annual fair. The militiamen then marched with their weapons, banners and drums through the main streets of the city, then to congregate in the city square to demonstrate their ability and strength to the people.

The Civic Militia was probably less prestigious than history has led us to believe. All burghers and residents of a city were, by law, obligated to have a weapon of some kind, the rich having more and better weapons than those with a lesser income. They were to carry these weapons in defence of their city, when and as often as the law subscribed.

The Civic Militia represented the core of this civil defence system: the richer citizens being properly armed and subject to regular practice, which the ordinary citizens were not. Amsterdam had three Civic Militias. Until about 1475 they were a rather motley assembly, but by the turn of the century they were more properly armed and organised. While at one time they were called on to march in only two processions per year, by the end of the 15th century regular processions were held for almost any occasion: in time of war to demonstrate for peace, in time of peace to observe their gratitude for such, when there was threat of attack,or plague, etc.. Understandably, the militiamen were not always inclined to join in yet another procession but this was effectively curtailed by fining any man who did not appear with 'a thousand stones' and whoever defected during a procession was fined 'five thousand stones'.

35. Parade of the Civic Militia on the Dam Square in Amsterdam, during the Annual Fair in 1686. Engraving by D. Marot
(Palace on the left, weighing house in the centre, homes of C. Benningh to the right, behind the weighing house)
Municipal Archives of Amsterdam, Netherlands

The Civic Militia was otherwise only called to action in time of war. Otherwise, they were obliged to keep watch on the city by night, under the authority of the Captain, and in the winter to break the ice on the canals. Four Captains were appointed for each city district, whose task it was to maintain artillery and a stock of gunpowder and lead in the watchtowers. A gong was sounded in case of alarm. By the beginning of the 16th century there were 16 Captains to a district. The Captains were, in effect, really only watchmen, and thus the term 'Nightwatch', (as a subject of Rembrandt's famous painting) is apt - the night watchmen. (Authorities claim that Rembrandt's painting was not actually a 'Night Watch', but was termed as such because the painting had darkened considerably since its rendition.)

Group portraits of the Civic Militia became very popular in the 1600's and the paintings were hung in the militia headquarters. Usually various highly decorated and costly artefacts and symbols were included in the painting: a chalice, a staff, chains of office or drinking horns.

Several very well known historic paintings of the Civic Militia feature Bannings. Two of these paintings feature a 'Jan Banning', both of whom appear to be the same person. The resemblance is less obvious in the first painting (1585) but striking in a sketch done of the painting by Jacob Colijn at a later date, which was rendered because the painting is in bad condition and partially obscured by a heavy layer of wax, so the sketch is often used as a reference.

The second painting is dated 1604, representing a farewell celebration for Captain Pieter van Neck. As Van Neck died in 1601, historians conclude that the painting was started before that date and completed later, possibly due to the plague in Amsterdam in those years. The identity of Jan Banning is the existing genealogy is unknown, as there were several; the most likely candidate being Jan Banning Claesz., born in 1563, but membership in the Militia is not specifically mentioned for any.

36. Corps of Captain Reynst, Pietersz and Standard-bearer Claas Claasz. Cruys
Dirck Barendsz. 1585
Jan Banning is third from the left, top row
Amsterdams Historisch Museum, Amsterdam, Netherlands

37. Officers of the Amsterdam Company of Captain Pieter van Neck (fragment)
1604 , Aert Pietersz.; from left to right: Jan Banning, Jan Valckenaer,
Pieter van Neck (Captain), Jurriaen Jansz., Frans van Nes, Hans
Goedewaert, unknown, Jacaob Lucaszc. (lieutenant)
Amsterdams Historisch Museum, Amsterdam

Dr. Frans Banningh Cocq, (*G2.E.VII.I.1*) (doctor of law) legendary as
the central figure in Rembrandt's 'Nightwatch', is more famous today
than he was at the time that he posed for posterity. This is primarily
because the 'Nightwatch' was in itself a controversial work of art, in
addition to being a Rembrandt and one of the largest canvasses ever
painted. Frans Banningh Cocq was Knight, Lord of Purmerland and
Ilpendam. Seen in perspective, many Banning family members held
positions of equal importance but received less public acclaim. Frans
Banningh Cocq's mother, Lysbeth Benningh (*G2.E.VII.1; 1581-1623*)
was an only child of Frans Benningh (1544-1582) and Maritge Haeck
(d.1621). Lysbeth married against the wish of her parents and relations
(they presumably felt that the marriage was beneath her station) on 16
Sept. 1603 to an apothecary who came from Bremen, Germany. This Jan
Jansz. Cocq (1575-1633 - alleged to have been orphaned) settled in
Amsterdam in 1590 as a servant to Steven Jansz, apothecary of 'In de
Witte Doos'('In the White Box'). A perhaps exaggerated description of

Jan. Janz. Cocq depicts him 'et ostiatim mendicasse dicitur'[161] ('people say that he went begging from door to door'). However, he seems to have done well for himself, becoming a burgher of Amsterdam on 9 May 1603 and immediately setting up his own chemist's shop, *'In the Glowing Oven'*.

38. Frans Banning Cocq (1655)
Copper engraving by J. Houbraken (1779) from a
drawing by H. Pothoven
courtesy of Th. F.M. Weyn Banningh

Two sons were born of the marriage between Jan Jansz. Cocq and Lysbeth Fransdr. Benningh. The youngest, Jan, was deaf, and drowned in 1658. The eldest son, Frans (b. 23 Feb. 1605), studied law in Basel, Switzerland, and appended his mother's surname to his own. However, he spelled the name as 'Banninck', as demonstrated by his signature on both his marriage contract and his doctoral degree. It is written as 'Banning' on the shield on the 'Nightwatch', and he has most frequently been referred to with this spelling, and as 'Banningh' in the centuries which followed. After his return to Amsterdam the young Dr. Frans Banningh Cocq rapidly made a name for himself in civil office. He married Lady Maria Overlander (b. 24.6.1603). The publication of their nuptial banns is described as follows:

"This 4th of April 1630 registered here: Frans Banning Kock, of Amsterdam, doctor, from the Breestraat, assisted by Jan Kock, his father

---

[161] J.E. Elias, *De Vroedschap van Amsterdam 1578-1795*, Part I, Vincent Loosjes, Haarlem, p. 406

and Marie Overlander of Purmerlant, of Amsterdam, assisted by Volckert Overlander, Ex-Burgomaster, Lord of Purmerlant, her father, and Geertruyt Hooft, her mother.
The 22nd of April 1630 married by Ds. Otte Badius[162].

Two life-size portraits of Frans Banningh Cocq and his wife were commissioned on the occasion of their marriage, in 1630. These portraits hung undisturbed in their residence, the Castle Ilpendam, for over two centuries. They were auctioned in 1872 to a tax collector, Burchard Theodoor Elias, for three hundred guilders. Apparently Mr. Elias, the eleventh of fourteen children, felt rather inferior to his siblings, who lived in more fortuitous circumstances in Amsterdam than did Elias himself. He rectified this situation and satisfied his yearning for social recognition by claiming that the portraits were of his own ancestors, mr. Floris Elias and Deborah Pancras, wed in 1650. The paintings passed into history as such and remained in the family, coming into possession of Professor Doctor Gerhard J. Elias, professor at the Technical University of Delft in 1918, through inheritance. The couple remained childless and in June 1975 his widow, Viktoria Maria Margarete Schloss, willed them to the township of Delft. Here they were hung in the ancient town hall bearing the inscription of Floris Elias and Deborah Pancras. It was not until 2002 that questions arose concerning the identity of the portrayed couple, when an art historian astutely noted that the apparel worn was twenty years out of date, considering that the couple was alleged to have been wed in 1650. Through research at the National Bureau for Art Historical Documentation, it was revealed[163] that the portraits were actually those of Frans Banningh Cocq and Maria Overlander. This created quite a storm of publicity in the Netherlands. The artist is as yet unknown.

[162] H. Bontemantel, *De Regeering van Amsterdam, soo in 't Civiel en Militaire (1653-1672),* Dr. G.W. Kernkamp, M. Nijhoff, the Hague, 1897, I, p. 480,481
[163] P. Hofland, *Delftsche Courant,* Sijthoff Pers, Delft, 1 Feb. 2003, B3

39. Marriage portraits of Maria Overlander and Frans Banninck Cocq,
1630/31, artist unknown
Gemeente Musea Delft, collection: Stedelijk Museum Het Prinsenhof, Delft, Netherlands

Mr. Volckert Overlander , Knight, Lord of Purmerland and Ilpendam (given his title of nobility by King James I of England in 1620) died on 18th October 1630, soon after the marriage of his daughter. Following his death his possessions, and his title, were passed on to his son-in-law Frans. After having been appointed as commissary to several municipal functions, Frans Banningh Cocq was appointed in 1642 as Captain of the Civic Militia. In the same year the masterwork of Rembrandt Harmensz. Van Rhijn (1606-1669) was commissioned, 'The militia company of Captain Frans Banning Cocq' , more commonly known as 'The Nightwatch'. Banningh Cocq is the central figure, elegantly attired in dark garments, black hat, white collar and red sash, in sharp contrast to the persons on his left and right sides.

The author D. Wijnbeek[164] wrote in a commemorative book about the 'Nightwatch' in 1944 that Banningh Cocq was manifested on the canvas more as a magistrate than as a military figure. The celebrated poet Jan Vos (1620-1667) also lauded him as such in a poem[165]. Wijnbeek

---

[164] D. Wijnbeek, *De Nachtwacht, de Historie van een Meesterwerk*, N.V. Uitgeverij Holdert & Co., Amsterdam, 1944
[165] D. Wijnbeek, *De Nachtwacht, de Historie van een Meesterwerk*, N.V. Uitgeverij Holdert & Co., Amsterdam, 1944, p. 83

notes that the militiamen were considerably displeased with the painting. Rembrandt had portrayed them as warriors, but in those days soldiers had a rather lowly status. They had expected a traditional, more static and stately group portrait, but the portrayal was freely rendered by Rembrandt so as to appear more a glorification of Banningh Cocq among a number of devoted subjects.

The Civic Militia with whom Banningh Cocq is proudly portrayed supposedly consisted of 34 figures, but only 17 were actual militiamen and 17 (including the dog) were 'supporting cast'. This was a deliberate departure from convention. The scene was not rendered in the style of conventional group portraits, as had previously been done by other artists, but as the dramatisation of an event. Rembrandt's motive seems to have been to create a setting, a composition of colour, of light and dark, rather than to objectively portray those who commissioned him.

Only fortuitous citizens could afford a place on the canvas. The sitters thus objected most forcefully when it became apparent that, while they had contributed equally, some were portrayed not full-face, but in three-quarter view or in profile, by which they reasoned that they should really pay three-quarters or half of the original fee. It was later deemed necessary to add a shield to the background specifying the names of the militiamen portrayed. Out of a company of some 120 men, only these 17 were prepared to pay to have themselves portrayed, and we must therefore view them as representative of the whole company. A sash was the only uniform article of attire worn by the Civic Militia; otherwise their choice of clothing and weapons was their own.

Now lauded as one of the most prominent paintings in the world, when it was unveiled the 'Nightwatch' met with disapproval and disappointment. Rembrandt's reputation suffered accordingly and he did not receive any prestigious commissions for group portraits after this one. Some time after it was completed, it was moved to the town hall, but proved too large for the wall to which it was consigned. This was easy enough to remedy. A few details more or less seemed irrelevant, and a large portion was simply cut off the side and the top to fit the wall.

Wijnbeek asks in 1944: what significant role did Banningh Cocq play in history other than representing the focus of the 'Nightwatch'? His father's past was obscure and entirely lacking in social status. His mother's family was affiliated with the old aristocracy of Amsterdam. His wife's family belonged to a longstanding line of eminent citizens. He undoubtedly demonstrated excellent insight into governmental affairs, and is said to have pursued his offices with flair and enthusiasm. However, he does not seem to have lacked in vanity and was not always taken seriously by his colleagues, apparently flaunting titles which did not always seem to justifiably earned. His knighthood by the King of France is one title mentioned for which no heroic deed or justification can be cited, Banningh Cocq never proved any service to France and it is inferred that he must have dug deep into his pocket in exchange for this badge of office.

40. Seal of Frans Banninck Cocq,
(Municipal Archives of Amsterdam)

41. Clay pipe depicting Frans
Banningh Cocq, 1880-1905
(collection Pijpenkabinet, Amsterdam)

Frans Banningh Cocq was noted to be very artistic and he had considerable interest in art and painting. His family album (now in possession of the Rijksmuseum of Amsterdam) contains numerous sketches and notes. The album consisted of two oblong parts, measuring 19cm. x 15cm.. The title page reads: "Family register of the Gentlemen and Ladies of Purmerlant and Ilpendam, in consanguinity as well as affinity." Banningh Cocq even went to the trouble of having notes on his official decorations authorised by a notary. Accompanying a sketch of the Nightwatch in his family album he writes:

"Sketch of the painting in the large Hall of the Cloveniers Doelen with therein the Young Lord of Purmerlandt as Captain, commanding his lieutenant, the Lord of Vlaardingen, to order his Company of Civilians to march[166]."

---

[166] J.A.W. Banning, *Genealogie van het Geslacht Banning*, Ferd. Banning & Zonen, Groenlo, 1934, p. 128

118

42.   Page from the family album of Frans Banningh Cocq
                   sketch of the Nightwatch
               Rijksmuseum, Amsterdam, Netherlands

Six years after the 'Nightwatch' was painted, when Banningh Cocq took
office as Superior Officer of the Longbow Association (1648), he was
portrayed with other notable citizens; this time rendered by Bartholomeus
van der Helst (1630-1670). B. van der Helst's portraits were very much in
demand, especially because of the striking likenesses he created. Frans
Banningh Cocq recorded in his family album:
"The gentlemen overlords of the Longbow Association 1653. Dr. Frans
Banningh Cocq (extreme left with the gold goblet), and Joan (Johan) van
der Pol, Burgomasters and governors of the towne of Amsterdamme,
Albert Pater, Councilman and ex-Alderman, Dr. Joan (Johan) Blaeu,
Councilman and governing Alderman of the towne of Amsterdamme[167]."

---

[167] J.A.W. Banning, *Genealogie van het Geslacht Banning*, Ferd. Banning & Zonen,
Groenlo, 1934, p. 129

43. Four overlords of the St. Sebastiaans-Doelen by Bartholomeus van der Helst, 1653. Frans Banningh Cocq is portrayed on the extreme left.
Amsterdams Historisch Museum, Amsterdam, Netherlands

The family album also includes a drawing of a stained glass window in the Reformed Church of Ilpendam with the subtext:
"Window donated to the church of Purmerlandt
MDCXXXXII by the young Lord of Purmerlandt."[168]
His coat-of-arms is featured on four pillows on the so-called 'hofbank' (the bench or pew reserved for more noble members of the congregation) in the St. Sebastian church in Ilpendam, as well as in the windows above a chapel in this church.

The great Old Church in Amsterdam has a stained glass window featuring the coat-of-arms of Frans Banningh Cocq.

No Roman Catholic priest had been in Ilpendam since the reformation. Priests were admitted again in 1645, with the approval of Banningh Cocq as 'local Lord', albeit within limits, because the new priest had to be a 'Hollander' and not a monk. Banningh Cocq was, however, rather ambiguous in his tolerance of the 'papists', as he withdrew his permission only a year later.

In 1648 he was knighted by the King of France (Louis XIV):
"and in 1648 benighted by the King of France in the order of St. Michael, being conferred with the chain of office by the French ambassador Henry Brasset in accordance with the missive dated 3rd November, presented to

---

[168] J.A.W. Banning, *Genealogie van het Geslacht Banning*, Ferd. Banning & Zonen, Groenlo, 1934, p. 131

His Honour by the King, according to the attestation of said Brasset, dated 26th of the same, month November 1648".[169]

The knighthood is rather shrouded in mystery, because no one has been able to discover why Banningh Cocq should have received it. As mentioned earlier, Wijnbeek infers in his book about the 'Nightwatch' that in these social circles a knighthood from the King of France might simply have been a result of handsome remuneration.

On 16 Sept.1650 Banningh Cocq was appointed burgomaster for the first time. His last appointment is described as follows:

"Appointed as Burgomaster on the first of February 1654: Cornelis Bicker, Lord van Swieten, Jan Huydecooper, Lord van Maarseveen, Nicolaas Tulp who, out of the departing Burgomasters have appointed: Frans Banningh Cocq, Lord of Pumerlant"[170]. Banningh Cocq had recorded his genealogy; after his death his brother-in-law, Pieter de Graeff, included it in a small museum of family history at the Castle Ilpendam, possessions which were auctioned in 1870. A record of the auction still exists.

44. Ilpenstein Castle, Ilpendam, built in 1622 (demolished in 1872) engraving by C. Pronk
photo: Iconografisch Bureau/Rijksbureau voor Kunsthistorische Documentatie (Netherlands Institute for Art History), the Hague

---

[169] J.A.W. Banning, *Genealogie van het Geslacht Banning*, Ferd. Banning & Zonen, Groenlo, 1934, p. 80
[170] J.A.W. Banning, *Genealogie van het Geslcaht Banning*, Ferd. Banning & Zonen, Groenlo, 1934, p. 126,127

Dr. Frans Banningh Cocq, Knight, Lord of Purmerland and Ilpendam, died on New Year's Day 1655, a month short of his 50th birthday. His marriage remained childless. His widow, Lady of Purmerland and Ilpendam (died 27 Jan. 1678), conveyed by will and testament her properties and rights to her nephew Jacob de Graeff, Esquire. The Domains Purmerland and Ilpendam remained in possession of the noble De Graeff family until the auction in 1870.

Jacob Benningh is the standard-bearer and central figure in Bartholomeus van der Helst's most famous work: 'De Schuttersmaaltijd', ('Banquet of the Civic Militia') completed in 1648. The Jacob central to this painting was most likely directly related to Gerrit, Cornelis Gerritsz., Jacob Jansz. and Jan Jacobsz., all of whom, in their own generations, owned property on the Nieuwendijk in Amsterdam – as did this Jacob – where, for generations, they pursued the textile trade and held prominent positions in the city. Although he is not mentioned specifically in the genealogy, his name occurs in the Amsterdam municipal archives. Jacob was baptized on 6 January 1608, a son of Balthasar Benning and Grietje Jacobs. He would have been around the age of 40 at the time the painting was rendered, which he is judged to be, as compared to Witsen who is aged 43 in the painting. Between 1647 and 1649 a Jacob Benningh on the Nieuwendijk ('by the Dam Square') was taxed for the exorbitant sum of 300 guilders, which implies that he must have had considerable wealth and status. On 31 July 1651 Jacob Benningh 'from the Dam Square' was buried in the Old Church.

The standard-bearer was one of the most important positions in the Civic Militia. The person appointed to this position was deemed to be "a young man from a respectable background and beyond reproach."[171], and "a dedicated bachelor, as far as these can be found"[172]. Apparently the reason for this was so that he could dedicate himself fully to his task, unencumbered by other loyalties. He was expected to be strong, to wield the heavy banner. After all, he who held the standard upheld the honour of the men. In those days, he was expected to be courageous, because he led the militia in a charge, encouraging his comrades to action. He was required to be handsome or hold physical appeal, as somewhat cynicallydescribed by Schmidt Degener: "In spite of the scarcity of Batavian Adonis's, most militia portraits reveal that the aspired ideal was met."[173]

[171] D. Wijnbeek, *De Nachtwacht, de Historie van een Meesterwerk*, N.V. Uitgeverij Holdert & Co., Amsterdam, 1944, p. 111

[172] D. Wijnbeek, *De Nachtwacht, de Historie van een Meesterwerk*, N.V. Uitgeverij Holdert & Co., Amsterdam, 1944, p. 111

[173] D. Wijnbeek, *De Nachtwacht, de Historie van een Meesterwerk*, N.V. Uitgeverij Holdert & Co., Amsterdam, 1944, p. 112

The 'Schuttersmaaltijd' represents a celebration of the Treaty of Munster, on the 5th of July 1648, signalling an end to the 80 Years War. The citizens of Amsterdam had avidly supported peace with Spain, especially for economic considerations. Not wanting to aggravate the Spaniards with large-scale victorious festivity, they emphasised the end of the war and the return of peace during the official celebration. The Amsterdam civic squadrons celebrated the amity with a banquet and a shooting competition held at the headquarters of the Longbow Association. Commissions were given for two paintings to adorn the headquarters of the Crossbow Association, one by Govert Flinck and one by Bartholomeus van der Helst. The latter illustrates the officers of the company of Captain Cornelis Jansz. Witsen and Lieutenant Johan Oetgens van Waveren at the militia banquet held on 18th June at the headquarters of the Crossbow Association.

Until 1850 this painting of Civic Militia was considered by experts, among which the English painter Joshua Reynolds, to be superior to the 'Nightwatch' by Rembrandt.

The painting should not be seen as a realistic rendition of the occasion, but rather as a more symbolic banquet of peace, emphasizing the Amsterdam politics of reconciliation. The officers and others are portrayed at a long table. The most important militiamen are seated in the foreground, the others in the back. On the right, Captain Witsen and Luitenant Van Waveren shake hands. This handshake symbolises the newly concluded 'eternal pact' expressed in a poem by Jan Vos, which is written on a piece of paper on the drum in the foreground. Witsen also offers Van Waveren the drinking horn of the Guild of St. Joris as the 'horn of peace'. Two sergeants, Thomas Hartog en Dirck Claes Thoveling, are depicted behind the Captain. Jacob Benningh, wearing a blue sash, is seated in front of the table at the centre of the canvas. He holds the standard showing the Amsterdam 'virgin' over his shoulder.

45. The Peace of van Munster, Bartholomeus van der Helst   1648
Jacob Banning is the standard-bearer , seated centre foreground
Collection: Rijksmuseum, Amsterdam

Johannes Banninck of Amsterdam, who has to date not been placed in the genealogy, was buried on 8 December 1787. Considering the fact that Johannes died some six months earlier, on the 30th of May of that year, the sinister circumstances of this burial were recalled and detailed in an article published in the *Geïllustreerd Volksblad voor Nederland (Illustrated Newspaper for the Netherlands)* more than a century later, on 8 December 1898[174]. The article reads:

" 8 December 1787
JOHANNES BANNINCK BURIED"

"The year 1787 was a year of turmoil. The Patriots were at the height of power and took this advantage to usurp government officials not in their favour from position. They also converged on Amsterdam and replaced nine loyal City Councillors by their own Patriots. It is not surprising that the loyal Orangists would tolerate this without a show of resistance and they therefore held meetings and submitted petitions to restore their rights, and in the easily incited situation in those days it was not at all surprising that these meetings did not convene peaceably. Especially in [the Amsterdam district of] Kattenburg, where the population was almost exclusively made up of Orange supporters, boisterous gatherings were held at various inns.

The Patriots, however, were the first to take action and on the 19th May plundered the inn "'s Lands Welvaren' on the Reguliersgracht, Arentsen's lace shop in the Halvemaansteeg and the book shop of Orangist Hendrik Arends on the Singel. When they realized that they were unchallenged they took possession of the houses of the Burgomasters Rendorp and Beels; the home of Burgomaster Dedel was occupied for some time by riflemen.

When the Kattenburg residents became aware of the situation, they decided to take revenge on the Patriots in their midst and plundered in turn some seven houses. As soon as this became known in the city, a governmental order was issued to chastise the Kattenburgers. However, they surged onto the bridges, making them inaccessible. Canons were hauled in from both sides, shots were fired and dead and wounded fell.

At nightfall the attackers attempted to cross over in three barges, but their plan was discovered and thwarted. However, the following morning they positioned six canons on a covered barge, constructed a rampart of bales of tobacco and thus approached the opposite side. A brief but vicious attack took place, whereby again several Kattenburgers perished. Some bodies were retrieved, but four were found by the attackers and taken to the Waag [Weighing House]. Aided

---

[174] *Geïllustreerd Volksblad voor Nederland*, 8 Dec. 1898, archives from the Central Bureau of Genealogy, the Hague

by riflemen, the Patriot attackers now invaded Kattenburg and thirty-five houses of respected loyal citizens were plundered and destroyed.

Who knows how the losing faction would have fared, had the government not finally realized the necessity to take action to stop the plundering. Several Patriotic rogues, unimpressed by the order, were arrested, but released after a few days. Plunderers on the side of the loyalist faction fared worse. Hans Jurriaansz, a Swede, was hanged on the Dam Square, and his body, together with that of Johannes Banninck, one of those killed at the Kattenburger Bridge, was transported to the Volewijk [district] on the other side of the Ij basin and hanged on the gallows; the body of Banninck hung by the legs. Eight days later four other Kattenburgers were flogged and convicted to several years imprisonment.

However, change came. The Patriots eventually dared to openly insult the Consort of the Governor and her brother, the King of Prussia, demanded justice. The Patriots refused to comply and 20,000 Prussian soldiers came to incarcerate them. The Patriot faction was instantly repressed and removed, and Banninck's next-of-kin promptly requested atonement for their blood relative.

The request was granted and on Saturday 8th December the hangman and a town clerk crossed the Ij, accompanied by a force of justice. The body was removed from the gallows, laid in a casket and then the town clerk raised his arms three times over the casket and pronounced the body honest [innocent]. The casket was then placed on a fittingly bedecked yacht, with flags at half-mast, and transported to the inn ''t Onvolmaakte Schip' in Kattenburg and, in the late afternoon, carried to the grave with a following of over 2000 people. Several ships' carpenters led the procession with banners and music. The funeral cortège halted at the place where the man had died and raised the banner over the bier. While the coffin was lowered into the grave, the musicians sounded the Wilhelmus [national anthem].

Before us lies a copy of a letter inviting friends to the funeral. At the top was a crown, a portrait of Banninck and an obelisk, and then the following text:

"In Amsterdam, Anno 1787. On Saturday 8th December, we request the presence of Mr. ...., at the interment of
the Body of JOHANNES BANNINCK
Who, on the 30th May of this Yeare, on the Kattenburgerplein, unfortunately dyed by the Bridge, as a Defender of the Countrie's Most Tyme-honoured and now Restored Constitution, who through erroneous concepts of that tyme was fated to hang by the Legs on the Gallowes over the Ij, which also befell; but now through Laying on of the Hands by a Town Clerk, in the name of Justice and Honour has been declared restored, to escort the above-mentioned Body, from the

Wijnhuis [Wine House = Inn] known as Het Onvolmaakte Schip, on the corner of the Kleine Kattenburger Straat and Plein."

Two prominent Benninghs from Amersfoort are included in this chapter, also having made names of repute during the Golden Age. It is not known whether or not they were related to the Amsterdam Bannings:

Johannes Benningh[175] (Benningius), born in Amersfoort on 6 February 1594[176], a historian and diplomat, was promoted to Doctor of Law in both civil and ecclesiastic affairs in Leuven, Belgium, lecturing there for a number of years. It is not known to which genealogy he belongs. He later became a Member of the High Court of Mechelen, and in 1611 President of Luxemburg. He was known as a man of extraordinarily shrewd genius, gifted with an exceptional memory, of whom great expectations could have been held had he not died suddenly at the age of 38 on 30 January 1632 (and not in 1711 at the age of 117, as the Dutch *Vaderlandsch Woordenboek (National Dictionary)* of 1787 states[177]). He was buried in Douay, Belgium. The only surviving publication in his name is *Historia Luxemburgensis, è diplomatibus documentis antiques* which may or may not be the same as his *Historische, Geografische Ontlediging van het Hertogdom Luxemburg* .

Jacob(us) Benningh[178] (Benningius), brother of the above mentioned Johannes, was born in Amersfoort in the second half of the 16th century. He was very experienced in law and was appointed Professor of Law at Douay (Belgium), where he died in 1611.

---

[175] Goudhoeven, *Chronycke*, 1636, p. 225/ Aa., A.J. van der, *Biografisch Woordenboek der Nederlanden*, J.J. van Brederode, Haarlem, 1852, p. 99

[176] The *Vaderlandsch Woordenboek* (Jacobus Kok, Johannes Allert, Amsterdam, 1787, p. 371) lists his date of birth as 13 February 1594, while *the Biographical Index of the Benelux Countries* of 2003 lists his year of birth as 1567.

[177] *Vaderlandsch Woordenboek*, Jacobus Kok, Johannes Allert, Amsterdam, 1787, p. 371

[178] Goudhoeven, *Chronycke*, 1636, p. 225/ Aa., A.J. van der, *Biografisch Woordenboek der Nederlanden*, J.J. van Brederode, Haarlem, 1852, p. 99

Until the middle of the seventeenth century the Amsterdam Bannings held prominent positions in public life, to which the following rhyme bears witness:

"The BENNINCX, olde lineage, out of whose grafts and scions,
The most Gentlemen of Amsterdam have come forth."[179]

It is said that this old, distinguished Amsterdam family died out in the 18th century[180]. They did not die out so much as disperse, for various reasons of a religious, economic or political nature.

Although Amsterdam was no longer the scene of their status and success, the Bannings were not that easily erased from history. Their old grandeur began to revive as Bannings from other family branches carved a niche for themselves in history.

Among the Bannings of note are the great Belgian statesman Emile Banning, a confidante and close friend of King Leopold II of Belgium, and Henricus Adrianus Banning, the influential 19th century man of letters and editor-in-chief of the Dutch periodical *Katholieke Illustratie* (*Catholic Illustration*), which counted thousands - both Catholic and non-Catholic - of admiring readers, because of its appealing style of journalism.

Another editor-in-chief of renown was Ferdinand Banning, founder of the Catholic publication for the (Dutch province of the) Gelderse Achterhoek of whom, through his forceful journalism, it was said that he contributed significantly "to raising to the cultural and moral standards of the population of this region to its present level"[181].

Professor Willem Banning made a profound impact on political life in the Netherlands in the 20th century, a force to be reckoned with where labour government and theology converged. Dr. Frans Banning was both physician and temperance man, one of the pioneers of Catholic temperance in the Netherlands.

The 1934 genealogy asserts that Banning had once again, throughout the last century, become an influential and respected name, a lineage represented by statesmen, mayors, academic and religious men; industrialists, publishers, technical experts and numerous other capable men and women living throughout the world.

*   *   *

---

[179] J.B. Rietstap, *Wapenboek van den Nederlandse Adel*, 1887, p. 283
[180] Prof. dr. J.H.F. Kohlbrugge, *De Nederlandse Leeuw*, edition 12., no. 4-5, 1912, column
[181] J.A.W. Banning, *Genealogie van het Geslacht Banning*, Ferd. Banning & Zonen, Groenlo, 1934, p. 12

Hermanus Banning (*G2.A,V.bis and G5*; *5 Sept.1790 –5 Dec.1880*) went to Russia as a petty officer in the cavalry forces of the French Emperor Napoleon I (1812). When he first signed up for duty in 1811, he was told to report to the garrison in Amersfoort, the Netherlands. After a stay of several days he was ordered to march to Paris. His parents, aware that they might never see him again, accompanied him to Vreeswijk and after a 'heart-rending' farewell, he set off on foot to Paris. Some 15,000 Dutchmen were ordered to join the Emperor's forces.

From Paris, Napoleon's army of half a million soldiers set out through Switzerland and Austria to Russia, toward their doom. They had to subsist largely on stolen goods during their journey eastward. The Russians applied 'scorched earth' tactics to discourage the advance, having set their capital city on fire two days before the French army invaded it on 16 September, including their own hospitals with some 20,000 wounded. The long French supply columns were attacked repeatedly. At the beginning of November, after the tsar had rejected all Napoleon's ultimatums in St. Petersburg, the exhausted Great Army began its retreat. Winter set in early that year and temperatures soon dropped to 18 degrees (C) below zero. Roads became slick with ice and the horses froze to death. The soldiers were poorly clad. On 26 November the troops reached the marshy banks of the Beresina River, a tributary to the Dnjepr.

The Russians, who planned to ambush and defeat the trapped army at this point, destroyed the only bridge. Under heavy fire and handicapped by ice floes in the river, the French army still managed to construct two improvised bridges. One of the soldiers present described the following events, "Everyone wanted to get across the river first, the strongest threw the weakest into the water, the baggage and wounded, with sable in hand they opened a path; a frenzied madness took possession of them. Worst of all, the bridge caught fire, and we could see the battalions crossing the burning beams disappear in the flames or throw themselves into the icy current."[182] When some 5000 soldiers remained on the east bank, the other bridge was also set ablaze and they were "trapped like rats". Only a small number reached the logistics support point of Koningsbergen on 19 December. The campaign had resulted in a slaughter of its own troops.

The destiny of the 15,000 Dutch soldiers has always remained obscure. The 3rd regiment of Grenadiers was annihilated during the defence of Krasnoi on the return home, with only 40 survivors. The men of the engineering corps, who had to assist in building the bridges across

---

[182] J. and M. Banning, *Genealogy of Ulft*, 2001, unpublished

the Beresina, stood in freezing water up to their armpits. Few survived. Of the 15,000 Dutch recruits an estimate of only a few hundred returned.

46. Hermanus Banning, 1790-1880
courtesy of Th. F.M. Weyn Banningh

Of the 200 recruited soldiers from Utrecht only three - including Hermanus Banning - returned. Three horses had been shot from under him. Hermanus suffered all the hardships of the terrible journey. On the return, carried by his horse, he survived the journey across the Berensina, where so many thousands met their death. Younger generations of Bannings listened avidly as he recounted his adventures, whereby he often showed his watch, which had also survived the Beresina, and the many military honours he received. One such distinguished honour was bestowed on him personally by Emperor Napoleon. Hermanus Banning was a lifelong fervent supporter of 'his' Emperor and he spoke ardently about him. Hermanus Banning survived his beloved Emperor by many years, dying suddenly on Saint Nicholas day in 1880 at the age of 90.

Coincidentally, another Banning in this line - **Joannes B.W. Banning** *(G2.C.IV;1791-1858)* - also served as an officer in the French army under Napoleon. He fought in the battle at Leipzig (1813) and was taken prisoner there. He returned home after the treaty of Paris was signed in April 1814 and settled in the Dutch city of Maastricht where he lived until 1831. When Maastricht was relinquished to the Netherlands by the French he was forced to leave the country and seek refuge in Belgium, because of his revolutionary principles. It was in Belgium that his son, the diplomat and historian Emile Th.J. Banning, was born in 1836.

Dr. Emile Th.J. Banning *(G2.C.V; 1836-1898)* took his doctorate in the liberal arts and philosophy (1860), and served as archivist-librarian after 1863 at the Ministry of Foreign Affairs in Brussels, later director-general. He was known as a passionate advocate for Belgian colonial expansion and became, as such, a trusted confidante of King Leopold II (1835-1909). Emile Banning, who played a significant role in the fight against slavery, is perhaps, although in deed but not in name, founder of the Congo as a private colony of Leopold II. In view of the fact that the colonisation of the this region cost the lives of some one million Congolese, this might be considered a dubious honour. A share company was founded in the spirit of the nineteenth century, upholding culture, trade and industry.

Emile Banning settled in Brussels in 1861, after completing his studies at the University of Berlin. After having worked for some time for the Royal Library in Brussels, he was employed at the archives of the Ministry of Foreign Affairs. As a learned polyglot he was manager of the bureau of translation for several years. Emile Banning brought order to archives in a state of total chaos and deterioration. He created a library which counted 100 volumes in 1863 and 16,000 volumes by 1899, the only one in Belgium which had a section on the history and geography of Africa.

Emile Banning was not only a very gifted writer, but also a poet and moralist, the brilliant pioneer of politics of colonial expansion in Belgium. As the right hand to King Leopold II, he undertook an extensive survey of the island of Formosa in 1865. Long before the British developed an Intelligence Service to aid them during the second world war, he set up the first Intelligence Service, by which, via the press, channels of contact were established between national and international intellectual movements.

It was subsequent to this, when Emile Banning met with King Leopold II in 1867, that the idea was discussed for a comprehensive news source for international intelligence and comparable politics, as both gentlemen were fired by the concept of expansion of their country. Although the plan had not acquired shape, Banning continued to publish colonial propaganda in cooperation with a number of newspapers, in particular *L'Echo du Parlement* (1862-1885). In 1876 he accepted the position of secretary to the International Geographic Conference, which represented the major force behind Belgian enterprise in the Congo.

In the last years of his life Banning came into conflict with the king because of his economic policies there. The current Bandudu (Zaire) was called Banningville in the colonial age (until 1966). The 'Rue Emile Banning' in Brussels was named in his honour in 1900, as well as the 'Emile Banningstraat' in Antwerp. Numerous (12) decorations and knighthoods were bestowed on him:

Commandeur de l'Ordre de Léopold (Belgium)
Officier de la Légion d'honneur (France)
Commandeur de órdre de l'immaculée Conception (Spain)
Grand Officier de l'Ordre de Charles III (Spain)
Grand Officier de Notre Dame de Villa Viciosa (Portugal)
Commandeur avec plaque de l'Ordre Royal de la Couronne Royale d'Italie (Italy)
Grand Officier de l'Etoile de Zanzibar (Africa)
Commandeur de l'Ordre de St. Anne (Russia)
Commandeur avec plaque de l 'Ordre de François-Joseph (Austria)
Commandeur avec plaque de l 'Ordre de l 'Aigle rouge (England)
Commandeur avec plaque de l'Ordre de la Couronne Royale de Prusse (England) en Chevalier (Knight) de l'Ordre de St. Maurice et Lazare (Italy). England honoured him with a silver inkwell with the coat-of-arms of England and an inscription.

Emile Banning was consulted and involved in planning an extensive system of Belgian fortification proposed by General Brialmont. The proposal was elaborated and finally approved in 1887. It included the construction of twelve forts in Liege, nine in Namur and fortification of the Fortress of Antwerp.

47. Dr. Emile Banning   1836-1898
source: Fortuné Koller, Annuaire des Familles Patriciennes de Belgique[183]

His passing in 1898 was widely mourned throughout Belgium.
The independence of the Congo was declared on 30th June 1960.

Marie Alphonse Joseph Hubert Banning *(G2.C.Vbis; 1844-?)*, brother
to Emile (above), also had a distinguished career in Belgium. He was
Directeur Honoraire of the Belgian Ministry of Foreign Affairs and
Captain of the Infantry in the Belgian army, Officer in the Order of King
Leopold, decorated with the North Star of Sweden and Civilian Cross 1st
Class.

---

[183] Fortuné Koller, Annuaire des Familles Patriciennes de Belgique volumes 1-6, Edelweiss,
Belgium, 1940-1945, p. 16

Cornelis Martinus Joannes Banning *(G2.C.VI.7; G5.V6.6;1863-1895)* was a son of the above mentioned Hermanus Banning, who went to Russia. He was a stained-glass artist whose windows are featured in the Castle de Haer in Haarzuilen, Utrecht and in the St. Dominicus Church of Utrecht. His promising career was cut short when he died at the age of 22.

Henricus Adrianus Banning *(G2.B.IV)*, was born in Utrecht on 25 August 1818. Not only did he run a bookstore at a very young age, he worked for the editorial department of the daily newspaper *De Tijd, (The Times)* writing the column *National Affairs*, until the publication *Katholieke Illustratie (The Catholic Illustration)* was founded in 1867 and he was named editor, and soon after Managing Editor. He wrote numerous short stories which were published both in the *Katholieke Illustratie*, which won him tremendous popularity, and as a separate series · of 17 volumes (1885). He also wrote several historical novels, many of which were reprinted several times and are still read today. As a competent polemist he wrote *Het Dompertje*, as Managing Editor he assumed the role of 'Old Valentine' leading an inexhaustible battle against modern conceptions and dubious or 'dangerous' theories. As a practiced journalist he made *Het Huisgezin (The Family*, of which he was editor) a household name among Catholic readers. He was also a board member of the *Reading Library for Christian Families*. Henricus Adrianus Banning was versatile as a writer, a critic, scientific and political writer in a widely encompassing field of endeavour, who devoted much time and thought to detail. It is said in the province of Flanders that "he taught the people to read". He was decorated with the knighthood in the Order of Oranje-Nassau in 1905, and on 22 March 1889 with the Golden Cross of Honour 'Pro Ecclesia et Pontifice' by Pope Leo XIII. His final years were spent in the country home *de Braaken* in Vucht. He died on Sunday 10th January 1909 at the age of 90.

1818. H. A. BANNING. 1898.

48. Henricus Adrianus Banning, 1818-1909
Central Bureau of Genealogy, the Hague, Netherlands

In 1923 the township of Soest elected to name one of their main streets in his honour: on 1 Jan. 1924 the 'Soesterbergsche Straat' was renamed 'Banningstraat'. Until 1944 there was a full-size, very beautifully painted portrait of Henricus Adrianus Banning in the first-class waiting room of the railway station in 's Hertogenbosch. Further research has revealed that the portrait was probably destroyed during the bombing raids on 1944, when the whole station was demolished. His biography is included in numerous biographical dictionaries.

The alleged Banning character, as profiled by Mary Elizabeth Banning and by Pierson Worrall Banning, is perhaps personified in a passage from the genealogy[184] about **Dr. Franciscus Bernardus Banning** *(G2.A.VII.ter; b. 29 Dec.1867)*. F.B. Banning took his medical degree in 1891. He was Officer in the Order of Oranje Nassau, Knight in the Order of St. Gregorius the Great, Commissioner of Orphanages in Nijmegen, member of the city council, Curator of the Roman Catholic Emperor Charles University, one of the founders of the Roman Catholic union for the temperance movement in the Netherlands and chairman of the Nijmegen Covenant of the Cross (temperance):

"The Nijmegen Covenant of the Cross was celebrating its silver jubilee, with numerous people attending, including religious and international leaders. The main force was a small army of representatives wrought with impatience in the face of the calm commands issued by those in charge, and who oft preferred a vicious guerrilla war to the ponderous methods wielded by the authorities in achieving their goal."[185]

Dr. F. Banning

49. Dr. Franciscus Bernardus Banning
Central Bureau of Genealogy, the Hague, Netherlands

The heart and soul of the ever truculent troop was Dr. Banning. He had joined the movement at a young age and his ambition - in those

---

[184] J.A.W. Banning, *Genealogie van het Geslacht Banning*, Fred. Banning & Zonen, Groenlo, 1934, p. 164
[185] *De Katholieke Illustratie*, (periodical) 3 Nov. 1920

days extraordinary – "inspired enthusiasm in others, ignited the meek to action, convinced passive observers of their backwardness"[186].

The Nijmegen doctor dedicated himself to the life-long cause, not only against alcoholism, which he referred to as an evil curse to Catholicism, but against anything which represented an obstacle to the course of Catholic ideology. As a commissioner of orphanages, member of the electors' association and a dedicated worker in the electors' association and in *Geloof and Wetenschap* (*Faith and Science*), as committed labourer for public health in numerous functions, but especially as chairman of the Covenant of the Cross, he served 'the noble cause'. His democratic ideas were certainly not cathedral rhetoric; he met with common folk and taught them where their own strengths and weaknesses lay.

Dr. Gerard Brom, in his 'New Covenant of the Cross', called him 'a man of fire and brimstone', and Dr. Ariëns spoke of him as 'a warrior, who was anything but amenable.' Banning made enemies, because the born orator and zealous propagandist did not shy from uttering harsh words and was not much conversant in the art of 'tact'. However, this did not quell the appreciation of his opponents and he had many loyal friends among his supporters.

"The knighthood which he received will probably remained modestly untouched in the drawer - the new knight considered decorations as ballast - but he himself will not retire. The blows of battle may have turned him grey, but the sacred fire is not yet extinguished. He continues to work for the good Catholic cause!"[187]

Anna Wilhelmina Banning (*G2.A.VI.bis.6*; *1865-1925*) older sister to the above Franciscus Bernardus Banning, was one of twins. (The other twin - the firstborn Franciscus Bernardus - died 18 days after birth.) Anna Wilhelmina Banning was the first female municipal councillor in the city of Oldenzaal, where she was born.

---

[186] J.A.W. Banning, *Genealogie van het Geslacht Banning*, Ferd. Banning & Zonen, Groenlo 1934, p. 164
[187] J.A.W. Banning, *Genealogie van het Geslacht Banning*, Ferd. Banning & Zonen, Groenlo 1934, p. 165

50. Frans Banning, by J. Th. Toorop, 1915
collection: Museum Het Valkhof, Nijmegen

Frans Adriaan Marie Banning (G2.VIIter.1), the son of Dr. Franciscus B. Banning, was born in 1891. He studied law in Utrecht and was also a board member of the Catholic student association Veritas. He died on 5 Nov. 1915, while working on his dissertation about criminal law, only 24 years of age. This promising young man was portrayed by the renowned Dutch artist Jean Th. Toorop (1858-1928), who was not only a friend of his father's, but also his patient. Apparently Toorop needed some persuasion to do this posthumous portrait as he was not accustomed to working from photographs. However, in this case he had no alternative and as Toorop had been acquainted with the young man, he was able to draw on his personal memories.

Hendrikus Adriaan Constant Banning (*G2.A.VIII.ter*) was born on 30 March 1900 in Nijmegen. Son of Dr. Franciscus Bernardus Banning (*G2.A.VII.ter*) and Maria Constantina Catherina van der Knaap, he married Johanna Hermanna Broekhoven (b. 24 April 1901 in Hengelo) on 16 May 1930. H.A.C.Banning appears to have made a lifelong profession

51. Mayor Hendrikus Adriaan Constant Banning
(1900-1970)
Central Bureau of Genealogy, the Hague, Netherlands

of being a mayor. On 20 January 1927, at the age of 26, he became mayor of Horssen, on 31 August 1929 he became mayor of Weerselo and in 1940 mayor of Leidschendam, a position he relinquished in 1943 when a more Nazi-inclined[188] person was appointed in his place. However, when the war ended in 1945, Mayor Banning returned to his post, where he remained until his retirement in 1965. Only two months prior to his death on 21 August 1970 the town council renamed the 'Laanzichtweg' in Leidschendam as the 'Burgemeester Banninglaan' ('Mayor Banning Avenue'), in his honour[189].

Ferdinand Joseph Frans Marie Weyn Banningh (G2.VIII.1), born 12 June 1925 in Groenlo, Netherlands, followed his military training in Wolverhampton, England. In 1946 he joined the Military Police in the Netherlands. As sergeant, he was assigned to a post in Bandoeng, Indonesia, in May 1947, and in 1948 became sergeant major of the Royal Military Police, as well as police instructor. As cornet and commander of the Military Police and Chief Investigator of Dutch East India, he was stationed in Makassar.

---

[188] Gemeente Leidschendam-Voorburg,
http://www.leidschendam.nl/smartsite2906.htm?CurPage=3669#4; accessed July 2004
[189] Gemeente Leidschendam-Voorburg,
http://www.leidschendam.nl/smartsite2906.htm?CurPage=3669#4; accessed July 2004

51a. Lt. Col. F.J.F.M.Weyn Banningh is decorated with the Bronze
Cross by H.R.H. Prince Bernhard of the Netherlands, in the
Royal Palace in Amsterdam, on 29 April 1953
photo: courtesy of the archives of Marechaussee Contact, Netherlands

With the rank of Lieutenant Colonel, F.J.F.M. Weyn Banningh served
with distinction in Korea and, by royal decree, was awarded the Bronze
Cross on 29 April 1953 for action against terrorists.
Ferdinand J.F.M. Weyn Banningh died on 17 Oct. 1984 in Groenlo.

Johan Carel Anne Bannink (*19.09.1877-15.03.1938*) was an Honorary
Major General and another Dutch mayor of repute. Born in Lochem, he
descended from the line of Banninks second to inhabit the homestead 'de
Banninck' in Colmschate, Deventer, from whence Gerrit, the first
Amsterdam Banning, is believed to have come in 1385. J.C.A. Bannink
was mayor of Zierikzee from 1929 until 1934. According to his obituary
in the *Zierikzeesche Nieuwsbode (Zierkzee Newsbulletin*[190]) of 18 March
1938:
"When the name Bannink is uttered, it inspires amiable reflection on a
sincerely good and noble person. All those who came in contact with
Mayor Bannink, for whatever reason, were impressed by his
forthrightness, simplicity and readiness to help. He wanted the best for
everyone and his desire to be a good friend to all people was the highest
aspiration that he set for himself in life. That people could have lesser
motives was a concept foreign to him, because Mayor Bannink could
hardly imagine that there were people whose intentions might be less than
unselfish."

"He was always generous and a friend to the poor. His kind heart
and also his wallet were always wide open for those of lesser fortune.

---

[190] *Zierikzeesche Nieuwsbode (Zierkzee Newsbulletin)*, 18 March 1938

Many will doubtless think back on him in these days with gratitude and will honour his memory."

"Our retired Mayor died suddenly and unexpectedly. He has been called to greater things and been beckoned to the Eternal Light. And we, his friends, pray that peace be with him. Peace which exceeds all comprehension and shall last forever more."

52. Johan Carel Anne Bannink
Mayor of Zierikzee 1929-1934
Collection: Municipal Archives of
Schouwen-Duiveland, Zierikzee

The same newspaper printed an article in 1965 outlining his foresight, looking back on predictions that he had made in 1935 concerning modernisation and change to the city in the decades to follow. The article states: "The deceased J.C.A. Bannink has undoubtedly earned an exceptional position on the list of mayors this city has had. This became apparent yet again when we discovered an article in which Bannink, with well-chosen words, outlined his vision on the future of the city of Zierikzee."[191] The article concludes with the comment that numerous of his predictions had been borne out.

J.C.A. Bannink did not live to see his vision materialize; he died in the Hague at the age of 60, three years after he retired from office. One development that he did not envision was that the municipality, in 1959, would name a street in Zierikzee after him: the 'Banninklaan', a wide avenue rendering access to an expansive park for sports and recreation which he had initiated.

One other namesake was recorded in Utrecht at a very early date, but seems rather out of place in this list of notable persons
Theodorus Gerardusz. Banninck was a notary 1462 ('clericus Traiectensis publics notaries'). He is mentioned in the Italian city of Triuli in that year[192], working for the chancellery of the Patriarch (Italy). He was registered as a notary in the Bishopric of Utrecht and therefore was likely born and/or educated in this area. It is not yet known to which lineage he belongs.

*　　　　　*　　　　　*

---

[191] *Zierikszeesche Nieuwsbode (Zierkzee Newsbulletin)*, 21 May 1965
[192] Monthly edition of *Oud Utrecht (Old Utrecht)*, 6th year, 1931, no. 3, p. 30

Sicke Benninghe[193], (**Benninge**) born in the latter part of the 15th century, was a chronicler of Groningen, in the north of the Netherlands. In 1504 he was a member of the 'Hoofdmannenkamer voor Stad en Ommelanden', ('Head Officers Council for the City and Environs'), representative of the free guilds on the municipal board, and a member of Council. He wrote his historical chronicles of events occurring in Friesland and Groningen in 1467, and from 1492-1527. The first printing was in the *Analecta medii aevi* of Brouërious à Nidek under the name *Kronijk van Beningha (Chronicles of Beningha)* A much more detailed edition was later published by J.A. Feith and was included in the *Werken van het Historisch Genootschap (Works of the Historical Society)* (new series no. 48). Another chronicle included in Benningh's work, covering the period of about 1400-1477, is known as the *Kroniek van Lemego (Chronicles of Lemego)*. Sicke Benningh wrote *Chronikel der Vriescher landen en de Stad Groningen (Chronicles of the Frisian lands and the City of Groningen)* around the year 1500.

The 'Sicke Benninghstede' ('Sicke Benningh-stead') in Groningen was once a homestead for the prominent Bennema family, and still exists. There is mention of Sicke Banninck and Wybbe Elzink involved in a legal transaction on 25 July 1480.The following note was found at the Bureau of Heraldry in the Hague, Netherlands, concerning a Benninghe in Nordhoorn which, since it is very close to Groningen, could well have been related to Sicke Benninghe.

"Benninghe, Meyste,... (?) Yelto B., pastor in Nordhoorn and Hidde Jensema, present their seals as ...? and agents of marriage articles, for Ekele Ukema son of Meyne Feringhe (sic) and Tadde X. Syltge, daughter of Syrts Allertsma and Thocsius - 12/12/1596 N7. with the seals in wax of Yelto B and Hidde J., physician Allersma."

Laes Rinties Benningh[194], born ca. 1658, lived in the north-east of the Netherlands, but his lineage is unknown. Laes Rinties Benningh was a die-cutter and jeweler. He worked primarily with silver and was specialized in medals. He lived in Deventer, Emmerich, Leeuwarden and Harderwijk, where he died on 23 Oct. 1717.

---

[193] Winkler Prins *Biographical Encyclopaedia*, Elsevier, 6th edition, 1948, p. 675
[194] Mr. N. de Roever, A. Bredius, *Oud-Holland, Nieuwe Bijdragen v.d. Geschiedenis der Nederlandse Kunst, Letterkunde, Nijverheid, enz.*, Gebroeders Binger, Amsterdam, 5th Edition, 1887, p. 233

Maurits Arnoldus Banning *(G3.1)*

A complete Frisian genealogy of "Maurits Arnoldus Banning 1687-1708) was compiled by J. Banning in 1984.

The genealogy mentions that: "It seems probable that one of the Gelderland (province of the Netherlands) Bannings settled in Workum around 1725. A certain Johannes Harmanus Banning - the ancestor of most of the Frisian Bannings now alive - came to Pingjum from there in 1778, to live here permanently."[195]

However, it later became apparent that the Frisian Bannings came to Workum from Germany, at an earlier date, as direct descendants from the German Bannings of Tecklenburg. (See chapter on East Frisia, Germany and Scandinavia.) The following reference was found in a publication on the German lineage of Nordbeck:

"The clergyman Johannes Nordbeck (1649-1690) married Mechteld Sutoris (died 1652) in 1640 in Nordhorn and later Henrike Schlichte, daughter of a wine merchant, in 1657."[196]

Egbertus Noordbeek (1649-1720) was born of this marriage, in 1673 he was a clergyman in Tjalleberd and called to Workum on 1 Apr. 1687. Rudolphus Noordbeek (1658-1719) was born of the second marriage, and became pastor in Lemmer in 1680 and on 28 Feb. 1697 in Leeuwarden. When they died they were interred in the family tomb in Workum, a grave marked with a stone featuring the coat of arms of Noordbeek. This gravestone broke during the restoration of the church in 1960 and was destroyed afterward. The most significant passage in the above mentioned publication was nevertheless that which referred to a daughter from a second marriage of Johannes Noordbeek, that is:

"Machteld Noordbeek, born in 1662 in Nordhorn, married in Gildehaus, [Germany] in 1684 to Mauritz Arnoldus Banning, Clergyman in Gildehaus and from 3 Apr.1687 in Oude and Nieuwe Mirdum (Friesland), became Emeritus (retired) on 22 Aug..1708, thereby succeeded by his son Johannes Banning. This Johannes Banning was baptised in September 1685 in Gildehaus and died in 1735 in Oude Mirdum."[197]

This announcement corresponds fully with what was found in another source[198] .

> "1687. **Maurits Arnoldus Banning** is approbated
> on the 3rd April, became member of the church
> council on 7th June, and emeritus in 1708 of the
> 22nd August in the College."

---

[195] J. Banning, *Stamboom van Maurits Arnoldus Banning*, 1984, p. XIII

[196] J. Banning, *Stamboom van Maurits Arnoldus Banning*, 1984, p. XIII

[197] *Naamlijst der predikanten in de Hervormde Gemeente van Friesland, sedert de Hervorming*, 1886

[198] J. Banning, *Stamboom van Maurits Arnoldus Banning*, 1984, p. XIII

> "1708. **Johannes Banning**, son of Maur. Arn., has
> been approbated as candidate on 20th November,
> member of the church council on 9th April 1709, and
> died in 1735."

Mr. F.E. Hunsche of Ibbenbüren (Germany) wrote in a letter dated 26 May 1982, to the author of the genealogy:[199]

"Confirming the receipt of your letters, I can inform you, that I have repeatedly searched for [records of] Mauritz Arnoldus Banning in Tecklenburg. His birth and baptism cannot be confirmed in Tecklenburg, as unfortunately the Church records are inadequate and do not go this far back. His parents are also still unknown. One brother was probably Adolf Friedrich Banning, merchant in Tecklenburg, born in 1650, married 11th May 1686 in Tecklenburg to Anna Elisabeth Detmeyer. There is also an entry for Fr. Banning in Tecklenburg in 1714. The Lengericher merchant's family descends from the merchant Adolf Friedrich B. The name Banning appears to be concentrated at that time in Burgsteinfurt and Tecklenburg. It is safe to assume that the name bearers specified here are related. The assumption that Mauritz Arnoldus was born in Tecklenburg is thus justified."

Although the date of birth remains as yet unknown, it is estimated in the genealogy as 1657. The date of his death is also unknown.

Correspondence between D. van Dijk (1894-1978) and the author of the Frisian genealogy shed new light on this. In an extensive letter dated 26 May 1964, which also included some misconceptions, D. Van Dijk rendered further information on the ancestors of the Frisian Bannings:

"Arnoldus Banning of Workum and Machtel Banning of Balk were confirmed in marriage in Workum (26.1.1751). It is likely that Arnoldus was a son of Ds. Johannes Banning, 1708-1735 of Oudemirdum, where father Mauritius Arnoldus was from 1686-1708."

Dr. David Koss, Barrington Illinois (USA), wrote in 1986 to the author J. Banning, after the Frisian genealogy was published:

"Recently in reading the Tecklenburg church books I found the following: 'Died 13 Apr. 1693, the olde woman Banningsche, aged 71 years 11 months.' J. Banning asserts that this may have been the mother of Maurits Arnoldus.

The 1934 genealogy includes a quotation from the same records, also citing the death of 'the olde woman Banning' on this date.

---

[199] J. Banning, *Stamboom van Maurits Arnoldus Banning*, Dedgum, 1984, p. XVII

Mr. H.J. Warnecke in Steinfurt (Germany) wrote on 20 December 1977 about M.A. Banning:
"A new communicant is mentioned in the Communion Records at Christ's feast (Christmas) 1675 in Burgsteinfurt. He was most likely a student of the Gymnasium Arnoldinum (Arnoldinum High School) and as such probably about 18 years.of age. The entry states literally: 'Moritz Arnold Tecl (aburgensis)' [Born at the time in Tecklenburg.] The Tecklenburg Church records commence, however, at a much later date; the names of the elders can therefore no longer be easily traced. The family, or otherwise the 'Tecklenburger', apparently descended originally from Hof Banning [Banning Homestead) in Wetteringen."[200]

The first reference to the Bannings of this homestead in Wettringen, Germany, is dated 1507. Further information is found in the chapter on East Frisia, Germany and Scandinavia.

Maurits Arnoldus Banning is recorded in the Charter of 7 July 1668- 25 May 1697 of the council books of the *Classis Sneek der Gereformeerde Kerk*[201] (*Council Records for the Gereformeerd Church for [the Frisian town of] Sneek*. A list of those present was signed by:

His name and profession are noted as follows in the *Acta classis Snecanae ordinaries habita den 3 April Anno 1687 (Charter of the council of Sneek of 3 April 1687)* as follows:

M.A. Banning made a more memorable appearance in the archives, concerning the somewhat disputed termination of his religious career. The following records of the discussions have survived.

His health compelled Ds. Banning to request emirate at an earlier date, as appears in the *Acta Classis Snecane ordinarie habita* of 7 Aug. 1708[202]:

[200] J. Banning, *Stamboom van Maurits Arnoldus Banning*, Dedgum, 1984, p. XVII
[201] J. Banning, *Stamboom van Maurits Arnoldus Banning*, Dedgum, 1984, p. XIV
[202] J. Banning, *Stamboom van Maurits Arnoldus Banning*, Dedgum, 1984, p. XIV, XV

or, for the sake of legibility:

"Deputies from the township of Oude Mirdum, both councillors of the old and the new churches, have appeared before the honourable Classis, and have, on behalf of the township, presented the issue of the most considerable weakness of the brain of its instructor Rev. Banning, such that he is completely incapable of fulfilling his duties as clergyman, and therewith transferring a writ instrument, as testimony to his weakness, signed by various men and simultaneously including therein a congenial appeal of the honourable Classis on behalf of the representatives to obligingly request of the honourable Gentlemen that his Honour use his favour to be included amongst those of the Emerites."

Also testifying are the Reverends Noordbeeken (mentioned above), respectively clergymen of Workum and Leeuwarden, both brothers of the 'housewife' of Reverend Banning, who further attest that this is in accordance with their fervent desire and moreover declare that they are both prepared 'to confirm this in writing.'

Rev. Banning was obviously displeased with this state of affairs, which, considering his apparent request for early retirement, seems rather odd. An excerpt from the *Acta Classis Snecanaie ordinaria habita of 9th Octobris 1708:*

146

"Rev. Banning, expressing discontent, testifies that he was included amongst those of the emirates without having thus been informed by the Honourable Gentlemen, and received no other information whatsoever from the honourable council, as that this case had been fully concluded without mention of those persons who had effected such, and without mention of the reason; and requests therefore that he himself might be read this Acte Classis aloud, which His Honour is permitted: against which charter His Honour again presented argument, but then requested a decision to be reached in which those words regarding great weakness of the brain be eliminated, or at least be modified: as being (according to his view) untrue."

Finally, the appeal of his son Ds. J. Banning, appears in the *Acta Classis Snecanae Extraordinarie habita of 20 Octobris 1708:*

Which, as far as can be deciphered, translates as:
"Following appeal of the Holy Lords in the name of P. Rev. Presidem:
Art j: appeared before us the Commissioners of Oldemardum, Niemardum, and Zindde? Del, submitting a letter of appeal concerning Rev. Jos. Banning S.S.M. Candidatus, requesting Approbation of this same appeal, whereupon the letter of appeal, having been read and considered, and having heard the testimony of he who submitted the appeal, that this appeal submitted, do declare in fear of the Lord, that in this testimony no unlawful means have been used."

All of which is rather archaic and legally couched language which appears to say that Maurits Arnoldus Banning had requested early retirement due to his health, but that he later contested having made this request and did not agree. It seems he was more-or-less forced into retirement because he was no longer considered mentally competent, and was also not informed of this decision. It seems he finally acquiesced to the proposal of retirement on condition that the state of his mental competence be eliminated from the wording.

Arnoldus Banning, *(G3.III.f),* a son of Johannes Conradus Banning *(G3.II.b)* was active in freight shipping. He was married to his cousin Machteld Banning *(G3.II.a.2).* Arnoldus is mentioned in the *Dutch Database of Sont Registers*[203], recording passage of his vessel from his home port in Friesland, between 1753 and 1763:
"- on 22 April 1753: departing from Amsterdam for the Baltic Sea, with a cargo of ballast;
- on 20 June 1753, departing from Riga, Latvia, for Hoorn, Netherlands, with a cargo of seed;
- on 13 August 1753, departing from Amsterdam for the Baltic Sea, with a cargo of ballast;
- on 17 September 1753, departing from Koningsbergen, Russia, for Bilbao, Spain, with a cargo of barley;
- on 12 June 1761, departing from Amsterdam for St. Petersburg, Russia, with a mixed cargo;
- on 7 November 1761, departing from Danzig, Poland, for Amsterdam, with a cargo of ash;
- on 10 May 1762, departing from Amsterdam for St. Petersburg, Russia, with a cargo of stone;
- on 16 July 1762, departing from St. Petersburg, Russia, for Amsterdam, with a cargo of talk (talcum)?;
- on 23 October 1763, departing from St. Petersburg, Russia, for Amsterdam, with a cargo of tally (?)."

Arnoldus Banning will have navigated the waterways of the Sont unaware that a namesake had been involved in the safe passage of ships here two centuries earlier. A certain Joost Benninck had been sent by the burgomasters of Amsterdam on a mission to warn the sailors on the Sont against some impending doom, but unfortunately no further details are given.[204] Another Banning, Willem, son of Claes Jansz. Banning of the Amsterdam genealogy, (who died in Moscovia (Russia) in 1594), died on the Sont, date unknown. (The Sont was the waterway above the north coast of Holland to the Baltic Sea, a major sea passage for trade between

---

[203] Database der Nederlandse Sontregisters, National Archives, the Hague, http://www.nationaalarchief.nl/sont, accessed Feb. 2004
[204] J. ter Gouw, *Geschiedenis van Amsterdam*, Scheltema & Holkema, Amsterdam, 1879, Part VI, p. 12

the Hanseatic cities, and was regularly closed in times of political conflict.)

Harmanus Banningh, *(G3.II.a; 11Dec.1692-1 Mar. 1778)* (Hermanus) the father-in-law of the above Arnoldus, (Arnoldus married his cousin Machteld, with the same surname) is specified as a notary in the *Matricula Notariorum*, a list of notaries of Friesland[205] dated 14 Feb. 1714:

"Hermanus Banning today 14th February 1714 showed a Declaration which proves that he, by command of the Honourable Commissioners and the Honourable Lord Commissioners as Provincial Boards has thereto been specially authorised by the Dutch States, has been a Notary and that he subsequently presented the full oath."[206]

Coenraad Banning, *(G3.III.f.4; 2 Oct. 1756)* another notary of Workum in the 18th century, was a son of the above Arnoldus.

53. Pages from the family bible of the Frisian Bannings, from 1854-1948
private collection

---

[205] J. van Leeuwen, *Matricula Notarium, Naamlijst van Notarissen in Friesland, 1606-1850*; S. Koopmans, *Het Notariaat in Friesland vóór 1811*, Leeuwarden 1883
[206] J. Banning, *Stamboom van Maurits Arnoldus Banning*, Dedgum, 1984, p. XXV

Willem Banning *(G3.VIII.w; 1888-1971)* is one of the most well-known Bannings in the Frisian genealogy.

54. Willem Banning
  photo by Corn. Leenheer, collection IISG
  (International Institute of Social History, Amsterdam)

Willem Banning was born as the son of a Makkum herring fisherman. He attended the government college of education in Haarlem (1903-1907) and afterward was employed as a private tutor in Hoorn (1907-1909) and as a teacher in Nieuwendam. After completing his final exams at the high school of Leiden he studied theology from 1923 and took his doctoral degree in theology many years later with a dissertation entitled *'Jaurès as a philosopher, a contribution to social moral ethics (1931)'*. Banning, as a Christian socialist and member of the S.D.A.P (Social Democratic Labour Party) (1914), became a clergyman in the Dutch Reformed Church in Haarlo (1917) and later in Sneek (1921-1928). From 1928 to 1940 he was chairman of the Labour association of Woodbrookers. Held prisoner in Sint-Michielsgestel during the Second World War, he later initiated a reformation movement in the Reformed Church. In 1945 he became chairman of the Dutch National Labour Movement. He presided over the founding congress of the Labour Party (19 Feb.1946). Appointed after the war as Head Instructor of the institute *Church and World* in Driebergen, the "Frisian Willem Banning with the stubborn cowlick" became associate professor at the University of Leiden in 1946, in order to teach religious sociology. On 16 May 1952 he was subsequently appointed associate professor in the juridical faculty, in order to teach ethics of sociology there.

55. The Temperance Movement on the Move: 1900-1925
Willem Banning is fourth from the right
photo: collection IISG (International Institute of Social History), Amsterdam

"Prof. dr. W. Banning "

"Banning is widely published. A common denominator to all his publications and activities is the dogmatic search for a link between mystical perception of faith and socio-political involvement. Friend and foe alike considered him as the man ardent to unite Christianity with socialism.

A study into the relation between his spirituality and his socio-political engagement is the title of a dissertation written by H. Zunneberg (Utrecht 1978). This dissertation is accompanied by a characteristic photograph of Banning, lost in thought.

Professor Doctor W. Banning's 65th birthday celebrations (21 Feb. 1953) drew a great deal of public interest. Prime Minister of the Netherlands Dr. W. Drees was one of the many who came to congratulate him. He conversed for some time with Banning and presented him with the decorations belonging to the knighthood of the Order of the Dutch Lion[207]. In 1962 Professor Dr. Willem Banning received the D.A. Thieme award and in 1963 he was awarded the Albert Schweitzer prize.

When he turned 65, Banning retired from public life. "I have experienced too often the tragedy of people who stay on, that is why I irrevocably withdraw from all official functions; anyone who might need me afterward - fine, he can call on me." People did just that: as a

---

[207] J. Banning, *Stamboom van Maurits Arnoldus Banning*, Dedgum, 1984, p XVIII-XXII

'freelance worker', he still undertook many endeavours, "proving yet again that life after retirement is often really a beginning."

56. Willem Banning in action , addressing the
Liberal Christian Student's Union at Whitsuntide, 1911
photo: collection IISG (International Institute of Social History), Amsterdam

In the magazine *Tijd en Taak (Time and Task)*, Ds. J.M. de Jong wrote: "Boy oh boy, it certainly is a good thing that Banning is so powerful of mind in his sixty-fifth year and so sound of body that he is enabled to continue to work and to live among the people, within the premises of the church, in the socialist movement, such, that one does not have the least inclination to look back in order to sketch his impact on country, church and socialism."

"Banning was one of the prominent socialist ministers before the war. He was a religious-socialist. He was a devoted member of the Social Democratic Labour Party, spoke at meetings and gatherings at a time when this was a dubious and rather brash undertaking for a clergyman. He was a servant of the church, although a rather radical servant, who was most outspoken in an age when the spiritual life of the socialist party was a persuasion, whereby Christians felt they were left on the perimeter. There, in the reading room of Bentveld, there, at the table with the unemployed in the crisis years, in a manner which they understood and with a word that touched them, there he was himself and there lay his vocation."

"More clearly than ever before, he saw the isolation in which liberal Protestantism, religious humanism, had come to rest, threatening to remain outside of the powerful stream of spiritual revival, such as the

152

breaking of new ground in the ecumenical movement and in municipal restoration. And so it ensued, in the sector of the church where Banning had his followers, that people would say "He's not our familiar Banning any more!" Because he created unrest where people had once felt peace, radical, disturbing sounds from the old evangelism which were once familiar to him too, now sounded more emphatically from his mouth. A world war had transpired and the direction of consciousness and political strife was forced to capitulate in the face of authority of this worldwide Evangelism. This left its mark. "People will stumble and be hurt, strongly and deeply...[208]."

In the national daily *Het Parool*, dated 21 Feb.1958, Johan Winkler wrote:
 "This is Banning: Christian and socialist, church leader and party leader, professor and minister, sociologist and theologian, Frisian from Makkum and Dutchman from Driebergen. It is the multiplicity that has made of Banning a highly unique, unifying personality, who in the last decades of our national history was always there when drastic conversions occurred, both on religious and social, both on political and cultural turf. He was, after all, always the man who had fuelled such a conversion, who had, more than anyone, personified and then almost as a matter of course felt compelled to grasp and to work out what aspect of the new zeal required leadership."
 "He was born in Makkum, his father was a fisherman and the family lived in a 'side alley of an alley, a room which served as living quarters, kitchen and bedroom.' The description is Banning's own and I quote it from a small, significant and entertaining little book that he gave to his friends a couple of weeks before his seventieth birthday:
' In retrospect of life and strife of, at any rate, part of a generation that was idealistically young at the beginning of the twentieth century, elucidating the evolution of one of these idealists.' "

W. Schermerhorn, (Prime Minister of the Netherlands in 1945/46) said in an article entitled *Banning as a Politician*, in the periodical *Vrij Nederland* dated 16 Jan. 1971:
 "Whoever contemplates the relation between Banning and politics will encounter an odd contrast. No attention is paid in his 'Retrospective' to his political development on any more than a couple of pages in succession, and then usually only as a part of the general context. On the other hand, it mentions that many acknowledge that Banning was a major influence on our country after 1945. He does not express this last anywhere in his 'Retrospective'. People might conclude that he had a natural modesty which prevented him in expressing this, although he was

---

[208] J. Banning, *Stamboom van Maurits Arnoldus Banning*, 1984, p. XIX-XX

very much aware of his own esteem. Banning was thus not so much a political leader in the usual sense, but he most certainly exercised leadership and on occasion decisive leadership. Was this the result of the fact that his political insight was not founded on some system or other of thought, but was drawn from that spiritual core that always rendered him with a sense of direction and made it possible to always remain active? In the middle of the confusion of the socialist movement of the past years I have often wondered: How would the Banning of 1945-50 react now? Could he again give direction to the socialist world for which it has been waiting - unsuccessfully - to date?"

In the national daily *Trouw* of 9 January 1971, Dr. J.J. Buskes wrote:
"Yesterday morning I received notice that Banning passed away peacefully. The fuel in the lamp was gone and the light which shone so brightly for years is extinguished. He was not only a moving person, but a person on the move. He never adhered to an established principle. He was not a man for whom religious dogmas and political and social convictions were always immutable, not a man of singular conviction. Answering a call, he set out, not knowing where it would lead him, not without having to surrender without pain certain insights, not to acquire new insights without gratitude. However, throughout all change which occurred during his lifetime, there was something which remained steadfast and the secret of his life was: the worship of God's justice and goodness.
We were friends and companions since 1920. When we celebrated his 70th birthday in 1958 I said at the banquet:
"If Banning was not an adherent teetotaller, then there would be a bottle of red wine on the middle of the table. Life on earth is seldom cause for celebration. For Banning it has always been a battle. God saves the wine for later. At Banning's celebration we drank water, but that water will be clear and pure and, on this particular occasion, tastes like the most delicious wine pressed from grapes of the most noble vines. I wish to thank Banning on behalf of us all, that he always gave us the vision of the glory of God in our daily life."
I wish to thank him once again for what he has given us and to thank God that, for Banning, He has saved the best wine for the last."

*   *   *

Cornelis Banning, (*C3.V.I.d2;30 Apr. 1894 – 7 July 1964*) Born in Bolsward, son of Arnoldus Banning and Maria Dirkje Essers, Cornelis Banning completed his medical exams in Amsterdam at the age of only 23. He was a general practitioner in heart and soul in Zaandam, where he was the first physician to own an automobile; his colleagues always visited their patients on bicycle. In spite of the demands of his practice, he took his doctoral degree in 1931 with the dissertation *Nutrition in Zaandam in 1929-1930*. He spent six months in the United States studying public health conditions; his conclusion on return being that, in comparison, the situation in the Netherlands 'wasn't bad at all!'.

He was appointed Chief Inspector of Public Health by Royal decree on 11 July 1939. In 1939 the war was imminent and, with the first world war in mind, it was thought prudent to have a man at the head of the Public Health Service who was utterly familiar with nutrition and related problems. As a protestant he felt it was pleasing to be appointed at the recommendation of the Catholic minister Romme.

The highlight of the celebratory meeting (26 Sept. 1956) of the White-Gold Cross in the province of North Brabant on the occasion of its 40th anniversary was undoubtedly the appointment to Knight in the Order of St. Gregory of Dr. C. Banning, Chief Inspector of Public Health in the Netherlands, a protestant, who, in his governmental position had accomplished great achievements for the confessional private health work, and he was deeply moved by the distinction. He was also Knight in the Order of the Dutch Lion.

Dr. Banning was also a delegate of the World Health Organisation from 1946-1948, Chairman of the Commission of Health in Zaandam and vice-chairman of the Public Health Fund of Zaanland.

His crass remarks were legendary, such as "They used to laugh at me when I said, 'Millions for antibiotics to combat infection? Wonderful! But let us begin by impressing on people that they should wash their hands after visiting the toilet. Perhaps we might then even avoid an epidemic'."

Foreign colleagues, either as 'medical officer of health' or as 'inspecteur de la santé publique', asked Banning regularly for an explanation of the extraordinarily favourable health statistics of the Netherlands. His answer was as follows: (*yearbook for Housewives in 1958*): "I attempt to give our foreign visitor an impression of the typical Dutch housewife and what goes on in a good family. Our women are traditionally scrupulously clean in home and hearth. In the home, generous application of water, scrubbing and polishing is considered the most normal activity and this is, in my view, the basis for household hygiene. The woman who knows that dust in her home is unhygienic, who knows that leftovers in the kitchen or pantry or in her garden are an indoor and outdoor feast for rats, mice and flies and therefore ensures that her kitchen and garden are clean, is by definition a good housewife. She helps to protect those of her household against contagion and germs."[209]

Banning resigned from function on 1st May 1959 on reaching the age of retirement, but until 1st September he remained active as an

---

[209] J.Banning, *Stamboom van Maurits Arnoldus Banning*, Dedgum, 1984, p XXII

employee because his successor was ill. The Red Cross honoured his services with a gold medal (3 Sept. 1959).

*   *   *

Although the Banning branches are peopled with numerous learned men and labourers, athletic prowess seems to be scarce. Specific mention is therefore made of **Jan Titus Banning** *(G3.VII.p.2; 19 Oct. 1874-12 Nov. 1919)*. Consul of the Dutch National Athletic Union in Edam, Consul of the Dutch National Soccer League, Jan Titus Banning was provincial skating champion of Overijssel, Groningen and North Holland from 1899-1901. The *Revue der Sporten (Sports Review)* of November 1919, writes: "Banning was among the good skaters in the years 1899-1900. He was an especially stylish speed-skater. He placed in numerous important competitions and often won in remarkable ways."

The *Sportkroniek (Sports Chronicle)* of November 1919 writes: "Banning was a very well-known person in the Dutch Skater's Union, and triumphantly won numerous championships, he also upheld the honour of our country successfully in the international skating arena (i.e. Davos, Switzerland). Co-founder and vice-chairman of Edam's Sports Commission, he soon became a leading power, whose advice was cooperatively followed."[210]

Arnoldus Banning (G3.VIIIr.1) was the eldest of four children born to a shipmate, Hermanus Banning, on 11 Oct. 1902 in Makkum, Friesland. He was ten years of age when his family emigrated to New England in the USA. Arnoldus began to paint in 1920 and became a respected local artist in Massachusetts, where he died in 1991.

56a. Winter landscape by Arnoldus Banning
private collection

[210] *Revue der Sporten*, November 1919

Anna Bosma-Banning (*G3.VII.b.2; 23 Oct. 1913-.?.*) It was only in the past half-century that women began to emerge from obscurity on the basis of their own individuality. A correspondent from the national daily *Trouw* wrote on 25 Nov.1967: "Not to speak Frisian anymore because so many non-Frisians have settled here? None of that. We'll just learn Frisian."[211] These are the words of Mrs. Annie Bosma-Banning from Drachten some twenty years ago, when, in her hometown, a major industry was at the beginning of the stormy developments of this once relatively unknown Frisian town."

"These words gave an unusual twist to the life of this woman, wife of a businessman and mother of two children, one she could not have foreseen. She studied for a teacher's degree in Frisian and, without any teaching experience, set about teaching Frisian to non-Frisians. She taught not only the newcomers to Drachten, but also taught her native language to people far outside of Friesland. This resulted in a course of the Frisian language by gramophone record, a total of 24 lessons and a total playing time of 168 minutes. It was expected that the course would not only draw interest in Friesland but also, for example, in Scandinavian countries where there was an active interest for Frisian at university levels."

"If you take the viewpoint of 'out with Frisian', this would only be wrong and a nuisance, because there would be no replacement. An educated person should of course speak other languages and while I definitely do not consider Frisian the be-all and end-all, I do feel that one should begin with the roots of the native language. If I aspire to be a good Dutch citizen, then I should also be a good Frisian. If I had not brought up my children with the Frisian language, then I feel I would have denied them something that I could later on never have made up for. Disappearance of the Frisian language would, I feel, have been an impoverishment.",[212] says Mrs. Bosma-Banning."

---

[211] J. Banning, *Stamboom van Maurits Arnoldus Banning*, Dedgum, 1984, p. XXIII
[212] J. Banning, *Stamboom van Maurits Arnoldus Banning*, Dedgum, 1984, p. XXIV

4   GENEALOGY OF THE AMSTERDAM
REGENT'S FAMILY OF BANNING

The following is a translation of Genealogy E from *'Genealogie van het Geslacht Banning'*, published in 1934.

Note:

1. The ending 'z.'or 'zn.' after most of the male names is an abbreviation of 'zoon'(son), and means that the person is question, such as Jan Jacobsz., was Jan, Jacob's son. The ending 'dr.' following most of the female names is an abbreviation of 'dochter' (daughter); therefore Margriet Dircksdr. was Margriet, Dirck's daughter. This use of the patronymic was very common until the end of the 18th century.

2. Spelling of names varies in the original documents and in research published throughout the last centuries: for the sake of simplicity all family members referred to in this genealogy are specified as 'Banning', as was done in the original 1934 genealogy. Although there were many variations, the most common were 'Banningh' and 'Benningh'.

3. The Dutch Mr. should be read as Master – a title of law, and should not be read as the English Mister.

4. According to the research of J.P. Ouweltjes in 2001, the second generation of this line did not commence with Gerrit Gerritsz., but with Jan Gerritsz., which, if true, would mean that the Amsterdam family was more widespread and wealthier than that set out below. Research is still begin done. For the findings to date by J.P.Ouweltjes, see the section entitled 'New Light on the Oldest Generations of Banning in Amsterdam – Ties to Assendelft", and the corresponding genealogy.

5. The Dutch words for nephew/cousin (neef) and niece/cousin (nicht) are the same. It is therefore often impossible to know exactly which familial relationship is referred to. In these instances both have been specified in the translation.

6. The families Boelens, Bam, Cat, Bicker, Heyn, Codde, Buyck, de Graeff, to whom numerous Bannings were wed, were all influential, prosperous and well-established families who held prominent positions in Amsterdam. They were portrayed by famous artists, 'the old masters', paintings which are now world renowned and displayed in international museums. The Banning family also belonged to this inner circle, historically termed as 'the Regent's' or 'Magistrate' families of Amsterdam'.

The first Bannings in Amsterdam appear at the end of the 14th century, as one of the earliest surnames in that city. The following are recorded:

DIRCK SYMONSZN.,BANNING, Bailiff from 13 Dec.1388 – 19 Jan.1390, 26 Apr.1391 - ...... and from 1393-1396. Chief Officer 1393., died 1405.
JAN OUDE (BROECK) BANNING, Symonsz., Alderman 1419, 1420 and 1423, Burgomaster 1420.
GERRIT BANNING, textile merchant on the Nieuwendijk, came from the house 'The Banninck' in Colmschate near Deventer, follows I.

I. GERRIT BANNING, married Unknown
From this marriage:
Gerrit, Gerritszn., follows II

II. GERRIT BANNING, Gerritsz., born +/- 1370, married 1398 to Baert Verburch, Aemsdr. daughter of Adam Ver- (van der) burch and ..... van Brakel.
Three children are known from this marriage:
1. Gerrit, Gerritsz., follows III.
2. Dirck, Gerritsz., follows IIIa
3. Claes, Gerritsz., follows IIIb.

III. GERRIT BANNING, Gerritsz., (born +/- 1400), Alderman 1461, 1463, 1465 and 1467. Married to Katrijn Paulusdr. van Neckeren, (sister to Jan Paulusz. van Neckeren, Alderman 1437).
From this marriage:
1. Gaeff, Gerritsz., follows IV
2. Jan, Gerritsz., follows IVa

IV GAEFF BANNING, Gerritsz, Alderman 1473, died shortly before May 1487, lived at 'de Plaetse' (Dam Square) in a house 'with an orchard', Alderman 1473, married Elisabeth Jansdr. (de Vlaming) van Oudtshoorn , alias Elisabeth van Haudshoorne, named Janszoons, died 10 Dec.1515, daughter of Jan Woutersz. and Wendelmoet Dirksdr. van Wormer. She remarried Mr. Willem Andriesz..
One son was born of the first marriage: Gerrit Benningh, who died young.

IVa JAN BANNING, Gerritsz., born +/- 1430. Alderman 1471 and 1474, married to N. Jacobsdr., daughter of Jacob Hendrick Auwelsz..
From this marriage:
1. Gerrit, Jansz., follows V
2. Mr. Jan Banning, Jansz., well-known historical personage in the

land reclamation of Amstelland, Shield-bearer and aide to Emperor Maximilian of Austria and Archduke Charles, Alderman 1492, Bailiff from 1 Oct.1495 to 15 June 1509, Councillor in the Provincial Council of Holland (before 1513) married 1st Unknown, and 2nd Imme Reijers, ("a farmer's daughter from Diemen but extremely wealthy"). He and his wife built a country estate on the Amstel River, outside of Amsterdam, called Brillenburg (later Kostverloren and later again Ruijsschenstein), and founded the Clarissen Convent in 1513 in Amsterdam. They had no children. Jan Benningh had two sons from his first marriage: Christoffel and Jasper, whose names were mentioned in his last will and testament which came to light only in 2003. Before that time he was assumed by historians to be childless.

3. Katrijn Banning, married Frans Claes Heynenz., Alderman 1510, Burgomaster and Councillor 1525, son of Claes Heyn "in den Arm".

From this marriage (amongst others);

a. Nelle Frans Claesdr. Heyn, married Claes Boelensz., born +/- 1480, died shortly before Nov. 1528, son of Boel (or 'Boeltgin') Jacobsz. Bicker and Nelle Jonge Jacobsdr..

From this marriage (amongst others)

    a.a. Nelle Claesdr. Boelens, married Pieter Pietersz. Codde, born +/- 1490, died shortly before Aug. 1557, Regent of the Nieuwe Zijds Home for Charity 1548, son of Pieter Pietersz..Codde and N. Zijbrantsdr.. Also born of this marriage Lijsbeth Pietersdr. Codde, who married Michiel Jansz.Banning.

    b.b. Katrijn Claesdr. Banning, buried in the New Church, Amsterdam 26 Apr.1588, married Jan Claesz. Cat, [Bontemantel mentions 'Jan Benninck Cadt' as captain of the Militia on 8 Sept. 1580] apothecary on the Middeldam 'in den Cat', Burgomaster 1579, Regent of the Hospice 1556, buried in the Old Church 12 Jan. 1593, son of Claes Bouwensz. 'in den Cat' and Volcken Jansdr..

b. Gerrit Banning, died before 1541, married Bennicht Pauw.

From this marriage:

    a.a Katrijn Banning, married 1553 Willem Jacobsz. Tromper, in Rotterdam

c. Stijn Banning, Fransdr., died after 1575, married 1st Cornelis Buyck, Sijbrandtsz., Alderman and Councillor 1525, Burgomaster 1536, Dike-grave of the Nieuwer-Amstel, conferred with the status of Shire by the city in 1541, widower of Geerte Gerrit Valckendr., died 17 Nov. 1560, son of Sijbrant Sijbrantsz. Buyck and Ael Jacobsdr.Meijster; married 2nd Simon Bauckesz., Sakema, Captain of the

Crossbow Association 1553, widower of Griet Jansdr.
Verburch, buried in the Bethany Convent 28 Jan. 1566, son
of Baucke Albertsz. Zythiema, alias Schipper Baucker
Albertsz., and Hillegond Thomasdr. Sakema.
4. Mr. Jacob Banning, follows Va

V. GERRIT BANNING, Jansz., (born +/- 1460), died shortly before
June 1504, Councillor 1498, married 26 July 1491 Katrijn Dirck
Heijmanszoonsdr. Ruijsch, daughter of Dirck Heijmansz.,
Alderman 1451, Regent 1479, Burgomaster 1483, and of Katrijn
Hendrick Auwelszoonsdr., alias Catrina Dircksdr.
From this marriage four children of which three are known:
1. .... Banning
2. Jacob Banning Gerritsz, follows VI.
3. Jan Banning Gerritsz, follows VIa.
4. Cornelis Banning Gerritsz, follows VIb.

VI JACOB BANNING, Gerritsz, (born +/- 1485), Councillor 1511,
Alderman 1526, married Maria Jacobsdr. Verheyen, [prenuptial
agreement between Antonis Willemsz. and Marie Jacobsdr.
Banning] [D. Francke refers to her as Maria Jacobs van 's
Gravenhage van Amersfoort] born in Amersfoort, died in
Amsterdam and buried in the Old Church 10 Apr. 1573.
From this marriage, amongst others.:
1. Jacob, Jacobsz, follows VII
2. Jan, follows VIIa
3. Marij Jacobsdr. Banning, buried in the Old Church 9 Febr. 1565,
married 1st Anthonius Willemsz., (Wou) [genealogists assert that
Antonius Willemsz, Bontekoe (Councilor 1578 until his death;
elected by the delegates of the Militias 27 May 1578; died 28 May
1594. Son of Willem Luytsz. Huydecoper and Lijsbeth Pietersdr.)
was married to Marij Jacobsdr. Banning, who was said to be
remarried to Evert Roswinckel. Genealogist Elias found an
Antonius Willemsz. who was married to the specified Marij
Jacobsdr, but according to the records he died long before his
namesake Bontekoe]; son of Willem Pietersz. and Ael
Hendricksdr. Wou, married 2nd Evert Horswinckel (or
Roswinckel).
4. Cornelis Banning, Jacobsz. married Pietertge Willemsdr.., (Wou),
daughter of Willem Pietersz. and Ael Hendricksdr. Wou.
5. Baertge (= Beatrix) Banning Jacobsdr., married Egbert Heynck.
6. Gerrit Banning, Jacobsz., married Lijsbeth Fransdr. van
Amersfoort.

VII JACOB BANNING, Jacobsz., textile merchant on the
O.Z.Voorburgwal, was 'Commissioner of the Grain Exchange '
from 10 Nov. 1565 to 22 Mar. 1566, Tax Commissioner from 26
May to 3 July 1578; Councillor 1578 until his death, (elected by
the delegates of the Militias 27 May 1578), Alderman 1578,
Regent of the Orphanage 1579, Warden of the Cloth 1580, buried
in the Old Church 7 Aug. 1581, married Wijburch Jansdr. van
Hoppen, daughter of Jan Claesz. van Hoppen, Alderman and
Councillor 1549, Burgomaster 1560.
From this marriage, amongst others:
1. Agnieta Jacobsdr. Banning, married Sebastiaen Egbertsz, alias
Sebastianus Egberti, born 1563. Councillor 1602-1618
(dismissed by the Governor Maurits 3 Nov. 1618), Alderman
1593, Alderman 'vice presus' 1594, 1597, 1598, 1600, 1601,
1603 and 1604, Burgomaster 1606, 1608, Representative
Councillor 1609-1611 of Holland and West Friesland, Steward
1613, Master of the Orphanage 1620, Professor of Anatomy in
the 'Atheneum Illustre' in Amsterdam 1595, Medical Doctor.
Died in Amsterdam as husband of Margriete van Dronckelaer,
buri in the Old Church 16 Apr.1621, son of Egbert
Meynertsz.and Dieuwer Jacobsdr. Dr. Sebastian Egberti was
widely renowned and is featured in several group portraits by
famous Dutch artists.
2. Elisabeth Banning, married Johannes Halsbergius who, subsequent
to his promotion to his being ordained, was appointed on 4 May
1589 in Amsterdam to preach and to further train in the ministry,
after which he was ordained as a minister on 7 June 1590 and in
1599 became instructor to all the churches of Amsterdam, died
at the beginning of 1607, suddenly in the prime of his life.

VIIa JAN BANNING, Jacobsz. Commissioner of Marital Affairs 1593,
1594 and 1595. Buried in the Old Church 1 Aug. 1597,
commissioner 1595, married 1st (around 1555) Griet Simonsdr.
Cluft [D.Francken: Margriet Sijmons Klugter], died shortly
before January 1574, married 2nd Lijsbeth Fransdr. van
Campen, born Utrecht 1562.
Various children from these marriages:
1. Simon, follows VIII
2. Cornelis Banning, married 1st Evertje Bolhaue(e)r; married 2nd
3. Agniesje Colijn; childless.
4. Jacob Banning, died unmarried
5. Dirck Banning, died unmarried

6. Josina Banning, died unmarried
7. Frans Banning, married Maritien Hendrickx (dr.).

VIII   SIMON BANNING, married Geertruyd van Blanckesteyn.
        From this marriage:
        1. Jan Banning, married Aeltje Willemsdr.
        2. Hendrick Banning, married 1st Susanne Clermont, 2nd
           Lysbeth Cornelisdr.
        3. Susanna Banning, married Leonora (?)..........
        4. Simon Banning.

VIa JAN BANNING, Gerritsz, Knight of Jerusalem 1519, Alderman
     1531, Head of the Polder Board of Amstelland 1537, Captain of
     the Longbow Association 1525, died 1557. Married Trijn
     Stansdr., died shortly before August 1579, very elderly, daughter
     of Stans Claes Stansz., Councillor 1484 and Alderman 1493, and
     Katrijn (Truy) Gerritsdr. van Alckmaer.
     The following seven children were born of this marriage:
     1. Gerrit, Jansz, follows VII.1
     2. Claes, Jansz, follows VII.1a
     3. Stans, follows VII.1b
     4. Lijsbeth Banning Jansdr., buried in the New Church 1 May
        1573, married Wigbout de Wael, born 1519, merchant 'in den
        vergulden Bril' in 1557 on the Nieuwendijk near the 'Plaetse'
        (Dam Square) , later (1582) on the 'Plaetse' itelf. Commissioner
        to the Prince of Orange until the reorganisation of the Convoys
        in the province of Zeeland 2 Febr. 1581 – May 1582, Councillor
        1582 –1583, Alderman 1582, died 13 May 1583, son of Jan de
        Wael, Jacobsz. 'in 't gulden Paert' and Alyd Wigboutsdr.
     5. Brechtgen Banning Jansdr., born 1531, buried in the New
        Church 11 Febr. 1595, married Pieter Rodingh, Albertsz., born
        1526, Treasurer 1578, Clerk to the Treasury 1580 to Apr. 1581,
        Councillor in the College of Superintendents to the Admirality
        on behalf of his Excellency Count Maurits of Nassau, March
        1592 – 30 Dec. 1593, Lieutenant of the Civic Militia 1578,
        Regent of the St. Jorishof 1578. Son of Albert Kors, Alderman
        1529 and Brecht Pietersdr. Rodingh.
     6. Maria Banning, died unmarried.
     7. Grietge Banning Jans, married Jacob Willemsz Stachouwer,
        born in Deventer, soap-boiler in Amsterdam on the Water "in 't
        Roode Scharlaken", son of Willem Elbertsz., from Deventer..

VIb CORNELIS BANNING, Gerritsz., brewer on 'd' Achtergracht' ,
     Alderman 1518, 1522, 1523,1525 and 1527; Councillor 1519 until

his death; Burgomaster 1534 and 1536, Church Warden of the New Church 1513, 151,1519,1520 and 1521; Regent of the Orphanage 1523; Treasurer 1525, 1526, 1528, 1529, 1530, 1531, 1532, 1533, 1535, 1543 and 1544. Extremely accomplished diplomat. Died 16 May 1547, due to wounds "self-inflicted in a state of madness", married Aefge Vranckendr. de Wael, died 1563, daughter of Mr. Vranck de Wael Jansz..
From this marriage three children:
1. Katrijn Cornelisdr. Banning (the Elder), married Pieter Pieter Gerbrandszoon Ruijsch, Alderman 1555, bailiff 1566, Burgomaster 1574, Councillor 1576. Died in Leuven, Belgium, 2 July 1578.
   From this marriage:
   a. Cornelis Banning, died 'a young man';
2. Hillegont Cornelisdr. Banning, married Young Jan Duvensz. (Duyvesz.) born 1510. Stockfish merchant in the Warmoesstraat. [D. Francken: asserts that 'Anna Banning was married to Mr. Jan Duyvensz., Medical Doctor, 1574, Alderman and Councillor, and that they were the parents of Cornelis Banning Jansz. Duyvesz. and his sister Lijsbeth. The Municipal Treasury Account of 1544, however, records that the city purchased its stockfish from "Young Jan Duvensz., Cornelis Banning's brother-in-law." This stockfish merchant was the father of Burgomaster Cornelis and at the same time uncle of the doctor.
   From this marriage:
   a. Cornelis Banning Jansz. Duyvesz, Dike-reeve (1580) and Dike-grave (1586) of the Nieuwer-Amstel, Councillor 1584 - 1617, Alderman 1584, 1586, 1588, 1590, 1596 and 1597, Commissioner of Marital Affairs 1600 and 1608, Burgomaster (7 Apr.) 1601, 1607, 1610, 1611, 1613, 1616, Regent of the Orphanage 1602 and 1609, representative Councillor of the States of Holland and West Friesland from 1 May 1603 to 30 Apr.1606, Treasurer 1608, Commissioner of the Bank of Exchange 1614 and 1615, Regent of the Civic Orphanage 1594 - 1596. Lived on the Coninxgracht (Singel) at the time of his death, 30 Mar. 1617, married 1st Hillegont Jansdr, married 2nd in Utrecht, June 1582 to Sophia Foeyt, born in Utrecht, daughter of Floris Foeyt Arentsz. and Emerentia Lam Jacobsdr.
      Children (from the second marriage):
      a.a. 'Lady 'Anna Banning, born 1584, died in The Hague, 31 July 1624, buried there in the Groote or St.

Jacobskerk. Married in The Hague, after having filed banns on 7 Feb. 1604 in Amsterdam, to Joachim (van Cuyck) van Mierop, Receiver-General of Holland and West Friesland 1608 (succeeded his father) – 1643. Son of Cornelis (van Cuyck) van Mierop, Lord of Hoogwoud, Eerstwoude, etc., Receiver General as above; Polder Board of Delftland, and Elisabeth van Alckemade.Died in The Hague 23 July 1643 and buried there in the Groote or St. Jacobskerk, [Epitaph on the gravestone features a woman with a torch held over her right shoulder, holding two coats of arms: "Here lies buried Mr. Joachym van Mierop in life Receiver-General of Holland and Westvrieslandt, died 23rd July 1643, with his housewife Lady Anna Bannincx died the last day of July MVIcXXIIII"] ;

b.b.Emerentia Banning, born 1586, died Leiden 11 May 1667, buried in the Pietersskerk in Leiden, married in The Hague, after filing banns in Amsterdam 18 March 1606 to Mr. Jacob van Brouckhoven, born 1577, died 16 June 1642, buried in the Pieterskerk, Forty in the Council of Leiden 1610, Burgomaster of Leiden 1620, Delegate of the Council, Delegate of the States General, Steward of Rijnland, son of Toy Jansz. van Brouckhoven, Bailiff of Leiden 1575, Burgomaster of Leiden 1589, Reeve and Dike-grave of Rijnland.

b.   Lijsbeth Jans Banningendr. alias Lijsbeth Jan Duvenzoonsdr., baptized in the Old Church 9 August 1567, married 1st Jan van Bekesteyn, living in the Warmoestraat, (baptised 19 May 1566), son of Jan van Bekesteyn and Machteld Stans Claeszoonsdr.. Married Febr. 1585 2nd Jan van Heussen, born in Arnemuyden, living in 1577 in Embden, afterward Burgomaster of Naarden, widower of Aefgen Wael [daughter of Vranck de Wael and Jannetgen Jan Pilgramsdr., not to be confused with Aefge Vranckenndr. de Wael, married to Cornelis Banning Gerritsz., daughter of Mr. Vranck de Wael, Jansz.) . After the death of Lijsbeth Jan Banningendr. he married Trijntje Laurensdr. van Neck.

3. Katrijn Cornelisdr. Banning, (de Jonge) (died childless), married Jan Verburch, Jacobsz., ropemaker, (lived on the water on the north corner by the Karnemelksteeg 'in the green Field') Regent of the Nieuwe Zijds Home for Charity 1578, Commissioner 1583, Councillor 1584 until his death, Burgomaster 1584, died Oct. 1604. Son of Jacob Oom Jansz, alias Jaepoom Jansz. and Neel Jansdr.

Verburch. He remarried Katrijn Cornelisdr. de Vlaming.

VII.1 GERRIT BANNING, Jansz., died 'aged 44 years', married
Jannetge Lam Jacobsdr., born in Utrecht, died 1604, after being
remarried to Gerrit Fransz Bogaert.
From this marriage:
1. Jan, Gerritsz, follows VIII
2. Cornelis Banning, died unmarried
3. Gerrit Banning, died unmarried
4. Enmegen (?) Banning, died unmarried
5. Sophia Banning, born 1561, married Dec. 1591 Claes Ment,
Cornelisz., living at the time of his marriage 'in the brewery
'van den Arend', and was thus probably employed by the
brewer Pieter Dircksz. Hasselaer, whose brother-in-law he
became through this marriage, son of Cornelis Jansz., furrier
'in 't roode Cruys', van Lis. Regent of the Hospice, Church
Warden of the Old Church 1567.
6. Catherina Banning, Gerritsdr., died before 1615, married in
Utrecht 29 Sept. 1599 (?), Adriaen van Helsdingen, he
remarried Utrecht 29 Jan. 1615 Hillegont Houwenaers, van
"Culenberch", son of Steven van Helsdingen and Jonge Maria
Boelens.
7. Margriet Banning, born 1565, buried in the Old Church 4 Mar.
1641, married in Amsterdam 19 Apr. 1587 to Pieter Dircksz.
Hasselaer, widower of Aecht Pietersdr. van Beverwaerde, born
in Haarlem 1554. Highly esteemed merchant and ship owner.
Known especially for his courageous action as Standard-bearer
of the Haarlem Militia during siege of the city by the Spaniards
in 1572/73. Councillor 1594 until his death, Alderman 1595,
Captain of the Militia, Governor of the Dutch East India
Company, died in Amsterdam 27 Aug. 1616, son of Dirck
Simonsz. Hasselaer and Aechgen Hoos, Pieterdr. from
Haarlem.

VIII JAN BANNING, Gerritsz, died 1602; married Heijltje van
Rheenen.
Children born of this marriage:
1. Geertruyd Banning, married Jacob Storm of Brouwershaven,
merchant of Venice.
2. Gerrit, follows IX
3. Anna Banning, marriage [recorded in 'Notes from the
oldest marital records of the city of Naarden 1600-1637]
11 Oct. 1615 in Naarden to Pieter Backer.

IX   GERRIT BANNING, married Alyd van Vollenhoven.
Children born of this marriage:
1. Jan   Banning, unmarried
2. Julia   "   , unmarried
3. Duifje   "   , unmarried
4. Havick   "   , unmarried
5. Heyltje   "   , unmarried
6. Geertuyd (Gerretje) Banning, married in the Old Church 22 Aug.
   1645 to Jan Vlasblom, died 1 Febr. 1681.
7. Mr. Gijsbert Banning, died 1661, unmarried
8. Sophia Banning, married Artus van Mansdale
9. Havick Banning

VII.1a   CLAES BANNING, Jansz., lived on the Burgwal 'in den
blaeuwe Rose', was probably a tradesman for Moscovië (= Russia;
one of his sons was in Moscow at the time of death of his father) died
30.8.1594, married Annetge Willemdr. Delff, daughter of Willem
Cornelisz. Delff and Wijve Claesdr. Bicker.
From this marriage:
1. Grietje Banning, married Jan Boudewijnsz. van Lockhorst
2. Baertie (= Beatrix) Banning, died unmarried
3. Jan Claesz., follows VIII
4. Jacob Banning, died unmarried
5. Vincent Banning, married Brechje Claesdr. van
   Vierhuysen.
6. Jannetje Banning, died unmarried
7. Willem Banning, 'obiit in de Sond' (died in the Sont)
8. Gerret Banning, 'obiit in the East Indies' (died in the East
   Indies)

VIII.   JAN BANNING, Claesz., born 1563, lived on the Nieuwezijds
Achterburgwal, married 15 May 1591 to Lijsbeth Lambertsdr.
Coppens, born 1568, daughter of Lambert Coppens and Lijsbeth
Reijers.
From this marriage six children::
1. Wijbrich (Weyntje) Jansdr. Banning, born 1592, buried in the New
   Church 9 Nov.1629, married 24 Apr. 1618 Balthasar Jans(s)en, born
   in Hamburg, Germany 1591, died shortly before November 1646, in
   1618 druggist in the Halsteeg, thereafter merchant and confectioner
   in the Warmoesstraat 'in de witte Roosecrans'. The joint capital of
   both he and his wife after their deaths in 1646 amounted to the sum
   of florins 280,000.-.
From this marriage:
1. Magdalena Janssens (dr.) Banning, married Paulus van Ijppelaer.

2. Jan Banning, Janssens (z).
3. Balthasar Banning, Janssens (z).
4. Elisabeth Janssens (dr.) Banning, baptised in the New church 13 Febr. 1629, married 29 Dec. 1648 to Jacobus Reijnst., born 2 July 1621, widower of Adriana Gillon. Lived on the Keizersgracht in 1645 and 1648 and in 1652 on the Singel, [was the owner of the homestead Duyn en Bergh near Velsen, which his father purchased on 26 May 1634 for the sum of florins 11,700.], Regent of the Charity Orphanage 1647, Lieutenant of the Civic Militia 1650, Regent N.Z. Home for Charity 1651, Captain of the Civic Militia 1652, Commissioner 1654, Governor of the Dutch West Indies Company, died 4 Sept. 1667, after being remarried to Maria Pater. Son of Hendrick Reyns. (Head Cashier of the Bank of Exchange 1616, Councillor 1626, until his death (29 June 1648), Captain of the Longbow Association 1626, Captain of the Civic Militia 1626, Alderman 1627, Governor of the Dutch East Indies Company 1636) and Elisabeth Princen.
5. Geertruyt (Margriet) Jansdr. Banning, married Johannes van Collen (van Ceulen), born in Aken (Germany) around 1609. Lived on the Keizersgracht. Buried in the Zuiderkerk 6 June 1646, son of Abraham von Collen (van Collen, van Ceulen), Master Builder in Aken, Germany 1597—1598. Was banned in 1598 by Emporer Rudolf II for religious reasons, because of confession of Protestantism, and moved to Amsterdam, where he lived on the Keizersgracht, he was an elder of the Dutch Reformed Church there (1605) and Maria Seullin.
6. IJsbrant Banning, follows IX
7. Lijsbeth Banning, married Mattheus van Halewijn
8. Stijntje Banning, died unmarried
9. Claes Banning, died unmarried

IX IJSBRANT BANNING, married in France to Francisca Rensi. From this marriage five children:
1. Christina Banning, born 1657, buried in the Zuiderkerk 21 May 1703, married Reijnier van Kuyck in Amstelveen 2 Apr. 1675, baptized 7 Mar. 1647. Lived on the Heerengracht and at his death on the Oude Schans, merchant and manufacturer of gunpowder, Standard-bearer of the Civil Militia 1668, Church Warden of the New Church 1693. Buried in the Zuiderkerk 6 Dec. 1703, son of Adriaen van Kuyck, van Heusden (merchant and manufacturer of gunpowder, Master of Equipage to the Admirality in Amsterdam, Commissioner and Superintendent of Rigging 1649; Lieutenant of the Civic Militia 1650; Church Warden of the Zuiderkerk 1652) and Hillegonda Reael.
2. Margrieta Banning, married Jan Bruet
3. Jan Banning, died unmarried

4. .... Banning
5. .... Banning

VII.1b STANS BANNING, well-known instigator of the iconoclastic
fury and image-breaking in Amsterdam (1566), married
Lijsbeth Gerritsdr. Stachouwer of Deventer, daughter of Gerrit
Stachouwer of Deventer, and Nelle Egbertsdr.
From this marriage:
1. Jan Banning, died unmarried
2. Margriet Banning, died unmarried
3. Nelle (Aeltje) Banning, married Philip Adriaen Texel
From this marriage:
   a. Stans Banning, Texel, Reeve of Loosdrecht, married
   Volckertje Jacobsdr. van Haerlem.
   From this marriage:
   a.a. Jan Banning
   b.b Jacob Banning
   c.c Nelletje Banning
   d.d. Lijsbeth Banning
   e.e. Geertie Banning
   b. Lijsbeth Banning, Texel, married Dr. Nicholaas Bodicher
   (Bodecherus), Preacher in Loosdrecht until 1611, after
   which in Alkmaar.
   From this marriage:
   a.a Joan Bodecheer Banning, alias Janus (Johannes)
      Bodecherus Banningius, born in Loosdrecht 1606,
      was appointed Professor of Science in Nov. 1630
      after a trial period of one year during which he
      lectured on Ethics at the University of Leiden. Five
      years later he was appointed Professor of Physics. In
      1638 he was temporarily relieved to serve for a
      number of years as political Councillor in Brazil, for
      the Dutch West Indies Company, a function which he
      apparently did not undertake. He was a celebrated
      literator and poet and his work is still read today.
      Died in Leiden in 1642 (insane).

Va   Mr. Dr. JACOB BANNING, born +/- 1470. Councillor and
      Pensionary, Notary 1513, 1515, Secretary 1504, 1505 and 1517,
      died before 1529, married Erm Jacobsdr., who is recorded as
      living on the Vijgendam as a widow in 1541, daughter of Jacob
      Simonsz.
      From this marriage three children:
      1. Jan Jacobsz, follows VI.1

169

2. Griet Jacobsdr. Banning, ("Griet meest(er) Jacob Ban(n)incx daughter) married 1st Dirck Cornelisz. Kater, died 5 Sept. 1536, of 'an injurie', inflicted by Claes Velserman, married 2nd Hillebrant Luijtsz., timber merchant 'in de Rave', widower of Aecht Gerritsdr. van Hoorn, son of Luyt Luytgensz. 'a prosperous man on the island of Wieringen'.
From the first marriage a son: Pieter Dircksz Kater.
From the second marriage, amongst others:
a. Jacob Banning, Hillebrandsz., was a timber merchant in 1564 on the N.Z. Kolk, married (before 1566) Foeck Jellesdr., daughter of Jelle Withmersz. van Ameland 'mariner to foreign parts' and Appolonia Bauckesdr. Zythiema.
From this marriage:
a.a Jacobgen Banning, married 1st Willem Arentsz. Lakeman, of Haarlem, son of Arent Meynertsz. Fabricius, Burgomaster of Haarlem 1595, and Maria Lakeman. Married 2nd Cornelis Jansz. van der Tin, Alderman and Councillor of Haarlem 1637, died there in 1647.
From this marriage, amongst others:
a.a.a. Jacob Banning, Notary in Haarlem, Secretary of Commissioners of the Klein Bank of Justice in Haarlem 1618, Councillor Haarlem 1631, Secretary there in 1632. Died in Haarlem 16 May 1660; married 6 Jan. 1643 Geertuyd Olycan, baptized in Haarlem 20 Aug. 1603, died without issue 16 Nov. 1666, daughter of Pieter Jacobsz. Olycan, Alderman and Councillor of Haarlem1615; Burgomaster of Haarlem 1630, Delegate of the States General 1631, Councillor 1624, and Maritge Claesr. Voocht.
3. Bartholomeus Banning, Jacobsz., follows VIe.

VI.1 JAN BANNING, Jacobsz. born +/- 1500, textile merchant on the Nieuwendijk 'on the south corner of the Jan Corten Lane', 'in 't Vliegende Varcken' [in the Flying Pig] , Warden of the Cloth 1546, attested in Gouda 1546, died of the plague 1567, buried in the New Church 13 Apr.1567; married Lieff Adriaensdr., died of the plague in May 1567 (eight days after her daughter Anna Jansdr. Banning), daughter of Adriaen Michielsz.
From this marriage six children:
1. Jacob Jansz. Banning, follows VII.
2. Michiel Jansz. Banning, follows VIIb
3. Mijen Jansdr. Banning, died in Emden in or shortly before

1578, married (before 1555) Matthijs Matthijsz, died in Emden in 1578, 'peddlar' in the Warmoesstraat 'in de drie roode Roosen' [in the Three Red Roses].
Their daughter was, amongst others, Dieuwer Matthijsdr., who married Pieter Claesz. Calff.

4. Geert Jansdr. Banning, died shortly before May 1569, married Pieter Matthijsz, dealer in hides on the Jan Hanssenpad, buried in the New Church, Amsterdam 6 June 1567.
Their only son died young.

5. Erm Jansdr. Banning, 'the third daughter of Jan and Lieff, who was still a spinster, departed this life....... six or eight days or thereabouts after her mother'.

6. Anna Jansdr. Banning, died a spinster in 1567 '14 days or thereabouts after her father, just as he, her mother and her sister of the plague'.

VII JACOB JANSZ. BANNING, textile merchant on the Nieuwendijk on the corner of the Dirck van Hassseltsteeg 'in 't vliegende Varcken', Warden of the Cloth 1563, 1564, Regent of the Lieve Vrouwe Hospice 1576-1578, Councillor 1578 until his death (elected by the delegates of the Militias 27 May 1578), Regent of the Civic Orphanage 1590-1592, died 3 Nov. 1604, married Lijsbeth Jandsr. Ruysch, buried in the New Church 22 Mar. 1600, daughter of Jan Jacobsz. Ruysch.
From this marriage:

1. Dieuwertje (Debora) Jacobsdr. Banning, buried in the New Church 28 Nov. 1620, married 10 Jan. 1580 to Govert Dircksz. Wuytiers, born 1548; textile merchant, in 1579 on the Nieuwenldijk on the corner of the Dirck Hasseltsteeg 'in 't Vliegende Varcken', at his death on the Warmoestraat 'in Engelenburch', Councillor 1579 to 1583, verwoonde his poorterschap in 1583 (zijn poorterschap ontvrijt anno 1583), Alderman 1581, buried in the New Church 6 Oct. 1615, son of Dirck Govertsz. Wuytiers and Aecht Cornelisdr. Barckman (Barchman) [the parents of the noble lineage of Barchman-Wuytiers]
From this marriage six children, amongst which:

a. Jan Banning Wuytiers, born 1591, ordained as a Roman Catholic priest in 1619; died 4 Oct. 1647 and buried in the Old Church on 8 Oct. 1647.

VIIb   MICHIEL JANSZ. BANNING, died shortly before June 1565,
married Lijsbeth Pietersdr. Codde, died before 1607, remarried
Otto Vogel (Alderman 1586, Regent of the Old Men and Women's
Home 1579). Daughter of Pieter Pietersz. Codde, Regent of the
N.Z. Home for Charity 1548, and Nelle Claesdr. Boelens (sister of
Katrijn Claesdr. Banning X Jan Claesz. Cat). She remarried Otto
Vogel.
From the first marriage one son: Michiel Michielsz Banning, born
June 1565, died Haarlem and buried in Amsterdam, New Church
29.10.1593.
From this marriage:
1. Michiel Michielsz. Banning, born June 1565, died in Haarlem and
   buried in Amsterdam in   the New Church 29 Oct. 1593.

VIb   BARTHOLOMEUS BANNING, Jacobsz., merchant on the
Vijgendam ' in de blinde Werelt', buried in the New Church on 21
Nov. 1563. Married Lijsbeth Fransdr. van Campen, buried in the New
Church 27 Sept. 1573, daughter of Frans van Campen, Jacobsz. and
Trijn Hillebrantsdr. den Otter.
From this marriage:
1.   Frans Bartholemeusz. Banning, follows VII
2.   Erm Bartholomeusdr. Banning, married 10 June 1581 to Willem
     IJsbrantsz Kieft. widower of Stijn Jansdr. Ruytenburch, merchant
     and owner of a malt manufactory on the Singel outside of the
     Gasthuismolenpoort. Son of Ijsbrant Jansz. Kieft.

VII   FRANS BANNING, Bartholomeusz. born 1544, Alderman 1579,
1581 and 1582, Captain of the Civic Militia 8 Sept. 1580. Buried in
the Old Church 28 Aug.1582. Married 28 Dec.1578 to
Maritge Hendricksdr. Haeck, died 8 Apr.1621, after being remarried
to Hendrick Hendricksz van Bronckhorst, daughter of Hendrick
Jansz. Haeck (living in the Warmoesstraat 'in de Kanis'
widower of Alijd Pietersdr. Bicker) and Claesgen Ijsbrantsdr. Hem.
     From the first marriage one daughter:
1. Lijsbeth Fransdr. Banning, born 21 Jan 1581, buried in the Old
   Church 1 Oct. 1623, married 16 Sept. 1603 to Jan Jansz.
   Cocq, born in Bremen, Germany in 1575, served the
   apothecary Steven Jansz. in 'de witte Doos ' [in the White
   Box] in the Warmoesstraat; he became a burgher on 9 May
   1602 and thereafter opened his own apothecary on the
   Dijkstraat, 'in de gloeyende Oven'. [In the Glowing Oven] .At
   the time of his death on 22 Aug. 1633 he lived on the
   Heerengracht.
   From this marriage:

1. Dr. Frans Banning Cocq, Knight, Lord of Purmerland and
   Ilpendam, born 23 Feb. 1605, President of the
   Conglomerated Polder Boards and Lieutenant Forester of
   Purmer and Wormer, Commissioner 1632, Councillor 1634
   until his death (1655); Alderman (1634?)1637,1640, 1642,
   1645, 1646, 1648 and 1649; Commissioner of Minor
   Affairs 1634, 1635, 1641,1643, 1644 and 1650;
   Commissioner of the Bank of Loans 1638 and 1639,
   Captain of the Civic Militia 1642; Colonel, from Jan. 1646
   to 25 Aug. 1650, Captain of the St. Sebastiansdoelen or
   Longbow Association 1648, Burgomaster 16 Aug.1650,
   1651, 1653 and 1654 (until his death on 1 Jan. 1655),
   Treasurer 1652, Regent of the Orphanage 1652. Knight in
   the Order of St. Michael as conferred by the King of France
   on 26 Nov. 1648. Died 1 Jan. 1655, married 23 Apr. 1630
   to Lady Maria Overlander of Purmerland, born 24 June
   1603, died 27 Jan, 1678, daughter of Mr. Volckert
   Overlander, Knight, Lord of Purmerland and Ilpendam
   (conferred by King James I of England, was raised to
   nobility in 1620; also Regent of the St. Pieters Hospice
   1600, Captain of the Kloverniersdoelen, Councillor 1605
   until his death on 18 Oct. 1630 in The Hague, Alderman
   1603, Burgomaster 1628, Councillor to the Admirality of
   Amsterdam 1614-1621, Councillor 1629-1630, Captain of
   the Civic Militia 1616, Studied in Leiden and acquired his
   doctorate in 1595 in Basel, Switzerland as Doctor of Law,
   merchant and ship owner) and of Geertruyd Hooft.

2. Jan Cocq, born 24 Apr. 1607 in Haarlem, near the 'Groote
   Houtpoort', drowned in 't Ij in Amsterdam in 1658,
   'surdaster celebs ' (was very deaf, remained unmarried)

IIIa   DIRCK BANNING, Gerritsz. born 1404, married 1428 to
       Geertruyd van Vliet, born 1412 (?), daughter of Gerrit van
       Vliet, Jansz., Knight, and Machteld van der Merwe.
       From this marriage:
       1. Margriet Dircksdr. Banning, born 1430, died 12 Jan. 1500,
          married Hendrick Coenenz. van der Schellingh, born 1427,
          died 13 Sept. 1495, son of Coen Tijmansz. van der
          Schellingh and Christyne Heynsdr. Schouten.

IIIb   CLAES BANNING, Gerritsz., born +/-1410, married Unknown.
       From this marriage:
       1. Jan Claesz., follows IV

IV   JAN CLAESZ. BANNING, born +/- 1440, married Unknown,
       who died shortly before August 1503.
       From this marriage:
       1. Matthijs Banning, Jansz, born 1482, died before 1526.
       2. Elisabeth Jansdr. Banning, born 1484, married Mr. Laurens
           Jacobsz, died. 1527.He remarried Geert Egbertsdr..
           From the first marriage one daughter:
           a. Elisabeth Jansdr. Banning, born 1484, married 1st 1540
               Jacob Ruysch (Jacob Ruysch moved to Weesp with his
               family in 1549, where he became a brewer in the brewery
               of 'den Sleutel'), son of Ruysch Jansz., alias Ruysch Jan
               Bethsz., Alderman 1497, Councillor 1498, Burgomaster
               1513 and of Dieuwer ...., married 2nd on 31 Jan. 1553
               to Pieter Bicker, born 1522, Brewer on the O.Z. Achter-
               burgwal in the brewery 'den Sleutel', 'between the olde
               and the new nun's convents', Regent of the Leper's Home
               1581 (Pieter Bicker remarried Marij Pietersdr. van Neck,
               thereafter Joostken Florisdr. van Teylingen from Alkmaar
               and finally Lijsbeeth Pietersdr. Nooms from Edam, widow
               of Gerrit Jansz. Ruytenburch, alias Gerrit Jansz. 'in den
               rooden Hondt'). Buried in the Old Church 2 April 1585,
               son of Mr. Pieter Bicker, Gerritsz., Alderman 1534 (he was
               extremely wealthy) and Anna Pietersdr. Codde.
       3. Willem Banning, Jansz., born 1487.(Elias: probably the same
           as Mr. Willem Banning, priest, who died shortly before
           1542, leaving behind a son by Katrijn Jacob
           Huygenszoondr., named: Jacob Huygensz., who died in
           1578, after having married in 1555 the daughter of Thijman
           Burgen).
       4. Jan, Jansz. follows V.

V JAN BANNING, Jansz, born 1490, died 1556, (at the end of his life it
   appears that Jan Banning Jansz. had financial difficulties. His close
   relatives received a 'reduced share of mother's inheritance' for the
   children from his first marriage in Feb. 1539) married 1st Katrijn
   Gerrits Cop, died shortly before January 1532, daughter of Gerrit
   Jansz. Cop and Geert Jans, married. 2nd Maria Dirksdr..
   From the first marriage:
   1. Jan Banning, died young
   2. Jan Banning, died young
   3. Duyf Jansdr. Banning, born 1525, married Jacob Pelser Jansz.,
       alias Jacob Jansz. 'in 't Lam', buried in the Old Church 27 Apr.
       1596, peltry (fur) merchant in the Warmoestraat 'in 't vergulden
       Lam' (in the Gilded Lamb), advocate for reformation of

Amsterdam, was suspected of having brought down the statue of Saint Rochus in the iconoclastic fury and image-breaking in the Old Church in August 1566, son of Old Jan Jansz. 'in 't Hart'. He remarried Trijn Jeroensdr., buried in the Old Church 15 Feb. 1600.

4. Aecht Jansdr. Banning, buried in the New Church 14 June 1600, married Jacob Jansz. Coeckebacker, born 1525, herring merchant on 'de Kolk' 'in de drie Haringen', buried in the Old Church 18 May 1595.

From this marriage:

a. Jan Banning Coeckebacker, Regent of the Nieuwezijds Home for Charity 1632-1644; merchant and ship owner in Amsterdam.

5. Gerrit Jansz Banning, born 1529.

6. Matthijs Jansz. Banning, born November 1531, was abroad in 1556. Seven children were born of this marriage; whose names are not mentioned.

5. New Light on the Oldest Generations of Banning in Amsterdam
- ties to Assendelft -

by J.P. Ouweltjes

Introduction

The family name Banning occurs in Amsterdam from the 15th century. In the sixties of that century we find a Gerrit Banninc as alderman of Amsterdam, and a decade later we find his sons Jan en Gaeff in the same function. By means of considerable land ownership in a favourable location, this family grows to enormous wealth in the rapidly expanding city. It is therefore not surprising that we encounter descendants of Gerrit Banninc later in the Amsterdam magistrate.

Older generations of this family have already been described extensively (ref. Elias) The number of authentic sources, however, is limited. This is why earlier genealogical research has been consulted, which refers to sources which can no longer be verified. The oldest Banning generations have already been thoroughly researched by Mr. Gerard Schaep Pietersz., who was regent of the Burgerweeshuis (Civic Orphanage) in Amsterdam. His work is still held up to critical analysis on the basis of sources available today.

Ties to Assendelft

Recent research conducted by Dudok van Heel indicates that land ownership of the Banning family in Amsterdam was considerable [ref Dudok van Heel]. However, it has recently come to light that this family also owned extensive property in Assendelft.

In Assendelft land ownership by the Bannings was concentrated around the Kerkbuurt [Church Area]. The largest share of land was located in an area which had, in sequence, the names 'Banen weer'(1480), 'Schout Gabbe weer' (end of the 15th, beginning of the 16th century) and the 'Jan Banningen weer' (from the 16th century)[213]. A document from 1480 reveals considerable information about the existing situation at the time.

Jan Nikolaas Banninksz. sold half of "Gerit Caycx ven" in the 'Banen weer' to the brothers Jan Banninck and Gaaf Gerard Banninksz.,

---

[213] A 'weer' was a number of properties enclosed by navigable water and is usually named after the owner or previous owner. The 'weers' were created during the period of land reclamation for purposes of good drainige of the peat bogs and were situated at right angles to the main drainige channel.

bordered in the northeast by land owned by Agatha, widow of Jan Banninck, and her children, bordered in the southwest by land owned by Pieter Bouwensz. and Simon Jan Willemsz.[214]. The name "Gerit Caijcx ven" which is used in 1480 bears reference to an ancestor named Gerit and would date land ownership of the Banning family from the end of the 14th century.

This tract of land, which we encounter at the end of the 16th century as "the Bincaijck" in 'Jan Banningen weer', then came into possession of the children of Garbrant Jan Baningen[215]. The land to the southwest of this tract is then known as "Bouwens ven" and appears to lie in the ' Claes Maerts weer'.

We encounter a certain Sijmon Jan Bannincxz even earlier in Assendelft, whose widow is mentioned in 1443 as owner of an adjoining tract of land there. The exact location of this land is unknown.

The ties between Amsterdam and Assendelft are still very much in existence in the year 1500, as appears from a large inheritance left to the children of Jan Gerritsz. Banninck and his wife, who was a daughter of the Amsterdam bailiff Jacob Heijndrick Auwelsz. [ref Heereman van Zuydtwijck]. It is apparent that they still owned a number of properties there, and various loans are registered in their name to several citizens of Assendelft.

Mr. Gerard Schaep Pietersz. refers to a certain Benning Gerritsz. as the oldest known ancestor. This person is alleged to have been born around 1375. It is worth noting that we do not encounter him in Amsterdam archives. It would therefore seem plausible to assume that he played only a minor role in the history of Amsterdam. However, this supposition would not correspond with early land ownership in Assendelft and therefore calls for a critical reassessment of Schaep's conclusions.

Because of the existence of Sijmon Jan Bannincxz. in 1443 and the frequent mention of the Christian name Jan, it would be most plausible that not Benningh Gerritsz, but Jan Gerrit Bannincxz. would be the oldest known ancestor of this family. This Jan Gerrit Bannincxz. is mentioned in a document dated 1416, whereby he is obliged to pay a yearly tenancy for his house in the Coppe Lanensteeg in Amsterdam, located where the Beurspassage is today and not far from the site where the homes of later generations of Banning in Amsterdam were located. According to current theory, Jan would have been the father of Sijmon

---

[214] J.H. Kort, *Stukken van de familie de Mérode vroeger op het kasteel Salmonsart (Bergen Henegouwen)*, [*Articles concerning the family de Mérode at one time in the castle Salmonsart*] O.V. [1984], p. 59.The actual text cites the name as "Berit Cayx ven", very probably a typing error (Berit=Gerit)
[215] GAZ, ORA 2006 fol.201v, 27-2-1637 and fol.263, 5-3-1638

Jan Bannincxzoen, Gerrit Jan Bannincxz., who owns the same house in the Coppe Lanensteeg in the year 1457 [ref De Melker], priest Jan Banninc and one Claes Banninck. How Simon fared beyond that point in unknown. Gerrit Banninc was a merchant in Amsterdam, recorded as such in the 'land tax register' of Kampen in 1440[216], alderman of Amsterdam on several occasions: 1461...67, his children own land in Assendelft, he is most probably the same as Gerrit Jan Bannincxz. who assumed a debt in 1456 for the 'banne' of Wormer of the sovereign involved in the rebellion of Kennemerland at the time of the Hoekse and Kabeljauwse uprisings[217], married unknown. The existence of Claes Banninck is based on the existence of Jan Claesz. Banninck, who was involved in the sale of land in Assendelft in 1480. *Claes Banninck* was married to *Margriete Claesdr.*, she remarried around 1465 to Gerrit Claesz. van Westzanen. We know of Claes Banninck and Margriete Claes from a number of inheritance affairs brought before the Court of Justice, which occurred at the beginning of the 16th century between the children of Jan Claesz. Banninck and Willem Karstantsz who was married around 1489 to a daughter from the second marriage of Margriete Claes[218]. Finally, we encounter a Jan Banninc in Amsterdam around the middle of the 15th century, priest in 1454 and also Memorial Master of the Onze Lieve Vrouwen Parish (New Church). In 1439 he is one of those mentioned as seller of the house on the south corner of the Coppe Lanensteeg (Municipal Archives of Amsterdam, Topographic Collection, charter dated 6 Nov. 1439). The same charter reveals that a portion of the house had once belonged to Elisabeth, widow of Jan Banninc. We therefore now know the name of Jan Gerrit Bannincxz.'s wife, hitherto unknown..

Family name Banning in the Zaan region

The earliest records date from the 15th century and come from Assendelft. This Banning family, members of the Dutch Reformed Church since the reformation, remain in Assendelft until the 17th century. After 1660 a branch settled in Westzaan who made their fortune in the shipping industry, which at that time reached a peak. The name Banning disappeared from Assendelft at the end of the 17th century. The family name Banning died out in Westzaan at the end of the 18th century.

---

[216] See for example Het Kamper Pondtolregister, Economisch Jaarboek [The Kamper Land Tax Register, Economic Yearbook] [1919], p.229 en F. Ketner, Hendel en Scheepvaart van Amsterdam, [Trade and Shipping of Amsterdam] p.79.

[217] SAW, OA Wormer, inventory 376, 20-10-1456

[218] See G.W. Bomhof, F.M. Kolvenbach, *Amsterdammers voor de Grote Raad (1465-1580)*, *[Amsterdammers for the Main Council]* Amsterdam [1977], p.55, no.87, 16-1-1535(1534),and J.Th. de Smidt and T. Lindijer, *Haarlemmers voor de Grote Raad van Mechelen 1458-1578, [Haarlemmers for the Main Council of Mechelen]* Haarlem [1999], p.68

During the construction of the genealogy which follows, it became clear from the genealogical data mentioned that Banning also occurred in other places in the Zaan region early on. The following data are based on the land tax registers of Assendelft, the land transport records and Baptismal, Marriage and Burial records of the relevant places and documents from the old notary archives.

In the northern part of Assendelft we encounter a certain Pieter Claesz. Ban, born around 1521, and another person of the same period (possibly a brother) Jan Claesz. Alckes alias Banning. From his son Claes Jansz Banning alias Op de Heijd, we encounter descendants in Krommenie and Westzaandam (all Dutch Reformed). Also mentioned is Jan Jacobsz. (Rode) Banning in Assendelft, brother of Jan Jacobsz. Rood, both children of Jacob Jansz. Rood and Aef Engels. We also encounter a Lijsbet Jan Benningen, a sister of Aernt Claesz and Cornelis Claesz, children of Claes Maerten Keijssers.

The frequent occurrence of the name Banning (or derivatives) in various families in Assendelft, as well as various tracts of land known by that name in the same region, make it plausible that the following genealogy was, in actual fact, even more extensive.

Finally, we also encounter Cornelis Benning Jan Duves in Assendelft, and his sister Guerte Benings. Cornelis belonged to the Amsterdam magistrate at the beginning of the 17th century. Cornelis owned several tracts of land in the south of Assendelft (country estates). His presence in Assendelft can be explained because his father, Jan Duves, originally came from Assendelft.

In Krommeniedijk the brothers Jan and Cornelis Jansz. Banning are recorded, born approximately 1590 and perhaps nephews/cousins of Cornelis Dircksz. Banning, also residing there (all Baptist).

A certain Pieter Jansz. Banning then lived in Koog aan de Zaan. His son Jan Pietersz. Banning alias Schoenmaker was born around 1598 and has descendants in Koog aan de Zaan, Wormer, Jisp and Wormerveer (all Baptist).

****

179

57. Kerkbuurt (Church area) in Assendelft at the beginning of the 18th century, viewed from the south. The Jan Banningen weer is seen in the foreground.
Municipal archives of Zaanstad

Banning Genealogy of Assendelft

I *Jan Gerrit Bannincxz*, date of birth estimated at around 1375, probably a merchant, died before 6.11.1439, owns land in Assendelft and in Amsterdam, married around 1400 to *Elisabeth NN*.
The Coppe Lanensteeg was later called the Baafjessteeg, and is situated at about where the Beurspassage is today.
From this marriage:

1. *Sijmon Jan Bannincxz*, died before 6-12-1443 when his widow is mentioned as owner of adjacent land in Assendelft[219]. Little is known of Sijmon. He is possibly the father of Jan Banninck, died before 1480, who was married to Aagt NN. Perhaps the tract of land in Assendelft named "Sijmon Benninck meed" referred to him[220].

---

[219] C.J. Gonnet, Het Zijlklooster te Haarlem (Convent der Kanonessen-Regulieren ten Zijl) met Cartularium van het Zijlklooster, [The Zijl Convent of Haarlem (Convent of the Regular Sisters of Zijl) with Cartularium of the Zijl Convent] Haarlem [1891]., inventory no. 59, p.78, 6-12-1443: Govairt Allaertsz appeared on behalf of Claes Tamesz, bailiff of Assendelf, before the regular sisters within the Zijl of Haarlem, two maden of land situated within six maden in Jacob Janszoens weer in the ban van Assendelft, bordered on the north by Willem Heijnricxz and on the south by Sijmon Jan Bannincxzoen – widow with her children.

[220] GAZ, ORA 2007 fol.39, 19-8-1639

180

2. *Gerrit Jan Bannincxz,* merchant in Amsterdam, recorded in the 'land tax register' of Kampen in 1440[221], alderman of Amsterdam on several occasions: 1461...67, married Unknown. The descendancy of Gerrit Banninc is described in another source[222] and is therefore not included in this one. (See Amsterdam genealogy)

3. *Claes Banninck,* follows II.

4. *Jan Banninc,* priest and Memorial Master of the New Church in Amsterdam (Municipal Archives, archive Begijnhof, Memorial Masters of the New Church no. 932, 952-954), died after 23.6.1454.

II. *Claes Banninck,* estimated year of birth around 1410, owns land in Assendelft and Amsterdam, married to *Margriete Claesdr.,* she remarried around 1465 to Gerrit Claesz van Westzanen. We know of Claes Banninck and Margriete Claes from a number of inheritance affairs brought before the Court of Justice, which occurred at the beginning of the 16th century between the children of Jan Claesz Banninck and Willem Karstantsz who was married around 1489 to a daughter from the second marriage of Margriete Claes[223].

From this marriage:

1. *Garbrant Claesz,* follows III.

2. *Jan Claesz Banninck,* inherits tracts of land in Assendelft and owns land in Amsterdam, lives in Amsterdam, married around 1480 to Unknown. Jan Claesz Banninck lived in Amsterdam. His children, Matthijs, Elisabeth, Willem en Jan were born there. After his mother Margriete Claes died, Jan Claesz also stayed for several months in her home in Haarlem[224]. His descendants have been described elsewhere[225].

III. *Garbrant Claesz,* born around 1445, owns land in what was later called the 'Jan Banningen weer' which at the time was called the 'Schout Gabbe weer'[226], bailiff in Assendelft (1475), possibly

---

[221] See for example Het Kamper Pondtolregister, Economisch Jaarboek [The Kamper Land Tax Register, Economic Yearbook] [1919], p.229 en F. Ketner, Hendel en Scheepvaart van Amsterdam, [Trade and Shipping of Amsterdam] p.79.

[222] GAZ, ORA 1993, fol.213v, 3-2-1581

[223] See G.W. Bomhof, F.M. Kolvenbach, Amsterdammers voor de Grote Raad (1465-1580), [Amsterdammers for the Main Council] Amsterdam [1977], p.55, no.87, 16-1-1535(1534),and J.Th. de Smidt and T. Lindijer, Haarlemmers voor de Grote Raad van Mechelen 1458-1578, [Haarlemmers for the Main Council of Mechelen] Haarlem [1999], p.68

[224] J.Th de Smidt and T. Lindijer, Haarlemmers voor de Grote Raad van Mechelen, [Haarlemmers for the Main Council of Mechelen] Haarlem] [1999], p. 56, item O

[225] GAZ, ORA 1993, fol.213v, 3-2-1581

married a sister of Gerrit Florisz. Two sons of Floris Garbrantsz, i.e. Garbrant and Cornelis, were involved in the division of land in 'Huijch Blockhuijs weer'[227]. Also appearing were the heirs of Willem Huijchen, who according to the letter of instruction of 25 Feb. 1503, was a brother-in-law of Gerrit Florisz,[228] Mr. Jan Duves acted on behalf of his father, Jan Duves, timber merchant, and Gerrit Dircksz Comes.

Father of:

1. *Floris Garbrantsz*, born around 1480, mentioned in the 10th land tax register of Assendelft 1543, owned a house and some land in the south of Assendelft in the Horn[229]. It has been established with certainty that Trijn, Garbrant, Cornelis and Anna were his children. We encounter Garbrant Florisz. together with a certain Joost Jansz Backer several times, who lived in Amsterdam . None of Floris' children carry the family name of Banninck.

2. *Gerrit Garbrantsz*, alias *Snijers*, tailor, mentioned in the 10th land tax register of Assendelft 1543, lived in the Horn in Assendelft. It is because of the registration of a small piece of land in the Jan Banningen weer, that is still recorded at the end of the 16th century as Gerit Snijers ventge[230], that we also know that he was a son of Garbrant Claesz. Gerrit's children are Claes Gerrit Gabben and Gab Gerrit Snijers. They also no longer use the name Banning.

3. *Jan Garbrantsz Banninck, follows IV.*

[226] GAZ, ORA 1997 fol.64, 14-1-1594

[227] GAZ, ORA 1995, fol.121v, 22-1-1587

[228] GAZ, ORA 1993, fol.213v, 3-2-1581

[229] For the genealogical line commencing with Floris Garbrandsz see: A.G. Molendijk-van der Ploeg, *Van Assendelft tot Rijperman*, [*From Assendelft to Rijperman*] Gens Nostra 1987, p.11.

[230] GAZ, Polderarchief Assendelft [Polderarchives Assendelft] inventory no.65, end16th century

58. Seal of Garbrant Claesz., bailiff of Assendelft in 1475.
Text on the outer edge reads: 'Garbrand Claesz ....nksz'
Archiefdienst voor Kennemerland, Haarlem

IV. *Jan Garbrantsz Banninck*, weigh-master in Assendelft[231], owns a
house and land in the Jan Banningen weer, as well as several
estates in the surrounding properties, recorded in the 10th land tax
registers of 1543, 1555/57 and 1562, died after 26 July 1562.
Jan Banninck's land ownership was considerable. Most of his
property was located in the Jan Banningen weer. In the adjacent
properties he rented land. In 1543 he owned 15 morgens of land in
Assendelft. In 1555 he shared his lands with a certain Gerrit
Cornelisz. and the extent of the property is 27 morgens and 33
rods. Jan also rented land from Havick Pietersz., living in
Haarlem and Claes Ponssen living in Oostzaan. In 1557 and in
1562 there is little change in this situation.
From this marriage:

1. *Aecht Jan Banningen*, died after 8 Oct. 1582, inherits in the "Jan
   Banningen ven" located in Claes Maerts weer' (directly to the
   south of the Jan Banningen weer), married *Jan Claes Caijcx*,
   recorded from the 10th penning 1543.
2. *Marij Jan Banningen*, alias *Marij Jan Gabben*, also inherits in
   the "Jan Banningen ven" in Claes Maerts weer, died before
   1581, as appears from the land tax register of 1555 she lived in
   Amsterdam, married *Engel Gerrit Meijnerts,* died after 1581.
3. *Garbrant Jan Banningen*, follows V.

V *Garbrant Jan Banningen*, inherits in the Jan Banningen weer, died
   before 1579, married to unknown. Little is known about Garbrant.

---

[231] GAZ, ORA 1995 fol.60v, which includes a sealed letter of losrentebrief d.d. 26-7-1562

We assume that he lived in the Jan Banningen weer. Because of his father's advanced old age he is not himself named in the 10th land tax registers. The exchange of land which occurred between the children of Jan Baningen and the son of Aelbert Willem Jansz., son of Willem Jansz. Smit[232] and the fact that, amongst the children there is a Garbrant and a Willem, makes it plausible that the wife of Garbrant was a daughter of Willem Jansz. Smit. From this marriage:

1. *Willem Garbrantsz* alias *Willem Costers*, sexton, died before 1569, married *Neel IJsbrants*, alias *Neel Costers*, alias *Neel Duijffgens*, died around 1581, daughter of IJsbrant Backer and Duijff .... Their children were Willem Willemsz., innkeeper in the Kerkbuurt, Jan Willemsz Costers, Duijff Willems (alias Duijffgen Backers, alias Duijff Costers, alias Duijffgen Wullem Gabben), and Lijsbet Willems alias Lijsbet Costers, married to Willem Jansz. vant Laentgen.

2. *Daughter*, married *Cornelis Heijndrick Gerits*, of age in 1572, carpenter, owns a mill on the Delft on the Jan Banningensloot, in 1624 weighing master, lived in the Kerkbuurt, died before 30 Mar.1628, son of Heijndrick Geritsz., bailiff of Assendelft 1542...46, and Neel Sijmons[233].

3. *Trijn Garbrants*, alias *Trijn Jan Banningen*, married *Pieter Cornelis Aerians*, died before 13 Apr.1608, son of Cornelis Adriaensz and Anna Aernts.

4. *Jan Garbrantsz.*, follows VIa.

5. *Cornelis Garbrantsz.*, follows VIb.

VIa. *Jan Garbrantsz*, alias *Jan Jan Banningen*, owns a house and land in the Jan Banningen weer, died before 27 Febr. 1637, married around 1590 to *Neel Jans Clous*, daughter of Jan Willemsz alias Jan Clous and Guerte Cornelis. We know little about Jan Garbrantsz.. The land transport deeds indicate that he was prosperous, considering the amount of money and land involved after his death on division of the inheritance between his wife and two sons. From this marriage:

---

[232] This concerns a part of the Delftcamp in the Kerckweer and the Hooge Veen in Jancke Maerts weer.

[233] Children of Gerrit Hendriksz are described in G. Schwartz, M.J. Bok, *Pieter Saenredam – De schilder in zijn tijd*, [*Pieter Saenredam – The painter in his era*] [1989]. Children of Cornelis Heijndrick Gerits were Hendrick Cormelisz, who was a miller in Alkmaar, Garbrant Cornelisz, timber merchant in Assendelft, Jan Cornelisz living in Medemblik and Willem Cornelisz, baker in Assendelft, from which issued a son Jan Willem Keesen alias Schuijtevoerder.

1. *Jan Jansz. Banning*, follows VIIa.
2. *Willem Jansz*, alias *Smit*, smith to the south of the Kerkbuurt of Assendelft, died after 4 Jan.1646, married *Baertje Jans*, daughter of Jan Sijmonsz Verwael, living in Westzaan. Willem Jansz. became acquainted with his wife because Jan Sijmonsz Verwael remarried Trijn Jong Willemen, from Assendelft., who lived next to Willem in the Dirck Jannen weer[234].Descendants, amongst which the sons Jan, Cornelis and Hendrick, use the surname Smit.

VIb. *Cornelis Garbrantsz*, alias *Cornelis Jan Baningen*, smith[235], owns a house and land in the Jan Banningen weer, acquired through his wife several pieces of land in the south of Assendelft, died in Assendelft 5 Sept.1640 (church membership registers), married around 1590 to *Marij Cornelis*, daughter of Cornelis Dirck Jan Baernts and Aagt Jans.In March and April 1638 the house and several pieces of land are sold by the children of Cornelis Garbranstz.. Altogether a sum of over *f* 4400,- is involved in this transaction. Perhaps because of this high amount, the sons Pieter and Jan sought their fortune elsewhere. Very little is heard afterward of the sons Garbrant and Dirck.
From this marriage:
1. *Garbrant Cornelisz. Banning*, acquired a tract of land from his brother Jan[236]in 1649, does not own a house in Assendelft.
2. *Pieter Cornelisz. Banning*, follows VIIb.
3. *Dirck Cornelisz.*, alias *Houwertjes*, fisherman, died after 16 Sept.1666[237].
4. *Jan Cornelisz. Banning*, follows VIIc.
5. *Daughter*, mentioned at the sale of the parental home[238].

VIIa. *Jan Jansz Banning*, carpenter, born around 1590, died in Assendelft 22 Oct. 1639 (lidmatenreg.), married *Aagt Gerrits Boet*[239], died after 2 Aug.1641, daughter of Gerrit Gerritsz. Boet and Griet Heijndricks. On 10 Febr. 1640 Aagt sold two

---

[234] GAZ, ORA 2004 fol. 90v, 6-2-1626
[235] GAZ, profession of Cornelis appears from the index to ORA 1999 fol.163, 1-4-1605 (last will and testament)
[236] GAZ, ORA 2009 fol.108, 8-1-1649
[237] GAZ, ONA 158 A 33, 16-9-1666
[238] GAZ, ORA 2006 fol. 261v, 5-3-1638
[239] She is already mentioned in J.H. Beudeker, *Genealogie van het geslacht Boet uit Assendelft*, [Genealogy of the Lineage of Boet from Assendelft] [1991] under generation IVa-6, but without mention of her marriage to Jan Jansz Banning.

tracts of land in the Jan Banningen weer. The children Gerrit and Willem are mentioned in the Assendelft land transport deeds after 1682 as heirs of Neltje Gerrits Boet. They are then also known by the surname Boet. The children of their brother Jan also receive their inheritance, but more on that later.
From this marriage:

1.   *Gerrit Jansz. Banning*, follows VIIIa.
2.   *Jan Jansz. Banning*, follows VIIIb.
3.   *Willem Jansz. Banningh*, follows VIIIc.

VIIb.   *Pieter Cornelisz Banning*, born around 1595, miller in the Beemster watermill on the south ring-dike, deacon of the NH-church in Beemster (1646), married in Beemster 17 Dec.1623 to *Neeltje Pieters*, young daughter of de Volger of Beemster. The situation arose that Pieter married Neeltje Pieters in 1623 and that he was already a miller of a watermill in the Beemster. When the eldest son Ariaen was born a year later, the family, however, lived in Assendelft again, according to the tenancy book. Pieter Cornelisz. does not come to the Beemster with attestation until 1626. In the following years we encounter Pieter several times in the church membership lists of the Dutch Reformed Church of Beemster. On 3 Mar. 1646 he was elected deacon of this church.
From this marriage:

1.   *Ariaen Pietersz Banning*, born in Assendelft around 1624, filed wedding banns in Beemster on 1 Dec.1646 to *Lijsbet Pieters*, young daughter of Mijzen, filed wedding banns in Beemster on 21 Sept.1659 to *Neel Pieters*, young daughter of Oosthuizen.
From the first marriage two sons are born with the name Jan and a daughter baptized by the name of Anna. We do not encounter the name Banning after this in Beemster.
2.   *Trijn Pieters*, baptised in Beemster 10 Jan. 1627
3.   *Cornelisje Pieters*, baptised in Beemster 8 Mar.1631
4.   *Cornelis Pietersz. Banning*, baptised in Beemster 1Jan.1634, filed wedding banns there on 20 Jan. 1656 with *Guurtje Jacobs*, young daughter of Oostzaan. In the baptismal records of Beemster no more children are found from this union.

VIIc.   *Jan Cornelisz. Banning*, born around 1605, married in Assendelft around 1632[240] to *Machtelt Floris*, daughter of van Floris Jan Floren and Duijff Engels. The church membership register indicates that Jan Cornelisz Banning leaves Assendelft for

---

[240] GAZ, ORA 2005, compare fol. 243v (13-6-16310 to fol. 468 (16-6-1634)

Purmerend in April 1638 together with his wife Machtelt Floris. It is no longer easy to trace how their life went on from there, as no land transport registers of Purmerend for that period have been saved. The last we know of Jan is that, in the year 1649, he sold the only piece of land in Assendelft still in his possession to his brother Garbrant. Many of his children, if not all, return to Assendelft and since then carry the surname Houwertjes[241]. After their uncle Garbrant died, the piece of land returned to their possession some time during the period between 1649 and 1672[242].

From this marriage:

1. *Floris Jansz Houwertjes*, fisherman, lives in the Kerkbuurt in Assendelft, fees paid for burial there on 2 Nov.1712 (class *f* 3,-), married in Assendelft around 1662 to *Catelijne Jans*, baptised in Haarlem 24 Nov.1641, daughter of Jan Heijndricksz. and Sijntje Jans, who was a midwife in Assendelft.

   His children were Jan, Sijntje, Garment (Garbrant), Aeltje and Machtelt. Descendants of Floris call themselves Houwertjes (Zaandam, Knollendam), in the 19e century the name altered to Ouweltjes for some of the family members (Oost-Knollendam)[243].

2. *Dirck Jansz Houwertjes*, fisherman, lives in the Kerkbuurt, died before 25 Apr.1682[244], married in Assendelft in about 1670 to *Anna Willems Comen*, fees paid for burial there on 4 Febr.1715 (pro deo), daughter of Willem Aelbertsz alias Comitje.

   From this marriage several children, of whom only Willem is known by name. Descendents call themselves Houwertjes (Assendelft).

3. *Allert Jansz Houwertjes*, baptised in Assendelft 16 Aug.1637, fisherman, lives in the Kerkbuurt, died before 6 Febr.1699, married to *Guurtje Jacobs*[245], fees paid for burial in Assendelft 24 June1705 (pro deo).

4. *Jan Jansz Houwertjes*, alias *Baes*, baptised in Purmerend 17

---

[241] GAZ, ORA 1982, 31-7-1692: Allert Jansz Houwertjes "says not to have known that small fish were in his *houwertjes* "

[242] GAZ, ORA 2012 fol.164v, 26-2-1672: bordered on the southwest by the children of Jan Cornelisz Houwertjes. The piece of land specified which came into possession of the children of Jan Cornelisz Banning is called "drie veenakkers" [three peat bogs] in Hillegond Roelofs weer and is purchased by him on 23-2-1635 (ORA 2006 fol.38v, 23-2-1635). We encounter it further on amongst the possessions of Allert Jansz Houwertjes (Verponding [Land tax] Assendelft 1657, inventory no..2)

[243] Genealogical data of Houwertjes and Ouweltjes in possession of the author

[244] GAZ, ORA 2013 fol.154v

[245] GAZ, ONA 158 A 33, 16-9-1682

Sept. 1643, fisherman[246], lives in the Kerkbuurt in
Assendelft, fees paid for burial there 4 Oct.1717 (pro deo).

VIIIa. *Gerrit Jansz. Banning*, alias *Boet*, alias *Mante*, merchant, fees
paid for burial in Assendelft 12 Jan.1698 (class ƒ 6,-), married
to Unknown.A declaration is drawn up in Assendelft on 15
July 1673, in which the 40-year-old Hendrick Jansz. Peet
declares that together with Gerrit and several others he visited
the inn 'de Swaan' in Grootebroek to settle a debt. Gerrit
Jansz. 's claim involved an amount of 2276 guilders, besides a
quantity of goods in Emden and 21 casks of brandy wine
which had been confiscated in Haarlem[247].
From this marriage:

1. *Jan Gerritsz. Banning*, living in the Krabbelbuurt, fees
   paid for burial in Westzaan 12 Nov.1696
   (class ƒ 3,-), married there 6 May 1696, fees paid in
   Westzaandam 21April 1696, to *Gleijntje Jans*, who
   came from the Krabbelbuurt. They are the parents of
   Dieuwertje Banning, burial fees paid in Westzaan 20
   Dec.1696 (class ƒ 3,-)
2. *Jacob Gerritsz. Banning*, follows IXa.
3. *Sijmon Gerritsz. Banning*, alias *Boet*, follows IXb.

VIIIb. *Jan Jansz. Banning*, ship's carpenter, owns a shipyard together
with his brother Willem carpenter's yard on the Westzaner
Overtoom, died before 16 March 1686, married in Westzaan
(church) 27 Febr.1661 to *Aagje Dirks*, baptised in Westzaan 14
Dec.1633, fees paid for burial in Westzaan 22 Mar.1699 (class
ƒ 15,-),.He purchased a shipyard on the Westzaner Overtoom,
together with his brother, on 23 Febr.1662 , as well as a house
adjacent to the shipyard for himself. On 30 Mar.1710 he sells
an oil press, a shed, some land and tools called 'de
Timmerman' [the Carpenter] to his daughter Aagje , for
ƒ 2350,-, located to the east of the houses.
The baptismal registers indicate that the family still lives in the
Krabbelbuurt in 1662. They later lived on the Hoogendijk.
In any case, Jan died before 16 Mar.1686. The state orphanage
records of the day indicate that the children Jan, Dirck and
Aagje inherited an amount of 450 guilders from their
godmother Neltje Boeth, who died in Assendelft[248].

---

[246] GAZ, ORA 1982, 11-5-1674: Jan Jansz Houwertjes alias Baes fined for fishing by illicit
means.
[247] GAZ, ONA 156, fol. 13, 15-10-1673
[248] GAZ, ORA 1919, 16-3-1686, Staatboek van de Weeskamer te Westzaan

Guardians of the children are Willem Jansz. Banning and Claes Dircksz.. Op 10 Jan. 1702 Jan and Aagje reappear to declare receipt of their share. Their brother Dirck has died in the meantime.

From this marriage:

1. *Jan Jansz. Banning*, baptised in Westzaan 19 Mar.1662 (witness Claesje Gerrits)
2. *Jan Jansz. Banning*, baptised in Westzaan 10 Febr.1664 (witness Claesje Gerrits), burgomaster of Westzaan, burial fees paid there on 10 July 1709 (class ƒ 30,-) Jan purchased a house in Westzaan on 14 Apr.1704 for ƒ 950,-.
3. *Dirk Jansz. Banning*, baptised in Westzaan 29 Oct.1666 (witness Jaanetje Dirks)
4. *Aagtje Jans Banning*, baptised in Westzaan 27 Oct.1669 (witness Neeltje Dirks), burial fees paid there on 26 Jan. 1718 (class ƒ 60,-).

VIIIc. *Willem Jansz. Banning*, baptised in Assendelft 17Apr.1638, lives in Westzaan in the Krabbelbuurt, master carpenter on the Westzaner Overtoom in a shipyard which he purchased together with his brother Jan. He is alderman, burgomaster and councillor in Westzaan, died after 14 June 1711, married 1st Unknown, married 2nd in Westzaan (church) 22 July 1674 to *Aeltje Jacobs*, young woman of Westzaandam. Purchased some land in the south of Westaan on 1 Nov.1685, together with the widow of his brother Jan, as well as the sawmill "Het Roode Hert", located on the Dijksloot in Westzaan, for the amount of ƒ 2300,-. These possessions are sold again on 13 Aug. 1693.

IXa. *Jacob Gerritsz. Banning*, lives in the Krabbelbuurt in Westzaan, smith, burial fees paid in Westzaan on 2 Nov.1722 (class ƒ 3,-), married there (church) on 19 August 1696 to *Jannetje Dirks IJff*, from the south end of Westzaan, baptized in Westzaan 11 May 1670, daughter of Dirck Jansz. IJff and Hillegont Jans. Purchases a house with a forge on 10 May 1708 in the Krabbelbuurt. Also owns a 1/3 share of a tan-mill in Westzaan, which he sells on 30 Oct.1722.

From this marriage:

1. *Jan Jacobsz. Banning*, burial fees paid in Westzaan on 12 Nov.1696
2. *Gerrit Jacobsz. Banning*, baptised in Westzaan on 6 Oct.1697 (witness Gleijntje Jans)

189

3. *Dirk Jacobsz. Banning*, baptised in Westzaan 25 Oct.1699 (witness Grietje Dirks), burial fees paid there on 25 Aug. 1705 (class *f* 3,-).
4. *Jan Jacobsz. Banning*, baptised in Westzaan on 3 Aug.1704 (witness Grietje Dirks), burial fees paid there on 24 Dec. 1705 (class *f* 3,-).
5. *Dirk Jacobsz. Banning*, follows X.

IXb. *Sijmon Gerritsz Banning*, alias *Boet*, lives in the Krabbelbuurt, baker[249], burial fees paid in Westzaan on 30 Oct.1734 (class *f* 15,-), marital fees paid there 3 Nov.1697 (class *f* 3,-), fees for marital banns paid in Assendelft 19 Oct.1697 to *Impje Davids*, came from Assendelft, burial fees paid there Westzaan on 21 July 1721 (class *f* 6,-), daughter of David Jacobsz. and Duijf Jans. This family is recorded in the genealogy of the Assendelft family Boet. Sijmon is specified there as a son of a certain Gerrit Jansz. Boet. From the baptismal and burial registers of Westzaan it appears evident that Sijmon belonged to the Banning family[250]. Sells 1/32nd share of the tan-mill "de Valck" on 12 Mar.1700 for 600 guilders 1/32 in Nauerna and on 1 Mar.1709 for 1100 guilders half of the oil press "de Pauw", located on the Twiskdijk near Nauerna. A deed of land transport dated 9 May 1715 in Assendelft indicates that he, together with Floris Kleijne, Pieter Kleijne and his brother-in-law Jacob Davitsz, were among the heirs of Griet Jans Kleijne.
From this marriage:
1. *Dieuwertje Sijmons Banning*, baptised in Westzaan on 21 Dec.1698 (witness Jannetje Dirks), burial fees paid there on 23-2-1699 (class *f* 3,-).
2. *Gerrit Sijmonsz. Banning*, baptised in Westzaan 11 Aug.1700, burial fees paid there on 7 June 1701 (class *f* 3,-)
3. *Dieuwertje Sijmons Banning*, alias *Boet*, baptised in Westzaan 27Apr.1702 (witness Jannetje Dirks), burial fees paid there on 26 Feb.1725 (class *f* 3,-), married in Westzaan 27 Mar.1723 to *David Jacobsz. Pel*, died after 3 Sept.1735.

---

[249] GAZ, ONA 5430, fol. 172, 4-5-1707
[250] GAZ, ONA 5857 A 1, 19-2-1718: Jacob Gerritsz Banning and Sijmon Gerritsz Boedt, nephews/cousins of the deceased Aegje Jans Banning on the father's side, each inherit *f* 4600,- to *f* 4800,-.

4. *Gerrit Sijmonsz. Banning*, baptized in Westzaan 31 Aug.1704 (witness Jannetje Dirks), burial fees paid there on 3 Mar. 1705 under the surname Boet (class *f* 3,-).

5. *Duijfje Sijmons Banning*, alias *Boet*, baptised in Westzaan 14 Mar.1706 (witness Gerrit Jansz), burial fees paid there on 7 July 1760 (class *f* 6,-), married there on 2 Oct.1729 to *Jan Jacobsz Nagtegaal*, from the south end of Westzaan, baptized in Westzaan 14 Dec.1701, burial fees paid there on 6 June 1780 (class *f* 30,-), son of Jacob Willemsz Nagtegaal and Anna Jans. The tombstone of Duijfje Banning and Jan Nagtegaal is located in the Reformed Church of Westzaan.

X. *Dirk Jacobsz. Banning*, baptised in Westzaan on 20 Nov.1707, lives in the Krabbelbuurt, merchant, owner of the mill *"De Banning"*, located to the east of 'de Reeff' across from the Krabbelbuurt, Alderman and Burgomaster of Westzaan, died there on 16 Mar.1771, burial fees paid there on 19 Mar.1771 (class *f* 6,-), married in Westzaan 27 Nov.1740 to *Neeltje Dirks Spat*, baptised in Westzaan 29 Mar.1711, burial fees paid there on 19 Aug.1766, daughter of Dirck Pietersz Spat and Neeltje Willems. Dirk Banning and Neeltje Spat drew up their will on 24 Febr.1766. This document indicates that Dirk is burgomaster of Westzaan[251]. Shortly after Dirk's death, the inheritance which he leaves to the children of Willem de Lange and (deceased) Jannetje Banning, his only daughter, are described on 13 Apr. 1771. This inheritance consists of a house and property in the Krabbelbuurt to the west of the road, five tracts of land, a snuff or tobacco mill behind the house on 'de Reeff', a house which is rented to Dirk Kuiper, and a share in the bluing mill. The document then describes the extensive contents.

From this marriage:

1. *Jannetje Dirks Banning*, baptised in Westzaan 23 May 1742, burial fees paid there on 9 Dec.1769 (class *f* 3,-), married in Westzaan 20 May1764 to *Willem de Lange*, baptized in Westzaan on 7 Nov.1742, burial fees paid there on 6 Dec. 1797 (class *f* 3,-), son of Cornelis Willemsz. de Lange and Maartje Paulus Schaap. Willem remarried on 27 Dec.1772 to *Claartje Riedes*.

2. *Neeltje Dirks Banning*, baptised in Westzaan 16 June 1743, burial fees paid there on 29 Sept. 1744 (class *f* 6,-).

---

[251] GAZ, ONA 5453, fol. 1039, 24-2-1766

3. *Jacob Dirksz. Banning*, baptised in Westzaan on 16 June 1743, burial fees paid there on 18 Dec. 1744 (class ƒ 6,-).
4. *Jacob Dirksz. Banning*, baptized in Westzaan 14 Nov.1745, burial fees paid there on 29 May 1748 (class ƒ 6,-).
5. *Stillborn child*, burial fees paid in Westzaan on 1 July 1757.
6. *Stillborn child*, burial fees paid in Westzaan on 5 June 1758

With thanks to Mr. L. Muts for providing access to the oldest records of land transport of Assendelft and to the personnel of the archives in Alkmaar and Koog aan de Zaan for their patience and advice.

Notes:
Abbreviations:
GAZ=Gemeentearchief Zaanstad [Zaanstad Municipal Archives],
SAW=Streekarchief Waterland [Waterland Regional Archives],
AvK=Archiefdienst voor Kennemerland [Archive Service for Kennemerland]
GAA=Gemeentearchief Amsterdam [Amsterdam Municipal Archives] ,
RAH=Rijksarchief Haarlem [Haarlem National Archives]

Although there is a possible relation between the Amsterdam Bannings and the influential Banning family in the Hague, this has not yet been verified. If so, the Hague Bannings most likely descended from:

(Matthijs Banning, Jansz., born 1482, died before 1526, mentioned in the Amsterdam genealogy as G2.E. IV.1)

ADRIAAN MATHIJSZ. BANNING, born 1512, Clerk in The Hague; Clerk of Secretary Plumeon; 1543, substitute of his secretary; 1551-1574 Secretary; 1558-1559 Substitute of the Bailiff; 1575 Rentmeester of the Sacraments-Guild House. Died in the Hague 27 October 1589, buried there in the Groote- or St. Jacobskerk. Married Aleud Plumeon (or Plumius), died in the Hague 27 Feb. 1590, buried there in the Groote- or St. Jacobskerk, daughter of Secretary Plumeon, mentioned above. From this marriage:

I MATHYS BANNING, Secretary of the Hague, died there 6 May 1612, buried in the Hague, Groote or St. Jacobskerk. Married Aleyd Jansdr. van Kuyl, died the Hague 6 Nov. 1627 and buried there in the Groote- or St. Jacobschurch. From this marriage:
  1. Willem Matthijsz. follows III
  2. Hendrick Banning, Matthijsz. (youngest son)

II WILLEM MATTHIJSZ. BANNING, born Delft 15 Oct. 1573. Notary in Rijnsberg (South Holland). Admitted to the Hague 10 March 1598. The protocols of "Notary Willem Benninck" are kept in the Royal Archives in the Hague. Charters for 1618, 1622 and 1628 – April 1629 are largely kept in Leiden, those from January 1629-September 1633 in Katwijk and in other neighbouring townships; Substitute Secretary of the Hague, died Sunday 31 Oct. 1655 (plague), married in Leiden in the Hooglandsche Church on Tuesday 3 Feb. 1604 to Maritghen van Thorenclyet, Willemsdr., born in Leiden on 20 May 1578, died 2 June 1654. Daughter of Willem van Thorenvlyet Pouwelsz., and Pietergen Nachtegael Jansdr. From this marriage:
  1. Matthijs, follows IV

IV   MATTHIJS BANNING, born Amsterdam Friday 9 Oct.1609,
        and baptized there in the New Church 25 October,1609, Notary
        of Leiden 1636-1669, died in Leiden 6 Jan. 1670, buried
        in the Hooglandsche Church. Married 1st in Leiden in the
        Hooglandsche Church on 29 Jan. 1636 to Cornelia van Oy, born
        in Leiden on 2 December. 1613, died there on 6 May 1658,
        daughter of Willem and Eva van de Boechorts; married 2nd in
        Wassenaar, 16 Mar. 1659 to Magdalena Doude, widower of
        Hermanus Piso. She died in Leiden 15 Oct. 1669 and was buried
        in the Hooglandsche Church.
        From the first marriage:
        1.   Willem Banning, born in Leiden on Tuesday 21 Oct. 1636,
             baptized in the Hooglandsche Church on 23 Oct. 1636. He
             died while taking the baths at Bordeaux (France) and is
             buried there in a "religious" cemetery.
        2.   Maria Banning, born in Leiden on Friday 25 Aug. 1651,
             baptized there on 29 Aug. 1651 in the Hooglandsche
             Church, married in Zoeterwoude 18 Mar. 1670 to Mattheus
             de Haes, born in Amsterdam 19 Feb. 1635, died there on 16
             Nov. 1704, buried in the Oude Zijds Chapel 21 Nov. 1704,
             son of Artus de Haes.
        Also belonging to this family are:
                JAN WILLEM BANNING, married Machteld Booth,
                born 1579, daughter of Mr. Christoffel Booth and
                Margaretha van Teylingen from Alkmaar,
                There were three children from this marriage.

                    *   *   *

7   VAN BANNING

Of all the variations on the name Banning, Van Banning is one which cannot be overlooked. There are diverse reasons[252] to assume that this family is directly related to those earlier described, but definite proof is as yet lacking. The author of the Dutch Banning genealogy published in 1934 was able to ascertain that the prefix 'van' was added to the name around 1750. The genealogy included in his book comprises eight generations, from 1757-1921, whose members were Catholic. The genealogy commences in 1757, in Amsterdam, and closes in 1921, in the Hague. Several of those specified occur in various archives both as 'Van Banning' and as 'Banning'. 'Van' means 'of', and consequently the name means 'of Banning'. Several members of this family held positions of note.

Joannes (Jan) van Banning *(G2.II.2)* was the most well known. He was born and baptised in Amsterdam 16 Nov. 1766, and invested as a Roman Catholic priest on 19 March 1791. He was Chaplain of Middelburg from 1791-1800, Professor of Theology at the Seminary in Warmond from 1800-1807, Pastor of Zoeterwoude from 1808 until his death in 1840, Provisor in Warmond from 1816-1819, Deacon of Rijnland from 1816, and coadjutor of Monsignor J.J. Cramer from 1818-1824 and, following his death,, Archpriest of Holland, Zeeland and West-Friesland 1824-1831. In the interests of national history, Joannes van Banning compiled *Necrologus virorum ecclesiaticorum utriusque cleri tum saecularis tum regularis, qui in Missione Batava defuncti sunt ab anno Domini 1730 ad annum 1830 toto hoc centum annorum spatio,* which was published in Leiden in 1833. On the request of his vice-superior he wrote *Elenchus pastorum saecularium districtus Hollandiae Zeelandize et Westfrisiae etc.*, in which he descriptively elucidates priests living in these areas at the time, their ages, their calling, knowledge, lifestyle and moral behaviour. Van Banning invested considerable time and energy in expanding on the *Liber Status Missionis,* a folio listing the pastors of the Staties of the bishopric of Haarlem who had founded and led the bishopric since the Reformation. Both of these last documents are held in the old archives of the bishopric in Haarlem. Joannes van Banning was also the author of *Considerationes super panem et vinum, quatenus sunt divini sacrificii missae material essentialis, auctore sacerdote catholico,* published in Rotterdam in 1839.

Joannes van Banning's extensive correspondance with various ecclesiastical institutions and other influential priests survives, largely in Latin, and provides great insight into ecclesiastical issues of that time, as

---

[252] J.A.W. Banning, *Genealogie van het Geslacht Banning*, Ferd. Banning & Zonen, Groenlo, 1934, p. 189

well as those involved in its pursuit. He died in Zoeterwoude on 14 June 1840, where his grave is still marked and a street – the Jan van Banningstraat – is named in his honour.

Theodorus Lucianus Johannes van Banning *(G2.VI)* was born in Halsteren or Tholen 21 Aug. 1857. He was Chief Councillor of the township of Rotterdam, member of the Committee for the Assessment of Customs Duties, member of the Committee for preparation of the Pawn Shop Law, Honorary Chairman of the Royal Harmony Corps of Maastricht. He died in Utrecht 25 June 1933.

Johan Petrus Dorothée van Banning, *(G2.VI.1)* the only son of Theodorus, above, was born in Rotterdam 1 April 1906. He acquired his Masters degree in geography in Sept. 1934 at the University of Utrecht, · also having studied history and later acquiring a doctorate of law. J.P.D. van Banning was a board member of the Royal Association *Het Nederlandse Lied* and a member of the Provincial States of the Netherlands. He was mayor of the township of Gennep and subsequently of Schaesberg in the southern Dutch province of Limburg until 1951, assuming office as mayor of Geleen until his retirement in 1971, also assuming temporarily the office of Mayor of Spaubeek in 1970.

JPD, as he came to be called, was a colourful and highly esteemed figurehead in his community, known for his dedication, his stern but just leadership and fondly but respectfully for a somewhat rigid enforcement of principles concerning the strict division of private and professional issues. In private life he was frequently seen riding an old bicycle without a chain guard or walking with rapid strides in trousers too short, heedless of his attire. In his professional capacity he often appeared at festive occasions wearing a dashing uniform and tricorne, proud to represent his office in style and earning, in more ways than one, the epithet of 'Magistrate'. He never allowed a clerk to take his personal correspondence to the post office with official pieces, but walked to the post office himself. He declined residence in the home provided by the municipality and sought his own for his family. He refused to ride in the municipal limousine for personal trips and was even rumoured to have carried two pens in his pocket – one for personal use and one for business use.

Under JPD's benevolent authority, Geleen grew from a population of 22,000 with 4,000 homes in 1951, to a population of 37,000 with 14,800 homes in 1971. He was dedicated to the establishment of schools and sports facilities, development of housing, the road infrastructure and a new shopping mall. He instigated numerous projects, such as the 'front garden competition' in 1956, which still survives today.

This was to promote cooperation between the township and residents and encouraged residents to make the most of their gardens and home fronting.

59. J.P.D. van Banning delivering a speech on the occasion of his investiture as Mayor of Geleen in 1951, in uniform and with the famed tricorne on the table in front of him.
Collection: Muncipal Archives Sittard-Geleen, Netherlands

Although JPD could be rigid in policy, he was notably lenient when those of lesser fortune required aid, such as families in need of housing or when, as mayor of Gennep, he became aware of the smuggling of Jews to safety during the war, an enterprise which officially he could not condone and for which he was reprimanded. Between 1936 and 1986 JPD wrote six books; five on the Dutch royal family - their genealogies, history and the position of the monarchy - and his last on the presidents of the United States. This book was to be presented at a public celebration of his 80th birthday but unfortunately he did not live to see this occasion. After a life characterized by enormous activity and enthusiasm, he died in February 1986. His last words were: "I am tired, I am going to sleep." He was admired and remembered even 15 years after having retired. The town council held a memorial reception in his honour later that year., where he was lauded and commemorated for his enormous and valued contributions, and the Van Banninglaan in Geleen was named after him.

Nicholaas Elisabeth Maria van Banning (G2.VIbis) was a brother to Theodorus, above, and born 16 Oct. 1858. He was Chief Councillor of the administration for the Dutch Railway and a member of the Municipal Council of Maastricht, where he died 18 May 1927.

Alphonse Claus van Banning is mentioned in the last generation of this family in the genealogy. He was born on 18 Sept 1912 in the Hague. When he died in Toronto, Canada, on 29 May 2002 at the age of 89, he was lauded as a hero of the Dutch Resistance and diplomat.[253] He was decorated as a Knight in the order of Oranje Nassau, War Cross with Bar, Resistance Cross, Distinguished Service medal of the Netherlands Red Cross, 'Nacht und Nebel' cross and La Croix du Combattant de l'Europe. He often joked that being the seventh child of eleven made him lucky and special.

60. Alphonse Claus van Banning
The Globe and Mail, 29 May 2002, Toronto

His boyhood was not unusual, growing up to be a middle-ranking civil servant. However, when Germany occupied the Netherlands in May 1940, he organised his own resistance group. He was arrested twice and released. The third time, his luck ran out and he was condemned under Hitler's 'Nacht und Nebel'('night and fog') decree, a sentence intended to be worse than death, since it's object was to make people simply disappear, no information being given whatsoever to their families concerning their fate, their whereabouts, or place of burial. Alphonse was sent to the concentration camps Natzweiler and later to Dachau. He survived only due to determination and luck. He developed an immunity to the dysentery which killed many of his fellow inmates, nursing the other prisoners. General G.S. Patton's[254] forces liberated the camp in April 1945 and Alphonse immediately registered to work with the International Tracing Service, collecting concentration camp documents in order to inform surviving family members what had happened to their loved ones.

Alphonse entered the Netherlands diplomatic service, acting as personal emissary for the Dutch Queen Wilhelmina. The family was posted to Australia, Rhodesia, Nyasaland and Brazil. His final posting was to Toronto, where he served the Dutch Canadian community for twelve years. In 1967 he organized the tour of southern Ontario for the

[253] *Toronto Globe and Mail*, Wed. May 29 2002, 'Lives Lived'
[254] General G.S. Patton was himself married to a Banning, Beatrice Banning Ayer of California.

198

Dutch Queen Juliana. He helped to spearhead the first 'Thank you Canada, We Do Remember' trips for Canadian veterans of the liberation, in honour of the veterans' contribution. Alphonse was also a founding executive member of the Netherlands Association of Ex-Political Prisoners, a group established to defend the rights of those who resisted the Nazi's, which honoured him at its 50th anniversary in the Hague. He was remembered as a man of exceptional courage, courtesy, charm and humour.

Although only a handful of Van Banning's are mentioned in history and there are relatively few of them, there are surprisingly many active today in politics, science and other fields of endeavour.

*   *   *

The Bannings and Coats-of-arms

There are probably more misconceptions about coats-of-arms in general than there are Banning coats-of-arms. Very few coats-of-arms existed before the 11th century and most came into existence after the 12th century. The status of coats-of-arms in early periods is described by Fox-Davies in *A Complete Guide to Heraldry*, where he writes that arms, and the right to them, developed in Great Britain as an adjunct of, or contemporaneously with, the extension of the feudal system.

"Every landowner was at one time required to have his seal – presumably, of arms - and as a result arms were naturally then considered to possess something of a territorial character." The arms were ascribed to a given family, "originating because that family held land and accepted the consequent responsibilities thereto belonging"[255].

Having the same name as that under which a coat-of-arms is registered does not give a person the right to bear that coat-of-arms. Although legislation per country may differ, in the Netherlands it is by law not permitted to use a coat-of-arms registered to any living family by anyone outside of that family or even to those within the same family unless they can prove to be a direct descendant of the person to whom the arms were originally granted. Many people have them framed as a keepsake or tucked into the family album. Unless one were to charge into battle with family arms emblazoned on a shield or standard, or use them for commercial purposes, there is hardly ground for prosecution, nor is it likely that anyone would take offense, let alone legal action. The reproduction of coats-of-arms and their sale has thus become a lucrative, widespread commercial and often misleading enterprise.

Officially, a coat-of-arms was registered for one person, and could be borne by that person and his direct descendants. Especially in Great Britain, the position of the descendant within the family was often clearly designated in the coat-of-arms with a mark of cadency. Simply stated, these marks of cadency registered the descent of related families, the distinction between the members of a family according to their age, thus indicating whether the bearer was an older or younger son or a descendant of an older or younger son.

The earliest marks of cadency date back far beyond other regularized methods applicable to younger sons.

The head of the family and the heir (oldest son) were the most important. When the father died, the heir dropped the mark of cadency and assumed the arms of his father. Until then, the position of heir, first

---

[255] Arthur Charles Fox-Davies, *Complete Guide to Heraldry*, T.C. & E.C. Jack, London/Edinburgh, 1909 p. 478

son, was designated by a 'label' of three points. A second son was represented by a crescent in the arms. Following this line, a crescent on a crescent, for example, meant a second son of a second son. The sign for a third son was a mullet, for the fourth son a martlet, for the fifth an annulet, for the sixth a fleur-de-lis, for the seventh son a rose, for the eighth son a cross Moline and for the ninth son a double quatrefoil.

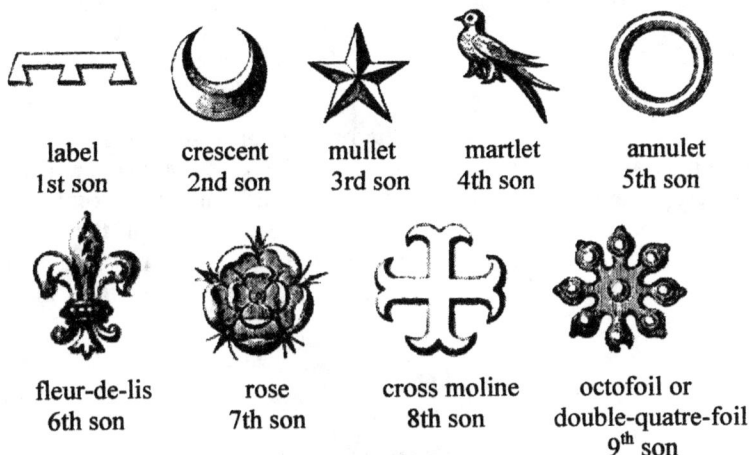

label	crescent	mullet	martlet	annulet
1st son	2nd son	3rd son	4th son	5th son

fleur-de-lis	rose	cross moline	octofoil or
6th son	7th son	8th son	double-quatre-foil
			9th son

61. Marks of Cadency [256]

Regarding the first six marks, John Bossewell in *Workes of Armorie* (1572) states: "If there be any more than six brethren the devise or assignment of further difference only appertaineth to the kingis of armes especially when they visite their severall provinces; and not to the father of the children to give them what difference he list, as some without authoritie doe allege[257]." Which means that only the king could use the seventh, eighth and ninth marks – the rose, cross Moline or double quatrefoil for his male offspring.

There are several official coats-of-arms once used by the various branches of the Banning family. The mullet, mark of a third son, was featured on the coat-of-arms – a cross Moline - used by Jan Gerritsz. Banning as seen on the painting of *The Church of the Nativity at Bethlehem* (see section on Amsterdam); Jan Gerritsz. Banning was indeed the third son of Gerrit. The most common feature in the Banning coat-of-arms is the cross Moline.

[256] Hugh Clark, *An Introduction to Heraldry*, Bell & Dandy, London, 1873, plate XLII, page 42
[257] Arthur Charles Fox-Davies, *Complete Guide to Heraldry*, T.C. & E.C. Jack, London/Edinburgh, 1909, p. 489

62 Coin struck under Stephen of Blois, King of England in 1135[258]	63 Cross Moline on a shield (Banning coat of arms)	64 Seal of Jan. Jansz Benningh, 1530 (Municipal Archives of Amsterdam)	65 Dutch Commandery of Harderwijk, 1570[259]

The symbolism of this cross is 'the mutual converse of human society' (said to represent a millstone or millrind). The cross Moline, or anchored cross, appeared frequently on French coins early in the 12th century and, amongst others, was used by the Crusader States in the 12th-15th centuries[260]. How and when it came to be used by the Bannings is unknown, although the earliest registered example dates from the 14th century.

Earliest known Banning coat-of-arms
rendered in blue and gold; 14th century

---

[258] courtesy of Marshall Faintich, Ph.D.

[259] Reverend Robert de Caluwé. *Guide Notes on Heraldry of the Sovereign Order of Saint John of Jerusalem Knights Hospitaller* , OSJ, Belgium, 2000, Illustration 344, page 41, from History of the Maltese Cross as used by the Order of St. John of Jerusalem, Dr. Michael Foster, http://www2.prestel.co.uk/church/oosj/cross.htm; accessed Apr. 2003

[260] History of the Maltese Cross as used by the Order of St. John of Jerusalem, Dr. Michael Foster, http://www2.prestel.co.uk/church/oosj/cross.htm; accessed Apr. 2003

The cross Moline in the Banning coats-of-arms is almost always blue, or azure, on a gold background. The names, as discussed in the introduction, have several different spellings. They are rendered here as found in the original source.

Dirk Symonsz. Benning, bailiff of Amsterdam, 1393-1395
(Nat. Bureau of Heraldry, the Hague, NL)

Willem Harmensz. Benning cheese merchant and alderman 1618-1625, Schiedam, NL
(Nat. Bureau of Heraldry, the Hague, NL)

Gerrit Banninck , alderman 1461 Amsterdam,; Jan Banning, alderman 1471; Gaeff Banning, alderman 1473 Jan Gerritsz. Banning, alderman 1474 Cornelis Gerritsz. Banning, alderman 1518, burgomaster 1534; 'Ýoung' Jan Banning, Captain of the Civic Militia 1523: Amsterdam
(Nat. Bureau of Heraldry, the Hague, NL)

Benning, Hamburg, Germany undated
(Nat. Bureau of Heraldry, the Hague, NL)

Banning of Gendringen / Ulft,
Netherlands
(Nat. Bureau of Heraldry, the Hague, NL)

Frans Banninck Cocq 1581
Burgomaster of Amsterdam,
Captain of the Civic Militia
(Nat. Bureau of Heraldry.,
the Hague,NL)

Banning / Bannyng / Bayning
Sir Paul   Bayning, Sheriff of
Essex, Baron of Horkesley,
1st Viscount of Sudbury 1617
(Banning and Allied families;
American Historical Society)

Paul and Andrew Bayninge[261]
Aldermen of London
detail from their grave monument
in St. Olave's Church, London
(photo courtesy Stephen Millar, London)

---

[261] The coat-of-arms features a black raven, which is likely from the family of Anne Raven, their paternal grandmother. The mullet above the raven may or may not indicate that Anne's father was a third son. The escallops featured in the other quarters are most likely from the Barker arms, which consisted of five escallops. (Anne Barker was their mother.)

Benning(h), Banning, Banninck, Bennynck
Jacob Benning(h), and (2nd) his son, Jacob Jacobsz. Benning(h). The first two
are registered in Amsterdam, also for Jan Banning, alderman 1563-1565,
and (2nd) Cornelis Benninck 1568, Amsterdam, the third in Haarlem. This Jacob
Banning used the coat-of-arms belonging to his father's family, Lakeman/
Fabricius, although Jacob retained his mother's name of Banning.
(National Bureau of Heraldry, the Hague, Netherlands)

Banning
(place not specified)
(Rietstap, 1903)

Benning or Banning
Amsterdam
(Rietstap, 1903)

Benning (Swedish)
Waldeck, Hesse (Ger.)
(Rietstap, 1903)

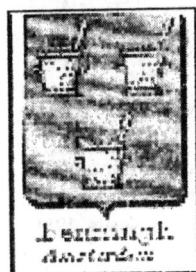

Benningh
Amsterdam
(Rietstap, 1903)

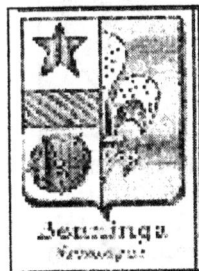

Benninga,
Groningen, Netherlands
(Rietstap, 1903)

Banninck, Zelhem
1728
(Nat. Bureau of Heraldry,
the Hague, NL)

Cornelis Banning Jansz.
Duvensz.,Burgomaster of
Amsterdam, 1600
(Nat. Bureau of Heraldry,
the Hague, NL)

Emerentia Banning,
Leiden, NL. 1643
(Nat. Bureau of Heraldry,
the Hague, NL)

Banningh (undated)
(Nat. Bureau of Heraldry,
the Hague, NL)

Frisian coat-of-arms
attributed to Bannings
of Friesland, NL ;
ca. 1850 (origin unknown;
private collection)

Coat-of-arms used by
Bernard Banninck of
Zutphen, NL 1714
(Nat. Bureau of Heraldry
the Hague,NL)

Lady Anna Benning or
Bannincx, sister to
Emerentia, married to the
nobleman J. van Cuyck van
Mierop, 1688, the Hague
(Nat. Bureau of Heraldry,
the Hague, NL)

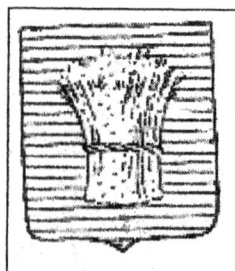

Dieuwertje (Deborah)
Jacobsdr. Banning
Amsterdam (+/-1560)
possibly also Gerrit
Benningh, (Benninck)
carved on his gravestone
in the Reformed church in
Coevorden, 1636 (now
indiscernible) (Nat. Bureau
of Heraldry, the Hague, NL)

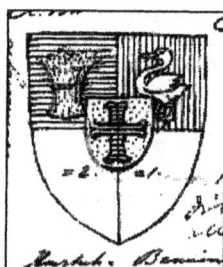

Benninck/Banninck
Banning. Benning
Jacob Banning, 1526
alderman, Amsterdam
Frans Benningh,
alderman Amsterdam 1579,
1581/2, Capt. of the Civic
Militia 1580

Weyn Banningh,
Groenlo, NL
(Gens Nostra, 1951)

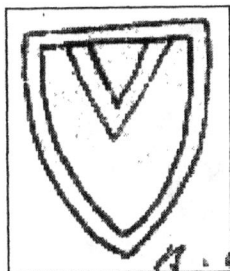

Sketch of coat-of-arms for Arnold(us) Banninck, alderman of Zutphen,NL 1343-1359 (that of his wife's family, Aleydis van Voorst) (Nat. Bureau of Heraldry, the Hague, NL)

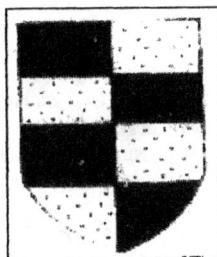

Banninck, Utrecht, NL undated
(Nat. Bureau of Heraldry, the Hague,NL)

Banning, Prov. of Gelderland Netherlands
(Gens Nostra, 1953)

SEALS

Zegel van schout Jan Benningh Jansz
Top. Coll. Arm dd 4.3.1504
Foto: Gemeentearchief Amsterdam

66. Seal of Jan Jansz. Benningh 1504, Municipal Archives of Amsterdam

Zegel van schepen Frans Banninck
Top. Coll. O.Z. Burgwal dd 26.4.1581
Foto: Gemeentearchief Amsterdam

67. Seal of Frans Banninck Cocq, 1581, Municipal Archives of Amsterdam

68. Seal of Garbrant Claesz. Banning, ca. 1475, bailiff of Assendelft, NL
Archiefdienst voor Kennemerland, Haarlem

207

Mark of identity used by
Garbrant Claesz. Banning
Amsterdam, 1569
(Nat. Bureau of Heraldry, the Hague, NL)

From the archives of the family Huydecoper, register 67, in Utrecht, Netherlands. Inv 295: lists of names and coats-of-arms of the Amsterdam aldermen from the 14th to the 17th century.

The triangular signs on the left and right of the first and second illustrations were marks of identity used by one individual and recognized as such.

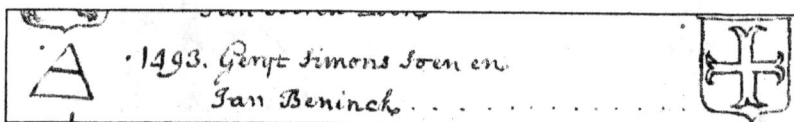

Sign of Gerrit Simonsz. and arms of Jan Beninck 1493

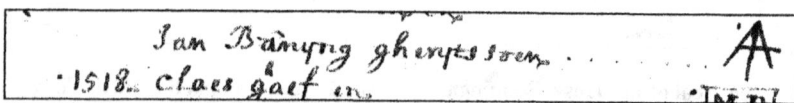

Sign of Jan Gerritsz. Banyng and Claes Gaef Banning 1518

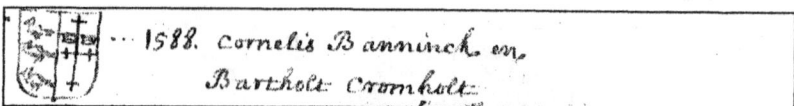

Coat-of-arms of Cornelis Banning and Bartholomeus Cromhout 1588

9   MEDIEVAL HOMESTEADS IN THE NETHERLANDS
(AND GERMANY)

Early records reveal some 40 properties in the eastern provinces of the Netherlands (and a few just over the border in Germany) between 933 AD and 1500 AD known by the name Banning and Benning, or derivatives thereof, some of which still exist today.

In most cases, such homesteads originally acquired their names from the owner, particularly to the north of the Ijssel River. When new tenants moved into a homestead, they often adopted the name of the homestead, and in this way numerous families who were not originally Bannings by birth came to be known by that name, as did their descendants, particularly in the 18th century. This has proven greatly confusing for genealogists.

Typical of the times, the spellings vary considerably, often in one and the same document, one and the same family, but in most cases are said to have derived either from Banning or the most common variant, Benning. Not only the spelling of Banning varies considerably, but also of a great number of place-names, homesteads and families mentioned in early feudal documents. All spellings are given here as in the original context. (Note: some homesteads may occur more than once under different spellings, but whether they are the same is unknown.)

On several occasions Bannings were long-term tenants on these landholdings. The first-known instigator of the Amsterdam magistrate family of Banning is said to be Gerrit Banning from the homestead 'de Banninck' of Colmschate near Deventer. Although Gerrit's origin has yet to be verified, there were indeed tenants by that name residing in 'de Banninck' in the 14th century to whom he could have been related. From the 16th to the early 18th century families of other names resided there, until in 1730 a builder, Harmen Harmsen Siemelink, married Egberdina Henriks Bannink, whereupon he moved into the Bannink and took the name of his homestead and/or that of his wife. His descendants, named Bannink, (of whom the genealogy is recorded) live there to this day.

The terms 'Kamp' and 'Esch' are occasionally used with reference to the homesteads. This was a very old division of land derived from 'Reebnings procedure' where land was apportioned in equal shares to the inhabitants. This method lasted longer in the north of Germany and Denmark, based on a Burgundian law and division of land amongst the Saxons. "The arable land was at first divided into separate fields (ager)called in German 'Wang', 'Kamp', 'Gewanne', or 'Esch'. This field was surrounded by a wooden fence or by a ditch, in the construction of which all were bound to assist. The chief of the village summoned all the inhabitants for this purpose, at certain fixed periods, and the work was the occasion for a public holiday. This practice was preserved up to a little over a century ago in the Dutch province of Drenthe and in Westphalia. There we find the Eschen distinctly marked out in the midst of the heath; as masses of offal are being constantly brought from the stables to manure it, the earth is raised several yards."[262]

The following homesteads are mentioned in historical documents. Where possible, they are presented in context, together with all relevant information found in the various archives, worded as in the original.

BANINGI[263] year: 933-966 place: Beuningen/Benningen (near Oldenzaal)

- Deeds and Charters of the Bishopric of Utrecht[264]/also the Charter of Grimheri in Eluiteri (Oldenzaal in Overijssel): "List of revenues from the abbey at Werden from estates in [the province of] Twente: "In *Baningi* Berhtgot VIII mo. de sigilo et III amphoras mellis et heriscilling XVI den. et herimalder II mo. et IIII avene." : (text is Latin and Germanic, referring to dues for feudal land): "In (the fief of) *Baningi*, Berthgot (has to pay to his lord) eight measures of grain and three amphorae of honey and 16 denarii herscilling (a war tax to be paid in denarios/coins) and two measures of herimalder (war tax in natural goods) and four of oats."

BANNING(E)HUS[265] house year 1298-1304 place: Uffelte
The oldest mention of Banning on record in the Netherlands is that of a Banning(e)house/ manor in the march of Uffelte, dated 1298-1304.

BANNING/BANNINCK/BANNINKSKAMP/KLEIN BANNINK[266] year: 1294   place: Zutphen, Bekveld, Hengelo, Zelhem
1294: The first person on record in the Netherlands, to date, is Arnoldus *Banninck*, alderman in Zutphen in 1294, and Arnoldus, (his son?), alderman from 1343-1358. The Bannings belonged to the prominent Zutphen families in the 14th century, according to a list published in the *Nederlandse Leeuw* of 1935: *Zutphen family names of prominence in 1390*. On the 13th line we find the specification "Reynoldum *Banninc* et eius uxorem."[267]. Other Bannings recorded in Zutphen, besides the three who were aldermen: Mechtelt Banninx, 1387, wife of Hendrick Vogel,

[262] Emile De Laveleye, T. E. Cliffe Leslie and G. R. L. Marriott, *Primitive Property*, 1878
[263] Dr. B.H. Slicher van Bath, *Mensch en Land in de Middeleeuwen*, Part I, Assen, Van Gorcum & Comp. N.V.,1944, p. 207
[264] Dr. Mr. S. Muller , Dr. A.C. Bouman., *Oorkondeboek van het Sticht Utrecht tot 1301*, Utrecht, A. Oosthoek, 1920, p. 104
[265] *Nomina Geographica Neerlandica*, Koninklijke Nederlandse Aardrijkskundige Gen., 1899,part V/B.J. Hekket, *Oost Nederlandse Familienamen*, Hengelo, 1983, p. 53
[266] *Zutphense Leengoederen* (Verpondingskahier 1650)
[267] J.B. Rietstap, *Heraldische Bibliotheek*, 1875, p. 35

Jacobsz..[268], Egbert Banninc's widow Aleijt in 1361, Johan Bannync's children in 1381, Lubbert Banninck in 1388, Reinier Bannink in 1390, Evert Banninck in 1400, Johan Banninck in 1434, Warner Banninck in 1457[269].

1405: Henrich Banningh, property transfer.[270]

9 Dec. 1437:[271] Arnolt Duke of Gelre released the property *Banninck* in the parish of Hengell from feudality and deems it hereditary property. Written receipt no. 416 presented by Anthonius Bannynck.[272]

20 Nov. 1476: Zutphen feudal rights: Bernt Wullinck received that property called Wullinck,in the parish of Zelem,in the hamlet of Zuerloe, with on one side Hakinck, and on the other *Banninck* homestead.

13 Dec. 1538: That property *Banninck* with all its appurtenances, located in the parish of Hengel, inherited by Zutphen rights Frans Kreyinck for his daughter Gertrud Kreyinx, widow of Johans van der Leeuwe, and to Herman Berner, 13 Aug. 1528.

69. Map fragment of Gelderland, illustrating the homesteads
'Bannink' and 'Kleine Bannink'
source : Historische Atlas Gelderland, Robas, Weesp, 1989

---

[268] *Register op de leenaktenboeken van het Vorstendom Gelre en Gro. Sche. Zutphen* (aldermen of Zutphen), article 7, no. 127, p. 420
[269] List IV: Aldermen's families, Zutphen, p. 261
[270] *Register op de Leenaktenboeken van het Vorstendom Gelre en Graafschap Zutphen,* 1917, article 8, no. 16, p. 35
[271] Jkr. Martens van Sevenhoven, *Archief der Geldersche Rekenkamer,* parts I & II, R 121
[272] Jkr. Martens van Sevenhoven, *Archief der Geldersche Rekenkamer,* parts I & II, inv. no. 416, enclosure 49

1 Nov. 1542: Henrick van der Lew, heir of his mother Gertrud, receives that property *Banninck*, located in the parish of Hengel, in the hamlet of Nortwyck, under Zutphen rights with one pound, 1 Nov. 1542.

4 Dec. 1550: tract of land split off from 98.99 Hengelo: The Langencamp with the small camp, so that that bordering on the Tackencamp, concerning 8 millseed lands, located in the Goischen fields, 4 between the homestead of Ellerdinck and *Banninck*, the other 4 on the opposite side of the road, with one stretching to Hoenkinck on the High way, divided off from the property of Bruynrinck and allocated by Zutphen rights to Johan van Seyst on behalf of Lijsbet Horstin, housewyfe of Arnt Obekinx, who transferred it to Gertrud, widow of Martins Quaden, 4 Dec. 1550.

There were numerous Bannings, most frequently Bannink, in the Eastern provinces of the Netherlands who took their name from the homestead they inhabited, most appearing for the first time in the 17th and 18th centuries. They were not always upstanding citizens: some seem to have been black sheep in the family and were recorded for their dubious conduct.

In September 1621 Jan Banninck, probably of Hengelo, died of shotgun wounds inflicted during a gunfight following a sojourn in the pub. The row occurred in a pub near the church, during and after the church service, and between boisterous rounds of refreshment the participants announced 'that they really should attend part of the service'. The row concerned the wife of one party, to whom Gerlich Banninck claimed to be betrothed. There were threats with knives and the Banninck brothers from Hengelo frequently fired rounds outside. Although they parted without further mishap, they had the misfortune to encounter each other on a bridge over the Hoijbeke. Tempers flared and more shots were fired, whereby one Lubbert Fruisinck and the tailor Henrick van Brummen, a companion of the Banninncks, were killed. Jan Banninck died the following night. Gerlich Banninck was seriously wounded in the face but survived. One Gerlich Banninck (most likely another, as the first would be either too old, or deceased) is mentioned as giving testimony in a trial in 1708 whereby accounts were recited of the bad reputation of the Banninck family, recalling that Jan Banninck sr., had an uncle Geerlich who had deserted his wife and children. Another brother, Arent Banninck (called Hog Arent because he had once stolen and slaughtered a pig and hidden the meat) also had a brother called 'Buckwheat Dries', a very roguish gentleman who had also once been flogged. There are numerous other incidences cited, such as the theft and destruction of the Judge's beehives, beating of their own womenfolk , false testimony and threats made to others. A descendant, also Jan Banninck, was imprisoned in Zutphen in 1707.[272]

---

[272] *Scholtambt Zutphen/Breukenboek* (inventory 0216, no. 16 ,81) *and Kondschappen van het Richterambt Hengelo*, archives Landdrostambt Zutphen, inventory 0217, (no. 897)

13 Oct. 1632: Aeltgen Mockincks requested her son Gerrit Hunteler to renew his pledge on half of the property of *Banninck*, 13 Oct.1632.

1650: land tax registers of Zutphen feudal lands: (the feudal lands were instigated in 1255). Weppeke (in Bekveld, Hengelo, once called Widapa [forest creek] and later Wideplo) lay on the Dunsborger Laak across from the *Banninkskamp*, which made up part of the property *Klein Bannink*, since divided. It bordered on the home camp of the Fokking farm. The Weppelerbeek or Dunsborger Laak flowed along the north and west boundary of the *Banninkskamp*.

1528: Kleijne Bannink [Small Bannink]in BEKVELD

Bannink, feudal property of Zutphen in Noortwijk, tenant Gerrit Hunteler in 1636 and the Brotherhood of Anthony in 1683.

70. Map of homesteads in Gelderland, showing the 'Banninkstraate' (street), the homesteads 'Groot Bannink', and 'Klein Bannink' (the polder) and the 'Banninkskolk' (gully)

source: Boerderij- en Veldnamenonderzoek van Hengelo(G), Staring Instituut, Doetinchem, 1988

1594: Hendrick Lamberts has a certain letter of commission approved for a third portion of the property *Banninck*, 1594 June 27/July 7).

1629: Margaretha Herdincks on behalf of Henrick Lamberts., her son Henrick Herdinck is holder, 1608 October 1. Heylgeji Herdincks, daughter of the deceased Henrick Herdinck (and Heylgen Hoefmans); Bernt Keynders, her uncle is holder, 1626 March 21.The division of goods of 4 March, drawn up on the death of Grietgen, sister of Heylgen Herdincks, whereby Henrick *Banninck* and his wife Geertgen Bernts., grandmother of Heylgen and Grietgen mentioned above, decide to forego their rights to the property in favour of Heylgen; was approved 1629 July The genealogy of Henrick Bannink, Hunteler and Jordens, is recorded.)

1645: Mention of one Derck Banninck, churchmaster, on the homestead Groot Banninck in Bekveld. Since he was also known as Derck Fockinck, and Derck Fockinck Banninck, it is not unlikely that he took the name Banninck from the homestead. His sons Jan and Berend are known by the name Bannin(c)k. The family purchased house and property on Klein Bannink in 1642.

GROTE BANNINCK[273] large fief/homestead year: 1421 place: Hargsen (Hervesen)

BANNINCK[274] feif/homestead year: 1421 place: Harfsen

It is assumed that Banninck was a large landholding, later divided into Grote (large) *Banninck* and Klein (small) *Banninck*, as shown on the maps above.

DE BANNINCK[275] [276] estate year: 1385 place: Colmschate, hamlet of Essen

The estate the *Banninck* in Colmschate, near Deventer, is where the Amsterdam Gerrit was said to have originated, although, as mentioned earlier, no evidence of this has yet been found in the archives. Wyssa *Banninx* lived here in 1385, and Evert *Banninek* was owner in 1403. The *Banninck* came into possession of Aleyt *Banninek* in 1443. Aleyt married Henric Ketel,(from a nobleman's family) and in 1481 son Henrick Ketel inherited the homestead from 'his olde mother Aleyt''. Gerrit Ketel . inherited it from his father Henrick in 1516, and his daughter Jutta Ketels

---

[273] B.J. Hekket, , *Oost Nederlandse Familienamen*, Twentse Uitgeverij W.G. Witkam, Enschede, 1975, p. 53

[274] Dr. B.H. Slicher van Bath, *Mensch en Land in de Middeleeuwen*, Part I, Assen, Van Gorcum & Comp. N.V.,1944, p. 255

[275] J.A.W.Banning, *Genealogie van Het Geslacht Banning*, Ferd. Banning & Zonen, Groenlo, 1934, p. 144-148

[276] *Oostgelders Tijdschrift voor Genealogie en Boerderijonderzoek*, 1998, Kwartierstaat Johanna Willemina Bannink, p. 137-139

took possession in 1519. Various tenants came and went, and in 1597 Herman Pinninck took up residence. Pinninck is deemed to be a variation on *Banninck/Banning*, but the origin of the name could as easily have been taken from the homestead as that Herman might have been an actual relation. The Pinnincks lived there until 1670, after which several names are mentioned, including that of Johan Jordens, burgomaster of Deventer and Commissioner of the province of Overijssel, in 1682. It remained in the Jordens family until some time between 1808 and 1851, when the entire estate was purchased by the family of Lord Sandberg tot Essenburg. In 1896 the manor house was completely rebuilt by the architect J.D. Gantvoort. It came into possession of Lord Storm de Grave in 1907, whose descendants still live there today. In 1916 The Bannink was described in a geographical dictionary as "house in the township of Diepeveen, Overijssel, ¼ hour directly east of Colmschate, railway stop on the railroad Apeldoorn – Almelo[277]".

In 1944 The Bannink, described as an estate located west of Bathmen on the road to Holten, consisted of 295 hectares.[278]

71. The estate Bannink in Colmschate, Deventer, in 2004
photo courtesy of A.J. Kloppenburg, Netherlands

The history of tenancy of The Banninck is recorded in the archives as follows:
1385: Feudal Registers of Gelre:[279]
"Wyssa *Banninx*,1385.Lambert dio Lewe holder.

---

[277] M. Pott, *Aardrijkskundig Woordenboek van Nederland*, 1913, p. 21
[278] K. ter Laan, *Van Goor's Aardrijkskundig Woordenboek van Nederland*, 3rd Edition, Van Goor Zonen, The Hague, Brussels, 1944, p. 33
[279] *Gelre Leenregisters*, Overijssel, no. 25

idem, in 1403.Evert *Banninek* holder.

Aleyt *Banninek* received that property of *Banninek*,in the parish of Deventer, in the hamlet of Essen, in 1443.

The last will and testament indicates that her brothers and sisters were: Roeloff, Jan, Heymen, Maria en Gijsberta. With his brother Esaye (feudal deed) With his brother Ijsbrand (feudal deed)."

Other Bannings of Deventer mentioned in the archives:

Alteti Banninge 1359[280]

Ludeken Bannynck 1451[281]

Lubbert Bannick 2 Dec. 1457 (Lubbert is the first Banning mentioned in the German city of Wettringen, where there was a homestead the Banninghof. (see below) His name occurs in the Hanseatic charters Book of Charters[282] as 'Lubbert Bannick of Deventer'. Whether this is the same Lubbert as he who died when run over by a horse in 1507 in Wettringen is unknown, but possible.

Griete Bannyngk 1480[283]

Albert Bannyng, (Bailiff) 1555[284]

29 June 1519: Jutta Ketels, heiress of her father Gerrits, received that property called *Banninck*, [Aleyt Banning was married into to the noble family of Ketel, which was how the homestead came into possession of Ketel] located in the hamlet of Essen, 29 June 1519.

17 Sept.1538: Housewife of Niclas Yerheyden, secretary in Deventer, takes pledge for feudal land called *Banninck*, in the parish of St. Niclas on the Berg within Deventer, located in the hamlet of Esschen, 1 July 15.

A farmhouse on the estate was also called homestead the Bannink. The building was probably built on the Bannink estate 1749. In 1730 a certain Harmen Harmsen Siemelink[285] (alias Bannink) was born, a builder who married Egberdina Henriks Bannink, whereupon he moved into the homestead and took its name and/or that of his wife. He died on the homestead in 1806, and his descendants, named Bannink, live there to this day. This genealogy is recorded. The farm lies on the Banningstraat.

---

[280] Mr. J.I. van Doorninck, *Cameraars-rekeningen van Deventer*, 1885, part II, 1348-1360, p. 671

[281] Mr. J.I. van Doorninck, *Catalogus der archieven van het Groote- en Voorster Gasthuis te Deventer*, 1879, no. 476, p. 203-4

[282] Stein, Walther, *Hansisches Urkundenbuch*, 1451-1463, Leipzig, Germany, Duncker & Humblot, 1899, p. 417-418

[283] Mr. J.I. van Doorninck, *Catalogus der archieven van het Groote- en Voorster Gasthuis te Deventer*, 1879, p. 292

[284] Mr. J.I. van Doorninck, *Catalogus der archieven van het Groote- en Voorster Gasthuis te Deventer*, 1879, no. 1043, p. 462, "Albert Bannynges-property on the Vorsterland, etc."

[285] H.A. te Hasseloo-Oldenmenger, *Kwartierstaat Johanna Willemina Bannink*, OTGB 98,137-139

Erve "Bannink" in Essen onder Colmschate

72. Farmstead 'the Bannink' in Essen, near Colmschate, Deventer,
photo courtesy of T.A. Kloosterboer, Deventer

BANNINCH[286] fief/homestead year: 1382-1383 place: Hengelo
The *Banninkstraat* is located to the west of Hengelo (Bekveld,
Gelderland)

BANNINC[287] fief/homestead year 1356 place: Lochem
1356: Banninc in Lochem
1356: Banninc[288].'Cubbinc, Verlehorst tenths[289], Odinc, the Laerer, the
tenths of Werensinc, of *Boync*, tenths of Wernerinc, farmland Custinc,
tenths of Westenholt,........,tenths of *Boninc*, for the tenth time.
Johan van Vorden Willemszoene ...and received the five marches (feudal
land), ca.1356.
10 Apr. 1822: died Lammert *Banning* age 61 (gardener?) born in Loghem
in Gelderland, resident of Groningen, married to Catherina   Plein?
Gealing?, son of deceased Jan *Banning*, in life porter, and Catherina
Steuren.'

---

[286] B.J. Hekket, , *Oost Nederlandse Familienamen*, Twentse Uitgeverij W.G. Witkam,
Enschede, 1975, p. 53/ Dr. B.H. Slicher van Bath, *Mensch en Land in de Middeleeuwen*,
Part I, Assen, Van Gorcum & Comp. N.V.,1944, p. 265
[287] B.J. Hekket, , *Oost Nederlandse Familienamen*, Twentse Uitgeverij W.G. Witkam,
Enschede, 1975, p. 53/ Dr. B.H. Slicher van Bath, *Mensch en Land in de Middeleeuwen*,
Part I, Assen, Van Gorcum & Comp. N.V.,1944, p. 267
[288] *Gelre Leenregisters*, Lochem, charter 64.
[289] Tenths were a historic form of tax, consisting of one tenth of the harvest, livestock, etc.,
to be paid to the bishop.

BANNINCK/BENEKINCH/BOYNCK/BENNINCK [290]
fief/homestead   **year: 1356 place:**   **Zelhem**

1356: 'Jolinc and Lunsinck, located in the parish of Zelem, to a five march feudal property Willem van Vorden one feudal property, one tract is called Lunsinck and the other Jolinc and *Banninck* and Cobbinc and that Voerhorst, in the parish of Vurden,1356.'

1382 Banninch in Hengelo was located in Zelhem . The *Benninkstraat* runs between Keijenborg and Zelhem..

78: ZELHEM

16 Oct. 1473: 'Henrick Wassinck Stevenssoon takes pledge for the property called Willinck, located in the parish of Zelm on the *Boynck*, with all its appurtenances, bordering on the property of Wengkinck on one side and that of Luttekeu *Boeninck* on the other; 16 Oct.1473.'

85: ZELHEM

16 Oct. 1473: 'Henrick Bettinck, heir of his father Willems, has received that property of Ludickinck with all its appurtenances, in the parish of Zeelhem situated in the Goy, bordered by that property *Boeninck* on the one side and that property of Tille on the other, under Zutphen rights.'

17 July 1676: '*Benninck*, Arent. Inventory of names specified in the documents of the Jurisdiction of Zelhem, 17 July 1676 transfer by Arent *Benninck* of a certain property in Zelhem; idem 6 Aug. 1680. Banned from the Homestead *Benninck* by Everhard van der Ketten and Hendrick Keties; 5 September 1680 idem.'

Arent Benninck: Baptised before 1656, died before 1729. The genealogy of this family, commencing with Jan *Benninck* in 1625, is recorded[291]. (see Benninkmolen, below.)

BANNINCK[292]   **fief/homestead**   **year: 1356**
place: Zodderloe/Oosterwijk

BANNINCK[293]   **year: 1420**   **place: Beekbergen/Loenen/ Schoten/Voorstonden**

1405: The inventory of Gherardus van Hengelo dated 1405 mentions 'bona *Bannincx* vel Everhardi Hadeconc' and his inventory of 1417 of 'bona *Bannynck* seu Hadekonc'.

11 Nov. 1420: Parish of Voorst (hamlet of Tonden).

The property, called *Bannynck*, with all its appurtenances (Hadekonc)x). Everen Hadekong and his oldest son sell to Gerit Schoetinc "three orchard lands, located above and below Tondermarce, with all its appurtenances".

---

[290] Dr. B.H. Slicher van Bath, Mensch en Land in de Middeleeuwen, Part I, Assen, Van Gorcum & Comp. N.V.,1944, p. 281 / Genealogy of Jan Benninck, commencing in 1625
[291] Parenteel van Benninck, Jan; http://home.planet.nl/~djo/frben3.htm, accessed Aug. 2003
[292] Dr. B.H. Slicher van Bath, Mensch en Land in de Middeleeuwen, Part I, Assen, Van Gorcum & Comp. N.V.,1944, p. 282
[293] Gelre Leenregisters, Vereniging Gelre, Prum, no. 40

18 June 1461: Steven *Banninck*, Everwiin's son on submitting a letter dated 10 June, whereby he is dismissed from services by Henrick van Middachten .

5 Apr. 1486: Henrick Hoebber on behalf of Steven *Bannynck* and his wife Elyzabet.

11 Nov. 1451: Parish of Voorst (hamlet of Tonden).

'That homestead and property, located at Schoten, with forest, creek, high and lowlands and with all its appurtenances, also if that is located in the parish of Oevoirst (*Banninck* op Schoten).'

26 July 1534: 'House, courtyard, pasture and fields, called *Banninck* at Schoeten, with a small hayfield, Ypenmaetgen, and as large as that in its stipulations and with all the same privelages, rights, appurtenances and all rightful goods in high and in lowlands, forest and creek, etc., located under the jurisdiction of Brummen, parish of Voirst and hamlet of Tonden.'

21 Nov. 1559: 'That property at Kampe, located in Loenen, in the parish of Bechberg. Wolter Haeek, burgher of Zutphen,1559 November 21.'

N.B. He is simultaneously granted the property *Banninck* at Schoten.

BANNYGHE[294]/BANINGHUS[295] fief/homestead year: 1360/1423
place: Rolde

'Johanni *Baninck* (1360 in Loen), living at the *Baningehus*, in the March of Loen, and the parish of Rolde, Drente.'

BANINGE-HUS[296] fief/homestead year: 1298-1304 place:
Loon, Assen

BANNINGHE[297] fief/homestead year 1298 place: Witten

'In the years 1298-1304 the parish of St. Peter in Utrecht received income from two fiefs in Witten, of which one was in the tenancy of a certain Herardi. In 1321 and again in 1369 the *Banninghe* property is mentioned, while the Chapter of the Cathedral in Utrecht, in addition to income received for a fief tenanted by the aforementioned Herardi, also received income in 1335 for Zilbingegoed in Witten.[298,]

At the time, Witten consisted of ten fiefs.

---

[294] Dr. B.H. Slicher van Bath, Mensch en Land in de Middeleeuwen, Part I, Assen, Van Gorcum & Comp. N.V.,1944, p. 289

[295] Nomino Geographica Neerlandia, Koninklijke Nederlandse Aardrijkskundige Genootschap, part V, 1899, p. 20

[296] B.J. Hekket, , Oost Nederlandse Familienamen, Twentse Uitgeverij W.G. Witkam, Enschede, 1975, p. 53

[297] Dr. B.H. Slicher van Bath, Mensch en Land in de Middeleeuwen, Part I, Assen, Van Gorcum & Comp. N.V.,1944, p. 290

[298] Drents Volksalmanak 1977, Gemeente Assen, p. 27

'Besides the aforementioned nine fiefs, the Bolen-fief (also called Boelen or Buelen fief) was located in Witten, which still existed in 1534. This Bolen-fief may have consisted, among other things, of half of the fields and meadows of the house *Banninghe*, sold to Bolo and Bertoldus de Witten in 1321, from which an income of two measures of winter rye was paid to the bishop each year.[299]'

BENNEKINC, BENNINK [300] [301] [302]   fief/homestead   year: **1188**
place: Delden / Deldenerbroek
23 Apr. 1400; No. 203: 'Jurisdiction of Delden/hamlet of Deldenerbroek: That property stretching to *Bennekinch*[303], that stretching to Rotgerinch, that of Haern, with all the privelages and rights belonging to property located in the parish of Delden.'
9 Apr. 1716. No. 206: 'The homestead *Bennink*, located on the . Deldenerbroek by the House of Baekenhage and presently occupied by *Gerrijt Bennink*. A section of the above jurisdiction.'
17 Mar. 1738: 'Half of the homestead named *Gerrit Benninck*, located on the Deldener Broick. Half of the homestead and property *Bennekers*, located in the parish of Delden, hamlet of Deldenerbroek.'

BENNIJNG, BENNINK, BENNEKINK[304] [305] fief/homestead
year: 1457   place: Woolde, Wollethe
Juridiction of Delden/hamlet of Woolde: No. 282
1379-1382 Feudal land *Beyminc* in the parish of Delden.
28 Sept. 1400-1417(?):Bynning in the hamlet of Wolde.
21 July 1447: Benning at Wolde.

BENNING[306]   fief/homestead   year: **1399**   place: **Essen**

[299] *Drents Volksalmanak* 1977, Gemente Assen, p. 28
[300] Dr. B.H. Slicher van Bath, *Mensch en Land in de Middeleeuwen*, Part I, Assen, Van Gorcum & Comp. N.V.,1944, p. 204
[301] list of properties of Count Hendrik van Dale (F. Philippi, & W.A.F. Bannier, *Das Güterverzeichniss Graf Heinrichs von Dale (1188)*, in: Bijdr. Med. Hist. Genoots. XXV,Utrecht 1904, p. 365-442
[302] K. ter Laan, *Van Goor's Aardrijkskundig Woordenboek van Nederland*, Van Goor Zonen, The Hague, Brussels, 1942 , 3rd edition, p. 39
[303] E.D. Eiken, *Repertorium op de Utrechtse en Overijsselse Leenprotocollen 1379-1805*, Zwolle, 1994, no. 203; 206; 282;
[304] Dr. B.H. Slicher van Bath, *Mensch en Land in de Middeleeuwen*, Part I, Assen, Van Gorcum & Comp. N.V.,1944, p. 207
[305] H.J. Krooskoop, *De Onbekende Middeleeuwen in Woolde, 14th century properties of the Bishop of Utrecht*, Oald Hengel 9,1984, no. 2, p. 23]
[306] Dr. B.H. Slicher van Bath, *Mensch en Land in de Middeleeuwen*, Part I, Assen, Van Gorcum & Comp. N.V.,1944, p. 209

BENNING/BENNINCK[308] **fief/homestead year: 1457 place: Borculo (Zutphen)**
The first person on record in the Netherlands, to date, is Arnoldus Banning, alderman in Zutphen, 1294, and his son or grandson (all three served as aldermen) listed from 1343-1358. The Bannings belonged to the prominent Zutphen families in the 14th century, according to a list published in the *Nederlandse Leeuw* of 1935[309]: *Zutphen family names of prominence in 1390.*

BENNING, BENNINYNG, BENNEKINCK, BENNIN(C)K[310]
fief/homestead   year: 1442   place: Haaksbergen
The origin of the Benninck family lies on the corner of the Hengelosestraat-Goorsestraat in Haaksbergen. A farm called Benninck was located here for hundreds of years, which had to be demolished for the new development 'Hassinkbrink'.[311]
In a charter held in the deanery of Daventria (Deventer) a certain *Sanderus Benninc* is named as fief in a dispute concerning tenths of land in the vicinity of 'Hokesberghe' (Haaksbergen).[312]
3 Nov. 1442: 'That property of *Bennyng* and all its appurtenances, located in the hamlet of Haexberge. [Haaksbergen]'
17 Sept. 1491: 'By charter, consent to the bishop to pay off a debt of 497 ½ Rhijn guilders, for which Mr. Reynalt van der Roer, Mr. Droene and his wife Lyse Stecke at one time gave as collateral to Beemt's ancestors the properties of *Bennekinck*, Wergerinck, des Stickershuys, Beeverdt and the tenths of Zegebertinck, all located in the parish of Haexberge [Haaksbergen], belonging to the house of Blackenborch.'
- *6 Nov. 1667* 'The homestead and property *Benninck*, now called Doornebusch, located in the andirons of Haexbergen, hamlet of Buirse. Jurisdiction of Haaksbergen/hamlet of Buurse: no. 382'
- *1 June 1701*, property division no 381: 'the homestead and property Bosch, consisting of a portion of the homestead *Bennink*, in the parish of Haxbergen, hamlet of Buurse. Engbert Bosch, testifies Engbert Bosch, just as Gerrit ten Dorenbos had held the homestead *Bennink* as part of the tenure.'
- *1723:* 'The tenancy of Willem ten Busch, following the death of his father Arent ten Busch, who was granted tenancy on 6 Feb. 1723, of a portion of the homestead and property of *Bennink*, called the Busch, was not registered in 1723.'

---

[308] *Zutphense Leengoederen*, Verpondingscohier, 1255-1650
[309] J.B. Rietstap, *Heraldische Bibliotheek*, 1875, p. 35
[310] Dr. B.H. Slicher van Bath, *Mensch en Land in de Middeleeuwen*, Part I, Assen, Van Gorcum & Comp. N.V.,1944, p. .215
[311] H. Bennink, *Parenteel Benninck* ,Van de Berg, Enschede, 1994
[312] Feudal registers of Haaksbergen/hamlet of Buurse: no. 381

- 22 May 1755: 'testifies Engbert Bosch, just as Gerrit ten Dorenbos had held the homestead *Bennink* in addition to other portions in tenancy.'

H. Bennink wrote a genealogy of the Bennink family[312] commencing with Johan Bennink in 1600, probably from the homestead of Benninc in Haaksbergen, where he is mentioned in the land tax registers.

BENNINGH[313] fief/homestead year: bef. 1380 place: Nyensteden

BENNINGEGOED (BENNYNGE)[314] homestead   year: 1440
place: Noordbarge, Emmen

The Benningegoed [Benninge property] (Bennynge) in Noordbarge is also referred to as bishopric property in 1440.

In the year 1381 the name 'Berghe' is encountered for the first time in official documents. The 'Germynghe house' is mentioned. Whether North or South Barge are meant here is not known. A document from 1440 clarifies this, in which is written: *'Bennynge'* homestead in Noordberge, or Noertberge. The name Bargum is also mentioned.

Researcher Garming has uncovered more than half of the names of residents of the parish of Emmen from 1645. In the registers of church members, those baptized, married and died, the following names of the first homestead owners of Nordbarge were specified: Alberinge, Rosinghe, Frijlingh, Ubbinge, Nijenhuisinge, Jolinge, Brink, Mantinge, Stratinge, Lutke Vrieling and *Beninge*.

1847: 'Eeme Bening from Emmen married Willem van Zomer, who was 65 at the time.[315]'

27 Febr. 1883: An old newspaper, the *Provincial Drentsche and Asser Courant* of Tuesday 27 Febr.1883 published an account concerning 'The farmer *Bening* of Noordbarge, in the township of Emmen'. Farmer *Bening* happened upon archeological finds on his property: a large basement or buried chamber of stone, containing crocks, iron implements and bones.

Farms in the Noordbarge area were demolished around the turn of the 19th century and replaced with homes. Four homes on the Huizenbrinkweg (no. 62-65) are located where the ancient residence of the *Bening* (*Beninge*) family once stood. The *Bening* family moved to another farm on the Oude Zuidbargerstraat, where they lived until 1938. In the red brick home to the south of this farmhouse the last generation of Bening

---

[312] H. Bennink, *Stamboom familie Bennink in Historisch Perspectief*, Eibergen 1989

[313] Dr. B.H. Slicher van Bath, *Mensch en Land in de Middeleeuwen*, Part I, Assen, Van Gorcum & Comp. N.V.,1944, p. 217

[314] Historic Emmen: http://www.historisch-emmen.nl/f_100_historie/f_100.htm, accessed March 2004

[315] Historic Emmen: http://www.historisch-emmen.nl/f_000_algemeen/f_000.htm, accessed March 2004

died out – three unmarried sisters, always referred to in Noordbarge as 'the *Bening* Womenfolk'.[316]

BENNINC[317]   year: 1460   place: Kuinre (Cunre)

BENNINK[318]   year: 1913   place: Gorsel in Gelderland
Railway stop

BENNINK[319]   year: 1913   place: Lichtenvoorde, Gelderland
Railway stop

BINKHORST[320] (Benninkhorst) year 933-966 place: Losser (Lutheri)
'Binkhorst has been located since 933 near Losser, today still a well-known family name; Bink=*Bennink*, Benno.[321]'
Also mentioned in the book of Deeds and Charters of the Bishopric of Utrecht[322]

BENINC (BENNYNC)[323] fief/homestead   year 1323 place: Rossum
(Rothem)
Jurisdiction of Oldenzaal/hamlet of Rossum: no. 861
'That house of   *Bennyng* in Rossem in the parish of Aldenzale [Oldenzaal].'
1382-1393: 'A section of the homestead, called *Benninc*, with all its appurtenances.'
10 July-31 Dec. 1405: 'That property at *Benneking* in Rossem.'
13 June 1662: 'That homestead and property *Bennekinck*, situated in the parish of Oldenzael in the parish of Rossum.'
No. 862: 'Concerning *Bennync* in Rossem half tenths--- in the parish of Aldenzale. [Oldenzaal]. Tenant: Sir Reynolt van Coevoerde, knight.'

BENSING (BENNING)[324]   fief/homestead   year: 1457   place:
Stegeren (Steygere)

---

[316] *De Provinciale Drentsche en Asser Courant*, 27 Feb. 1883
[317] Dr. B.H. Slicher van Bath, *Mensch en Land in de Middeleeuwen*, Part I, Assen, Van Gorcum & Comp. N.V.,1944, p. 220
[318] M. Pott, *Aardrijkskundig Woordenboek van Nederland*, 1913, p. 29
[319] M. Pott, *Aardrijkskundig Woordenboek van Nederland*, 1913, p. 29
[320] Dr. B.H. Slicher van Bath, *Mensch en Land in de Middeleeuwen*, Part I, Assen, Van Gorcum & Comp. N.V.,1944, p. 207
[321] Gens Nostra, Ned. Genealogische Vereniging, Amsterdam ,1963
[322] Dr. Mr. S. Muller, Dr. A.C. Bouman, *Oorkondeboek van het Sticht Utrecht tot 1301*, Utrecht, A. Oosthoek, 1920, p. 104
[323] Dr. B.H. Slicher van Bath, *Mensch en Land in de Middeleeuwen*, Part I, Assen, Van Gorcum & Comp. N.V.,1944, p. 226
[324] Dr. B.H. Slicher van Bath, *Mensch en Land in de Middeleeuwen*, Part I, Assen, Van Gorcum & Comp. N.V.,1944, p. 230

BENNEKINC[325] fief/homestead year: 1298-1304 place: Alberge(n)

BENNEKINCK (BENNIJNG)[326] fief/homestead year: 1420 place: Itterbeek (Itterbeke)

Domun BENNINCK[327] house year: 1284 place: Aalten
(see Dinxperlo)

BENNYNCK[328] fief/homestead year: 1356 place: Dinxperlo
'Jan *Beunink*, son of Conraad Benninck 'under Dinxperlo' marries Jenneken Tammel/Tambel in Aalten on 21 July 1700.[329]'
Bennynck Dinxperlo:[330] charter 46: 'whereby Jacob van Ittersum grants to the lord of Borculo the right to re-purchase the tenths of the properties Bennynck and Schurynck, below Ommen, 1497. 1 charter.'

BENNINC[331] year 1379-1382 Jursidiction of Ahaus, hamlet of Ortwick
1379-1382: 'Den Rotardinchof. List of feudal lords: Mathias van *Bonynghen*.'
11 Jan. 1395: 'Mathijs van *Banijnghen*. The Court of Raeterdinc with its appurtenances and *Benninc* [?], which is included, located in the Bishopric of Munster. *'Benninc'* is barely legible; perhaps it reads 'Benric'. The table of names of feudal lords includes 'Mathijs van *Boningen*.'
17 Oct. 1397: 'Herman Knuyff on behalf of Mathis *van Boningen*.'

BENNINCK property[332] place: hamlet of Vrageren, the Convent in Varel
1768: owners and lessees of tenths: Berent *Benninck*, Herman *Benninck* Cruese, widow of Jan *Benninck*, Coene *Benninck*, Lady (Mrs.) *Benninck*;

[325] Dr. B.H. Slicher van Bath, *Mensch en Land in de Middeleeuwen*, Part I, Assen, Van Gorcum & Comp. N.V.,1944, p. 232
[326] Dr. B.H. Slicher van Bath, *Mensch en Land in de Middeleeuwen*, Part I, Assen, Van Gorcum & Comp. N.V.,1944, p. 244
[327] Dr. B.H. Slicher van Bath, *Mensch en Land in de Middeleeuwen*, Part I, Assen, Van Gorcum & Comp. N.V.,1944, p. 253
[328] Dr. B.H. Slicher van Bath, *Mensch en Land in de Middeleeuwen*, Part I, Assen, Van Gorcum & Comp. N.V.,1944, p. 259
[329] *Gens Nostra*, Ned. Genealogische Vereniging, Amsterdam, 1993
[330] H.J.A.M. Schurinck, *Inventaris van het Archief der Heren van Borculo*, Gelders Archief, bloknr. 0378, charter 7.46
[331] E.D. Eijken, *Repertorium op de Overstichtste en en Overijsselse Leenprotocollen*, 1379-1805, no. 2003
[332] *Oostgelders Tijdschrift voor Genealogie*, 1984, p. 1

convent of Varel and Lord Bergklo Vicarage and the church of Groenlo: the property *Benninck*.

Cattle mortality in 1768: in the jurisdiction of Vrageren: 'two cows belonging to Berent *Bennink* died[333].'

BENNINCK[334]   year: 1433   place: Uelsen/hamlet of Haftenkamp
Jurisdiction of UELSEN / hamlet of Haftenkamp
30 Oct. 1433: 'duties: 8 bushels of rye, in the parish of Ulsen tenths on the Huede at *Benninck*, crude and fine.'

(Domum) BENNINCH [335], BENEKINK[336] fief/homestead   year: 1284
place:Huppel(o)/Winterswijk/Bedervoort
1 Apr. 1284: Charter no. 1243; 'The nobleman Baldewin von Steinfurt, together with his consort, sells half of the castle of Bredevoort and several adjacent properties to the Bishop Everhard and the Bishopric of Munster, including domum *Benninch*.'
1402: 'Keylwinck, Boefkinck and *Benekinck*, those homesteads and property, located in the jurisdiction of Bredenvoirt, received by Evert van Walien,1402.'
1424: 'Wernher van Walyen received the properties and their appurtenances, called Keelwinck, *Benekinck* and Boevekinck, located in the parisch of Wintersweek, in the hamlet of Huppeloe, under Zutphen rights, 1424. Willem van Waly inherited from his brother Evert van Waly in 1447.'
7 Oct. 1473: 'Idem takes pledge for these properties, called Kelwinck, *Bennekink* and Boevekinck, located in the jurisdiction of Bredevort,in the parish of Winterswiek and the hamlet of Hoeppele, bordering on the property of Hyink and that of Hermkinck on both sides, under Zutphen rights, 7 Oct.1473.Bernt van Walye, heir of his father Everts, 4 Apr. 1489. Sonnendach van Munster received this property in 1501.'
15 June 1534: 'Vith van Munster, bailiff of Anholt, heir to his father Sondachs, received those properties, called Kelwinck, *Bennekinck* and Boevekinck, with their appurtenances, highlands and lowlands, in wet and in dry lands, with forest, with creek, located in the jurisdiction of Brevoort, in the parish of Winterswick and in the hamlet of Hoeppelle, on one side bordered by the property Hyinck, and on the other the property

---

[333] Historisch Centrum Overijssel, Leenrepertorium 1923, no. 1924, p. 58
[334] Historisch Centrum Overijssel, Leenrepertorium 1923, no. 1924
[335] Dr. Roger Wilmans, *Westfälisches Urkunden-Buch*, H. Th. Wenner, Osnabruck, 1973 (original publication 1871) Part III,p. 654
[336] Dr. B.H. Slicher van Bath, *Mensch en Land in de Middeleeuwen*, Part I, Assen, Van Gorcum & Comp. N.V.,1944, p. 279

Hermekinck, under Zutphen rights, 15 June 1534. Sondagh van Munster, inherits from his father Vijts, 15 Oct.1549.'

1 Apr. 1570: 'Jacob van Munster receives by transfer from his brother Sondags that feudal land and the house Walyen with dry goods, called Kelwinck, *Bennekinck* and Boevekinck, with all its appurtenances in high and lowlands, wet and dry lands, forest and creek, in the jurisdiction of Bredevoort,in the parish of Winterswick, in the hamlet of Hoepele, located there from old times, under Zutphen rights, 1 April 1570.'

BENNYNG[337] fief/homestead yar: 1402 place: Miste

BENNINGHBROEC / BENNINGBROEK / BENNINXBROEK
village year: 1302

Province of North HollandName derived from the patronymic Benning i.e. Christian name Benno plus suffix *'-ing'*, meaning belonging to, and Broec/Broek, meaning 'marshy land'.[338] The village was founded in 1302. Benningbroek was at one time a more important place, merged in 1413 with the township of Sijbekarspel and accorded the status of a city, with it's own 'city' market. In 1450 it's privileges, which had in the meantime been lost as a result of rebellion, were reinstated.[339]

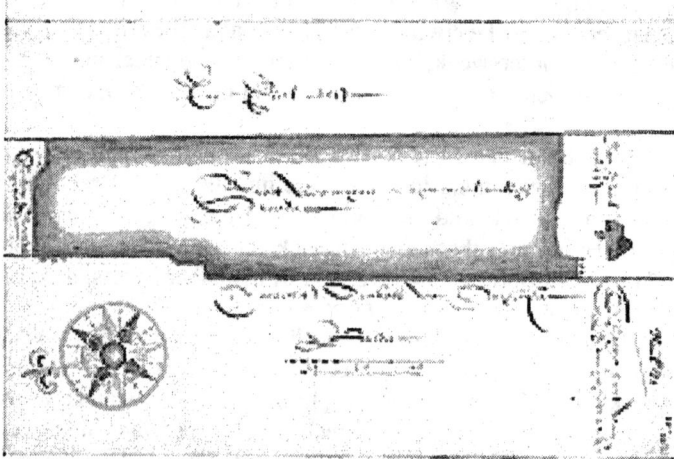

73. The High Land of Benninghbroeck, collection:Topographical-historical atlas, Map Book of the Almshouse Poor of the City of Hoorn[340]
Westfriese Archieven, Hoorn (ref. no. 65j.208(32))

---

[337] Dr. B.H. Slicher van Bath, *Mensch en Land in de Middeleeuwen*, Part I, Assen, Van Gorcum & Comp. N.V.,1944, p. 279

[338] *Prisma Woordenboek*, Het Spectrum B.V., 1995, p. 18-19

[339] A.J. van der Aa, *Aardrijkskundig Woordenboek der Nederlanden*, Jacobus Noorduyn, Gorinchem, Part II, B., 1840, p. 276-277

[340] *Kaartboek van de Huiszittende Armen der stad Hoorn*, no. 32, ca. 1650, 't Hooge Lant van Benninghbroeck

Since Benninghbroeck and Abbekerk lie in very close proximity to each other, it has been proposed that this lends credence to the assumption that the old and prestigious family Abbe was either related to the Benningh family (Amsterdam) or that they were at one time the same family, wherein the name took different forms.

BENNINGMEER / BENNEMEER[341] polder land year: 1302
Province of North Holland

Benningmeer (Benning Lake) was at one time a lake. When it was laid dry to become polder land is unknown. In 1840 it was described as holding only one farm. The Polder Board consisted at the time of two Mill Masters, of which only one at a time served, and they alternated every two years. It lay partially in the township of Abbekerk-en-Lambertshagen en partially in the township of Twisk, adjacent to Abbekerk, immediately to the south of (the above mentioned) Benninghbroeck. (See comment above, concerning Benningbroeck and the Abbe family

BOENEKINCK/BENNEKINCK/BENNINCK[342] property year: 1473 place: Bedevoort, Miste/ Winterswijk

17 Oct. 1473: 'Henrick Ubbink acquires the property of Ubbinck, in the jurisdiction of Bredervoort, in the parish of Winterswick, bordered by *Boenekinck* on the one side and by the property Berge on the other side, under Zutphen rights, 7 Oct.1473.'

16 Sept. 1531: 'Johan Drossart received the property *Bennekinck* with all its appurtenances, located in the jursidiction of Bredevoort, in the parish of Winterswick, as collateral feudal land belonging to the house of Bredevoort, 16 Sept.1531.'

'Idem, anno 1582, of the property called *Benninck*, located in the parish of Winterswick, with house and courtyard included.'

3 Dec. 1603: 'Idem, Frans Drost received the property called *Benninck*, with house, courtyard and all its appurtenances, in the jurisdiction of Bredevoort, in the parish of Winterswick, in the hamlet of Miste.'

29 Jan.1611: 'Wychmoet Huysinck, housewife of Hermans van Basten, acquires the property Ubbinck with all its appurtenances, located in the

---

[341] A.J. van der Aa, *Aardrijkskundig Woordenboek der Nederlanden*, Jacobus Noorduyn, Gorinchem, Part II, B., 1840, p. 276-277
[342] *Gelre Leenregisters*, no. 494

jurisdiction of Bredevort, in the parish of Winterswijck, in the Darp hamlet, between the properties of *Boenekinck* and Berge.'

9 Feb. 1711: 'Half of the homestead and property, called *Bennekink*, with house, courtyard and all its appurtenances, in the jurisdiction of Bredevoort, parish of Winterswijk, hamlet of Miste in Ekel, located as a special feudal land under Zutphen rights, with transfer rights of one pound, paid by Hendrik Walyen, heir of his father Wilhem, and thus granted, 9 Febr.1711.'

The names *Bennekinck* en *Benninck* were used interchangeably. In de deed of 1531 the first is written in the body of the text and the second in the margin the second.

BENNINGEHUS[343] **fief/homestead**   **year: 1298-1304**   **place: Beilen**

BENNIJNGEHUYS[344]   **house**   **year: 1181**   **place: Echten**
(read: Bennijnge house, or Bennynge house)

BENNINCKEGAE[345] **(kl) Finkega year 1408 place: Stellingroerf**
A note concerning dues for various parishes "in the region of Stellingwerff, that kerspel of Belsdyck, Pepergae, Steggerden, *Benninckegae, (Beninchergae)*, Noortwolde, Bente, etc.." [346]

BENNINC [347]   **year: 1323**   **place: Rot(h)men/Reutem**
4 July 1323 ' (in translacione sancti Martini)[348] Johannes de Almelo, knave, declares, in the presence of Johannes, Count of Benthem, Bernardus de Zebelinge, Everhardus de Bevervorde, knights, Henricus de Almelo, Otto en Bernardus de Welvelde, brothers, Rodolfus de Peze, Tidericus de Grimberghe, Hermannus de Enthere, Ecbertus Welghem, Wolterus de Haslo, Johannes de Reve, Bernardus Suederi, Johannes Welghem and Ecbertus Mostart, knaves, that his uncle Johannes, Count of Benthem, in cooperation with his relatives Bernardus de Zebelinge, knight, Henricus de Almelo, Otto and Bernardus de Welvelde, brothers, Rodolfus de Peze and Thidericus de Grimberghe, between himself

[343] Dr. B.H. Slicher van Bath, *Mensch en Land in de Middeleeuwen*, Part I, Assen, Van Gorcum & Comp. N.V.,1944, p. 283
[344] Dr. B.H. Slicher van Bath, *Mensch en Land in de Middeleeuwen*, Part I, Assen, Van Gorcum & Comp. N.V.,1944, p. 290
[345] Dr. B.H. Slicher van Bath, *Mensch en Land in de Middeleeuwen*, Part I, Assen, Van Gorcum & Comp. N.V.,1944, p. 303
[346] Schwartz, Worp, Kroniek II, 13, I p. 367
[347] Dr. B.H. Slicher van Bath, *Mensch en Land in de Middeleeuwen*, Part I, Assen, Van Gorcum & Comp. N.V.,1944, p. 226
[348] Historisch Centrum Overijssel, Almelo, charter 1636

(Johannes de Almelo) and Ecbertus his brother has effected a division of property, whereby the following goods were allocated to him, which he shall hold for his brother: the homestead (domus) Ambinc in Elsnen (Elsen), ...in Holthon (Holten), Groot Hunse and *Benninc* in Rotmen (Reutem), Vredinc in Otmershem; the crude and fine tenths from the fiefs of Stonebrinke, Hinvordinc,...... Lanzinc in Nozelo (Noetsele), *Bennekinc* in Alberghe, Hofstede,......and the tenths from the house of Bolto de Reve'

BOENINCK[349]   **fief/homestead   year: 1473   place: Gooi**

BOENINCK[350]   **fief/homestead   year: 1473   place: op den Boynck,   Lutteken**

BUNINC[351]   **fief/ homestead   place: Zweelo   year: 1335**

[349] Dr. B.H. Slicher van Bath, *Mensch en Land in de Middeleeuwen*, Part I, Assen, Van Gorcum & Comp. N.V.,1944, p. 281
[350] Dr. B.H. Slicher van Bath, *Mensch en Land in de Middeleeuwen*, Part I, Assen, Van Gorcum & Comp. N.V.,1944, p. 281
[351] Dr. B.H. Slicher van Bath, *Mensch en Land in de Middeleeuwen*, Part I, Assen, Van Gorcum & Comp. N.V.,1944, p. 293

BANNING MILL   windmill   year: 1890   place: Alkmaar

Hermanus Banning operated and lived in this mill from October 1890, previously to which it was known as Molen de Wolf. It was one of eight flourmills on the Alkmaar city embankments. The mill was demolished in 1911. Although there were Bannings in Alkmaar, most of whom have been traced, it has not yet been ascertained to which genealogy Hermanus Banning belonged.

FOTO M. KATER   TYP. O. DE WAAL

EEN VERDWENEN MONUMENT
MOLEN VAN BANNING

74. Banning Windmill 1890-1911 (photo by M. Kater)
courtesy of the Regional Archives of Alkmaar, Netherlands

230

75. Banning windmill (flourmill), Edam, Netherlands   ca. 1900
collection Zuiderzeemuseum, Enkhuizen, Netherlands

BANNING MILL   place: Edam   **before 1870**
This windmill was purchased in 1870 by Arnoldus Johannes Banning, a miller's son from Workum, Friesland, for 7,000 Dutch guilders. He sold it in 1912 and in 1918 it was demolished, leaving the ground floor intact.

BENNINKMOLEN   windmill   **(re) built 1921**
Doetinchem, Gelderland
The Benninkmolen, now a national monument, is one of the three remaining windmills in Doetinchem today, and is named after the Bennink family which operated and lived in the mill for three generations. At one time there was another mill located on this spot, built in 1856 by B. Vels, demolished in 1920 due to dilapidation. The *Benninkmolen* was constructed with part of a mill from Zelhem and from other mills, in 1921. It was fully renovated in 1980/84 after years of great considerable neglect, whereupon the name was changed from Velsmolen to *Benninkmolen*. Owners of the mill were J.F. Bennink, (1921-1949), Theodoor Bennink, born in Doetinchem 04 Aug. 1907, H.W. Molenkamp and the widow of J.F. Bennink (1949-1955), and F.H. Bennink (1955-1976) after which it became property of the municipality of

Doetinchem.[352] The genealogy of this Bennin(c)k family is recorded, commencing with Jan *Benninck* in Aalten/Zelhem in 1625.[353]

76. Benninkmolen , Doetinchem, Gelderland
photo courtesy of Hans de Kroon, Veenendaal, Netherlands

[352] Nederlandse Molendatabase, http://www.hippowebdesign.com/molens/molen.php?nummer=201, accessed March 2004
[353] Genealogical page of D.J. Oldenboom, http://home.planet.nl/~djo/home.htm, accessed March 2004

BENNINCHUS[354] **house   year: 1244   Kl. Marienfeld, Westphalia**
Charter 430 mentions Frowinus as priest of the 'Benninchus' (Benninc house'.

BENNING / BENNINCROTH[355] **property   year: 1302 Coesfeld, Westphalia**
Mentioned in charter no. 100. It is plausible that this property belonged to Bannings as aldermen of Coesfeld in the 13th century, of whom several are mentioned in this book, the first being in 1238.

BENNINK (BEMUNK)[356] **town?   year: 1193 near Ascheberg**
East of Ascheberg, Kr. Lüdinghausen, most likely in the proximity of the present colony Bünningman. Freeholding 1193.

BENNINCCAMP[357] **fief   year: 1318**
place: Mecklenbeck, Munster, Westphalia
The young man Johannes lord of Benninccamp is mentioned in a charter of the Charter Book of Westphalen, where some of the earliest Bannings mentioned came from (Coesfeld).

BENNINGH[358] **fief/homestead   year 1433   place: Emlichheim (Germany)**
1433: Jurisdiction of Emlichheim / hamlet of Emlichheim
'Maerleninge and Orphanse in Empninchhem. Those tenths of *Bennynck*, Oesmelinc and Kalewinck. '
1433: 'Those tenths of *Bennynck*, Oesmaling and Kalvyng.'
1455: mentioned as existing in 1455, the homestead *Benningh*.[359]

According to family information, the first Benninks in Emlichheim were recorded some time in the 14th century and appear in church records. One story holds that there were three Bennink brothers in Emlichheim at the

[354] Dr. Roger Wilmans, *Westfälisches Urkunden-Buch*, H. Th. Wenner, Osnabruck, 1973 (original publication 1871) Part III,p. 230
[355] Dr. Roger Wilmans, *Westfälisches Urkunden-Buch*, H. Th. Wenner, Osnabruck, 1973 (original publication 1871) Part III,p. 36
[356] Dr. Roger Wilmans, *Westfälisches Urkunden-Buch*, H. Th. Wenner, Osnabruck, 1973 (original publication 1871) Part III,p. 711
[357] Dr. Roger Wilmans, *Westfälisches Urkunden-Buch*, H. Th. Wenner, Osnabruck, 1973 (original publication 1871) Part III, charter no. 1226, 16 Feb. 1318, p. 447
[358] E.D. Eijken, *Repertorium op de Overistichste en Overijsselse Leenprotocollen 1379-1805*, charter 1867
[359] Dr. B.H. Slicher van Bath, *Mensch en Land in de Middeleeuwen*, Part I, Assen, Van Gorcum & Comp. N.V.,1944, p. 211

time, who stole everything that 'was not nailed down', being common thieves. It hardly seems credible that such relatively inconsequential deeds would be passed down as lore through the centuries, unless the fabled brothers had truly cleaned out the town and posed a major threat. This genealogy has been traced from 1677, commencing with Jan Bennink, civil servant and Bailiff of Coevorden (1710, 1718)

BANNINGHOF [360] fief/homestead year: place: **Wettringen, Munster, Germany**

The Banninghof near Wettringen in Germany, some 20 km. from the Dutch border, was partially rebuilt after a fire in 1982, whereby the stables were destroyed but most of the main house survived. Two stone plaques on the new façade commemorate frau Julia Banning and her husband Clemens, who took his wife's name of Banning as was · frequently done in Germany at the time. Another stone on the façade , dated 1913, commemorates their parents August Banning and his wife Helena.

77. A painting of House de Banninghof, Wettringen, Germany
photo courtesy of Frans van Heijingen

1507: Lubbert Banning: possibly the same Lubbert mentioned in the Hanseatic Book of Charters in 1457, as 'Lubbert Bannick of Deventer'

---

[360] J.A.W. Banning, *Genealogie van het Geslacht Banning*, Ferd. Banning & Zonen, Groenlo, 1934, p. I

(see estate The Bannink of Deventer, above). He died of injuries sustained when run over by his horse. [361].

1526: 'the young Banninck'[362] takes over the fief, making a payment of wine and ½ cask of butter.

1668: court records:[363] Description of the fief, mentioning the owner 'Deitert', originally from 'Kaldemeyer's' house, who has 'courted the deceased Banning's widow, Ine Frerich's daughter, married her and made a payment of wine'.

1729: description of property, followed by mention of the owner, Herman Banning, who came there nine years before, the husband of Adelheit Sundarps.

1750: description of the property, including a house, sheep stable, a barn and..... The farmer is named Jan Gerd Werning now Banning.

1828: Joh. Gerh. Banning, born 5 Nov. 1783, and his wife Maria Kath. Lammering.

For the genealogy of this family and further details see the chapter on East Frisia, Germany and Scandinavia.

[361] Wilhelm Brockpäler, *Wettringen, Geschichte eine Münsterlandischen Gemeinde*, Gemeinde Wettringen, Germany, 1970, p. 119, 120

[362] Wilhelm Brockpäler, *Wettringen, Geschichte eine Münsterlandischen Gemeinde*, Gemeinde Wettringen, Germany, 1970, p. 119, 120

[363] Wilhelm Brockpäler, *Wettringen, Geschichte eine Münsterlandischen Gemeinde*, Gemeinde Wettringen, Germany, 1970, p. 119, 120

10 EAST FRISIA, GERMANY AND SCANDINAVIA
Beninga of East Frisia

The Frisians were a sea-faring Germanic tribe, originating from the North Sea coast in the Dutch provinces of Friesland and Groningen,, West Frisia and East Frisia in Germany, and parts of the west coast of Sleswig-Holstein in Germany and Denmark. It is debated whether the original settlers of Friesland came from the Danish peninsula, or migrated to it, or whether they were Saxons, or Angles, depending on the historical interpretation.

We do know that the Frisian islands served as a stepping stone for migration from the continent to the British Isles, where Frisians settled in East Anglia, Lincolnshire and Kent around 500 AD. Frisian is the Germanic language most closely associated with English. Moreover, DNA studies[364] have shown central English and Frisian DNA to be statistically indistinguishable. The 6th century historian Bede (673-735 AD) refers to the Frisians as being among the more important of the Germanic peoples to come to Britain[365]. This is verified in the work of the sixth-century Byzantine historian Procopius[366] (490/510-560 AD) The Roman writers Tacitus[367] (ca. 56-117 AD) and Plinius[368] (23-79 AD) also mentioned the Frisians in their writings. Two key Frisian historical figures are mentioned in the early literature: King Finn Folcwalding (sixth century) appears in the Anglo-Saxon epics (*Widsith, Beowulf* and the *Finnsburgh* fragment) and King Redbad (679-719 AD), the pagan chieftain who, as the Frisian hero, defended the Frisian empire against both the Franks and Rome.

East Frisia lies in what is now the extreme northwest of Germany, where the Beninga's once reigned as one of the oldest and most influential chieftain families. Whether or not Beninga and Banning could in any way have been related is definitely subject for debate, as the names apparently evolved from different Germanic origins. Whether the Beningas, as they were most commonly known, should make up part of this book is thus uncertain. However, given all the variations in spelling encountered especially in the middle ages, they are included for the sake of interest and good order. A more recent union such as that between a

---

[364] M.E. Weale, D.A. Weiss, R.F. Jager, N. Bradman, M.G. Thomas, *Y chromosome evidence for Anglo-Saxon mass migration*, Molecular Biology & Evolution ,Oxford University Press, July 2002
[365] http://www.bbc.co.uk/education/beyond/factsheets/makhist/makhist4_prog4b.shtml; accessed June 2004
[366] http://www.bbc.co.uk/education/beyond/factsheets/makhist/makhist4_prog4b.shtml; accessed June 2004
[367] http://85.1911encyclopedia.org/F/FR/FRISIANS.htm; accessed July 2004
[368] http://www.fryskeside.nl/mainframe_bestanden/fryslan_best/frl_main8.htm; accessed July 2004

Benninga and a Banning in 1918[369] is interesting to note, but of no particular relevance here other than to indicate how close and intricate the bonds can be.

Eggerik Beninga, born in Grimersum in 1490 was a member of the chieftain's family of Beninga and a chronicler of Frisian history. He was Bailliff of Leerort in 1524. (It is coincidental that Sicke Benningh of Friesland, while unrelated, was a chronicler of Friesland at the same time.) Eggerik Beninga's *Cronica der Friesen (Chronicle of the Frisians)* was published in about 1550, the first Frisian history ever written. In 1723 his manuscript was described as "comprising not only the history of East Frisia, but also the neighbouring tribes to the east and the west, uniquely the most incomparable record of ancient and present day Friesland, both in the time of the heathens and since it has been Christianised, written by Eggerik Beninga, now enriched and reproduced with borders and margin illustrations, old seals and other features, printed by Eilhardus Folkardus Harkenroht."[370] . Eggerik Beninga died in 1562 and was laid to rest in a monumental grave in the historical church of Groothusen, Grimersum.

Although the East Frisian family is most commonly known as Beninga, spelling of the name varied considerably. The suffix *'-a'* is characteristic, also today, of Frisian names. There are numerous mentions of the family in the *Oostfriese Oorkondenboek 787-1470* and that of 1471-1500 (*East Frisian Book of Charters 787-1470* and *1471-1500*):

1354: (2 Aug.): Gerald and Thyadger Beninga (Gheraldus and Thyadgerus) sons of Lyuardi Beningha of the Beninghaburch
1379: (18 July) Geraldum Binga and Beninghones
1404: (13 July) the Benyngmans
1475: Garreldt Benyngha, (Garrelt Beninga, Gherald Beningha, Geralde, Geraldum, Bailiff of Hinte and landowner of Grimarzum/Grimersum),
Geraldo Bennyngen/Aylt Bennyngen
1478: (25 July) Wyard Beninge of Loppersum
1481: Affa Benyngha, landowner of Pylsym
1500: marriage contract between Folkert Beninga of Grimersum and None Kankena
1566:(23 March) birth of Aepke Beninga, Chieftain of Loppersum, later married to Anna Juechter (b.29 July 1567), lady-in-waiting to Countess Anna of East Frisia.

---

[369] J. Banning, *Stamboom van Maurits Arnoldus Banning*, Dedgem, 1984, p. 26: Popke Banning b. 12. Feb. 1918 married Elisabeth Anje Jacomina Benninga, b. 24 Nov. 1925.
[370] H. Meybohm, J. Beer, & Wolffram, booksellers, Beek & Wolfram, printed in Emden, 1723

Redward Beninga was the first known chieftain of that name in East Frisia, probably around 1325. His son Haitet Beninga was chieftain of Groothusen in East Frisia. His son, Haytet Beninga, (ca.1378-1448), who married Itze Pibinga, was also Chieftain. Chieftain Redward II was born in 1405 and died in 1442. Several estates in a cluster of towns are mentioned in relation to the family and are rather confusing to sort out: the castle of Beningaburg, the castle of Upleward, the Stiekelkamp estate (Beningafehn), Westerburg and the estate of Middelstewehr. Middelstewehr, comprising roughly 85 hectares, came into possession of the Beningas through marriage to the family of Cirksena, who owned it originally. Redward II was married to Doda Cirksena, and one Inel Beninga was married to a Hilleda Cirksena. A son of this union was Tido Beninga, who inherited the property in 1533 and sold it in 1582.

The family Beninga of Grimersum had their seat in the Beninghaburch (Beningaburg), located between Grimersum and Wirdum, first mentioned in 1354. The castle Beningaburg was built some time between the 11th and early 14th century. Apparently it was destroyed and rebuilt, being destroyed for a second time in 1435. Archaeological excavations of the medieval castle in 1999 and 2000 revealed that Beningaburg was designed for military defence and more a fortification than a castle , once situated by open waters, with entrenchments dug for larger ships.

One excavated area[371] measured some 44m. long and 11m. wide. A mighty, solid brick tower measuring 11.40m. by 10.10m. marked the east corner. It overlapped the trench of the western section, a hall construction of over 30m., partitioned on the inside. The configuration and foundation construction suggest that one was an earlier development, with notable differences. The older trench contained very few brick fragments, which were more numerous in the newer trench. Only some wall and floor remnants, foundations and brick paving remained preserved. Two older strata of construction were discovered some 3m. under the late medieval layer. Finds of ceramics indicate early medieval use. The main building measured 21,4m. by 11,40m. with walls of 1,40m. thick.

---

[371] http://www.ostfriesischelandschaft.de/af/wirdum00.htm; accessed May 2004

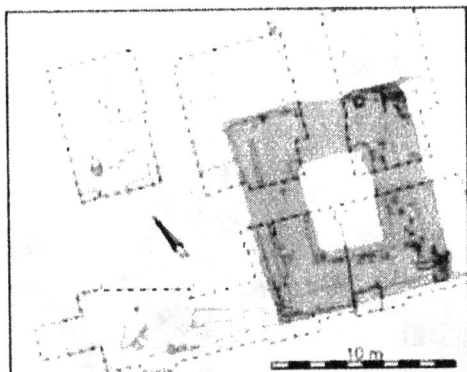

78. Reconstruction of a stone section of Beningaburg in
Wirdum after the excavation findings.
image: G. Kronsweide, Ostfriesische Landschaft[372]

Wood from a board construction could be dated to 1175 and
traced to the company Delag, of Göttingen, in south Nether-Saxony,
(north Germany). A rectangular oak post from a later phase, obviously
broken off, was dated 1238. Outbuildings and a refuse pit revealed
ceramic material, animal bones, bone artefacts, vegetable remnants and
charred grain. Other finds included a tiny gold object similar to a button,
and a long tine comb made of bone. The material found did not give the
impression that the former owners lived in great wealth.

The Beningas of Grimersum owned the castle and village of
Upleward[373] from the 14th to the 17th century. This magnificent castle,
gradually refurbished in Renaissance style, was once home to the
Chieftain family of Edelinga in 1409. A grandchild, Ubbo Tidena (1469),
was married to Hebrich Beninga of Grimersum, whose descendants bore
the Beninga name. The last chieftain of the family mentioned was Tido
Beninga II, chieftain of Upleward, Middelstewehr, Hamswehrum and
Uiterstewehr. He died on 21 December 1594. Tido's magnificent
gravestone was moved to the inner court of the Pewsum castle after
restoration. The castle was demolished in 1782. The gravestone can now
be viewed at the East Frisian Burgenmuseum in Pewsum.

---

[372] Emder Jahrbuch für historische Landeskunde Ostfrieslands 80, 2000, S. 218;
http://www.ostfriesischelandschaft.de/af/wirdum00.htm; accessed May 2004
[373] Krummhörn – Upleward; http://www.upleward.de/; accessed May 2004

79. The castle of Upleward in Grimersum, home to the Beninga Chieftains
private collection

The Stiekelkamp estate in Oldenburg[374] (Altenburg) was most likely what is referred to as Beningafehn, purchased in 1788 by the Lantzius Beninga family. It comprises 60 hectares of parkland and forest, age-old oaks and beeches obscuring the estate and former seat of the Lantzius Beninga family. Since the last owner, Maria Lantzius Beninga, died in 1969, ownership was transferred to the township. Poor structural condition led to renovation using the old stones, salvaged to create guest houses. The original ancestral hall has been preserved, featuring the furniture, a large tiled stove and numerous family portraits. It was restored in 1975 and is open to the public. The oldest portrait depicts Ajold Beninga, chieftain to Grimmersum, Wirdum and Jennelt, who died in 1483.

The forests, seriously damaged by a storm in 1972, are being replanted. The park, having withstood the ravages of the storm, is now a popular recreational area. It features rare species of vegetation carefully nurtured by Oberfürster George Boyung Scato Lantzius Beninga over 180 years ago: a tulip tree, acacias, cypresses, cedars, arbour vitae and Japanese screen firs. The forest cemetery serves as a family burial place for the Lantzius – Beningas.

The Beningaburg in Dornum[375] was built in the second half of the 14th century by the Chieftain Attena. A century later it fell into

[374] Unser Dorf Neukamperfehn;
http://www.neukamperfehn.de/Schone_Ecken/schone_ecken.html; accessed May 2004
[375] Dornum und seine Burgen; http://www.nordwestreisemagazin.de/dornum/Burgen1.htm; accessed May 2004

possession of the Kankena family by inheritance, and through marriage to the Beningas at the beginning of the 16th century. It was further developed after the middle of the 17th century and remained in Beninga possession until the beginning of the 19th century. Ownership changed hands several times after that.

Surrounded by old trees and a moat, the castle is now operated as a hotel and restaurant. Portraits of Beninga ancestors can be viewed in the ancestral hall.

80. entry to Beningaburg, Dornum
unsigned sketch, private collection

The Westerburg[376] belonged to the second son of Chieftain Attena, Eger, and was passed on to his son Hicko, whose daughter married Tanno Cankena. When Cankena was taken prisoner during the siege of Wittmund, he purchased his freedom by surrendering the castle to Ulrich Cirksena, the first count of Frisia in 1464.

Westerburg later came into possession of the Beningas. Countess Theda acquired it from Ayelt Beninga's widow. In a Friedeburg peace settlement she left the Westerburg to the brothers Hero and Hicko of Dornum, granting them all rights in 1481. It apparently suffered damage during the Saxon feuds and was not rebuilt. A mill was built on the historical grounds in 1719.

[376] Dornum und seine Burgen; http://www.nordwestreisemagazin.de/dornum/Burgen1.htm; accessed May 2004

The very first records found to date of Bannings and Bennings are from Germany. They held prominent positions as alderman in Coesfeld, Westphalia, which is known to have been a major Saxon settlement and later a Hanseatic city. The Book of Charters of Westphalia[377] names the following:

1238: Gottfried (Godefrido) Benninc, father of Conrado
1238: Konrad (Conradus) Benning, alderman of Coesfeld from 1238-
1258)
1247: Heinricus de Benninghusen (also Bennig-, Benninch)
1258: Conradus and Bernardo Benning
1275: Bernardo Benning (alderman of Coesfeld from 1258-1275)
1278: Ludolfo Benninc
1292: Thiderico Benynck
1295: Johannes de Benninchusen, Councillor of Geseke (read: Benninc-husen, or Benninc/Banning house)

German homesteads deriving from the name (see chapter on homesteads for further description) include:
Benninchus (read: Benninc-hus, or Benninc-house) in Westphalia, 1244[378]
Benninghausen, date of origin unknown, which as a town still exists
Benning/Benning-roth[379], Coesfeld, Westphalia, 1302
Bennink[380], near Ascheberg, 1193
Benninccamp[381], Westphalia, 1318
Benningh[382], Emlichheim, 1485
Banninghof[383], Wettringen, year of origin before 1507 unknown, still exists.

One *Lubbert Bannick*[384] is mentioned in Wettringen, of the homestead of Banninghof, killed when run over by his horse in 1507.

---

[377] Dr. Roger Wilmans, *Westfälisches Urkunden-Buch*, H. Th. Wenner, Osnabruck, 1973 (original publication 1871)
[378] Dr. Roger Wilmans, *Westfälisches Urkunden-Buch*, H. Th. Wenner, Osnabruck, 1973 (original publication 1871) Part III,p. 230
[379] Dr. Roger Wilmans, *Westfälisches Urkunden-Buch*, H. Th. Wenner, Osnabruck, 1973 (original publication 1871) Part III,p. 36
[380] Dr. Roger Wilmans, *Westfälisches Urkunden-Buch*, H. Th. Wenner, Osnabruck, 1973 (original publication 1871) Part III,p. 711
[381] Dr. Roger Wilmans, *Westfälisches Urkunden-Buch*, H. Th. Wenner, Osnabruck, 1973 (original publication 1871) Part III, charter no. 1226, 16 Feb. 1318, p. 447
[382] Dr. B.H. Slicher van Bath, *Mensch en Land in de Middeleeuwen*, Part I, Assen, Van Gorcum & Comp. N.V.,1944, p. 211
[383] J.A.W. Banning, *Genealogie van het Geslacht Banning*, Ferd. Banning & Zonen, Groenlo, 1934, p. I

The following review appeared in the daily newspaper *The Noord-Brabant Daily*[385] (October 1935):

"About an Inheritance"

"The court of Pittsburgh in the American state of Pennsylvania has decided on division of the inheritance of Karl Banning. This Banning, who died unmarried and is buried in his birthplace of Lengerich (Germany), had left behind a fortune of two and a half million dollars. With the exception of $ 30,000 the entire fortune will go to the German heirs, that is, after the inheritance tax has been paid in the United States."

A French daily newspaper wrote on this subject in August 1934[386]:

"MENDIANT MILLIONAIRE"

" A beggar from Pittsburgh, Carl Banning, 72 years of age, died recently. It was known that, 20 years ago, he had left a stockbroker's and put aside a small fortune, but people were convinced that Banning had long since lost all his savings in the many stock market crashes which occurred in the U.S. in the past 5 years: otherwise Banning lived in the worst of poverty.

The juridical authorities were astounded to discover amongst the papers of the deceased a minute account of all his monetary transactions. A perfectly executed will stipulates that the entire fortune left by the deceased had to be handed over to distant relatives living in Lengerich, Germany. The account showed that the beggar had amassed some 300,000 francs 20 years ago. Thanks to prudent investments, his fortune now is worth 45 million francs."

On Thursday 2nd August 1934, the Pittsburgh Press, Pennsylvania published a life sketch (abbreviated; translated from the Dutch genealogy of 1984[387]):

"As a young man in his early twenties Karl Banning let go of his mother's skirts to seek his fortune in a foreign country. In England he took a job in a steel factory, but was soon transferred to Pittsburgh, the land of unlimited opportunity. He led an uneventful life, prepared his own meals and repaired his own shoes. Diligent, judicious and above all thrifty, he amassed a small fortune. He left his job and invested his savings in first rate securities. The dividends poured in and he conscientiously pursued this policy, which was rewarded. The stock market was an open book to

---

[384] Wilhelm Brockpäler, *Wettringen, Geschichte eine Münsterlandischen Gemeinde*, Gemeinde Wettringen, Germany, 1970, p. 120

[385] J. Banning, *Stamboom van Maurits Arnoldus Banning*, Dedgem,1984, p. VI

[386] J. Banning, *Stamboom van Maurits Arnoldus Banning*, Dedgem,1984, p. VI

[387] J. Banning, *Stamboom van Maurits Arnoldus Banning*, Dedgem,1984, p. VII,VIII

him and his purchases became more extensive as time went by. Outside of a small, select group of friends nobody could imagine that his financial transactions would make him a millionaire after some years. Dressed in black, always carrying a sturdy walking stick, he was seen in the city centre as a greying old gentleman, a passer-by whom nobody paid mind. He hated driving in automobiles and preferred public transport by train. Once outside of the city he would step down and commence on a walk of hours in the extensive forests there. He revelled in the outdoors, which must have reminded him of the homeland he had left behind years before.

He had the worthy habit of donating an amount of a thousand dollars every year at Christmas to the mayor of Lengerich, so that schoolchildren could be surprised with a Christmas gift, In return, they presented 'Uncle Banning' with a large packet of thank you notes, which he saved carefully as a cherished keepsake.

When his health declined, he moved into an apartment in a respected hotel. On the evening of 26th July 1934, after dining with friends and after the usual conversation concerning economy, politics, literature and the theatre, he suffered a heart attack on arriving home. Even then, he invited those present to join him in partaking of a bottle of champagne, given as a gift by the Italian consul. Fortunately, there was a doctor among those present, who gave him morphine to reduce the pain, but he died several minutes later. He reached the age of 72. His last wish was to be buried in the small churchyard in Lengerich, beside the grave of his parents. His fortune was almost entirely left to the family in Germany."

Karl Banning (not specified in the genealogy) was a descendant of the German lineage commencing with Adolf Friedrich Banning & Elisabeth Detmeyer, who married on 11 May 1686 in Tecklenberg (Westphalia, Germany). Their only child, Johann Marcus (1688-1754) became a clergyman in 1719 in Ladbergen. He was married on 11 June 1720 to the widow Venna Maria Focke. Nine children were born of this union, of which the two eldest are mentioned specifically: Ernst Johann Adolf (1721-1790) and Moritz Hildebrand (b. 1722), great-great-grandfather to Karl Banning.

The first mentioned followed in his father's footsteps to become a clergyman and was married on 12 July 1757 to Henriette Sophie Deegen. Their sons Johann Matthias Marcus and Ernst Ludwig later also entered into the clergy. Moritz Hildebrand Banning chose the profession of his grandfather, Adolf Friedrich, and settled as a manufacturer in Lengerich. He was followed by his eldest son Johann Bernhard (b. 1748). A shop owned by the deceased Bernard Banning was still located in Lengerich in 1982.

More men in the family entered into the clergy: Hermann Moritz (1799-1866) and Ernst Bernhard Banning (1811-1874), both born in Lengerich, sons of Johann Bernhard Banning and Helene Friederike Ziegler. Hermann Moritz Banning was a clergyman in Gütersloh from 1838-1843, after which he was sent to Unterbarmen (Wuppertal). Amongst other things, he was a close associate of Heinrich Barth, a well-known philosopher and explorer (Africa) and fervent supporter of Evangelism.

80a. Hermann Moritz Banning clergyman (1799-1866)

Source: *Geschichte der Vereinigtevangelischen Gemeinde Unterbarmen vom Jahre 1822 bis zum Jahre 1922"*, Thümmel, Schreiner und van den Bruck, Barmen (Wuppertal), 1922

Felix Heinrich-Wilhelm Banning provided P.W. Banning with most of the information on the German Bannings, included in the First Banning Genealogy in 1909. Felix H-W. Banning was born 3 Aug. 1861 in Düren, Rheinland. He married his cousin Lizzie Banning, born 4 Jan.1864; they had six children. Felix H-W. Banning was a prosperous manufacturer of paper machinery.

81. Felix Heinrich Wilhelm Banning, (1861-?)
The First Banning Genealogy, P.W. Banning, Chicago, 1909

Düren (Rheinland), den 4 November 1885.

Lieber Willy!

[handwritten letter text, German cursive]

Felix.

82. Letter from Felix Banning to his brother-in-law, Willy Peters,
written on company stationary in 1885
courtesy of his grandson, Ing. J. Banning, Düren, Germany

In 1976 the Tourist Association of the city of Tecklenburg issued the book *Tecklenburg 1226-1976*[388], written by Friedrich Ernst Hunsche, on the occasion of the 750th anniversary of the city .

After the Westphalia Peace Treaty was signed, putting an end to the thirty year war (1618-1648), the city gradually began to flourish again, partly thanks to the reviving textile industry. Public life was well organised, including the instigation of a civilian watch. Housing was divided into a number of precincts for this purpose. The author Hunsche was selective and restricted himself in his book to the publication of watch schedules for the years 1693, 1727 and 1816. According to the watch schedule of 1693, the first precinct consisted of 21 houses surrounding the market square. Among the 24 houses of the seventh precinct a house was included belonging to a certain Adolf Friedrich Banning, which can accurately be assumed to have been the ancestor of this genealogy .

---

[388] F.E. Hunsche, *Tecklenburg 1226-1976*, Tourist Association of Tecklenburg, 1976

GENEALOGY OF BANNING OF TECKLENBURG, WESTPHALIA, GERMANY (Protestant)

I   ADOLF FRIEDRICH BANNING, married in Tecklenburg (Westphalia)11 May 1686 to Anna Elisabeth Detmeyer, widow of .... Föges.

From this marriage:
1. Johann Marcus, follows II

II   JOHANN MARCUS BANNING, born Tecklenburg (Westph.) 24 May 1688, becomes 'Pfarrer' (Clergyman) in Ladbergen (Westph.). Died there 11 Apr. 1754. Married there 1 June 1720 to Maria Focke.

From this marriage:
1. Ernst Johann Adolf, follows III
2. Moritz Hildebrand, follows IIIa
3. Ernestine Margarite Elisabeth Banning, born Ladbergen, (Westph.) 1 Nov. 1724.
4. Ernst Bernhard Banning, born Ladbergen (Westph.) 20 Apr. 1726 (emigrated to England around 1768, will written in 1797 London)
5. Friedrich Banning, born Ladbergen (Westph.) 20 Apr. 1729.
6. Lernhard Hermann Banning, born Ladbergen (Westph.), 15 Feb. 1731.
7. Christine Wilhelmine Margarethe Banning, born Ladbergen (Westph.) 7 Jan. 1733.
8. Alexander Banning, born Ladbergen (Westph.) 15 July 1734.
9. Maria Magdalena Banning, born Ladbergen (Westph.) 24 June 1736.

III   ERNST JOHANN ADOLF BANNING, born Ladbergen (Westph.) 28 Aug. 1721. Later became a clergyman and married there to ..... unknown.

From this marriage:
1. John Johann Matthias Marcus Adolf Banning, born Ladbergen (Westph.), follows in his father's footsteps as clergyman there.
2. Ernest Ludwig Banning, born Ladbergen (Westph.), follows in his brother's footsteps as clergyman there.

IIIa   MORITZ HILDEBRAND BANNING, born Ladbergen (Westph.) 17 Dec. 1722. Merchant, settles in Lengerich (Westph.). Married .... unknown.

From this marriage:

1. Johann Bernhard Banning, baptized Lengerich (Westph.) 1 Nov 1748 (sons Hermann Moritz b.1799 and Ernst Berhard b. 1811)
2. Maria Elsalein (Elisabein) Banning, born Lengerich (Westph.) 13 Oct. 1751.
3. Johann Adolf Banning, born Lengerich (Westph.) 12 June 1754.
4. Christine Marie Banning, born Lengerich (Westph.) 20 Apr. 1757.
5. Friedrich Mauritz Banning, born Lengerich (Westph.) 8 Oct. 1760.
6. Ernst Moritz Banning, follows IV

IV MORITZ BANNING, born Lengerich (Westph.) 6 May 1767. Apothecary there. Died Lengerich 16 May 1811. Married in Lengerich to Frederike Louise Smend..
From this marriage:
1. Ernst Bernhard Banning, follows V
2. Florens Ludwig Banning, follows Vb

V ERNST BERNHARD BANNING, born Lengerich (Westph.) 1796. Apothecary there. Died Lengerich 21 June 1834., married 1st: Wilhelmina Kriege, 2nd : Elisabeth Henriette Kandelhardt , 3rd: Sophie Elisabeth Kandelhardt.
From the second marriage:
1. Heinrich Ernst Banning, follows VI

VI HEINRICH ERNST BANNING, born Lengerich (Westph.) 29 Apr. 1833. Apothecary in Düren (Rijnland). Died there 12 Sept. 1872. Married in Düren to Antonia Schüll,.
From this marriage:
1. Felix Heinrich Wilhelm Banning, follows VII
2. Elli Banning, born Düren (Rijnl.) 8 July 1864, married there 15 Apr. 1885 to Wilhelm Peters, draper in Eupen.

VII FELIX HEINRICH WILHELM BANNING, born Düren (Rijnl.) 3 Aug. 1861, paper machine manufacturer in Düren. Compiled the German genealogy. Before 1914 he travelled to various countries in Europe and to the United States, searching for genealogical data. Many of the results are recorded in the First Banning Genealogy by Pierson Worrall Banning, Chicago 1909. Died in Düren 7 Mar. 1932. Married 10 July 1888 to LIZZIE BANNING, born in Hamm 4 Jan. 1864, daughter of Johann Ernst Gustav Banning (born 10 Jan. 1833, Lengerich, died 8 Feb. 1895, Hamm) and married to Elisabeth Mauve on 11 Mar. 1860 (Elisabeth was born 4 Jan. 1834, [daughter of Sophie Frederieke Banning, born before 1802, daughter of Ernst Banning and Friederieke Arnoldine Smend] and Friedrich Wilhelm Mauve]).

From this marriage:

1. Margarite Banning, born Düren (Rijnl.) 15 May 1889, married in Metz (war marriage) 3 Aug. 1914 to Fritz Martienssen, born 17 Sept. 1878, Captain of the Germany Imperial Army, died 26 Jan. 1926, son of Georg and Helene Mattis.
2. Elli Banning, born Düren (Rijnl.) 2 Oct. 1890, married in Düren 27 Feb. 1914 to Erwin Hoesch, Düren, manufacturer, son of Robert and Martha Schoeller.
3. Hans Banning, born Düren (Rijnl.) 6 Aug. 1893. Died Düren 3 Feb. 1894.
4. Felix Banning, follows VIII.
5. Hellmuth, follows VIIIb.
6. Wolfgang Banning, follows VIIIc.

VIII FELIX BANNING, born Düren (Rijnl.) 30 Jan. 1895. Engineer. Married in Hamm (Westph.) 14 June 1923 to Hilde Hobrecker, daughter of Eduard, and of Bertha Castingius.

From this marriage:

1. Hilde Banning, born 5 Apr. 1924.
2. Brigitte Banning, born 13 Aug. 1928.
3. Annemarie Banning, born 5 June 1930.

VIIIb HELLMUTH BANNING, born Düren 19 Jan. 1898. Engineer. Married in Essen 12 May 1928 to Grete Guthing, daughter of Wilhelm, and of Martha Aldendorff.

From this marriage:

1. Lore Banning, born 18 Mar. 1929.
2. Marianne Banning, born 24 Mar. 1930.
3. Hans Banning, born 18 Sept. 1932.

VIIIc WOLGANG BANNING, born Düren 19 Oct. 1902, merchant, married in Düsseldorf 3 Aug. 1929 to Hilla Clason, daughter of Ernst, and of Minnie Bachem.

From this marriage:

1. Johann Ernst Gustav Banning, follows VI

VI JOHANN ERNST GUSTAV BANNING, born Lengerich (Westph.) 19 Jan. 1833. Machine manufacturer in Hamm (Westph.) Died there on 7 Feb. 1895. Married in Hamm to his cousin Elisabeth Mauve (see VII).

From this marriage:

1. Lizzi Banning, born in Hamm (Westph.) 4 Jan. 1864, married

there on 10 July 1888 to FELIX HEINRICH WILHELM BANNING, born in Düren (Rijnl.) 3 Aug. 1861. Died in Düren 7 Mar. 1932. Son of Heinrich Ernst, and Antonia Schüll.

   2.   Heinrich Banning, follows VII

VII HEINRICH BANNING, born in Hamm (Westph.) 16 June 1868. Machine manufacturer there, married in Hamm in Aug. 1899 to Clara Witte.

From this marriage:
1. Hermine Banning, born in Hamm (Westph.) 7 Dec. 1900
2. Werner Banning, born in Hamm (Westph.) 2 Mar. 1903

The above genealogy brings us to Maurits (Moritz) Arnoldus Banning, clergyman of Oldemirdum in Friesland, the Netherlands (1687- ?). Although it had previously been assumed that the Bannings of Friesland originally came from the Dutch province of Gelderland, the following information confirms that their origins lay in Tecklenburg and descended from the same family as the German one specified.

Mr. F.E. Hunsche of Ibbenbüren (Germany) wrote in a letter dated 26 May 1982, to the author of the Frisian genealogy of Maurits Arnoldus Banning:[389]

"Confirming the receipt of your letters, I can inform you, that I have repeatedly searched for [records of] Mauritz Arnoldus Banning in Tecklenburg. His birth and baptism cannot be confirmed in Tecklenburg, as unfortunately the Church records are inadequate and do not go this far back. His parents are also still unknown. One brother was probably Adolf Friedrich Banning, merchant in Tecklenburg, born in 1650, married 11th May 1686 in Tecklenburg to Anna Elisabeth Detmeyer. There is also an entry for Fr. Banning in Tecklenburg in 1714. The Lengerich merchant's family descends from the merchant Adolf Friedrich B. The name Banning appears to be concentrated at that time in Burgsteinfurt and Tecklenburg. It is safe to assume that the name bearers specified here are related. The assumption that Mauritz Arnoldus was born in Tecklenburg is thus justified."

Dr. David Koss, Barrington Illinois (USA), wrote in 1986 to the same author:

"Recently in reading the Tecklenburg church books I found the following: "Died 13 Apr. 1693, the olde woman Banningsche, aged 71 years 11 months."

J. Banning asserts that this might have been the mother of Maurits Arnoldus. The 1934 Frisian genealogy includes a quotation from the same records, also citing the death of 'the olde woman Banning' on

---

[389] J. Banning, *Stamboom van Maurits Arnoldus Banning*, Dedgum, 1984, p. XVII

this date. The 'olde woman Banning' would thus have been born in May 1622.

The following records further identify this German branch with that of the Frisian branch of Maurits Arnoldus Banning.

"Machteld Noordbeek, born in 1662 in Nordhorn, married in Gildehaus, [Germany] in 1684 to Mauritz Arnoldus Banning, Preacher in Gildehaus and from 3.4.1687 in Oude and Nieuwe Mirdum (Friesland), became Emeritus (retired) on 22.8.1708, thereby succeeded by his son Johannes Banning. This Johannes Banning was baptised in September 1685 in Gildehaus and died in 1735 in Oude Mirdum."[390]

Mr. H.J. Warnecke in Steinfurt (Germany) wrote on 20 December 1977 about M.A. Banning:

"A new communicant is mentioned in the Communion Records at Christ's feast (Christmas) 1675 in Burgsteinfurt. He was most likely a student of the Gymnasium Arnoldinum (Arnoldinum High School) and as such probably about 18 years of age. The entry states literally: Moritz Arnold Tecl (aburgensis)(?) (Born at the time in Tecklenburg.) The Tecklenburg Church records commence, however, at a much later date; the names of the elders can therefore no longer be easily traced. The family, or otherwise the 'Tecklenburger', apparently descended originally from Hof Banning [Banning Homestead) in Wetteringen."[391]

These findings are corroborated with other records found.[392] Further information on this Frisian line is included in the chapter on the Netherlands. It seems safe to assume that Adolf Friedrich Banning was a brother to Maurits Arnoldus Banning, thus establishing the link between Friesland in the Netherlands and Germany.

Wettringen

No proof has yet been found that the Tecklenburg Bannings mentioned above came from Wettringen, but Bannings have lived there for centuries, the first being recorded in 1457.

Lubbert Bannick 2 Dec. 1457 (Lubbert is the first Banning mentioned in the German city of Wettringen, where there was a homestead the Banninghof. (see below) His name occurs in the Hanseatic Book of Charters[393] as 'Lubbert Bannick of Deventer'. Whether this is the same

---

[390] *Naamlijst der predikanten in de Hervormde Gemeente van Friesland, sedert de Hervorming, 1886*

[391] J. Banning, *Stamboom van Maurits Arnoldus Banning*, Dedgum, 1984, p. XVII

[392] J. Banning, *Stamboom van Maurits Arnoldus Banning*, 1984, p. XIII

[393] Walther Stein, *Hansisches Urkundenbuch, 1451-1463*, Leipzig, Germany, Duncker & Humblot, 1899, p. 417-418

Lubbert as he who died when run over by a horse in 1507[394] in Wettringen is unknown, but not unlikely.

The Banninghof in Wettringen (near the Dutch border) still exists, and Bannings live there still. A cornerstone (S.D.B. 1913) reveals the names of August Banning and Helena Leismann and a second, adjacent stone (1962) mentions the names of Julia Banning and her husband Clemens.

The following references to previous tenants of the Banninghof are taken from the book *Wettringen, History of a Münster Township*[395], under the heading *Registry of village homesteads and farmsteads; Banning*::

1507: "Lubbert Banning died when his horse ran over him. Costs for burial, because they were poor and Herford people, 11 Horn guilders and 2 ..?.

1526: "the young Banning took over the homestead; he pays ½ of a cask of butter."

1612: "A very accurate assessment of costs and the progress of labour in Höltings are recorded in the March Protocol of 1612. The names of the representatives of the march are read: Schulte Frohoff, Naern Strodemann, the Herford men Johanningh, Erlink, Raynck, Bower, Banning, Sundarp...."

1661: "(Village records: homesteads and farmsteads) Banning: Horsefarm, plowed land, size 1668; 48 agricultural land, 1765: 12-16 bushels of rye seed. 1828: 44 Mo.(?) division of Vollenbrok, amongst other things. 1849: 58 Mo. (?)1679 3 horses belonging to the lord."

1668: "(Court records) The property includes a house with a stable for sheep. There are 2 horses, 4 cows, 2 bulls. There is a small forest of oak and other kinds of trees. The farmer is called Deitert and is born of Kaltemeyer's house. He married Banning's widow, one daughter of Tie Frerich, and paid the fee of a cask."

1679: "Banning, Sundarp and Biefang, horsefarm owners, are in favour." (No further details are mentioned.)"

1729: "The house, bakehouse, sheep stable and a small forest. In the meantime the property has been put (must be put?) to good repair. The new field has been sown with 6 bushels of seed and all fields must be cultivated accordingly. At the outset there is a debt of 400 Reichstaler, at present there is an interest of 60 Reichstaler on capital."

"The farmer is named Hermann Banning, who came to the homestead nine years ago....... His wife is named Adelheit Sundarps. The fee of a cask was paid."

---

[394] Wilhelm Brockpäler, *Wettringen, Geschichte eine Münsterlandischen Gemeinde*, Gemeinde Wettringen, Germany, 1970, p. 120

[395] Wilhelm Brockpäler, *Wettringen, Geschichte eine Münsterlandischen Gemeinde*, Gemeinde Wettringen, Germany, 1970, p. 28, 29, 49, 54, 73, 79, 119, 120

1729: "Banning sows 6 bushels of seed in land for new cultivation."
(undated) "Herford and Steinfurt possession of goods in Wettringen: no lease need be paid at Herford, leaving only minimal requirements to the Meier. The three farmsteads mentioned are the old one of Banning, Sundarp and the no longer existing Kempenhus."
1791: (Court Proceedings) "Wessling, Banning, Raing, Ahling and the farmstead owner Buelter were punished, because they had in their possession 4 to 12 pieces of oak each, without permission. Elling and Janning did not have wood, other than a little oak. Banning, however, has the most, who was instructed to 'visit the shrubs'(?)"
1850: "Payment of promised funds of 2 Mar. 1850. In the middle of the 19th century most of the tenants of the other farmsteads have paid their debts. These included the farmers Wesseling, Lohaus, Große Specker, Böwer and Banning."

A fragment genealogy has been compiled of nine generations of Bannings of Wettringen. Names recorded in the above extracts concerning the homestead Banninghof, from the book *Wettringen, History of a Münster Township*, recur in this genealogy. This is an excellent example of how the name was often passed down through the female line, where the husband assumed the name of his wife.

GENEALOGY OF BANNING OF WETTRINGEN, GERMANY

I GERDT BANNING, born ....?, married 7 Nov. 1654 in St. Petronilla, Wettringen to Anna zum Thie, died 28 June 1705
from this marriage:
    1. Joan Banning, born 17 Nov. 1656, follows II
    2. Friderig Banning, born 1660

II JOAN BANNING, born 17 Nov. 1656 in Wettringen, married Nov. 1683 to Maria Bifang in Wettringen, born 1664 (the name Biefang occurs together with that of Banning in 1679, in the book by Wilhelm Brockpähler[396];)
from this marriage:
    1. Enne Banning, born 11 Apr. 1685, follows III
    2. Alheid Banning, born 4 April 1689

III ENNE BANNING, born 11 Apr. 1685 in Wettringen,, married ca. 1710 to Joan Bischoff/Banning in St. Petronilla, Wettringen.
From this marriage:

---

[396] Wilhelm Brockpähler, *Wettringen, Geschichte einer Münsterländischen Gemeinde*, Gemeinde Wettringen, Germany, 1970

1. Maria Banning, born 30 May 1711, follows IV
2. Anna Aleida Banning, born 22 Feb. 1715/16
3. Hermanus Banning, born 26 Nov. 1718
4. Joes Banning, born 26 Nov. 1718

IV MARIA BANNING, born 30 May 1711 in Wettringen, married 6 July 1745 to Joes Gerardy Werning in Wettringen, son of Hermann Werning and Aheleidt Sondarps. The name Sondarps occurs in relation to the Banninghof in the book by Wilhelm Brockpähler in 1612, 1679 and in 1729, where it is stated that Hermann Banning was married to Adelheit Sundarps. At his death in Wettringen on 3 May 1779, Joes Gerardy Werning was recorded as 'Jan Banning' (Joes is an abbreviation of 'Johannes'= 'Jan'). The book by Wilhelm Brockpähler contains an entry dated 1750[397] which states that 'Joh. Gerd. Werning became known as Banning, and that Maria had been born on the homestead (of Banninghof). Maria died in Wettringen 9 Nov. 1789.
From this marriage:
1. Anna Maria Banning, born 27 Nov. 1747, (died before 1753?)
2. Joan Herman Banning, born 27 June 1751, follows V
3. Anna Maria Cath. Banning, born 19 March 1753

V JOAN HERMAN BANNING, born 27 June 1751 in Wettringen, married 5 June 1822 in St. Petronilla, Wettringen, to Margaretha Essing, born 16 Jan. 1752, daughter of Engelbertus Essing and Margaretha Bruninck, died 12 April 1824. Joan Herm Banning died 5 June 1822.
From this marriage:
1. Joan Gerd Engelbert Banning, born 7 Nov. 1779; (died before 1783?)
2. Anna Maria Gertrud Banning, born 21 Sept. 1781
3. Joan Gerard Henrich Banning, born 5 Nov. 1783, follows VI

VI JOAN GERARD HENRICH BANNING, born 5 Nov. 1783 in Wettringen, married 24 Nov. 1812 in St. Petronilla, Wettringen to Maria Catherine Lammerding, born 15 Sept. 1789, daughter of Berent Engelbert Lammerding and Anna Aleid Santmann. Joan Gerard Henrich Banning died 4 June 1863 in Wettringen.
From this marriage:
1. Bernard Hermann Banning, born 22 Sept. 1813, (died before 1821?)

---

[397] Wilhelm Brockpäler, *Wettringen, Geschichte eine Münsterlandischen Gemeinde*, Gemeinde Wettringen, Germany, 1970, p. 120

2. Anna Maria Catherina Banning, born 19 Nov. 1815 (died before 1833?)
3. child Banning, born 23 Sept. 1818
4. Catherina Elisabeth Banning, born 7 Nov. 1819
5. Bernhard Banning, born 19 Dec. 1821, follows VII
6. Maria Anna Banning, born 17 March 1824
7. Gerard Henrich Theodor Banning, born 27 Apr. 1826
8. Joan Henrich Franz Banning, born 5 Apr. 1829
9. Anna Maria Gertrud Banning, born 26 March 1833

VII BERNARD BANNING, born 19 Dec. 1821 in Wettringen, married 25 Nov. 1862 in St. Petronilla, Wettringen to Maria Roling, born in Emsbüren, died in 1902 in Wettringen. Bernard Banning died 18 Feb. 1903 in Wettringen.
From this marriage:
1. Anna-Maria Katherina Banning, born 5 Nov. 1863
2. Maria Katherina Banning, born 8 Dec. 1865, married Theodor Biefang, born 7 June 1847 in Wettringen, died 18 Mar. 1903. Maria died ?.
3. Gertrud Banning, born 20 Apr. 1868, married .. Termühlen
4. Elisabeth Carolina Banning, born 16 Dec. 1872, married 18 June 1900 to Joseph Gerhard Bernhard Brüning, born 27.09.1862 in Dutum, died 13 Feb, 1940 in Dutum. Elisabeth died ?
5. August Banning, born 19 Aug. 1877, follows VIII

VIII AUGUST BANNING, born 19 Aug. 1877 in Wettringen, married Helene Maria Theresia Leusmann, born 19 Nov. 1876 in Dutum, daughter of Bernard Anton Leusmann and Julia Maria Merker, died 21, Apr. 1965 in Wettringen. August Banning died 19 Nov. 1917 in Wettringen.
from this marriage:
1. August Banning, born 1904, died 1904
2. Änne Banning, born 1905, died 1908
3. Maria Banning, born 1908
4. Ludwig Banning, born 1911, died 1945 in Feldlazarett, Denmark
5. Julia Banning, born 27 Oct. 1915, follows IX

IX JULIA BANNING, born 27 Oct. 1915 in Wettringen, married 16 May 1950, in Wettringen to Clemens Grieuwe G. Banning, born 25 Mar. 1910 in Hopsten, died 16 May 1950 in Wettringen. Julia Banning died ?
From this marriage:
1. Maria Banning
2. Hedwig Banning

3. Regina Banning
4. Ludwig Banning
5. Hubertus Banning

Information and an illustration of the Banninghof of Wettringen are included in the chapter on (Medieval) Homesteads.

Almost all of the Bannings recorded in Germany lived in the province of Westphalia. It is, perhaps, worth note that some of the earliest Bannings recorded in Europe were located in Hanseatic cities: Coesfeld, Munster, Danzig, Lübeck, (Germany); Deventer, Oldenzaal, Zutphen (Netherlands) London and Ipswich (England).

Albert Benningk[398], (born..., died 1690) of Lübeck, was a metal caster and bell caster. He is not to be confused with the Danzig bell casters of the same name, although no reason is given why. It is assumed that he is a son of Hermann Benningk, metal caster in Hamburg, mentioned from 1647-1668, in turn probably a son of Reinhard Benningk (died 1617), Hamburg metal caster, who married 1st Sophie Helms and 2nd Elisabeth Balcke. In 1665 Albert Benningk practiced his profession by appointment to the government. He left Lübeck in 1686 and was probably in Copenhagen, Denmark, until he died, in service to the Danish royal court. He was one of the most prominent masters of his craft in the 17th century, throughout the whole Baltic Sea area. Bells which he cast still hang in various cities, such as Travemünde (1673) and the cathedral of Ratzeburg (1670). One bell, dated 1669, is inscribed with his initials: "A.B. me fecit Lübecae" (made by A.B. in Lübeck) and is now held by the Vienna Heeresmuseum. Canons cast in 1669 and 1679 were once held by the military arsenal in Berlin, others in the military arsenal of Copenhagen. One of his most famous bells, in the Marien Church in Lübeck (1669), was rung regularly for 273 years, from Advent of 1669 until 1942, when the church was bombed by British fighters during World War II.

The bell which was temporarily stilled in the war was eventually compensated for by another, which had an unusual history. In the town of Staraja Russa, close to Ilmensee in Russia, the small church of the holy Mina lay behind the summer home of the writer Dostojewski, where he wrote his renowned 'The Brothers Karamazov". It was one of only two churches which survived out of thirty which the Bolsheviks had converted into garages, manufacturing facilities and storage. During World War II, in the summer of 1941, the village was stormed by German troops. During war time, the church tower afforded an excellent view over enemy lines. It was thus that an engineer from a military battalion, when examining the tower for soundness of its construction , happened upon a

---

[398] *Deutsches Biographisches Jahrbuch*, Deutsches Verlagsanstalt, Stuttgart, 1932, p. 52

church bell, which did not in itself seem remarkable. However, his attention was caught by a Latin inscription on the beautifully wrought bell rim, which hinted at it's history: 'ALBERT BENNINGK ME FECIT LUBECA ANNO 1672.' ('Made by Albert Benningk in Lübeck in 1672') The war records describe how the bell had seen turbulent times until the Bolsheviks came to power, churches were closed and the bell silenced. The record[399] continues: "German soldiers woke it now from its long slumber. The German commander, once having served as a soldier in the old Hanseatic city of Lübeck, displayed the bell to his men, and on a Sunday morning the troops were instructed in an unusual task: to construct hoists and pulley and to bring down the bell."

The commander conceived the idea of returning the bell to whence it came, as Lübeck had lost so many of its treasures to the war, in a gesture of homage and brotherhood, a symbol of stability and faith which survived centuries of turmoil. In December 1942 it was thus sent to Germany, and in January 1943 came to rest in the basement of the Holy Spirit Hospital in Lübeck. However, the well-intended transfer of the bell was a dubious enterprise, as seizure and removal of church property and works of art in the war – this also being unrecorded and beyond the public eye - was an offence under international law. When, on initiative of Russia, the bell was discovered in 1999 in the church of St. Catherine's in Lübeck, the German authorities immediately conceded that it was not rightfully theirs, suffered pangs of conscience and pledged to return it. After 60 years, the bell (58 cm high and weighing 100 kg.) was returned to its rightful place in the tower at Staraja Russa. An official letter from Lübeck accompanied the bell, reading: "This document was presented to the citizens of the city Staraja Russa on the occasion of the return of the bell of the old church of the holy Mina, on 18 February 2001. The Hanseatic city Lübeck thereby wishes you luck and peace for the future, as is described by Friedrich Schiller (1759-1805) in his *Song of the Bell*: "Holder peace, sweet unity, repose, repose, - friendliness over this city! May ne'er again the day appear, where the rough hordes of war rage through this quiet valley, where the heavens, which paint the lovely evening with gentle hues of red, are scorched with the wild and terrible blaze radiating from the villages, the cities!"

Gerhardus Benningk[400] (17th century) was of Danzig, West Prussia, and rather out of place in this or any other chapter, except for his affinity by name and profession – if not relation - with the above mentioned Albert. For that reason he is included here. We know of him only through the

---

[399] Wie "Schutzengel" zu Kirchenräubern wurden; http://www.webarchiv-server.de/pin/archiv01/1001ob13.htm; accessed June 2004
[400] Katholische Kirche Zuckau, Kreis Karthaus, Provinz Westpreußen; http://pom-wpru.kerntopf.com/kathkirche/zuckau.htm, accessed June 2004

inscription on a bell in an old 13th century parish church of Zuckau. The second in size of the three bells in this church is inscribed: "Divino auxilio fudit ME Gerhardus Benningk' (Gerhardus Benningk cast this bell with divine assistance)" and "Si deus per nobis, quis versus nos (is God for us, who is against us), Anno 1647".

Matthias Benningk[402] (1595) During the course of this research a text dated 1830[403] was found, written by a vicar and describing two bells in a church tower in Knäred, in south Halland on the west coast of Sweden. The inscription on the smallest bell reads: ' DJESSA + KLOCKE + DE +ERENTUESTEN + JUGCKEREN + GODICH + HNCKE + UND + AXEL + KORCK + HEBEN + MTIAS + BENNINGK + ME + FECIT + FORERET + THO YLLESSBY KERKE + ANNO 1595' which translates as: "This bell was donated by the honourable Godich Hinck and Axel Korck, Esquires, and made by Matthias Benningk for the Yllessby Church in 1595". The location of Yllessby is identified with what is now called Ysby, near Knäred. The bell was hung in a new church in Knäred which was opened in 1849, replacing a medieval church still in use in 1830, perhaps the one in Ysby described by the vicar. However, the new church fell down around the ears of the congregation during the very first service in 1849 and had to be rebuilt. The bell of Benningk tolled again from the present church , which was rebuilt in 1854 and still stands today.

Perhaps Matthias was related – a father or brother? – to the above mentioned Reinhard, grandfather of Albert, which would seem a reasonably plausible assumption. The bell caster's family might then have been Swedish in origin. If this is the case, the next question would be whether they were related to Abraham Benningk of the noble Swedish genealogy mentioned below. As yet, there are no further clues.

---

[402] Hallands historia och beskrivning; http://www.glimten.net/hok/Knered.HTM, accessed June 2004

[403] Hallands historia och beskrivning; http://www.glimten.net/hok/Knered.HTM , accessed June 2004

The Benningks seemed to have feet in both Germany and Sweden, and thus it is appropriate, in making the transition to Scandinavia, to close this section with a fragment genealogy of the Benning(k) family, several generations of nobles originating from Sweden, living in Germany in the 17th and 18th centuries. This excerpt is taken from:

The Noble family of Benning(k)[403]

Raised to aristocracy on 2 April 1751, registered in Sweden in 1752 under no.1908, became extinct 13 Feb. 1875.

A family who, after the year 1760, held prominent positions as councillors in Sweden, living afterward in Waldeck and in Hessen (Germany) until the 1870's, and subsequently died out due to lack of male heirs. The last male members of the family were Carl von Benning, born 18 Feb. 1804 in Rhena, who died without issue on 13 Feb. 1875 in Cassel; married 22 June 1844 to Clementine von Langenschwartz, heiress, born 1822 in Rhena; and Customs Officer Johan Henrik Benning. The *Riddarhusgenealgien (Swedish genealogy of the house of nobles)* specifies the Customs Officer Johan Henrik Benning as having been the son to burgher Abraham Benningk, born in 1594, deceased in 1673, and his wife Anna Bartels (sister of Lydert Adlersköld), deceased in 1670. However, this couple did not marry until 1658 and left only two daughters. Nothing is known about Abraham Benningk's earlier marriage, from which Johan Henrik could have been born, it is known that he married Ingrid (von) Ahlstedt in 1671, which marriage was childless. (The groom was 77 years of age at the time.)

---

[403] Gustaf Elgenstierna, *Den introducerade svenska adelns Ättartavlor, med tillägg och rättelser*, Norstedt 1925-1936 and Schwedische Adelsgenealogie, 1920, Vol. I, page. 298

Abraham Benningk, born 1594, died 1673, in Sweden. Married 1st: ? , 2nd
in 1658 Anna Bartels, died 1670, 3rd Ingrid (von) Ahlstedt in 1671
From these marriages: two daughters, unnamed, and a son:

Johan Henrik Benning: Customs Officer in Verden 1668; died in Bremen
in 1660.[author's note: one of these dates is erroneous: J.H.B.,
could not have been working in Verden in 1668 if he died in 1660]
– married Elisabet Amende.

From this marriage:

Otto Vilhelm Benning, customs Official in Verden, died there in 1715.
Married to Dorotea Knigge.

from this marriage:

Engelhart Didrik Benning, born 14 Aug. 1699 in Verden; secretary to the
abbesses of Herford, Princess Charlotta Sofia of Courland 1719;
appointed as her cabinet secretary to the Polish, English,
Hannoverian, Danish and Holsteingottorpska (?) courts; secretary
to Duke Carls of Hessen-Cassel-Schaumburg Chancellery 1729; in
service to Duke Ferdinand of Courland 1736 and councillor to
Parliament in Warsaw 1738; chancellor to King Frederik I, serving
his Hessen-Cassel affairs in Stockholm 1740; raised to Swedish
nobility on 2 April 1751   (introduced 1752 under no. 1908);
government councillor in Hessen Casselsktjanst;(?)died 2 March
1762. Married Louisa Henrietta Hufholz, born 1698, daughter of
Chancellor Johan Valentin Hufholz of Rinteln.

From this marriage:

Johanna Elisabet, born 6 March 1733 in Rinteln.

Ferdinand Ludvig, born 18 March 1736 in Rinteln; Captain of the
Grenadiers of the Hessian Royal Guard. Married 1st Tyroll, who
died in childbirth, as well as the child; married 2nd Catharina
Johanna von Campen, who in 1764 had (as yet) no children.
Ferdinand Ludvig was awarded with
the medal 'Pour le Mérite' in 1792, one of the highest German
honours bestowed. Another 'knighthood in the order Pour le
Mérite' was awarded to a Benning in 1815, but it is unknown
whether the same Ferdinand Ludvig was the recipient.

Charlotta Augusta, born 2 Oct. 1738 in Rinteln. Married to Captain of the
French service Peter von Flott.

Ulrika, born 18 Sept. 1741 in Rinteln

Fredrik Vilhelm, born 4 Sept. 1743 in Stockholm; lieutenant with the
Hessian regiment .

*   *   *

BANNING OF SCANDINAVIA

A century ago, genealogists claimed that the Bannings originally came from Denmark, as Vikings, and were said to proliferate there still. However, surprisingly few Scandinavian Bannings have turned up in the course of this research.

Closer enquiry revealed that there were only two Bannings (telephone connections) located in Denmark and five in Sweden in 2003. Since it is not logical to conclude that the Bannings have all fled the country since the claim of their great numbers was made, nor that Bannings do not possess listed telephone numbers in this day and age, and given that next to no evidence was found of their being there in great numbers in the first place, this claim shall be relegated to the realm of myth until proven otherwise.

In response to a request for information on the Scandinavian family, Professor Knud Banning (originally of Denmark) kindly granted permission to publish the letter he wrote from Sweden on 23 August 2003:

"Dear Elisabeth,
It is not possible that I can be of any help to you, because my Banning name is a bought one. My father was baptized Olesen, a very common Danish last name, and about 1915 his superiors in the Danish State Railways asked him to change it. He looked his new name up in a special list, he told me, bought it for a few croners and therefore it is certain that nobody else was named Banning – in that case, the name would not be on sale. My youngest daughter and I are now the only persons who use the name, but curious enough here in Helsingborg, in Sweden, where I now live, there is one person also called Banning, and contacting him some years ago, he told me that his father, too, had bought the name, around the same time as mine did. But I remember that very many years ago, I saw in the newspaper, published by the Danish minority in Flensborg, just south of the border to Germany, that "a pig had been stolen from the widow Banning in Slesvig town", about 30 km. from the border. It can easily be 50 years ago or so, when the food was scarce, and a pig was hard cash. Perhaps it could be of some use to you to have a look in old directories. Once I was interested in the name myself, and studying in London in 1962 I threw some glances in the telephone directories and found, as far as I remember, that the name was most common in the eastern parts of England. I got the impression that it was just there that my ancient relatives, the Anglo-Saxons, had lived. I see that you follow the same guidelines."

Best greetings from
Knud Banning, Professor Emer. Dr. Theology

A derivation of Banning, the name Benningius, such as that used by a few Dutch Bannings in the 16th and 17th centuries, also occurred in Sweden in the 17th century in a poignant fragment genealogy[404],[405]:

I PETRUS MATTIAE BENNINGIUS, vicar, was born in Karbenning, Uppland, October 1624. He married in 1652, in Orsa, Sara Floràea born in Ore 3 July 1628. They both drowned in the lake Orsasjön at Guto Island on their way home from a wedding the 8th of June (or July 1682. The couple had 4 children:

1. *Gudmund Persson Benningius* was born in Orsa 1656. In 1668 he was registered in the school in Uppsala, but already the following year he moved to Västerås and in 1674 he began in gymnasium (high school). There he attended one year. In 1679 he asked the royal commander of the county (similar to a governor) about a job as local police-officer in Orsa, to be able to support his aged father and his younger siblings. He was appointed to the work and married 1 January 1683 to Anna Göransdotter Zeidritz (Zedritz), born in Falun 1667. Her father was 'copperweigher'. Gudmund died suddenly 'by fear and strike' 7 March 1709. Anna was buried 2 June 1728 in Orsa. The couple had three daughters: Sara (b.1684), Margareta (b.1687) and Maria (b.1700).

2. *Mattias Björling Benningius* was born 1659 in Orsa. He attended school in Västeråsand and was then employed by the armed forces. After his father's death he wanted to leave the military in order to make a living for himself and his sisters in 'a small business'. That little business became so great that the city councilof Falun intervened. It was, however, settled that he was allowed to carry out 'civil business' on condition that he pay an annual fee to the township. He left business and returned into military service and on 14 November 1705 he was appointed as captain. He died in the field of wounds sustained on 6 March 1706.

3. *Marina Benningus* was born 1668. She married the vicar in Orsa, Johannes Laurentii Elfvius. He was born in Älvdalen 27 October 1661 and died 4 October 1715 in Orsa. Marina died in Orsa 2 September 1736.

4. *Margareta Benningius* was born 1669 in Orsa. She married 6 November 1684 with the vicar in Ore, Petrus Andreae Machlin. He was born in Möklinta 20 February 1653 and died in Ore on

[404] http://home.swipnet.se/~w-87123/Andreas%20Olai%20Floraeus%20&%20Margareta%20Gudmundsdotter.htm; accessed March 2004
[405] http://members.tripod.com/~masgen/ingelber.htm; accessed July 2004

Christmas Eve 1733. Margareta died 1756. They had one daughter: Sara (b.1688).

*   *   *

There is a village named Banninge in Floda Parish, Sweden. It lies in the administrative county district Oppunda, province Södermanland and is very small, originally having been just a farm. It is mentioned for the first time in the original sources on 6 July 1347[406], as 'Bandunge'. However, the name seems to have been derived not from a person, but from the geographical location, an elongated elevation - a band or belt of land – where the village is located. The Banningetorp, also in the parish of Floda, is the name of a farmstead (meaning: the Banninge (or Banning's) pastureland or enclosure).

---

[406] personal communication to the author from Floda Parish dated 21 June 2004

The first Bannings in England were likely a Saxon tribe or clan by that name, having come from the continent and settled in Banningham, (Bannyngham) Norfolk, in the 5th or 6th century. The name Banningham means 'settlement of Banning's dependants/family'[407] (in Saxon times most tribes were family units). It is feasible that these settlers were related to, or descended from, the Banings as a tribe in middle Germany, as referred to in Widsith[408]. Dr. Paul Cavill, of the University of Nottingham, says; "There is no very good reason why Banningham should not have been settled by people who claimed descent from this tribe: there just isn't any evidence to verify it, and a connection with the Baningas of middle Germany cannot be ruled out[409]."

83. Map of Banningham in, Norfolk, date
© Crown Copyright and Landmark Information Group Ltd, Exeter

Many of the early villages were founded by leaders or chiefs, and as a consequence the village bears their name. A personal name followed by the Saxon ' - ham', indicates so and so's village, or homestead, and '-ing' indicates 'people of', so that '-ingham' means village/homestead of the people of .[410]

Banningham (Banincham) was mentioned for the first time in the *Domesday Book*[411] as a market town, with the designation "11th century

---

[407] information from the Norfolk Heritage Centre to the author, Nov. 2003
[408] K. Malone, *Angelistica, Widsith*, Rosenkilde and Bagger, Copenhagen 1962, vol VIII, p. 130
[409] Dr. Paul Cavill, (Research Fellow, English Place-Name Society, School of English, University of Nottingham) personal communication 10 Dec. 2003
[410] Early Villages of the Marsh; http://www.saltfleetby.co.uk/east_lindsey_2.htm, accessed Feb. 2004

landowners place name, Norfolk." It is located 5 miles from the 11th century market town North Walsham, used in a sample study for DNA research concerning the early migration of peoples[412]. One of the conclusions of this study was that DNA profiles for residents of N. Walsham (and therefore by definition also for Banningham) was virtually identical to that of settlers in Friesland in the north of the Netherlands, an indication that there was, at one time, an affinity.

According to Blomefield's *History of Norfolk*[413] (first published mid-18th century), the name Banningham refers to 'the dwelling at the lows in the precinct' (precinct referring to the nearby town of Aylsham, since Banningham originally belonged to the manor of Aylsham).

Blomefield's *History of Norfolk* informs us that Banningham was held by Guert the Dane[414] (born 1030) before the Norman Conquest (1066). Guert was a noble of Danish origin, the brother of King Harold II. Their father, Earl Godwin of Wessex, was an Anglo-Saxon, a confidant of King Canute the Great (of England, Denmark, Norway, governor of Schleswig and Pomerania) to whom he was related by marriage. Guert's sister Edith was married to King Edward. Earl Godwin was a large landowner in England. Guert the Dane became Earl of East Anglia, one of the most powerful men in England and a large Norfolk landowner, which included the landholdings of Banningham. The landholdings were probably part of the bounty acquired when Canute and his father (a Jomsburg Viking) invaded England in 1013 and again in 1015. Guert was killed in the Battle of Hastings and his estates, which had been given him by his brother King Harold II, became the property of William I, who held them as Royal possession.

William I gave them to William de Warenne in 1066, a commander of Norman forces who fought with him at Hastings,. William de Warenne received as his share of the spoil some three hundred manors, nearly half that number being in the county of Norfolk. He was created Earl of Surrey in 1088 but died in the same year from an arrow. William had holdings in 13 counties all over the country, and in modern currency his holdings would be worth £57 billion[415], a record in Britain during the last millennium.

---

[411] Domesday Book, 1066; http://www.domesdaybook.co.uk/norfolk.html; accessed July 2004

[412] M.E. Weale, D.A. Weiss, R.F. Jager, N. Bradman, M.G. Thomas, *Y chromosome evidence for Anglo-Saxon mass migration*, Molecular Biology & Evolution ,Oxford University Press, July 2002, 19(7):p 1008 – 1021.

[413] Rev. Francis Blomefield, *An Essay towards a Topographical History of the County of Norfol*, completed by Rev Charles Parkin, London, 1807, Vol. VI, p. 326-328

[414] Rev. Francis Blomefield, *An Essay towards a Topographical History of the County of Norfolk*, completed by Rev Charles Parkin, London, 1807, Vol. VI, p. 326-328

[415] The Domesday Book Online, http://www.domesdaybook.co.uk/landownersu-z.html, accessed Feb. 2004

From the Warennes the manor passed to the Bigod Earls of Norfolk, and then in the 14th century to the Felbrigges. The last of the Felbrigges died in 1442 and the manor passed to John Windham, who had purchased a considerable estate there from John de Banningham and Joan his wife (the date of purchase is not given). The de Banninghams are first mentioned in the reign of Richard I (1189-99) when John, son of John de Banningham, lived there. John would have taken his surname from the village ("a family sirnamed of the town, and had continued in it ever since Richard the First's[416] time, when John de Banningham lived here."[417]) and would have held some status to distinguish him from the local peasant population. In 1281 John de Banningham, both senior and junior, were mentioned as owners, so they would have been descendants of the first John in the 12th century.

The following names occur in the London Metropolitan Archives: Geoffrey de Banningham in 1287[418], John, son of John de Banningham in 1296[419], Reginald de Banningham[420], rector of Stanninghall in 1322, and John de Banyngham in 1334[421]. Intriguingly, John de Banyngham is also mentioned in 1328[422] as brother to Sir Thomas Ketel, chaplain. Bannings of the Netherlands were related by marriage to the ennobled family of Ketel in that country in the 15th and 16th centuries. The case of Nicholas Bannyngham of Marsham[423], Norfolk, versus one Thomas Aleyn, mercer, of Abingdon is mentioned regarding 'feoffment[424]' of 'lands, etc.' in Marsham, the file dated 1386-1486.

The Windhams still held the manor in 1854; the Lord of the Manor of Banningham in 1937, listed under the lords of manors in Kelly's Directory of Norfolk[425] for that year, was Lieutenant Colonel Reginald Cossley Batt. No more Norfolk trade directories were published after this date.

Blomefield makes no reference to any Banning in this parish. Neither was the Norfolk Record Office able to find entries for the names

---

[416] King Richard I: 1157-1199
[417] Rev. Francis Blomefield, *An Essay towards a Topographical History of the County of Norfolk*, completed by Rev Charles Parkin, London, 1807, Vol. VI, p. 328
[418] Database Access to Archives, Report on family and estate papers of the Ketton-Cremer Family of Felbrigg Hall 13th-20th century;Catalogue Ref. WKC; ref. MS 15689, 37C1 - date: 1287; http://www.a2a.org.uk/, accessed Feb. 2004
[419] Database Access to Archives, - ref. WKC 1/36, 390 x 8 - date: 1296,
[420] Database Access to Archives, - ref. WKC 1/36, 390 x 8 - date: 1296; ref. MS 15730, 37C2 - date: 1322
[421] Database Access to Archives ; Catalogue Ref. LEST, ref. LEST/F 15 - date: 1333-1334
[422] Database Access to Archives ,Catalogue Ref. KIM, ref. KIM 2N/13 - date: 31 October 2 Edward III [1328]; Le Strange of Hunstanton
[423] Database Access to Archives; item details C. 1/28/45
[424] 'feoffment': legal term for a land transaction, where one party 'enfeoffs' the other with a fief, derived from the manorial system of landholding.
[425] information from the Norfolk Record Office, 20 Nov. 2003

Banning/Baning/Bayning in their indexes, nor in the indexes to wills proved in Norfolk 1370-1750.

Banningham was described in 1854 as: "a straggling village with 79 houses, 330 souls, and 908 acres of land, the property of various owners: W. H. Windham, Esq. is lord of the manor[426]."

It is assumed that Dutch Bannings settled in England around 1500, but there is as yet no evidence to support this, and they would not necessarily have been the first Bannings in the country. The first mention in England of a Banning found to date is that of Simon Baynyng of Itterby in 1364[427]. Simon was involved in a land transfer concerning selions[428] of land in Thrunscoe ('Thirnesco') held by his father William Baynyng's widow, Matilda Ploghman. Itterby, Thrunscoe and Oote made up the small town of Cleethorpes in Lincolnshire. (Cleethorpes is a Saxon name derived from Clee (clay) and Thorpe.) Lincolnshire was one of the locations settled by Saxons and Frisians.

A certain Thomas Bannyng is the second record found in England, listed in 1379 in the Marlborough Poll Tax[429], in Wiltshire, where many of the later Bannyngs appeared.

Robert Bannyng appears on 17 March 1384, with his wife Juliana, as previous owner in a land transfer[430] comprising two acres, half an acre, one rood with appurtenances in Leicestershire/Rutland.

Johannes Bannyng[431] is the fourth record found in England. He was rector of Easton Grey in Wiltshire on 26 January 1401/02, and quite likely an ancestor of the Wiltshire Bannings.

John Baynyng of London is the following record found, whose last will and testament at the National Archives is dated 4 January 1417.[432] His name in the margin of the will is written in the Latin form as 'Johannes Baynyng'. He names no family members in his will, other than his deceased first wife Agnes and his second wife Alice. John Baynyng was obviously an affluent citizen, owning wharves, lands and tenements

---

[426] Frances White's History, *Gazetteer and Directory of Norfolk* 1854, p. 414;

[427] The National Archives Online Catalogue, PRO ref. C146/3293, Vigil of Holy Trinity 1364
http://catalogue.pro.gov.uk/ExternalRequest.asp?RequestReference=PROB+11%2F2B, accessed Feb. 2004

[428] 'selion' : an area of undulating grassland known as 'ridge and furrow', a survivor of an early farming system

[429] Charles Wordsworth, *Marlborough Poll Tax 1379*, WNQ, vol 6, 1910, p. 535-546

[430] Database Access to Archives; Conant MSS, cat. ref. DG11/119, date 7 Richard II, Thursday of Gregory, pope

[431] Rectors at Easton Gray; http://www.oodwooc.co.uk/ph_egrey_vics.htm, accessed June 2004

[432] Will of John Baynyng of Saint Dunstan by the Tower, City of London, 15 July 1418, Register: Marche Quire Numbers: 30 – 55, Records of the Prerogative Court of Canterbury, ref. PROB 11/2b; translated by Nick Barratt

"in the street of Petit Wales in the parish of All Saints, London". (Petit Wales stretched from the Thames to the eastern end of Tower Street, now Tower Hill). Both executors and friends whom he names were wool merchants, and it would seem likely that John Baynyng was therefore active and prosperous in the wool trade and formed his alliances through his business. The homes and street of Petit Wales, which now no longer exists, are shown on a woodcut map of London dated around 1550. The Thames is on the south end and Tower Hill on the north, The Tower of London just visible on the east.

84. Segment of a map of London, woodcut, ca. 1550,
showing the street of Petit Wales
by permission of British History Online,
Institute of Historical Research, University of London[433]

Willelmus Banynge was a vicar in Temple Parish, Bristol, in 1448. His name is mentioned in connection with the 'feoffment' of Temple church lands[434] on 25 Aug. 1448 and the 'feoffment' of two shops on Temple Street[435] on 4 Apr. 1449.

---

[433] source: http://www.british-history.ac.uk/iframe
[434] Database Access to Archives, Cat. ref. Temple, ref. P.Tem/Aa/29
[435] Database Access to Archives, Cat. ref. Temple, ref. P.Tem/Aa/30

The name Detmar Bannyng, Hanseatic merchant, occurs in a Hanseatic Charter dated 1475[436], pertaining to toll fees to be paid at Ipswich.

There is a will registered in the Probate Registry at Canterbury for a David Bannyng of Dover, dated 1497[437], which names as his only next-of-kin his wife Katherine.

One Roberte Baynyng of Bromley, Essex, made up a will in 1523[438] mentioning his wife Elizabeth, daughter Jane, his brother John and his godson Thomas Baynyng, who may perhaps have been John's son.

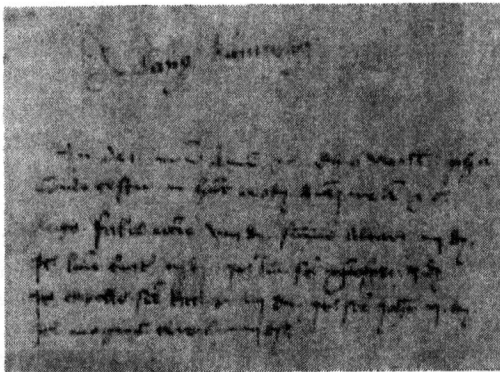

85. the name Anthany Bannyng on the frontspiece
of a 15th century manuscript held by St. John's College, Oxford
courtesy of: The President and Scholars of Saint John Baptist College
in the University of Oxford

The name Anthany Bannyng occurs as owner of a 15th century medieval manuscript[439], held by St. John's College, Oxford. Anthany (or Anthony) Bannyng was, in the 16th century, the second owner, after one 'Master Coxe off Bugbroucke'. The inscription comprises the opening of a will with several small bequests 'In dei nominee Amen &c. Ego Will'pha Condo testu. in hunc modum....'. 'Thomas Royland' is mentioned twice, and in one case he is identified as 'a knave'. The third owner, who donated the manuscript to the invaluable collection of St. John's College Library, was a Richard Butler, Doctor of Theology of Northampton. The identity of Anthony Bannyng is unknown.

---

[436] Walther Stein, *Hansisches Urkundenbuch*, volume 10, 1471-1485, Duncker & Humblot, Leipzig, 1907, p. 278
[437] *Wills and Administrations in the Probate Registry of Canterbury*, 1396-1558 and 1640-1650, ref. C 4 147 1497
[438] Archdeaconry of Colchester, Franys 154, FHL film #91232, item 2
[439] Prof. Ralph Hanna., *A Descriptive Catalogue of the Western Medieval Manuscripts of St. Johns College Oxford*, Oxford University Press, Oxford, 2002, p. 66,67

Three English lines of the family are included in Pierson Worrall's book. These commence with Robert Banning in 1539 (this Wiltshire line is designated with K in his book), William Banning in 1710 (Liverpool, designated as L) and James Banning in 1795 (Bristol, designated as M). A fourth line, currently being researched, is that of Charles Banning in 1836. The prestigious line of Richard (15th century, below) is not included in P.W. Banning's manuscript.

Dedham and London

With a notable parallel to the Bannings of Amsterdam, the Banning name came into distinction in England in the fifteenth century, their wealth and land ownership accrued from the cloth industry. The book *Fuller's Worthies of England*[440], first published in 1711, outlines the most prominent Bannings of England[441]. A certain Richard Bannyng settled in Dedham (County Essex) at the close of the 15th century. Richard came from Nayland in Suffolk, only some five miles removed from Dedham, and only some 15 miles removed from Ipswich where Detmar Bannyng was located in 1475. (A few generations later, in 1632, Paul Bayning, descendant of Richard, Viscount of Sudbury and Baron of Horkesley, was recorded[442] in the matriculation register of Oxford as "Baro de Nayland, Vicecomes Bayning de Sudbury". In the same extract: "J.H. Round[443] writes: "Horkesley (Essex) adjoined Nayland (Suffolk) and was included in the great manor of Nayland at the time of the Domesday.")

Richard Bannyng's son Richard would have been born toward the end of the 15th century, around the time that his father settled in Dedham. In spite of the fact that Dedham was a small town – popular but not populous - in the 15th and 16th centuries it was a prosperous market centre for the woollen trade, where Richard Bannyng probably gained affluence. *An Essay on the Position of the British Gentry*[444] makes note of landowners before the year 1500, whose descendants later became English peers. Only one hundred and twenty one English peers had ancestors who were proprietors of land in England prior to 1500, a minor proportion of the existing peerages today. Among the names mentioned is that of Richard's descendant 'Lord Bayning', indicating that Richard and perhaps even earlier generations of the family were noted landowners.

---

[440] *Fuller's Worthies of England*, London, 1711, Vol. VIII, p. 247
[441] notes held by the Essex Record Office, ref. D/DL/C43/4/10, no. 293, taken from *Fuller's Worthies of England*, Thomas Fuller, 16..,
[442] G.E.Cokayne, with Vicary Gibbs, *Complete Peerage*, St. Catherine Press, London, vol 2, 1910-1951, p. 37
[443] J.H. Round, author of Feudal England in 1895
[444] *An Essay on the Position of the British Gentry*, Burke's Peerage and Gentry, , 4th Edition, Part 1, 1862

The second Richard Bannyng married Anne Raven. The raven is illustrated in the quarters of the coat-of-arms on the monument for their grandsons, which can be seen further on. Richard and Anne had, in turn, at least one son; also Richard, whom we know of as a prosperous merchant in the cloth trade. Among his assets was the estate of 'Powers' in Little and Great Waltham, which he purchased from the Mildmay family. At the time of his death, Richard Bannyng III of Dedham held the manors of Sheddinghoe and Manningtree (both of which are mentioned in the Domesday book of 1086) of the King, "in capite by the tenth part of a knights fee, the manors of Old Hall and New Hall and the manor of Abbots in the parish"[445], which formed more or less the whole of the town of Manningtree.

Richard Bannyng III of Dedham and his wife Anne Barker had three sons, Paul (1539), Andrew (1543) and Robert. The existence of Robert is strangely obscure. He is mentioned in passing in an article on the family in 1944[446] and in the last wills and testaments of his brothers Andrew, (proved 11 Feb. 1611[447]), and Paul, (proved 12 Oct. 1616[448]). Robert does not seem to have married and it would appear that there was some agreement between his two brothers that Paul, who left him considerable land and/or the income thereof, would see to his needs. Andrew left him a token fee and instruction that a suit of apparel be purchased for him for mourning, but instructs his executors that Robert "should not want nor cannot want for anything that he shall reasonably require of my brother Paul."

It is curious that Robert otherwise makes no appearance whatsoever in any records, considering the impressive trail that his siblings left behind. A document held by the Church of St. Olave's mentions "Robert; ob. Powers, Great Waltham", which would seem to imply that he died at his grandfather's estate of Powers. The impression is that he may have been dependant on his brothers, perhaps because of some physical or mental condition. As the wills were written when the brothers were elderly, Robert would also have lived to old age. Paul refers to him as 'my loving brother Robert'. Since Paul and Andrew also refer in their wills to their cousins Marie (Mary) Bayninge (married John Watts) and Margaret (married William Washell), this would infer that their father, Richard, had a brother, or brothers, unknown to us, being the father(s) of these two girls. There are more Bannyngs mentioned in Dedham, and it seems likely that they, too, were cousins or more distant relations of Paul, Andrew and Robert. One Elizabeth Bayning was born in

---

[445] Morant, excerpt held by the Essex Record Office, ref. T/P51/3
[446] Hugh G. Gillespie, M.R.I., *The Re-discovery of an Elizabethan Merchant Adventurer*, Genealogist's Magazine, vol. 9, no. 11, Sept. 1944, p. 429
[447] National Archives, Surrey, cat. ref. PROB 11/117, image ref. 115/98
[448] National Archives, Surrey, cat. ref. PROB 11.128, image ref. 359/327

Dedham around 1540[449]. She may have been a sister but was more likely a cousin and although she died young, her offspring are not mentioned in the wills of Paul or Andrew. Elizabeth married Lewis Sparhawk in 1559 but died six years later.

Another possible cousin to Paul and Andrew may have been Thomas Bayninge, Yeoman of Little Bentley. In his will dated 1605, Thomas declares being of "sound mind and memory but sicke and weake of bodye"[450], and leaves his possessions to his brother John, but no other family members are specified as such. Thomas mentions Paul and Andrew Bayninge, (referring to them as 'Mr.', indicating some deference) He left to Mr. Andrew a small sum to buy a ring to remember him by, which was a common bequest at the time. No relation to the two is mentioned; Little Bentley was built and owned by Paul.

Paul Bannyng was born in 1539. As a London merchant (member of the Grocers Company), he was Alderman, Sheriff of London (1593-4) and Privateering Promoter. In a charter dated 31 August 1588[451], he is mentioned among other merchants of London as 'Pauwels Banninghe' and 'Pauwels Banninge'. His name occurs in historical documents in relation to two ventures: the purchase and sale of property in Tudhoe between 1597 and 1602[452], and investments in shipping[453]. He accumulated a great fortune, as did his brother Andrew, also a member of the Grocers Company. Paul was nominated Alderman and Sheriff on 20 Feb. 1593. Andrew was elected Alderman on 26 Mar. 1605, but it is suspected that this was without his knowledge, as he relinquished the post only three weeks later on payment of a fine. After their deaths in 1616 and 1610 respectively, the two brothers were interred at St. Olave's Church in Hart Street, London, where a very large monument in the chancel commemorates them. The name in the inscription is spelled as 'Bayninge'.

[449] Bayning: http://awt.ancestry.com/cgi-bin/igm.cgi?ti=0&surname=bayning&given=; accessed Feb. 2004

[450] The National Archives, Public Record Office, ref. PROB 11/106

[451] Rudolf Häpke, Niederländische Akten und Urkunden zur Geschichte der Hanse und zur Deutschen Seegeschichte, volume II, 1558-1669, Lübeck 1923, p. 421-423

[452] Jeremy Hutson, The History of Tudhoe Village, documents 1330-1569, http://www.dur.ac.uk/j.m.hutson/tudhoe/docs.html, accessed Feb. 2004

[453] Dan Byrnes, The English Business of Slavery, website book, chapters 8 & 9, http://www.danbyrnes.com.au/business/, accessed Feb. 2004

86. Monument in St. Olave's Church, London, commemorating
Paul (right) and Andrew (left) Bayninge
Photo courtesy of Stephen Millar, London

87. Paul Bayninge   88. Andrew Bayninge
details of the monument in St. Olave's Church
photos courtesy of Stephen Millar, London

Tudhoe Village lies about five miles south of Durham City and for most of its history was located in the parish of Brancepeth.[454]. Paul Bayning is mentioned as having purchased extensive property in this area, together with several business partners, including Brancepath Manor, and having sold this property in parcels up to 1602. The Essex Record Office holds a document dated 1588[455] listing properties belonging to Paul Bayning, citizen and alderman of London, Andrew Bayning, citizen and grocer of London and two other gentlemen, being: "Manor of Ilgars and Latchleys, 20 messuages, 20 cottages, 2 mills, watercourse, 2 dovecotes, 40 gardens, 40 orchards, 50a. land, 200a. meadow, 50a pasture, 100a. wood, 200a. gorse and heath Billericay, Buttsbury and Woodham Ferrers." These were only a small portion of their assets.

As a London Merchant specializing in trade with the Levant, Turkey and Brazil, Paul Bayning and two associates made an attempt to exclude other merchants from the Turkey Trade, which is revealed in the State Papers[456]. He is specifically mentioned in 1589[457] in relation to a venture proposing a voyage to the Far East by way of Cape Good Hope, using the ships *Susan*, *Merchant Royal* and *Edward Bonaventure*. The ships were owned by Paul Bayning and Thomas Cordell, of Venice Co., men also in Spanish trade and leading privateers. These ships (plus one other) were used in the 'pathbreaking' voyage of James Lancaster to the Indian Ocean in 1591-1592.

---

[454] Jeremy Hutson, The History of Tudhoe Village, Dissent and Rebellion in Country Durham, http://www.dur.ac.uk/j.m.hutson/tudhoe/index.html#pre1570, accessed Feb. 2004
[455] Essex Record Office, Estate and Family Records, Collection of John Avery, ref. D/DQs/61, 1587/8
[456] Hugh G. Gillespie, M.R.I., *The Re-discovery of an Elizabethan Merchant Adventurer*, Genealogist's Magazine, vol. 9, no. 11, Sept. 1944, p. 430
[457] Merchants and Bankers, 1550-1575,
http://www.danbyrnes.com.au/merchants/merchants5.htm, accessed Febr. 2004

Paul Bayning was one of the founders of the East India Company and became its first treasurer, being one of the largest subscribers to the original Charter of the Company and later purchasing the interests of others. The first meeting of East India Company Adventurers was held in London, 24 Sept. 1599. Seven of the original 24 directors of the East India Company of the charter of 31 December 1600 were Levant merchants.[458] Between 1601-1605, Levant Company charter officers included, amongst others, Paul and Andrew Bayning. After 1600 the East India Company had 125 shareholders (including Queen Elizabeth I). By 31 December 1600, the Company had obtained a royal charter, and now proposed voyages.

The East India Company's first fleet left with four ships from the Thames under Captain James Lancaster, in February 1601, for a voyage of two years, involving the ships *Red Dragon, Hector, Ascension* and *Susan*, sailing for Java and Sumatra. The *Susan*, commanded by James Lancaster, was owned by London alderman Paul Bayning and was perhaps named after his wife. Paul showed shrewd business ability in selling this vessel to the East India Company, as the minutes show: "The Susan to be purchased for 1600 pounds upon condition that Alderman Bayning, the owner, receive her again upon her return from the voyage for 800 pounds."[459] The *Susan* had the honour of conveying the first Ambassador from the Court of Queen Elizabeth to Turkey, William Harborne, in 1582/1583.

In 1607 the Court minutes of the East India Company make mention of a complaint to the effect that Paul Bannyng detained money which he owed to the company. He thereafter ceased to be one of the Committee of Directors, although this may have been due to age; he was 68 at the time, and it was not uncommon to find members greatly in arrears in paying their share in the adventures undertaken. Although he is mentioned again in 1612 as a member of another company called *The Governor and Company of the Merchants of London Discoverers of the North West Passage*[460] , he was 73 years of age and gradually handing over the reins of power to his son, Paul, age 24, for whom he had purchased a baronetcy in 1611.

Paul Bannyng of Bentley, Essex, Merchant, Alderman and Sheriff of London married Elizabeth Mowse, daughter of John Mowse of Creting, Suffolk, in 1574. She died of consumption on 21 Dec. 1579 at the age of 28, leaving no issue. In the following year, 1580, he married Susan(na) Norden, daughter and heiress of Richard Norden of Mistley.

---

[458] Brenner, *Merchants and Revolution*, charter of 31 Dec. 1600, Encyclopedia Britannica, 1928, p. 21, p. 86
[459] Hugh G. Gillespie, M.R.I., *The Re-discovery of an Elizabethan Merchant Adventurer*, Genealogist's Magazine, vol. 9, no. 11, Sept. 1944, p. 430
[460] Hugh G. Gillespie, M.R.I., *The Re-discovery of an Elizabethan Merchant Adventurer*, Genealogist's Magazine, vol. 9, no. 11, Sept. 1944, p. 430

The first ten years of marriage seem to have been harmonious, but in 1594 Paul had occasion to turn her out of his house in disgrace. Susan was apparently involved with an associate of her husband's, and Paul avoided bringing the man's name into the courts for fear of his business relations and possible revelations of his own business misconduct. There are numerous mentions of Susan's thwarted attempts to recover her portion of dowry and of the marital controversy. Paul refused to bring evidence against his wife in the Ecclesiastical Court and therefore a restitution of conjugal rights was ordered. A separation was decreed in December 1600 by a Commission at Lambeth, by no less than the Archbishop, the Lord Admiral, the Lord Chamberlain and others. In March 1602 it was Paul's turn to be elected as Lord Mayor of London, an office he refused, and he also ceased to be Alderman in the following May. In a letter dated 8 May 1602[461], John Chamberlain informed Dudley Carlton that "Several Aldermen have disrobed themselves. Alderman Bayning for spite, because he will not have his wife Lady Mayoress."

The unfortunate situation was concluded in court records on 18 Feb. 1606 with: "The King to the Archbishop of Canterbury and Bishop of London. To require Paul Bayning to allow a maintenance suitable to a lady, to Susan his wife, separated from him at his own wish; he promised to do so, but fails to perform.[462]" Perhaps it would be prudent, when considering their disparate interests, to consider the disparity of age between the two. If it is true that Susan was born in 1567, then Paul would have been 41 and Susan only 13 when they married in 1580 – although it was not uncommon for girls to be married at this age.

Paul Bannyng was said to have had his country home in Banningham (Norfolk). There is no substantiation to this whatsoever, and his family estates are listed in numerous locations in Essex and Sussex. He lived at Mark Lane, London, his 'messuage' being an old red brick mansion in an open court, shaded by spreading limes and plane trees. (Interestingly, this would have been at almost the exact spot that John Baynyng, mentioned above, held his wharves and lands in 1417). As Paul's brother Andrew lived in Mincing Lane, the homes very likely backed one another with an interconnecting passage. It appears to have been one of the best homes in the City and was lent to the French Ambassador during a visit early in 1600, also being requested for the Duke of Lennox in the following year. (Mark Lane and Mincing Lane are clearly visible running north from Tower Street on the map (illustration

[461] Hugh G. Gillespie, M.R.I., *The Re-discovery of an Elizabethan Merchant Adventurer*, Genealogist's Magazine, vol. 9, no. 11, Sept. 1944, p. 432
[462] Hugh G. Gillespie, M.R.I., *The Re-discovery of an Elizabethan Merchant Adventurer*, Genealogist's Magazine, vol. 9, no. 11, Sept. 1944, p. 432, 433

84.) above, showing the street of Petit Wales, as well as Hart Street and the Church of St. Olave's.)

Amongst Paul's domestic staff was a maid called Agnes Peirsonn , who died in the house in 1579 at the age of 30, the cause of death given as 'bewitched'. There was also a little black page boy, to whom Paul designated 5 pounds in his will and, on condition that the boy would follow instruction in the Christian Faith and Religion, he would receive another 5 pounds when he was fit to be baptised. This transpired on 27 Jan. 1617, when he took the name Mark Antonie, but the 5 pounds brought him little joy. Whether he become the victim of theft and murder, or succumbed to his great excitement is unknown, but he was buried the next day, 'A Christian'.

Paul also owned a capital messuage until 1592 just off Gracechurch Street, (in 1944 Lombard Court), which he sold to the draper Eligins Echard. In addition to his extensive other properties, he had a country mansion, Bentley Hall, built in Little Bentley.

In 1603 Paul attempted to remove his recalcitrant wife to Bentley Hall from London, but her response to this, recorded in a letter to "The Right Worshopfull Sir Julyeus Coasor" asserts "But iff my husband accordinge to his accustomed policie feed you with vayne hope that iff I will goe into the countrye and to that I answer absoluttlye that I will not goe out off the Cety..... etc."[463]

A few years into the marriage, however, while harmony still reigned, the country estate was the setting for the birth of their two sons: John, who died young, and Paul, born at Bentley Hall on 28 April 1588. Knighted in 1614, Sir Paul Bayning became Sheriff of Essex in 1617, and was conferred with the titles Baron of Horkesley in 1627 and Viscount Sudbury in Suffolk a few days later, by King Charles I. It is said that he altered the spelling of his name from 'Bayning' to 'Banning' after having been raised to nobility. However, all references found to date indicate the contrary. His ancestors spelled the name as Bannyng. His father, Paul, was recorded as 'Bannyng' in the numerous documents concerning his business ventures and marriage, as 'Bannyng' and 'Banning' in his own last will and testament proved on 12 Oct. 1616, in *The Oxford Tin Letter of 1599*[464], addressed to her 'Majestie Queen Elizabeth' as 'Pauwle Bannyng, Alderman', and in the London Subsidy Rolls[465] of 1598 his name also occurs as Pawle Bannyng, Alderman. The spelling 'Bayning'

[463] Hugh G. Gillespie, M.R.I., *The Re-discovery of an Elizabethan Merchant Adventurer*, Genealogist's Magazine, vol. 9, no. 11, Sept. 1944, p. 433
[464] Oxford Tin Letter; http://ist-socrates.berkeley.edu/~ahnelson/TINLETTS/990600A.html; accessed July 2004
[465] http://ist-socrates.berkeley.edu/~ahnelson/SUBSIDY/369b.html; accessed July 2004

does not occur until the beginning of the 17th century, simultaneously with the accruement of titles and affluence of Paul and Andrew. Even then, this second Paul is encountered in official documents as Bayning(e), Banynge, Bannyng and Banning.

Paul II lived at Mark Lane, London with his wife Anne Glemham (1595-1639) and their five children: Cecelia (1613-1639), Paul, (1616-1638), Anne (1619-1678), Mary (1623-1671) and Elizabeth (1624-1686). Sir Paul died at his home on 29 July 1629, aged 41, leaving vast estates in Essex and Suffolk and an enormous fortune of £153,000[466] and 15 shillings, excluding "jewels, plates and household stuffs". This was unparalleled wealth, as the sum of a thousand pounds, by the standards of the time, was more than an average workman would earn in a lifetime. Paul left considerable sums to charity, hospitals and the church. His generosity and noble character were eloquently eulogized by the poet William Strode (1602-1644) :

"On The Death Of The Right Honourable The Lord Viscount Bayning[467]
Though after Death, Thanks lessen into Praise,
And Worthies be not crown'd with gold, but bayes;
Shall we not thank? To praise Thee all agree;
We Debtors must out doe it, heartily.
Deserved Nobility of True Descent,
Though not so old in Thee grew Ancient:
We number not the Tree of Branched Birth,
But genealogie of Vertue, spreading forth
To many Births in value. Piety,
True Valour, Bounty, Meeknesse, Modesty,
These noble off-springs swell Thy Name as much,
As Richards, Edwards, three, foure, twenty such:
For in thy Person's linage surnam'd are
The great, the good, the wise, the just, the faire.
One of these stiles innobles a whole stemme;
If all be found in One, what race like him!
Long stayres of birth, unlesse they likewise grow
To higher vertue, must descend more low.
When water comes through numerous veins of lead,
'Tis water still; Thy blood, from One pipe's head,
Grew Aqua-vitæ streight, with spirits fill'd,
As not traduc'd, but rais'd, sublim'd, distill'd.
Nobility farre spread, I may behold,

---

[466] G.E. Cockayne, *Complete Peerage*, St. Catherine's Press, London, 1910-1959, Vol. II, p. 37 ,38
[467] Old Poetry; http://www.oldpoetry.com/poetry/26389; accessed July 2004

Like the expanded skie, or dissolv'd gold,
Much rarified; I see't contracted here
Into a starre, the strength of all the spheare;
Extracted like the Elixir from the mine,
And highten'd so that 'tis too soone divine.

Divinity continues not beneath;
Alas nor He; but though He passe by death,
He that for many liv'd, gaines many lives
After hee's dead: Each friend and servant strives
To give him breath in praise; this Hospital,
That Prison, Colledge, Church, must needs recall
To mind their Patron; whose rich legacies
In forreigne lands, and under other skies
To them assign'd, shew that his heart did even
In France love England, as in England Heaven:
Heav'n well perceiv'd this double pious love,
Both to his Country here, and that above:
Therefore the day, that saw Him landed here,
Hath seen him landed in his Haven there;
The selfe-same day (but two yeares interpos'd)
Saw Sun and Him round shining twice & clos'd.

No Citizen so covetous could be
Of getting wealth, as of bestowing, He;
His Body and Estate went as they came,
Stript of Appendix Both, and left the same
But in th' Originall; Necessity
Devested one, the other Charity.
It cost him more to clothe his soule in death,
Than e're to cloth his flesh for short-liv'd breath;
And whereas Lawes exact from Niggards dead
A Portion for the Poore, they now are said
To moderate His Bounty; never such
Was known but once, that men should give too much:
A Tabernacle then was built, and now
The like in heav'n is purchas'd: Learn you how;
Partly by building Men, and partly by
Erecting walls, by new-found Chymistry,
Turning of Gold to Stones. Our Christ-Church Pile,
Great Henrie's Monument, shall grow awhile
With Bayning's Treasure; who a way hath took.
Like those at Westminster, to fill a nook
'Mongst beds of Kings. Thus speak, speak while we may
For Stones will speak when We are hush'd in Clay."

It is interesting to note that William Strode refers to Paul Bayning's lineage, the 'three, foure, twenty-such Richards and Edwards' who preceded him. It is unknown whether this was figurative speech or not. There were certainly Richards in Paul's ancestry; the only Edward found to date was one Edward Bayninge who purchased Baynards Manor in Ewhurst, Sussex from Sir Francis Woolly in 1607, placing him in the same generation as Paul. He may or may not have been related, but the author may have been referring to the noble traits of monarchs.

89. Fragment of the last will and testament of Sir Paul Bayning[468], written 12 July 1629 (note the two different spellings: Banynge and Bayning, in the same document)
The National Archives, Surrey, (PRO) PROB 11/156

Deeds deposited in archives in 1675 showed the Bayning estates to be considerable, according to those registered[469] for the following: Manors of Great and Little Bentley, Landmer Hall, Great Leighs, Little Leighs, Lyons Hall, Boxted, Great Horkesley, Little Horkesley, Smalland Hall, Blunts, Guing Joyberd Landre, Algers, Leycockes, Lacheleyes, Newhall in Tendring, Little Bromley alias Overhall, Ockeley Hall, Hampstall, Vange, Barehall, Cahmpions, Mistley, Manningtree, Shedinghoe, Oldhall, Abbotts, Rivershall and Powers, Mistley, Manningtree, Weeley, Tendring, Thorpe, Kirby, Little Clacton, Colchester, Nether Mumford, Bradfield, Lawford, Little Bromley, Vange, Langham, Stoke, Nayland, Buttsbury, Stock, Woodham Ferrers, Boreham, Fairstead, Witham, Hatfield, Wickham, Rivenhall, , Ardleigh.

---

[468] Will of Sir Paule Bayninge (Lord, Viscount Sudbury, St. Olave, Hart Street, London, 91 Ridley; Page 23, Vol. VI, index of wills at the Prerogative Court of Canterbury 1629, Public Record Office, Surrey, ref. PROB. 11/156
[469] Essex Record Office, Estate and Family Records, Barrett Lennard family of Aveley, Kent, Sussex, Norfolk, Cumberland, Ireland; ref. D/DL/T1/902, 1691-169

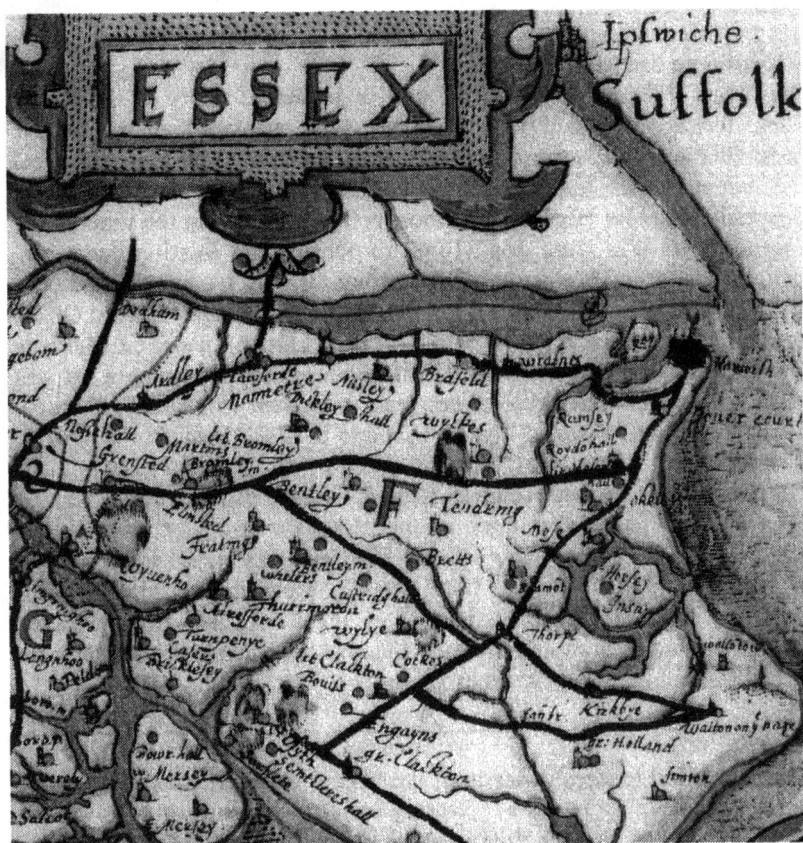

90. Part of Essex in 1594, showing the locations of Bentley, Bentley Manor, Dedham, Mistley, Tendring, Great and Little Clac(k)ton, Bromley Manor, Little Bromley and Elmsted, properties belonging to the Bannyng/Bayning family; John Norden's Map of Essex., 1594, private collection

Witching on the Moors

The areas of Essex and Suffolk, and in particular many of the towns where the Bayning family held estates, such as Manningtree, Mistley, Great Bentley, Colchester and Chelmsford, are known for their historical and heinous witch hunts at the time. The self-appointed 'Witch-finder Generall' Matthew Hopkins was most active here during the time of the English Civil War from 1642-1648, responsible for hunting down and hanging or drowning some 230 persons whom he proclaimed and 'proved' to be possessed by the Devil. . (A file in the Essex Record Office holding notes on the Bayning family also includes an essay on Matthew Hopkins and notes on witchcraft[470].) The simple act of owning a cat was sufficient proof to Hopkins to condemn a woman to death as a witch. Eventually the tide turned against him and it is said that, in the end, he was subjected to his own tortuous practice, dunked and drowned off Hopping Bridge in Manningtree, although other sources claim that he passed away "peacefully, after a long sicknesse of a Consumption[471]". According to the Church Registers he died and was buried in the village of Mistley on 12th August 1647. Today, according to local legend, Hopkins' ghost is said to haunt Mistley Pond. An apparition wearing 17th-century attire is reportedly seen roaming the vicinity, particularly on Friday nights near to the Witches Sabbats.

The names and tenures of many of the tenants of landholdings belonging to Sir Paul Bayning in the 17th century are also still on record, as well as several incidents in which they were involved:

On 23 November 1609 some 20 local people were charged with "riotoriously breaking and entering, with seythes, sticke, cudgels, stones and the like, the close of Paul Bayninge, esquire, at stock, called Whitehill Spring, and cutting down and carrying away wood and underwood growing therein, worth 10s. for assaulting Robert Fannynge and Richard Aslopp of stock, husbandman, his servants[472]."

"Inquisition taken at Little Bentley on 9 September 1603, before John Nashe coroner, on view of the body of Daniel Scofield. The jurors say that on 8 September a certain Edward Kelar 'did drive' a cart laden with 'lath tymber' drawn by 4 horses of Paul Banyng esq. of Bentley aforesaid on the highway there, when it happened that the cart 'ran downe a fulling grounde' so that the cart was 'over throwen' and a piece of timber fell on Scofield and crushed him, so that he died instantly. The cart

[470] Extracts of Records relating to Mistley and Manningtree, Essex Record Office, ref. T/P
[471] John A. Stearne, *A Confirmation and Discovery of Witchcraft*, London, 1648 (Exeter 1973)
[472] Essex Record Office, Sessions Rolls, Epiphany 1610, ref. no. Q/SR 189/94

and timber were worth 13s.4d., remaining in the hands of the said Paul Bayning, to the King's use. By misfortune[474]." (Note, again, the two different spellings 'Banyng' and 'Bayning'.)

In 1625 Sir Paul Bayning wrote a draft petition[475] to Charles I, reciting that Bayning, with Sir Baptist Hicks and Sir Wm.Herrick, lent James I £7,500, and that Bayning had not claimed repayment of his share, or any interest, and now, as the king's "occasions for money at this time are very urgent", offered to increase the loan to £10,000, on receiving sufficient security for payment.

91. Handwritten draft petition from Sir Paul Bayning to King Charles I[476], concerning a loan to the king, ref. D/DRg 2/47
Courtesy of the Essex Record Office, Chelmsford, England

[474] Essex Record Office, Calendar of King's Bench Indictments Ancient 724, Part I, Inquisitions. ref. T/A 428/1/137, no. 125 (around 1580)
[475] Essex Record Office, Estate and Family Records, Charles Gray of Colchester, De Vere-Bayning Papers, 1625, ref. D/DRg/2/47
[476] Essex Record Office, Draft Petition from Sir Paul Bayning to Charles I concerning a loan, ref. D/DRg/2/47

The loan, one of many he made, had been outstanding for several years, as is evidenced by a similar draft petition filed among the Herrick Family Papers at the London Metropolitan Archives. (The fact that the monarchy borrowed money was not unusual: the numerous wars, years of exile and other extensive political, familial and social obligations took a heavy toll on the royal treasury.)

Paul Bayning III , Viscount of Sudbury and Baron of Horkesley, was born in 1616. He paid the king £18,000 for the fine of his wardship[476]. He married Penelope Naunton (b. 2 Oct. 1620) on 25 August 1634, daughter of Sir Robert Naunton, Master of the Court of Wards and Liveries and once Secretary of State.

Among the manuscripts held in the British Library are numerous warrants and bills of payment such as: "warrant of the Committee of the Revenue to Thomas Fauconbridge, Receiver-General, for payment of the diet of prisoners in the Tower; warrant for payment for a watch and clock for the King (the King was extremely fond of clocks) 4 Dec. 1647; similar warrant for payment for boots and shoes for the King, 4 Dec. 1647; warrant of T[homas Wriothesley], Earl of Southampton, Lord Treasurer, for payment of expenses in preparing Nonsuch palace for the Exchequer during the plague, 24 July 1665; similar letter of Henry [Bennet], Earl of Arlington, Lord Chamberlain of the Household, on purchase of jewels for several foreign ambassadors, 18 Dec. 1678[477]' and many more. Among these papers is a bill from "Edward Basse, haberdasher, for goods supplied to Lady Banninge." [Penelope, wife of Paul, 2nd Viscount Bayning] 1635-1636.

Two daughters were born of this marriage: Anne, on 1 May 1637 and Penelope, on 3 Nov. 1638, less than five months after the death of her father at Little Bentley Hall in Essex on 11 June 1638, at the age of 22, "promising high performance to his country but alas cut off in the prime of his life[478]". He was buried in the Bayning vault at Little Bentley Church, on the north side of Little Bentley Hall. No doubt the five bells tolled mournfully which his grandfather had donated to the church, and again less than a decade later when his widow Penelope (who had remarried) was laid to rest at his side.

Viscount Bayning had founded Bayning's Almshouse in Gunpowder Alley in 1631, also proving himself a considerable benefactor of his own college at Oxford, Christ Church, and the scholars marked his

---

[476] *Complete Peerage* v51 2 (ed. Vicay Gibbs) p 37; Essex Record Office, Extracts of Records Relating to Mistley and Manningtree, 1662-1840, Notes on Bayning family, ref. T/P 51/3

[477] Miscellaneous Letters and Papers 1602-circa 1711, The British Library, Manuscripts Catalogue, London, ref. no. 32476

[478] Essex Record Office, *Extracts of Records Relating to Mistley and Manningtree, 1662-1840, Notes on Bayning family*, ref. T/P 51/3

passing with nearly thirty elegies. Amongst these are verses entitled "Death Repealed by a Thankful Memorial sent from Christ Church in Oxford celebrating the noble deserts of the Right Honourable the late Lord Viscount Bayning of Sudbury (1638)". Viscount Bayning had travelled widely in his mercantile pursuit, and this is noted in the verses:

"Not like our silken heirs, who only bound
Their knowledge in the sphere of hawk and hound,"
and:
"Thus big with foreign praises he's come home
But all was only here to find a tomb."[479]

The young Bayning heiresses were easy prey for potential suitors. Anne Bayning was married to Aubrey de Vere, the twentieth and last Earl of Oxford, when she was only ten years of age. The couple had no surviving offspring, but her vast estate was very necessary for the support of the sinking fortunes of the Earl's house, reduced to the verge of ruin by the unlimited extravagance of his predecessor, Earl Edward. Anne Bayning died without issue on 14 September 1659, aged 22. She was interred in Westminster Abbey. Penelope, too, died (1657) without offspring, although she had been married twice; first to John Herbert Esquire and second to John Wentworth, Esquire. She was 19.

Penelope and Anne inherited the manors of Sheddinghoe and of Mistley, cum Manningtree, shown in records of Chancery Proceedings where both ladies are named as Oratrices. According to the proceedings, there was an "anciently belonging way for carts, etc. into the said close of Hillfield, from the highway leading from the parish of Mistley to Manningtree through a close called the tenn acre piece in Mistely, in the tenure of a Joseph Burnish of Manningtree, tanner". The said way or passage had always been used by the owners of Sheddinghoe "by all the time whereof the memory of man is not to the contrary, without gainsaying, lett, interruption of any person whatsoever."[480] However, Joseph Burnish had of late begun to protest this right of way and denied them passage. Joseph was summoned to appear at court hearings. The outcome is unknown, although this can likely be found in the archives.

The Bayning estate became the property of the Earl of Oxford after the sisters died. He and his second wife had the stately and magnificent Bentley Hall, which had been erected by Paul Bayning during the reign of King James I, dismantled, and sold the materials. These now adorn many houses in Colchester and surroundings.

---

[479] Elizabeth Hamilton, *The Illustrious Lady*, Hamish Hamilton Ltd., Gr. Britain, 1980, p. 2
[480] Record of Chancery Proceedings, Essex Record Office, ref. T/P51/3

Cecily (Cicelia) Bayning (1613-1639), daughter of Paul Bayning I and sister to Sir Paul, married Henry Pierrepont, Earl of Kingston, Viscount Newark, (before 1630) who made a bid for the hand of her sister Mary when Cecily died.

Anne Bayning (1619-1678), daughter of Paul Bayning I, married Sir John Baber M.D. Physician in Ordinary to Charles II and related to Lord Craven; she became 2nd Viscountess Bayning of Foxley on 17 March 1674. She had previously married (1634) Henry Murray, Esq. one of the Grooms of the Bedchamber of Charles I. Her Will dated 18 November 1676[481] "confirmed 10 July marriage a Home and Lands called Syon Farm, near Syon House, Middlesex".

The London Metropolitan Archives contain the following references to Anne Bayning:

"The principal manor of Hackney, now known as Lordshold, was formerly held by the Bishop of London who surrendered it to King Edward VI in 1550, together with the manor of Stepney. Both manors were granted by the King to Thomas, Lord Wentworth, Stepney in 1550 and Hackney in 1551 and remained in the Wentworth family until the confiscation of the Earl of Cleveland's estates in 1652. In 1633, however, the Earl of Cleveland had mortgaged the manor to Sir Thomas Trevor and Thomas Trevor. The redemption sum was not repaid and the term was assigned to Anne, Viscountess of Dorchester in trust for Viscount Bayning, whose executors Sir Thomas Glemham and Henry Glemham assigned it to Richard Wallcott, Richard Wallop, William Smith and Francis Glover.[482]"

"5 Dec. 1678 Reciting above and sums owed to Anne, Viscountess Bayning, by R.P. and others which she bequeathed to her daughters., the wives in (2), and that R.P. has paid 3 others £1000 each (in lieu of share due in right of his wife), now (1) and (2) to (3) manors as above; void on repayment of £1000 by R.P."[483]

From miscellaneous letters and papers of John Holles, Duke of Newcastle upon Tyne and Earl of Clare: "Declaration and quitclaim by Sir John Baber, to John Duke of Newcastle, relating to a manor belonging to Baber's late wife, Anne, Viscountess Bayning, purchased by the Duke; date: 22 August 1698.[484]"

Elizabeth (1624-1686), daughter of Paul Bayning I, was the consort of Francis, Lord (Baron) Dacre, and second to David Walter Esquire, Groom of the Bedchamber to King Charles II,. On 6 September

---

[481] Will of Anne Viscountess Bayning dated 30 October 1678, ref. PROB 11/358

[482] London Metropolitan Archives, Tysson, Francis, catalogue ref. M/79

[483] London Metropolitan Archives, Settlements, Wills, Titles and Cognate Papers, Pierrepont of Nottingham, 5 Dec. 1678, ref. DD/4P/44/29

[484] London Metropolitan Archives, Papers of the Holles Family, 1571-1728, Catalogue Ref. Pw 2, 22 Aug. 1698, ref. Pw 2/647

1680 Elizabeth was created by King Charles II Countess of the island of Sheppey in the county of Kent for life. Elizabeth inherited the estate of Powers in Little and Great Waltham which her great-grandfather Richard had owned.

Mary Bayning (1623-1671) was only six when her father died. On a Monday morning in October 1639, a hard-fought duel took place in Hyde Park in London for the hand of Mary, when she was allegedly fourteen, but simple arithmetic indicates that she was two years older. The two contenders were William Villiers, Lord Grandison, and Mary's own brother-in-law, Lord Newark, who had recently become widowed when his wife, Mary's sister Cecelia had died the previous month. The only injuries sustained were, perhaps, to their pride, and although Lord Newark was the victor, the men were reconciled within the week and Mary was permitted to follow her heart. She married William Villiers (1614-1643) 2nd Viscount Grandison of Limerick (Ireland), nephew of George Villiers, 1st Duke of Buckingham and a confidant of both James I and his son Charles I, on 31 October 1639. (Buckingham was assassinated in France in 1628. His assassination later became part of the plot of Alexandre Dumas' classic *The Three Musketeers*[485].)

92. William Villiers, Viscount Grandison,
husband of Mary Bayning
engraving by H.R. Cook, 1643, private collection

William Villiers succeeded his father (Sir Edward Villiers, President of Munster) on 7 September 1626; his name was called in the House of

[485] Alexandre Dumas, The Three Musketeers, 1844, 'Great Villiers';http://www.kirkbymoorside.com/LocalHistory/Kirkby/Buckingham_House/BuckinghamHouse.htm; accessed Nov. 2003

Lords (Ireland) November 1634. He was one of four knights dubbed at Windsor, 20 May 1638, when the Prince of Wales was installed as Knight of the Garter. He did not take his seat in the House of Lords, but was introduced by proxy, 26 October 1640. He distinguished himself nobly in the Royal cause at the head of his regiment (as Colonel-General), and was mortally wounded, 24 July 1643, at the siege of Bristol. He died at Oxford from the gangrenous wound, on 30 September, and was buried 2 October 1643, in Christ Church Cathedral there, in his 30th year. His widow Mary married, 25 April 1648, at St. Bartholomew's-the-Less, London, Charles Villiers, 2nd Earl of Anglesey, a cousin of her first husband, who died 4 February 1660/1. She married, 3rd, Arthur Gorges of Chelsea, Middlesex, who died, 18 April 1668, and was buried there. She drew up her will on 30 March 1671, shortly before she died in that year at the age of 48.

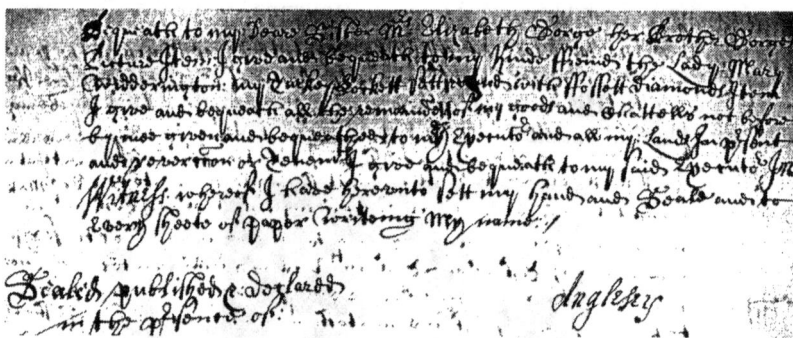

93. Fragment of the last will and testament of Mary Bayning, Lady Anglesey, dated 30th March 1671, ref. D/DL F94
courtesy of the Essex Record Office, Chelmsford, England

Bearing the name of her father and not of her mother, Mary Bayning's only daughter Barbara Villiers (1640-1709) would at this point have passed into some other history, were it not for the fact that she became one of King Charles II's most favoured mistresses, who bore him no less than five illegitimate children.

Barbara was only three when her father, William Villiers, died. Lord Clarendon mentioned the "rare piety, devotion, and personal courage of all kinds" of William Villiers and stated (prophetically) that "the very obligations of gratitude to the King on behalf of his house were such, as his life was but a due sacrifice[486]", and who wrote of him as "a young man of so virtuous a habit of mind that no temptation or provocation could corrupt him; so great a love of justice and integrity that

[486] Antonia Fraser, *King Charles II*, Wiedenfeld and Nicholson, London, 1979

the Court or camp could not show a more faultless person.[487]"

Barbara certainly did not inherit her father's virtue. She did, however, erect a fine marble monument at Christ Church, Oxford to his memory.

The bonny Barbara married Roger Palmer in April 1659, who was created Earl of Castlemaine two years later, and soon after this marriage her intimacy with Charles II began. The king was the father of her first child, Anne, born in February 1661, although this was not officially acknowledged until Anne's marriage in 1674[488] (at the age of thirteen), when she was created Countess of Sussex in her own right.

According to a note found in the archives[489], Anne later married her cousin, Thomas Lord Dacre, (created Earl of Sussex by the king on his marriage), son of her aunt Elizabeth and Francis Lord Dacre. Anne received £20,000 dowry from the King, and the bridegroom £2,000 a year pension[490]. Anne Countess of Sussex, said to be capricious of character, enjoyed a passionate friendship with her father's (the King) latest mistress, Hortense Mancini, in spite of the King's disapproval. The two young ladies took fencing lessons together, proceeding to St. James's Park on one occasion, with drawn swords beneath their nightgowns.

Bishop Burnet describes Barbara as "a woman of great beauty, but most enormously vicious and ravenous, foolish but imperious, ever uneasy to the king, and always carrying on intrigues with other men, while yet she pretended she was jealous of him[491]." Pepys claimed to be headily affected "just by the sight of her pretty linen petticoats edged with lace drying in the Privy Garden"[492].

---

[487] Antonia Fraser, *King Charles II*, Wiedenfeld and Nicholson, London, 1979
[488] Antonia Fraser, *King Charles II*, Wiedenfeld and Nicholson, London, 1979, p. 182
[489] Essex Record Office, no. 10 memorandum on the Bayning family, ref. D/DL F94
[490] Antonia Fraser, *King Charles II*, Wiedenfeld and Nicholson, London, 1979, p. 343
[491] G. Burnet, *Burnet's History of his Own Times*, Thomas Ward and Joseph Downing, London, 1724-1734, vol. I. p. 129.
[492] Antonia Fraser, *King Charles II*, Wiedenfeld and Nicholson, London, 1979, p..209

94. Barbara Villiers, Duchess of Cleveland (1640-1709)
courtesy of the UT Library Online[493]

Dryden addressed Lady Castlemaine in his fourth poetical *Epistle* in terms of great adulation, and Wycherley dedicated to her his first play, *Love in a Wood*. Her portrait was frequently painted by Sir Peter Lely and others, and many of these portraits are now found in various public and private collections.

Barbara was naturally much disliked by Charles's new queen, Catherine of Braganza. The queen's antipathy was quite understandable, as directly after their marriage the king reluctantly appointed Barbara, on her own insistence, as lady of the bedchamber to Catherine while Barbara was pregnant with Charles' second child. Barbara began to mix in the political intrigues of the time, showing an especial hatred towards Edward Hyde, Earl of Clarendon, who reciprocated this feeling and forbade his

[493]UT Library Online; Portrait Gallery; http://www.lib.utexas.edu/photodraw/portraits/#top accessed 12 July 2004

wife to visit her. Her house became a rendezvous for the enemies of the minister, and according to Pepys, she exhibited a wild paroxysm of delight when she heard of Clarendon's fall from power in 1667. Whilst enjoying the royal favour the Lady Castlemaine's liaisons with various gentlemen were satirized in public prints, and a sharp quarrel which occurred between her and the king in 1667 was partly due to this cause. But peace was soon made, and her influence, which had been gradually rising, became supreme at court in 1667. Accordingly, Louis XIV instructed his ambassador to pay special attention to Lady Castlemaine, who had become a Roman Catholic in 1663.

In August 1670 Barbara Palmer-Villiers, Lady of Castlemaine, was created Countess of Southampton, Duchess of Cleveland and Baroness Nonsuch, and she also received many valuable gifts from Charles. Her extravagance and her losses at gaming were so enormous that she was unable to keep up her London residence, Cleveland House, St. James's, and was obliged to sell the contents of her residence at Cheam. In about 1670 her influence over Charles began to decline. The pert, young actress Nell Gwynn supplanted Barbara in the King's favour and Barbara was asked to remove herself from her Whitehall apartments. Although believed to be still stunning at the age of 42, the women of the age were said to be "at their prime at twenty, decayed at four and twenty, old and unsupportable at thirty[494]". Indeed, when the despised Earl of Clarendon looked up at her window on his departure after falling from grace and witnessed her 'great gaiety and triumph', he remonstrated, "Pray remember that, if you live, you will grow old.[495]" The King had a ballad sung under her window beginning, "Alinda's growing old," to which the poet Marvell added, "Paint Castlemaine in colours that will hold, Her, not her picture, for She now grows old...[496]"

Barbara consoled herself meanwhile with lovers of a less exalted station in life, among them John Churchill, afterwards Duke of Marlborough, and William Wycherley; by 1674 she had been entirely supplanted at court by Louise de Kéroualle, Duchess of Portsmouth. Soon afterwards the she went to reside in Paris, where she formed an intrigue with the English ambassador[497], Ralph Montagu, afterwards Duke of Montagu, who lost his position through some revelations which she made to the king. She returned to England just before Charles's death in 1685, enjoying his friendly favour and light-hearted dalliance on the last evening before he became mortally ill. He died within the week. In July 1705 her husband, the Earl of Castlemaine, whom she had left in 1662, died; and in the same year – at the age of sixty-five - the duchess married

[494] Antonia Fraser, *King Charles II*, Wiedenfeld and Nicholson, London, 1979, p. 286

[495] Antonia Fraser, *King Charles II*, Wiedenfeld and Nicholson, London, 1979, p. 286

[496] Antonia Fraser, *King Charles II*, Wiedenfeld and Nicholson, London, 1979, p. 286

[497] Antonia Fraser, *King Charles II*, Wiedenfeld and Nicholson, London, 1979, p. 364/5

a notorious rake known as Beau (Robert) Feilding[498], who treated her abominably. The union was declared void in 1707, as Feilding had a wife living. Barbara died of dropsy at Chiswick on the 9th of October 1709.

By Charles II she had three sons and two daughters - five of the King's twelve surviving illegitimate children by seven mistresses[499]. The Queen, Catherine of Braganza, was barren and he therefore had no legal successors, although he acknowledged paternity of his children publicly and loved them dearly. They were all granted titles[500]. The name Fitzroy, which her children bore, was a thinly veiled allusion to their paternity: 'fitz' being the Norman French for 'son of', (as in Fitzgerald or Fitzpatrick) and 'roy' being the anglicised form of the French 'roi'(king). Barbara's second son, Henry Fitzroy, was created Baron Sudbury, Viscount Ipswich, and Earl of Euston at the age of eight-and-a-half and Duke of Grafton in 1675, just before his 12th birthday. When he was almost nine he married Isabella Bennet, who was about five years of age at the time, but this marriage was not binding. They were legally married for a second time in 1679 when he was sixteen, and she twelve years of age. He saw military service both on land and on sea and was killed while in command at the siege of Cork, at the age of twenty-seven.

Grafton is one of the four remaining Dukedoms today still representing the quasi-royal line, all of whom use the Baton Sinister or Bordure Compony in their coats-of-arms to signify their relation to Charles II – related by blood but unable to succeed to the throne because of illegitimacy. Barring further illegitimacy, this would mean that the current Dukes of Grafton, besides being of royal blood, have equally infinitesimal amounts of Bayning blood flowing in their veins.

[498] Antonia Fraser, *King Charles II*, Wiedenfeld and Nicholson, London, 1979, p. 462
[499] Antonia Fraser, *King Charles II*, Wiedenfeld and Nicholson, London, 1979, p. 411
[500] Antonia Fraser, *King Charles II*, Wiedenfeld and Nicholson, London, 1979, p. 413-415

95. Henry Fitzroy, 1st Duke of Grafton, grandson
of Mary Bayning, son of Barbara Villiers and
King Charles II, ca. 1678, artist unknown
National Portrait Gallery, London

Blood, however, is thicker than water. Henry Duke of Grafton would appear to have inherited some other characteristics from his mother as well, as he attracted scandal for his indiscreet personal life and love of pleasure. According to some accounts, his career was saved by the fact of his wife's own indiscretions, which allowed him to divorce her, but other accounts cite her as a sweet-natured, gentle and devoted wife.

Whatever the case, before Henry died Isabella produced him with an heir. Seven generations down the line and over two centuries later, Frances Maynard, a noted Edwardian beauty and daughter of Blanche Adeliza Fitzroy, became mistress to King Edward VII, following her family's longstanding devotion to the king and Lily Langtree's departure from his bedchamber.

There are numerous well-known portraits of Barbara Villiers, including one which she had painted of herself with Charles' illegitimate son, in a pose improbably - and improperly - reminiscent of the Virgin and Child. Taken as such, it became an altarpiece in a Roman convent until the nuns realised their mistake[501].

---

[501] History; Bath Baroque; http://www.bathbaroque.com/history.htm, accessed Feb. 2004

96. Barbara Villiers and son,
sketch after Sir Peter Lely, ca. 1670
private collection

It is perhaps poignant in this respect to note that Barbara's youngest daughter, Barbara (1672—1737), the reputed offspring of John Churchill, entered a convent in France. However, she became by James Douglas, afterwards 4th Duke of Hamilton (1658—1712), the mother of an illegitimate son, Charles Hamilton (1691—1754). She did return to the convent afterward and spent the rest of her life there, in piety. Barbara Villiers' first daughter Anne, Countess of Sussex, also spent some time in a convent, strategically incarcerated there by her mother. Barbara had became the lover of Ralph Montagu, the English Ambassador Extraordinary to the Court of France, but Montagu allowed himself the luxury of also trifling with her daughter Anne's affections. However, Anne, lured by Montagu, bounced out again and the vicious rivalry continued.

Barbara's daughter Charlotte - the King's favourite - was, however, a paragon of virtue. Charlotte Countess of Lichfield was known for her sweet nature and charm. Married off at the age of twelve, Charlotte had borne four children by the age of nineteen and gave birth to a total of twenty. The Earl and Countess of Lichfield enjoyed a married life of forty-two years. Their shared monument in Spelsbury Church commemorates the fact that "at their marriage they were the most grateful bridegroom and the most beautiful bride and that till death they remained the most constant husband and wife"[502].

---

[502] Antonia Fraser, *King Charles II*, Wiedenfeld and Nicholson, London, 1979, p. 414

BANNING (BANNYNG/BAYNING) OF DEDHAM & LONDON
(data printed in italics are unconfirmed and based on speculation)

.... BANNYNG, born ca. 1450, probably from Nayland, Suffolk. *Could this have been Detmar Bannyng, Hanseatic merchant in the neighbouring Ipswich in 1475?*
   From this marriage:
   1. Richard, follows I
   2. *other sons, unknown?*

I RICHARD BANNYNG, born ca. 1470 came from Nayland, Suffolk, lived in Dedham at the close of the 15th century. Data concerning marriage and death unknown.
   From this marriage:
   1. Richard, born ca. 1495, follows II
   2. *son Robert, born ca. 1495, perhaps the ancestor of the Bannyngs known of in Burbage, Wiltshire?*

II RICHARD BANNYNG, born ca. 1495, lived in Dedham at the close of the 15th century, married Anne Raven,
   From this marriage:
   1. Richard, born Dedham +/- 1520, follows III
   2. *son(s): possible fathers of:*
      - *Elizabeth, born in Dedham in 1540, who married Lewis Sparhawk in 1559, died 1565;*
      - *Robert, born 1540, who married Agnes Stibb, parents of a daughter Margaret;*
      - *Margaret, who married William Washell;,*
      - *Mary (Marie) Banninge, who married John Watts;*
      - *John, born around 1540-1545 in Little Bentley? John was father of James who died in 1584, might he have been the same John, Yeoman of Burbage, Wiltshire, born around 1640, who had 5 daughters, one son, John, and a brother Robert?;*
      - *Thomas, Yeoman of Little Bentley; will proved in 1605, mentioning only a brother John?*

III RICHARD BANNYNG, born in Dedham +/- 1520, married Anne Barker
   From this marriage:
   1. Paul, born 1539, follows IV
   2. Andrew, Alderman of London, born +/- 1543, died 11 Dec. 1610; buried in St. Olave's Church, Hart Street, London
   3. Robert , died at Powers estate in Great Waltham, elderly

IV PAUL BANNINGE, born 1539; 1st Viscount Bayning of Bentley, Alderman and Sheriff of London, married Elizabeth Mowse (b. 1551, d 21 Dec. 1579 of consumption) in 1574, married 2nd Susanna Norden in 1580; died 30 Sept. 1616, buried in St. Olave's Church, Hart Street, London

From the second marriage:
1. John, bapt. 17 Apr. 1582, buried 27 Feb. 1583 St. Olave's
2. Paul, follows V

V PAUL BAYNING, baptised 28 April 1588 at St. Olave's Church, London; Baron Bayning of Horkesley, Viscount Bayning of Sudbury, Sheriff of Essex; died 29 July 1629 at his home in Mark Lane, London, buried St. Olave's, London, married Anne Glemham, born 1595, daughter of Sir. Henry Glemham and Lady Anne Sackville, died 1639.

From this marriage:
1. *Scicilia* (Cecily) bapt. 8 Apr. 1613; married in 1630 Henry Pierrepont, Earl of Kingston-Upon -Hull, Viscount Newark, Marquess of Dorchester; died 19 Sept. 1639; had four children.
2. *Paul, follows VI*
3. *Henrie,* bapt. 12 Mar. 1616, buried 27 Apr. 1619
4. *An(ne)* , bapt. 23 Sept. 1619; 2nd Viscountess Bayning of Foxley; married 1st 26 Nov. 1635 Henry Murray Esq.(groom of the bedchamber to Charles I) and 2nd Sir John Baber MD (physician-in-ordinary to Charles II), died Oct. 1678, buried Savoy Church, Middlesex; from the first marriage, one child.
5. *Elizabeth,* born 1622? (no baptismal record), married 1st Frances Lennard, 14th Baron Dacre, 2nd David Walter Esquire; Elizabeth was created Countess of Sheppey for life, by Charles II; died 1686; from the first marriage, one child.
6. *Marie (Mary)* bapt. 24 Apr. 1624; married 1st William Villiers, Viscount Grandison; 2nd Charles Villiers, 2nd Earl of Anglesey; 3rd Arthur Gorges. Had one daughter: Barbara (1640 - 1709) Lady Castlemaine, Duchess of Cleveland, Baroness Nonsuch, Countess of Southampton.
7. *male child* of 'Sir Paul Baninge's' buried 22 Apr. 1627
8. *Susanna,* bapt. 19 June 1628, buried 25 May 1629 .

VI PAUL BAYNING, bapt. 4 Mar. 1615 at St. Olave's Church, London; graduated from Oxford University 12 Sept. 1633, 2nd Viscount Sudbury, Baron of Horkesley, married Penelope Naunton (daughter of Sir Robert Naunton, Master of the Court of Wards and Liveries and once Secretary of State) and Penelope Perrot, on 25 Aug, 1634. He died at Little Bentley Hall in 11 June 1638 and is buried in the family vault in the parish church of Little Bentley.
From this marriage:

1. Anne, born 1 May 1637. Married Aubrey de Vere, 20th Earl of Oxford. Died without issue on 14 Sept.1659. Buried in Westminster Abbey
2. Penelope , born 3 Nov. 1638 Married 1st The Honourable John Herbert and 2nd John Wentworth, Esq. Died without issue in 1657. Buried in Westminster Abbey.

*　　　*　　　*

Liverpool

Pierson Worrall Banning specifies several English Bannings in his genealogy of 1909 (ancestors of the first American Bannings), commencing with William Banning, 1710. He was a miller, his son John was a blacksmith and his other son William an innkeeper and property owner in Stafford. This innkeeper William was father to seven children, including John and Joseph, who lived in London and were both grooms to King George III. Son Thomas held the esteemed office of Postmaster in Liverpool from 1798 to 1819. Brother Joseph married Margaret Wrenshall; they had nine children. The family moved to Philadelphia U.S.A. in 1793, where Joseph opened a store on North Third Street and ran it together with his brother-in-law John Wrenshall from 1793 to 1799. Joseph lost two of his children to the yellow fever plague and returned to England in 1799, settling in Heller, Blackburn, where he died in 1829. He was a prominent Wesleyan Methodist.

Thomas the Postmaster married four times and also had seven children. His son Thomas Baines Banning (born 1784) was a physician to the Royal Infirmary and a graduate of Edinburgh. His brother William succeeded his father as Postmaster of Liverpool, from 1819 to 1847; a prominent figure in local affairs. Another brother, John Johnson, was a solicitor in Liverpool, and brother Benjamin was Vicar of Wellington and Rector of Eyton Selen. His name occurs in the Eyton estate and family archives in the following extract:

"1848 Loyalty and Religion the safeguard of the Nation. A sermon, preached before the members of a friendly society, on Tuesday, August 1, 1848. By the Rev. B.Banning, M.A. Vicar of Wellington and Rector of Eyton, Salop; Domestic Chaplain to the Earl of Morley.[503]"

Brother Charles Barber Greaves Banning is said to have carried on as Postmaster of Liverpool after his brother, from 1847 to 1875. If this is correct, then he must have taken the position late in life and maintained it until he was quite elderly. On succeeding to the property of Mr.Greaves

---

[503] London Metropolitan Archives, Shropshire Archives, Eyton Family, Part 3, Cat. ref. 665, 1848, ref. 665/3/172

of Manchester, through his wife, he assumed the name Greaves-Banning and obtained a coat of arms.

Joseph (born 27 January 1792; son of Joseph Banning and Margaret Wrenshall, above) was apprenticed as a violin maker, but soon after became a schoolmaster. When quite young he joined his uncle Thomas as his sole clerk in the Post Office of Liverpool. He later became Deputy Postmaster and Surveyor of Liverpool, a post he maintained for about fifty years, having over a thousand men under his authority when he retired in 1865.

Joseph's brother Jesse (1808-1893) was a professor of music and a composer in Liverpool.

Joseph's son Robert Joseph Banning (born June 17, 1832) was a physician. He was a Civil Surgeon during the Crimean War, and later Justice of the Peace. Alice Cooper was his second wife, whom he married in 1869. Dr. Robert Joseph Banning, of Shoeburyness, furnished Pierson Worrall Banning with most of his information on the English Bannings.

DR. ROBERT JOSEPH BANNING
L-180

ALICE COOPER BANNING
L-180

97. Dr. Robert Joseph Banning and his wife, Alice Cooper Banning,
The First Banning Genealogy, P.W. Banning, Chicago, 1908

Charles Henry Banning, brother to Robert, was educated for the Ministry, receiving his M.A. at Dublin. He was vicar successively of Streed, Highbury London and of Sprin Grove, Middlesex.

In July 1963 the auction house of Sotheby's published a catalogue entitled: *Sporting Prints, Views and other Coloured Prints. The Property of Mrs. H.D. Banning and other Properties. The Property of Col. R.L. Preston*[504]. The London Times of 15 February 1968, page 16, carried a notice of the death of "Mabel Tempest, aged 85 years, on 11 February 1968 at the Priory Nursing Home, Louth, Linc.,. widow of Henry Druce Banning, formerly of Blackheath". Mabel Tempest is to be identified as the same Mrs. H.D. Banning whose property was auctioned in 1963. Her husband's death was noted in this newspaper a decade earlier, on August 13, 1958 , page 10, under 'Wills and Bequests, "Banning, Mr. Henry Druce of Orchard Drive, S.E. (gross 69,364 pounds, duty paid 28,244 pounds)."

Henry Druce Banning (*G1.L.290*) was a descendant of Thomas the Postmaster, mentioned above. Whether he acquired his wealth through his songwriting, or whether this was a diversion he could afford while living in comfortable circumstances in not known, but the lyrics of numerous musical compositions are attributed to his name. Between 1910 and 1925 he wrote lyrics to the following songs, for various composers: '*A Spring Madrigal, The Sweet Maytide, The Twilight Hour, I sent thee Perfumes, The Fleeting Hour, The Call of the Woods, Song My Sweet when I to others sing, To thee in Paradise, Just a Spray of Rosemary, O pure white Flower, Roses I lay at your Feet, Awake! Awake! The First Spring Morning, Loving is so sweet, From out the Mist, When, my Sweet, I gaze on thee, Once in a Garden lovely, In the purple Glow, Blossom and Song, Forget not yet, O lonely Pines, Two Little Ditties. "Kitty" - What a Pity! - and Mabel* (his wife?) - *"The Linden Tree" , A Wild, wild Rose, The Ploughman's Courtship, Sweet, as I gaze, Western Wind so sweetly blowing, The Sweetest Song, Little Feet, Love in thy youth, Love in Celia's eyes, A Night Song, Butterflies, and finally, The Superior Sex: A Comic Opera in Three Acts, libretto by H. D. Banning, The Constant Lover, Grey Flowers of Dusk, A-Maying, Love's Window, The Byegone Hill, The Song you sang to me, Rose of the World and Time flies away.*'

Nothing more is known of Henry Druce Banning, but he has left us with the distinct impression of being both fortuitous and a romantic.

As Liverpool lies very near Wales, it is thought that the Bannings from Liverpool may have migrated from Wales, or the other way around; research is currently in progress. To date, only one Banning has been found in the records in Wales: James S. Banning, who wrote a letter dated 11 March 1844 to claim a reward for having presented evidence against one Shoni Sguborfawr for his role as one of the two infamous leaders of the Rebecca Riots in Carmarthenshire. These disturbances and popular protests occurred in parts of south-west Wales between 1839 and the end of 1843, when poverty-stricken farmers expressed violent discontent due to an increase in tithe payments, turnpike tolls and other levies enforced. The riots were suppressed when troops were called in and the instigators put under lock and key. William Chambers (junior), a magistrate at Llanelli who enjoyed a close relationship with the authorities, devoted his efforts to ending the violent, night-time activities of the so-called 'Daughters of Rebecca'. James Banning served as steward to William Chambers, who held a file of letters concerning the Rebecca Riots. Among these papers is the following letter which James wrote to George Spurrell, Magistrate's Clerk at Carmarthen:

98.   Letter from James Banning to George Spurrell, dated 11 March 1844
reproduced with permission of Llyfrgell Genedlaethol Cymru /
The National Library of Wales

The letter reads:

"Dear Sir,
Having seen by the Welshman newspaper that 1500 £ was distributed to different Constables witnesses &tc I hope I am not forgotten being one of the principal witnesses against Shoni. I take the liberty of writing to you, trusting that if I am forgotten you will represent my case to the proper authorities - stating the dangers of my life & property during the disturbances, can Mr. Tierny do anything for me in the case if you will be kind enough to mention it him, I know he will, I will handsomely reward you for your trouble, please to write me a line for Return of post & if my presence is rqd [required], I will come over any day. Please address as

below, a house I have opened and which I would be most happy to see
you any time you may come to Llanelly,
I am Sir,
Yours obediently,
J. S. Banning
New Bailey Mews
Park Street
Llanelly
March 11th 1844"

It is unknown whether James received his reward.

Wiltshire

The spelling of the name Banning was often inconsistent in the
British Isles, although less so than on the continent. The families found
seem to be concentrated in particular areas, giving the impression that
there is a relation between several. The spelling Bannyng, as was used by
the Richards and Pauls Bannyng/Bayning, is found most frequently in
Wiltshire. Since some members of the Wiltshire family eventually
emigrated to the United States, Pierson Worrall Banning included what is
known of their genealogy in his work.

In the 16th and 17th centuries Wiltshire, too, was a prosperous
area for the production of wool, as was East Anglia. Bannings from Essex
and Suffolk may have migrated here for this purpose, as we know they
were active in the wool trade. Certainly London, as a trade centre, was
easily accessible and the existing waterways, such as the River Stour and
the Thames, would have provided a natural network for transportation
inland.

Although the earliest mentions in the archives are of Thomas
Bannyng in 1379 and Johannes Bannyng as Rector of Easton Grey in
1401/2, the line set out by Pierson Worrall commences in 1539 with one
Robert Banning from Burbage, Wiltshire, known to be an 'old man' in
1565. Until the end of the 17th century, the first generations outlined by
Pierson Worrall are more-or-less restricted to single persons, as follows:

I.   Robert Banning, Burbage Wilts., mentioned in 1539, old
        man in 1565

II.   John Banning, living at Burbage in 1565

III.   John Banning, 1613 - ?

IV.   John Banning, of Burbage and Magdalena Cell. Oxford
        registration B.A. 1630, M.A. 1634. Subsidiary Roll 1642.

V.   Stephen Banning, wife Mary, died 1688

VI.   Stephen Banning, 1714 –

VII.   John Banning, of Mitton, Wilts., married Elizabeth Noyes of
        Wooton River, Wilts., heiress of Noyes, in 1694. Died 1716.
        Six children:
        1. Elizabeth , born Sept. 1695 in Mitton, died unmarried
        2. Mary, born 1698, in Mitton, died unmarried
        3. Frances, born 1702, in Mitton, died unmarried
        4. John, born 1705, in Mitton, married Mary Ayers
        5. Martha, born 1707, married Simon Alexander of Mitton
            in 1737, two children
        6. Susan, born 1712, married Jasper Easter, of Wooton,
            Dec.. 1736

After this the genealogy becomes more populous, and more detailed.,
until about 1860. Efforts to find verification of the above persons in the
archives have remained, to date, largely unrewarded.
        Some of the miscellaneous Wiltshire Bannings who were found
in various archives are the following:
- *Roberte Bannyng*, North Wiltshire Muster lists in 1539[505] (ancestor of
  the above).
- *Elizabeth Banning*, born ca. 1524, married William Piper in 1545
  The Wiltshire Tax Lists of 1545 and 1576[506] mention:
- *William Bannyng*, paying 8 shillings in the Benevolence of 1545 at
  Burbage Sturmy; (Wilts.)
- *John Baininge*, at the Subsidy of 1576 at Burbage (Wilts.), as well as
  Rauffe Bainning of Wooton Rivers and *Richard Baininge* at
  Marlborough. This Richard Banninge (also Bannyng) was a baker at
  Marlborough, Wiltshire. According to his last will and testament,[507]
  dated 8 Feb. 1593, he was married to Alice, and they had three sons –
  Daniel, John and Robert, and three daughters – Johane, Jane and
  Millicent.
- *John Banning,* married 29 October 1604 to Alice Felp, (Burbage,
  Wiltshire); with children: Alis, baptized 16 June 1606; Edith, baptized
  1 Nov. 1608; John, baptized106 June 1609; William, baptized 20 Nov.
  1612.
- *Thomas* Banning, born ca. 1675, married Elizabeth (Milton, Lilborn,
  Wiltshire), with children: Anthony, baptized 16 May 1692; Anna,
  baptized 22 July 1698

---

[505] The Hundred of Kynworthstone;
http://freepages.genealogy.rootsweb.com/~dutillieul/ZWiltsMuster/Places/Clenche.html;
accessed May 2004
[506] personal communication from R. Heaton, 25 Jan. 2004
[507] The National Archives, Public Record Office, Will of Richard Banninge or Bannyng,
baker of Marlborough, Wiltsire, 8 Feb. 1593, ref. PROB 11/81

Other Bannings of Wiltshire are known to have registered wills now held at the National Archives of the United Kingdom.

- *John Baninge* or Banynge, Yeoman of Burbage, Wiltshire. In his will dated 29 Apr. 1579[508], John declares being 'sicke of bodye, but of good and excellent remembrannce'. He bequeathed his possessions to his brother Roberte, his son John and his five daughters: Johan, Elizabeth, Katherine, Agnes and Mary, and his wife was Elizabeth. He also bequeathed one bushel each of wheat to John Baninge and Thomas Baninge, and to Edmonde Baninge twenty pence, without mentioning any relation. A certain William Baninge (amongst numerous others) is specified as owing him twenty-four shillings.
- *Thomas Banning*, Blanket maker of Corsham, Wiltshire, 16 June 1766[509]
- *Annamoriah Banning*, Widow of Corsham, Wiltshire, 18 June 1772[510]
- *Ambrose Banning*, Carpenter, Gunner, Wiltshire, 30 June 1827[511]
- *John Banning*, Blacksmith of Collingbourne Ducis, Wiltshire, 23 May 1848[512]
- *Rebecca Banning* of Ogbourn Saint George, Wiltshire, 09 February 1853[513]

Captain Stephen Thomas Banning (*G1.K.44*) was born in 1859, at 21 Great Tower Street in London, a descendant of the Wiltshire Bannings. He was a son of John Stephen Banning (*G1.K.35*), a wine merchant of repute and Common Councillor of the City of London. (John Stephen provided P.W. Banning with the first data of the Wiltshire Bannings). Stephen Thomas married Isabel Margaret Moriarity on 26 Apr. 1886 (born in 1862, from Duncistin County, Kerry, Ireland. He was Lieut. Col. of the Royal Munster Fusilliers, J.P. Co., Ireland, and barrister at Law of Middle Temple, having acquired his M.A. at the Royal University of Ireland. The following reference is found of him and his fiancée in the archives: "Corkery family: 1893: Four invitations to Capt. and Mrs. Banning and Miss Moriarty from the Lord Lieutenant, to attend functions at the Castle, Dublin."[514]

Captain Percy Stuart Banning (*G1.K.58*) was born in 1887. He was assigned to the 2nd Battalion of Royal Munster Fusiliers and killed in action at Ypres, Belgium on 4 Nov. 1914, at the age of 27. Captain

---

[508] The National Archives, Public Record Office, ref. PROB 11/
[509] The National Archives, Public Record Office, 16 June 1766, ref. PROB 11/919
[510] The National Archives, Public Record Office, 18 June 1772, ref. PROB 11/978
[511] The National Archives, Public Record Office, 30 June 1827, ref. PROB 11/1727
[512] The National Archives, Public Record Office, 23 May 1848, ref. PROB 11/2074
[513] The National Archives, Public Record Office, 9 Feb. 1853, ref. PROB 11/2166
[514] London Metropolitan Archives, Devon Record Office: Corkery family, Catalogue ref. 5277 M, 1893, ref, 5277M, F2/ 6a-d

Banning was the only son of Lt. Col. S.T. Banning C.B.E., L.L.D. (late Royal Munster Fusiliers)and Mrs. I. M. Banning, the husband of Mona Mary Henry (formerly Banning), of 50 Kensington Mansions, Earl's Court, London. He is buried at Ypres Town Cemetery in Ieper, West-Vlaanderen, Belgium.

Bristol

Other than the mention of Willelmus Banynge as vicar of Temple Parish in Bristol in 1448, only the scant data compiled by Pierson Worrall Banning are available concerning Bristol Bannings. The first mentioned is James Banning, whose son James Banning was born about 1795 in Bristol. He lived in Everleigh for many years as a farrier and eventually moved to Workingham, where he lived and died. He had six sons: Frank, Jake, John, Charles, Frederick and Harry, who would probably have been born some time between 1820-1840. Frank was father to William Banning, and William in turn was known to have lived in Euston Square in London around the end of the 19th century. William provided Pierson Worrall with these data.

Miscellaneous

Various other Bannings in England are known to have registered wills now contained at the National Archives of the United Kingdom.
- Elizabeth Banning, Widow of Thornbury, Gloucestershire 10 February 1680[515], who mentions brothers Thomas and Anthony, brother-in-law Stephen and her son William Banning
- Thomas Banning, Labourer of Hampstead, Middlesex, 16 December 1776[516]
- Ann Banning, Spinster of Wandsworth, Surrey, 17 January 1783[517]
- Joseph Banning, Coachman of Edmonton, Middlesex, 17 August 1801[518]
- Thomas Banning, Gentleman of City of London, 2 July 1807[519]
- Thomas Banning of Mill Street, Harrington near Liverpool, 28 June 1833[520]
- Thomas Banning of Fetcham, Surrey, 6 May 1829[521]
- Robert Banning, Servant of Saint Marylebone, Middlesex, 28 November 1837[522]

---

[515] The National Archives, Public Record Office, 10 Feb. 1680, ref. PROB 11/362
[516] The National Archives, Public Record Office, 16 Dec. 1776, ref. PROB 11/1025
[517] The National Archives, Public Record Office, 17 Jan. 1783, ref. PROB 11/1099
[518] The National Archives, Public Record Office, 17 Aug. 1801, ref. PROB 11/1361
[519] The National Archives, Public Record Office, 2 July 1807, ref. PROB 11/1464
[520] The National Archives, Public Record Office, 28 June 1833, ref. PROB 11/1817
[521] The National Archives, Public Record Office, 6 May 1829, ref. PROB 11/1755
[522] The National Archives, Public Record Office, 28 Nov, 1837, ref. PROB 11/1886

- Stephen Banning of London, 13 June 1613[523], mentioning his wife Hellen, brothers Anthony and Eustathius and three daughters, of whom one was Mary

The London Metropolitan Archives and National Archives contain numerous mentions of Bayning and Banning, which only hint at history. These include the following:

Warwickshire, Ilmington, 6 March 1899: Draft conveyance from Joseph Keyte of Pebworth, coachman, to Joseph Banning of Pebworth, baker, of two cottages in Ilmington[524].

Gloucestershire, Pebworth, 9 February 1898: Draft agreement between Thomas Banning of Pebworth, farmer, and Mrs. Susan Malin, wife of John of Pebworth, labourer, relating to the lease of lands in Ullington in Pebworth[525].

1605-1876 deeds, copy wills and other papers relating to property in Bretforton. Banning, Ashwin, Wagstaff and other families[526].

Quarter Sessions Rolls (Worcestershire) Charles I: "Sheriff Sir John Rous, 10 January 1637: Presentment by Robert Edlington Constable of St. Michaels in Bedwardine that daywarding is duly observed that Thomas Rorcke, Thomas Banning and Elizabeth Tranter sell ale without license and that the highways are in good repair &c." [527]

Records of the Private Bill Office, House of Lords: Private Act, 17 George III, 1777 An Act for naturalizing Ernest Bernard Banning[528]. The will for Ernest Bernard Banning , Merchant of Saint Mary at Hill, City of London, was proved on 07 November 1797[529]. This Ernest B. Banning came originally from Tecklenburg , Westphalia, in Germany, as appears from the bequests to his brothers and sister, nieces and nephews in that country. His genealogy is included in this book. (See chapter on East Frisia, Germany and Scandinavia).

Middlesex Sessions Papers for October 1794: case v Richard Rich on prosecution of John Banning, for assault[530].

---

[523] The National Archives, Public Record Office, 13 June 1613, ref. PROB 11/121
[524] London Metropolitan Archives, Shakespeare Birthplace Trust Records Office: S.C. Warden and Tompkins, Solicitors, of Stratford-upon-Avon, catalogue reference DR 153, Ilmington, 6 Mar. 1899, ref. DR 153/468
[525] London Metropolitan Archives, Shakespeare Birthplace Trust Records Office: S.C. Warden and Tompkins, Solicitors, of Stratford-upon-Avon, catalogue reference DR 153, Pebworth, 9 Feb. 1898, ref. DR 153/610
[526] London Metropolitan Archives, Worcestershire Record Office: Ashwin's of Bretforton,Catalogue Ref. 705:273, 1605-1876, ref. 705:273/7775/19/iv
[527] London Metropolitan Archives, Worcestershire Record Office: Quarter Sessions [10 Charles I - 19 Charles I], Catalogue Ref. 1,1637, FILE - 13 Charles I: Sheriff Sir John Rous.
[528] London Metropolitan Archives, House of Lords Record Office, Catalogue Ref. HL, 1777, File - Private Act, 17 George III, c. 21 - ref. HL/PO/PB/1/1777/17G3n43
[529] The National Archives, Public Record Office, 7 Nov, 1797, ref. PROB 11.1297
[530] London Metropolitan Archives, Middlesex Sessions of the Peace, Court in Session, Catalogue ref. MJ, Papers for 1794, Affidavits and Notices, ref. MJ/SP/1794/OCT/039

Southampton Council/Corporation/Quarter Session papers: "27 March 1697, Recognizance of Sarah, wife of John Chapman, mariner to appear at the next Quarter Sessions. John Chapman, Thomas Swift and Philip Banning, cordwainer, sureties"[531].

Lancashire County Quarter Sessions: "Record Book of Dissenting Meetings : Date: 13 May 1820, Place: Blackburn, Premises: Field at Melling occupied by Joseph Banning" [532]

Lancashire County Quarter Sessions: "Michaelmas (13 September) 1898, Manchester: Chorlton upon Medlock. Copy notice and grounds of appeal of Harry Hill, tenant, John Taylor and Company Limited, licensees, and Henry Hannotte Vernon and Thomas Edmondson, trustees of the will of Mary Mollineaux, owners, against refusal to renew beerhouse licence for premises in Ivy Street, known as the Sun Inn, previously held by Alexander Banning".[533]

"1735: A settlement upon the marriage of William Bund and Mary Parsons of (various arable fields, meadows, roads and cottage), a further piece of meadow called the Banning adjoining meadow called the Rotten on the north; several other closes called the Long Rudge, The Upper Tyning (now converted into a cherry orchard), etc..[534]"

"Portland of Welbeck: Estate and Household Accounts: John Hutchinson: Provisions: Receipted bills of greengrocer (Thos. Banning or Joseph Broughall), poulterer (Mary Moor or Stephen Bowyer), butcher (Edward Mason or John Heathcott), cheesemonger (Joseph Berks or Robt. Day), fishmonger (W. Watson (Oxford Market) or Edward Truelove), greengrocer (John Broughall), baker (Wm. Gebbard), and pastrycook (Isaac Harrison or John Taylor); also miscellaneous vouchers for truffles, muffins, cheese, whey, wheat, crawfish, dairy produce, braw, etc."[535]

"Sale particulars, Gloucestershire, Bourton-on-the-Water 20 June 1876: 'Oven Field' being 1 acre meadow in occupation Mr. Banning."[536]

---

[531] London Metropolitan Archives, Southampton Archives Office: Southampton Council/Corporation Records: Quarter Sessions Records, Catalogue ref. SC9, 27 Mar. 1697, ref. SC9/4/28e

[532] London Metropolitan Archives, Lancashire Record Office: Lancashire County Quarter Sessions [QDL - QEC], Catalogue ref. Q, File: Record of Dissenting Meetings, 1819-1820, ref. QDV/4/70d&71

[533] London Metropolitan Archives, Lancashire Record Office: Lancashire County Quarter Sessions Petitions [QSP 4530-4585], Petitions, Cat. ref. Q, Manchester, Michaelmas, 13 Sept. 1898, QSP/4553/17

[534] London Metropolitan Archives, Worcestershire Record Office: Worcester City Library Collection [899:749/8782/11/B14/1 - 899:749/8782/84/iv/5], catalogue ref. 899/749, 1735, ref. 899:749/8782/57/20

[535] London Metropolitan Archives, Nottinghamshire Archives: Portland of Welbeck (5th Deposit): Estate & Household Accounts, Catalogue ref.

[536] London Metropolitan Archives, Shakespeare Birthplace Trust Records Office: Sale Particulars Catalogue ref. ER6, 20 June 1876, ref. ER6/146/1

Clayton Family Papers: Papers of Sir Robert Clayton (1629 - 1707), Scrivener: 1632 – 1677: Memo. endorsed "Totall of the estate of the Coheires of Lord Banning in the several Counties" [537].

From the Essex Archives: On 25 October 1609: "Recognizance of John Banning of Little Holland, husbandman, to prefer a bill of indictment at the next general gaol delivery against Richard Kyche and William Cronwall of (blanke), charged with stealing eight geese from Banning[538]."

"Examination of Philip Subbs, gent., and Thomas Bannyng, yeoman, both of Little Clacton, for John Clerke of Thorrington, yeoman, to keep the peace towards Robert Went of Great Bentley, husbandman. Before John Argall, esq".[539]. (Little Clacton and Great Bentley were estates owned by Paul Bayning.)

Bannings were not always regarded as upstanding citizens. In June 1767 Elizabeth Banning was accused and found guilty of theft, recorded in the Old Bailey Proceedings[540] as follows:

"327. (L.) Elizabeth Banning was indicted for stealing a looking glass, a brass fender, a poker, a fire shovel, a pair of tongs, and a tin kettle the property of Thomas Simpkins , in a certain lodging room lett by contract, &c May 23. +

Thomas Simpkins . I lett the prisoner's husband a ready furnished lodging, he and she were in it a month or better; they left it about a fortnight ago. There was a warrant out against him, and the woman was left in the room; I went to see that the things were safe, and desired her to get another room; after that I heard she was gone. I went and found the key under the door; I then missed a great many things, feathers out of the bed, pillows and bolster, all the covering, fireshovel, tongs, and poker, a looking glass, copper tea-kettle, and more things. After that I was informed the prisoner was in Bunhill-row near the Three Tuns; I took her up on Monday last; she was committed yesterday by Sir Thomas Rawlinson . I charged her with taking the things; she acknowledged she had taken them; the shovel, poker, and tongs, and other things, were pawned in Bunhill-row, where I found them.

Alexander Renshaw . I am a pawnbroker. On the 18th of April the prisoner pawned a lookingglass with me for 3 s. and on the 19th of May a sender for 2 s. the prosecutor saw them both at my house, and owned them.

---

[537] London Metropolitan Archives, Centre for Buckinghamshire Studies: Clayton Family Papers, Catalogue referenced 135, Papers of Sir Robert Clayton, Scrivener, 1629-1707, ref. D135/A1/5
[538] Essex Record Office, Sessions Rolls, Epiphany 1610, ref. Q/SR 189/72
[539] Essex Record Office, Sessions Rolls, Easter 1609, ref. Q/SR 187/85
[540] Old Bailey Proceedings Online; www.oldbaileyonline.org;accessed 7 July 2004; 03 June 1767; trial of Elizabeth Banning, ref: T17670603-45

Honer Hillier. I am servant to Mr. Marshal in Bunhill-row. The prisoner pledged a tin kettle there the 23d of May; there were other things: she brought a little before a shovel, tongs, and poker.

Prisoner's defence.

I carried them there through necessity, my husband being out of work; he said he would go into the country and get work, and I have not heard of him since."

The verdict was guilty, and the punishment for Elizabeth was transportation. This would seem unduly harsh compared to other punishments of the day, such as months of hard labour, whipping or imprisonment at Newgate. However, transportation for theft is a mild exercise of justice compared to that which was conferred on James Banning in January 1774[541]:

James lodged at the dwelling house of Mr. Binns, where he · shared a bed with a shoemaker, William Croft. According to William's testimony: "I lay in the same-bed with the prisoner; I missed him three times out of bed that night; I heard him say the day before that he had no money at all; Foster told him we had been after him to Staines, the prisoner said, you do not imagine I should have been so great a fool as to go there though I have a brother there; I took the great north road. The prisoner said nothing in his defence. " The accusation was theft "of a watch with a silver case, value 40 s., a brass watch key; value 1 d. and nine guineas and 8 s. in money numbered, the property of William Foster, in the dwelling house of John Binns, Dec, 6th." The verdict was guilty, and James was sentenced to death.

. One Joseph Banning also received a sentence of death in September 1785[542], although the crime he committed is not mentioned.

*   *   *

A certain John Banning was born in England about 1650. His first child, John, was born in England about 1671. There is a record in the Register of St. Martin in the Fields, County Middlesex, England, of the baptism on 31 October 1673 of Frances, daughter of John and Elizabeth Baning[543]. Her father's will stated: "and as for my daughter Frances, through God's goodness she is provided for and I have given her what I have to bestow

[541] Old Bailey Proceedings Online; www.oldbaileyonline.org;accessed 7 July 2004; 12 Jan. 1774, trial of James Banning, ref:: T17740112-17
[542] Old Bailey Proceedings Online; ; www.oldbaileyonline.org: accessed 7 July 2004; 14 Sept. 1785; Punishment summary from Old Bailey Proceedings; Richard Clark, Session VII, Parts I-XII, 943-1181; ref. s17850914-1
[543] Mary Banning Friedlander,The Banning Line, http://freepages.genealogy.rootsweb.com/~mbfriedlander/banning.html, accessed Feb. 2004

upon her[544]." John emigrated to America, appearing in the records there for the first time in 1685, mentioned as having attended a town meeting of New Shoreham, Block Island RI. A wealthy landowner, Peter George, gave him three acres of land, perhaps as a wedding gift when he married a second time to the widow Abigail Niles in 1689. The family is further described in the section concerning Bannings in America.

Captain Augustus Banning, DSO, Merchant Navy Officer, could not be found in an existing British genealogy, but his image was captured on canvas by the artist B. Hailstone in 1945 and presented to the Imperial War Museum, War Artists Advisory Committee, in 1946. The portrait is now held by the Government Art Collection of the United Kingdom.

The only information found was that Augustus Banning was Captain of the *Beachy*, a 1,600 ton steamship owned by the Clyde Shipping Company. The *Beachy* was acting on a rescue mission to a convoy in the North Atlantic on 11 January 1941 when, about 500 miles west of Ireland, the ships were attacked by Germany aircraft and the *Beachy* was hit and sunk. Five men were killed and six, including Captain Banning, were wounded.

---

[544] Mary Banning Friedlander,The Banning Line, http://freepages.genealogy.rootsweb.com/~mbfriedlander/banning.html, accessed Feb. 2004

99.   Captain A. Banning, DSO, Merchant Navy Officer
portrait by Bernard Hailstone 1945
© Queen's Printer and Controller of HMSO, 2003. UK Government Art Collection

English Bannings emigrated to the United States some time in the 17th century. One line which connected the two continents is descended from a certain Robert Banning, born around 1490 and died after 1565 in Burbage, Wiltshire, England. Robert was allegedly the father of John, father of John, in turn father of John, who had Stephen, father of Stephen, born around 1600, who died in 1688 in Wiltshire, England. His son was Edward, thought to be born before 1650 in England, who is the first Banning known to have emigrated to America, where his death is registered in 1710, in Maryland.

*   *   *

The holy wars and the sharply contrasting religious beliefs in Europe were partially the cause of European colonization on the east coast of America. Roman Catholics founded the colony of Maryland under Lord Baltimore (1634). The present American harbour, and industrial city of Baltimore, in the state of Maryland was founded in 1662 but given its present name in 1729.

Emigration to America occurred from England, Scotland and Ireland, as well as from the Netherlands. Banning descendants spread practically throughout all of the United States and contributed a significant share not only to the founding of a nation, but also toward its growth and prosperity.

The United States probably has more Bannings today than any other country. In 2003 there were over 1,300 telephone numbers registered to Bannings in the USA. In only two or three centuries since the first Bannings settled here they seem to have prospered and in any case proliferated significantly more so than in Europe, from whence they came.

In 1909 *The First Banning Genealogy* appeared, as fifteen typewritten copies, of which one edition was donated to the 'Koninklijke Bibliotheek' (Royal Library) in The Hague, Netherlands. The author, Pierson Worrall Banning, born 13 Sept. 1879, renders a description of ten American and three English branches. He also mentions in part the German branch of Felix Wilhelm Banning.

100. Frontspiece of 'The First Banning Genealogy' presented
to The Royal Library in The Hague, inscribed by the author
The First Banning Genealogy, P.W. Banning, Chicago, 1909

312

101. Pierson Worrall Banning
The First Banning Genealogy, P.W. Banning, Chicago, 1909

P.W. Banning describes the characteristics of the Bannings:
"The Bannings have always taken an active part in the wars of countries in which they lived and an honourable record stands to the credit of many of them."

"There are certain characteristics or traits that have remained with the greater part of the Banning families. Among these might be mentioned the following, without pretending to include all. Determination and willpower almost to the point of stubbornness; loyalty to their friends and families to the last, with the greatest opposition but fairness to their enemies; clannishness, with strong feeling for those of their friends in need and ability for hard reliable work. In many cases the facial characteristics show a wonderful resemblance, especially in the firmness of the mouth. Dark hair and brown eyes are very common, although clear sharp blue eyes are often found. As a family they are healthy, probably from the hard active lives so many of them lived."[545]

[545] P.W. Banning, *The First Banning Genealogy*, Chicago, 1909

The first Banning recorded to have come to America was Edward. *(G1.A)* The archives of the state of Maryland (vol. 7, 1678-1683) mention a provincial tax remuneration to be paid to Edward Banning, Talbot County in November 1678.[546] It is thought that Edward was the father of James Banning, and possibly of John and Samuel who settled in Lyme, Connecticut around 1700. However, a will written by an Edward Banning Sr., of Talbot County, dated 1704[547], does not include James or Samuel among the names of his children. It seems plausible, therefore, that this assumption was mistaken. It is unknown as yet who James and Samuel did descend from.

Edward Banning was thought to have been born around 1620 in England[548]. Notes in the Bristol Record Office, England, mention an Edward Banton[549] (Banning) bound to a certain Darrell Sam for a period of four years. It is therefore assumed that he came to the United States as an indentured servant around 1635. He purchased 50 acres of land known as 'Goose Neck' on the north side of the Choptank River, Talbot County on 13 Jan.1690[550].

Edward presumably descended from Stephen Banning of England (see chapter on England), who died in 1714 'as an old man'; he must indeed have been very old if his son was born around 1620!) Edward's brother John married in 1649 to Elizabeth Noyes of Wooton Rivers, Wiltshire, heiress of Noyes. John died in 1716 and she in 1719. Of their six children, one was John, born in 1705 in Milton, Wiltshire, who married Mary Ayers in 1744. The relationship between Edward's family and that of Stephen in England is illustrated by a story passed down through the generations. A grandson of Edward was sea captain Jeremiah Banning. On one of his voyages to England, he brought back various items given to him by his relatives, including a sampler given to him by Mary Ayers, the wife of his father's cousin. This sampler is still in existence and is said to depict Edward's relationship to the early English line of Robert Banning, 1539. One of the facts stitched into the sampler is the marriage of John Banning to Mary Ayers[551].

Edward died in Maryland USA in 1714 (other records state that he died on or before 07 Aug 1710 in Talbot County, the date that his will

---

[546] P.W. Banning., *The First Banning Genealogy*, Chicago, 1909; Province of Maryland Publick Levy and Payments of 1678, http://www.combs-families.org/combs/records/md/1678.htm; accessed July 2004
[547] Will of Edward Banning Sr.;
http://freepages.genealogy.rootsweb.com/~mgjga/Jackson/Wills/edwbanningwill.html; accessed Jan. 2004
[548] P.W. Banning., *The First Banning Genealogy*, Chicago, 1909
[549] Genealogy of Plunkett, Balis,
http://freepages.genealogy.rootsweb.com/~nplunkett/Balis/balis8.html; accessed Feb. 2004
[550] http://www.mandellstreit.com/genealogy/families/bannings/ May 2004
[551] Genealogy of Plunkett, Balis,
http://freepages.genealogy.rootsweb.com/~nplunkett/Balis/balis8.html; accessed Feb. 2004

was proved). His personal possessions and estates, described in this last will and testament dated 9 August 1704[552], identifies as his children William, John, Edward, Andrew, Thomas and Eliza(beth). Charles and Susannah, his youngest children, are not mentioned.

"Will of Edward Banning, Sr. of Talbot County
In the name of God Amen. This ninth day of August in the Eighth year of the Reign of our Sovereign Lady Queen Anne and the year of our Lord God one thousand seven hundred and four I Edward Banning, Sr. of Talbot County in the Province of Maryland being in perfect health of mind and memory, Blessed by God but not of body and confessing the mortality of all mankind do make and ordain this my last will and testament in manner and form following. I bequeath my soul into the hands of Almighty God that gave it hoping that by the meritorious death and passion of Jesus Christ my Blessed Redeemer to have full and free pardon and Remission of all my sins and my body to be buried in Christian buriall according to the direction of Executrix and Executor hereafter nominated- -
Item I give unto my beloved wife Susannah free liberty to Enjoy and live upon my now dwelling Plantation so long as she continues a widdow not molesting my son William Banning.
Item If my said wife marry my will is that she shall only enjoy the third of the said plantation.
Item my will is that assisting my wife to share the fruit of the orchard to the value of half the labor of my son William shall have half the fruit through all the orchard to be equally divided.
Item I give unto my well beloved wife Susannah all my moveable estate whatsoever after my debts are paid.
Item I give unto my two sons John Banning and William Banning after my wife's decease or marrying again my now dwelling plantation and their heirs forever to be equally divided betwixt them and my will is when they come to enjoy the said land that they shall pay unto my son Edward Banning fifteen hundred pounds of Tobo a piece.
Item either of my said two sons John or Wm shall die without heir then their part shall go to my son Andrew Banning.
Item I leave my two younger children which I had by my former wife Viz Thomas and Eliza to my said wife Susannah. Thomas until he comes to the age of one and twenty years and Eliza until she comes of the age of sixteen years.
Item I leave my said beloved wife Susanna and my son William my Executrix and executor of my last will and testament disowning and

[552] Jackson-Chambers Genealogy,
http://freepages.genealogy.rootsweb.com/~mgjga/Jackson/Wills/edwbanningwill.html, accessed Feb. 2004

disallowing all wills by me formerly made and publishing and declaring this to be my last will and testament.
Witness my hand and seal the day and year first above written
Edward B. Banning
his mark
signed sealed and published and declared in the presence of us
Robert Pearson
Richard R. Roberts
John Bradshaw"

In the book *Jeremiah Banning, Mariner and Patriot*[553], William Banning is mentioned as coming to Maryland from the British Isles as an indentured servant. In view of the above information, which mentions Edward having come to the United States as a youth, it is more than likely that William was born in the United States. On 8 May 1745, a Samuel Chamberlaine gave William Banning and his wife Jane a lease to farm a fifty acre lot called Goose Neck on the west side of Plaindealing Creek – perhaps the same, or close to, the land purchased by his father in 1690. According to the terms of the lease, the couple could have this land "for and during their natural lives upon payment of one ear of Indian corn upon the 30th day of April yearly and every year."[554] This would have been an exciting day of independence for William and Jane and their three sons Jeremiah, Henry and Anthony. However, before the first payment of corn was due on the leased land, William Banning died. In 1746 Jane Banning married Nicholas Goldsborough, a longstanding family friend and wealthy landowner. A note in *Old Kent, The Eastern Shores of Maryland, published in 1876*[555], however, states that Jane Spencer was the widow of James Banning, and not of William. This error was apparently due to an incorrect reading of the Administrative letters of the estate of James Banning[556], who was said to be her son, and not her husband. It seems very unlikely that Jane had sons other than Jeremiah, Anthony and Henry, as Jeremiah's own logbook and will mentions only these two brothers. Jane's marriage to William is said to be established by church records and deeds.[557] Having no children of his own, Nicholas Goldsborough adopted the boys and, in his will dated 20 Oct. 1756, left them his property. The names of the adopted children were Jeremiah,

---

[553] Jane Foster Tucker, *Jeremiah Banning, Mariner and Patriot*, published under auspices of the Oxford Bicentennial Commission, Maryland, 1977
[554] Jane Foster Tucker, *Jeremiah Banning, Mariner and Patriot*, published under auspices of the Oxford Bicentennial Commission, Maryland, 1977, p. 2
[555] P.W. Banning, *The First Banning Genealogy*, Chicago, 1909, genealogy A.
[556] L. Banning, *The Banning Branches*, Heritage Books, Maryland, 1997
[557] P.W. Banning, *The First Banning Genealogy*, Chicago, 1909, genealogy A.

Henry and Anthony. The confusion of ancestry ends here, where the story of Jeremiah begins.

As a boy, **Jeremiah Banning** (*G1.A2; 1733-1798*) had his heart set on going to sea and was apprenticed as a hand on a ship at the age of 17. Becoming a most accomplished mariner, he soon took command of various vessels and sailed for almost 25 years, combining trade interests on shore with shipping to Europe and other destinations.

Throughout the years his prosperous circumstances increased. It has been said that he also pursued the slave trade, but only one instance can be cited when he carried slaves, having acquired a coloured family for his own use and five others presented to him in return for services rendered. The slaves were given sufficient liberty on board that three managed to steal a lifeboat from deck during the night and rowed out to sea with five bars of Jeremiah's gold. The sailors pursued the fugitives, but on discovery two jumped overboard where they were promptly devoured by sharks and although the third was apprehended, he drowned accidentally several years later in a cove adjacent to Jeremiah's home. As did most plantation owners of the time, Jeremiah owned slaves but was known to treat them uncommonly well and many were devoted to him. Of the slave boy Juba, whose family he purchased in Senegal in 1763, he wrote in his will: "As to my favourite boy Juba, who never that I know of told me a falsity or betrayed a confidence, and from his pleasing spirited and cheerful disposition greatly leads me to provide for his future welfare and happiness.[558]" Juba was apprenticed to a house carpenter to learn the trade and outfitted with clothing and tools to pursue this profession, and his freedom.

Jeremiah came to deplore the enforced captivity of human beings and decreed in his last will and testament that all his slaves be released on occasion of his death and that they enjoy a fitting education and generous material aspects to live as free citizens, at the cost of his inheritance, "and never permit them to want"... This was done as he requested. Jeremiah's brother Anthony (*G1.A4, 1740-1787*), with whom he did business, owned a plantation where there were also a large number of slaves.

---

[558] Jeremiah Banning, *Log and Will of Jeremiah Banning*, privately printed, W.F. Austin, New York, 1932

Jeremiah Banning

102. Jeremiah Banning : drawing by John Moll, taken from a daguerreotype, published in 'Jeremiah Banning, Mariner and Patriot', by Jane Foster Tucker, 1977

Jeremiah was a courageous man who did not shy away from adventure at sea. With a record height of 1.96m he was a dreaded opponent, a pillar of strength who had to contend with considerable adversity. He survived smallpox; recording in 1756: "the whole family subject to the disorder took the infection and five died[559]," although his omission of the names in his journal seems surprising. We do know that his stepfather died on 14 November 1756 as a result of smallpox. Jeremiah survived perilous storms at sea, where his vessel was sometimes the only one of a convoy which was not shipwrecked, and he never lost a single crewman at sea. Only one was thrown overboard in a storm but survived after a daring rescue. Perhaps this record was due to good fortune, but also justifiably attributed to his courage and expert seamanship.

---

[559] Jeremiah Banning, *Log and Will of Jeremiah Banning*, privately printed, W.F. Austin, New York, 1932, entry made 1756

He was entertained by the King of Senegal, shrewdly evaded bankruptcy at the hands of corrupt businessmen in England, and taken prisoner by the French with his crew in Barbados. This incarceration is vividly described in Jeremiah's journal (in which he consistently referred to himself in the third person): "…..the miseries, distress and horrors of a jail, a jail in a suffocating and burning climate, crowded with 378 men, groaning with the pain of their wounds in battle and the worse, torturing flux (dysentery), suffocation, and almost every calamity and distress incident to man. The dead, the dying, and the effects of the flux were the beds and pillows for the living."

"Those that died were often 24, sometimes 48, hours before removed. They were then thrown over the high wall of the fort at St. Pierre within which the prisoners of war were confined. At the foot of the walls stood Negroes, ready to haul the corpse to the sea-side, where they were slightly buried in the sand, and soon after which the hogs would root up the carcasses and devour them."

"Those unacquainted with the too frequent rigors pursued in war and how the hearts and feelings of men inured thereto may become callous, would be ready to conclude the above exaggerated. But the truth is, Captain Banning and his crew suffered more than language can relate – such as putrid meat and but little of that, water from a stream wherein the women washed their linen, etc., and consequently strongly tinctured with soap suds. The hot scorching sun pouring down on their heads in the prison yard. Driven within the walls thereof, at the going down of the sun, the stone pavement thereof to be their bed, swarming with millions of lice. Parched up with heat and not one drop of water in general – bad as it was – to be got after night to slake their thirst. But what was, as before observed, more intolerable than the rest, was that of being obliged to lie down among the excrements of the flux – the dead – and the dying."[560]

Everyone in the jail – 378 men – died except himself and a young boy. When it was thought he could no longer endure the torturous confinement, he was summoned to the fort officer. Filthy, emaciated and ragged, Jeremiah made a supreme effort to stand erect, and listened in disbelief as he was told that a redemption had been concluded. He was conveyed to Guadeloupe and eventually recuperated in St. Kitts, the first English colony in the Caribbean.

On another occasion in 1761 Jeremiah's ship was captured again by the French and taken to a Spanish port. Jeremiah was loathe to experience another dreaded incarceration. With insufficient daylight to enter the port, the ship was compelled to anchor offshore to await the

---

[560] Jeremiah Banning, *Log and Will of Jeremiah Banning*, W.F. Austin, New York, 1934, entry: 1761

dawn. At midnight a British 50-gun ship espied the hapless ship at anchor and towed it to freedom.

Jeremiah recorded these and other highlights of his career in a journal which he called "A narrative of the principle incidents in the life of Jeremiah Banning, written in 1793". The original manuscript still

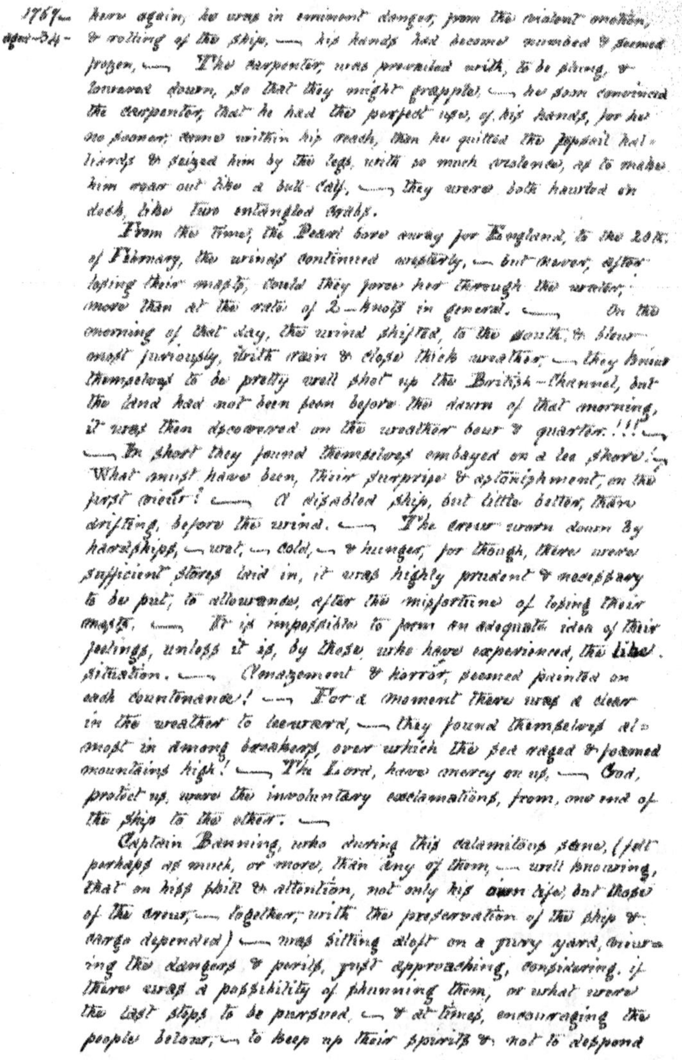
1767— here again, he was in eminent danger, from the violent motion,
Age-34- & rolling of the ship, — his hands had become numbed & seemed
frozen, — The carpenter, was prevailed with, to be slung, &
lowered down, so that they might grapple; — he soon convinced
the carpenter, that he had the perfect use, of his hands, for he
no sooner, came within his reach, than he quitted the topsail hal-
liards & seized him by the legs, with so much violence, as to make
him roar out like a bull calf, — they were both hawled on
deck, like two entangled crabs.
From this time, the Pearl bore away for England, to the 20th.
of February, the winds continued westerly, — but never, after
losing their masts, could they force her through the water,
more than at the rate of 2—knots in general. — On the
morning of that day, the wind shifted, to the south, & blew
most furiously, with rain & close thick weather, — they knew
themselves to be pretty well shot up the British-Channel, but
the land had not been seen before the dawn of that morning,
it was then discovered on the weather bow & quarter.!!! —
— In short they found themselves embayed on a lee shore! —
What must have been, their surprise & astonishment, on the
first view! — A disabled ship, but little better, than
drifting, before the wind. — The crew worn down by
hardships, — wet, — cold, — & hunger, for though, there were
sufficient stores laid in, it was highly prudent & necessary
to be put, to allowance, after the misfortune of losing their
masts. — It is impossible to form an adequate idea of their
feelings, unless it is, by those who have experienced, the like
situation. — Amazement & horror, seemed painted on
each countenance! — For a moment there was a clear
in the weather to leeward, — they found themselves almost in among breakers, over which the sea raged & foamed
mountains high! — The Lord, have mercy on us, — God,
protect us, were the involuntary exclamations, from, one end of
the ship to the other. —
Captain Banning, who during this calamitous scene, (felt
perhaps as much, or more, than any of them, — well knowing,
that on his skill & attention, not only his own life, but those
of the crew, — together, with the preservation of the ship &
cargo depended) — was sitting aloft on a jury yard, survey-
ing the dangers & perils, just approaching, considering, if
there was a possibility of shunning them, or what were
the best steps to be pursued, — & at times, encouraging the
people below, — to keep up their spirits & not to despond

103. Page from the Log of Jeremiah Banning, written 1733-1798
transcribed by Emily E. Banning in 1880
(privately printed by W.F. Austin, New York, 1932)

exists today in a museum in the United States. His relative Emily E. Banning made a literal copy of the journal in 1880 and is cited[561] as follows: "The original record of Jeremiah Banning's life, written by himself in 1793, having become difficult to read, from age and faded ink, it became necessary to copy it. This I have faithfully done." Emily rendered her copy not only faithfully but in an elegant script which was printed privately in 1932 by W.F. Austin (a descendant) of New York, and included the text of Jeremiah's last will and testament.

In 1773, at the age of 40, Jeremiah was compelled to abandon his sea-faring life due to gout, but by no means become idle, and he was obviously a prominent citizen in Talbot County. His appointment as Lieutenant Colonel was effected on 9 April 1775 and soon after as Captain of another company. In 1776 he was appointed Major to the 37th Battalion of Militia, assessor of Mill-Hundred (Hundred was an old English term to denote a district which contained at least ten estates which would provide 100 fighting men), and in 1977 Magistrate of his county, then Colonel of the 38th Battalion of Militia and Naval Officer of the Port of Oxford. His subsequent promotion was as Chief-Justice of the Orphans Court. In 1779 he was elected as one of the select vestry of St. Michael's Parish (without having solicited such) and appointed one of the Commissioners of Taxes and authorised to sign paper money issued by the State Council. In 1785 he was appointed by law as first commissioner for laying out the town of Talboton (since called Easton); in 1787 appointed Armourer of the Eastern Shore. In a very contested election in 1787 he was chosen to represent Talbot County in a general convention to be held at Annapolis to ratify and confirm the Federal Government of the United States. Three days before his 58th birthday in 1791 he was commissioned by President Washington as Collector of the Customs for the Port of Oxford and two months later Inspector of Revenue for the same port.

Jeremiah also devoted time to the management of his considerable landholdings. He resided on an isthmus in an attractive and sizeable stately home with the fitting name 'The Isthmus', where, in the extraordinarily significant days preceding the freedom war (1775-1783) historical personages were received hospitably. The military leader and statesman George Washington was party to secret meetings here with other notable persons, such as the French Marquis De La Fayette, who fought on the side of the freedom fighters, and William Morris the financier.

---

[561] Jeremiah Banning,, *Log and Will of Jeremiah Banning*, W.F. Austin, New York, 1934, introduction

Correspondence with George Washington still exists in the United States archives:[562]

"*Easton, September 7ʰ 1793*
To the President of the United States-
Sir: I am injoined by such of the citizens of Talbot County as were present at a meeting held this day in Easton, to communicate to you the enclosed resolutions; and at the same time to accompany their sentiments by expressions of their esteem and attachment to your person; and of their heartfelt wishes for your constant health and happiness. In compliance with this injunction I have accordingly done so; and I beg to assure you, sir, that in the exercise of this duty I feel the most distinguished pleasure.
I have the honor to be, sir,
Your most obedient servant,
Jere Banning, Chairman.

The President replied as follows:
"*Mount Vernon, 16ʰ Sept., 1793.*

To Jeremiah Banning, Esquire, Sir:
The approbation which the General Government has met from my fellow citizens, throughout these States, cannot fail to excite in me the liveliest satisfaction; and the assurance given by them of their firm intentions to unite in keeping our country in a state of peace at this important period, is an additional and pleasing testimony of the unanimity and good sense of the citizens of the United States.
While I beg of you to assure the citizens of Talbot of the reliance I place in their disposition towards the General Government manifested in these resolutions, I also request you to make known to them the pleasure I receive from their expressions of esteem an attachment for my person: and to you, sir, for your polite manner of transmitting these resolutions, my best thanks are offered.
Go. Washingon"

However, the most honourable incident in the life of Colonel Jeremiah Banning was on 5 Nov. 1777, when he co-signed the Articles of Confederation, through which the United States of America came into being.

---

[562] Jeremiah Banning, *Log and Will of Jeremiah Banning*, W.F. Austin, New York, 1934, introduction

Although Jeremiah once lost his heart to a damsel in a foreign port, he never married. Records do not reveal when he adopted the three children of Mary Gossage – Robert, Freeborn and Clementina, but he undertook responsibility for their upbringing and left to them the bulk of his estate.

His mansion apparently still stands on the beautiful Tred Avon River across from Oxford. Seeking a place where he could escape the activity of a large household in order to administer his estate and other affairs, he had erected a curious little frame building on the lawn at the water's edge which he called 'The Office'. In the mornings his faithful servants Juba and Anthony would carry him there, where he could look out over the water and take up his quill to render his memoirs to paper. Jeremiah died two days before Christmas in 1798, at the age of sixty-five. He is buried in an unmarked grave on his estate.

Henry Geddes Banning *(G1.A. 26)*, a grandson of Jeremiah, was born 8 Mar.1816 in Talbot County. He married Emily Eschenburg on 17 April 1847. Henry came to Wilmington, Delaware as a young man, becoming one of its leading citizens. He soon won general recognition and esteem for his integrity and clear-headed business capacity, known for his public spirit and sense of civic responsibility.

104. Henry Geddes Banning
The First Banning Genealogy, P.W. Banning, Chicago 1909

An example of this was his membership, among some of the most substantial businessmen of the city, of one of the earliest fire companies in the southern part of Wilmington - the Fame Hose Company – organised in 1839. Henry G. Banning was near the top of the list. The company maintained only a hose carriage until a steam fire-engine was added some years later. Before the advent of this 'modern' piece of equipment, members of the volunteer fire department responded to fire alarm calls armed with long leather water-buckers, and participation in a volunteer fire company meant arduous physical labour for all hands when the alarm sounded.

In 1872 Henry G. Banning was elected President of the National Bank of Delaware, chartered 9 Feb. 1795, one of the oldest banks of the country. He was its fifth president and held the office for thirty-three years. Tenure of office for such a long period of time was a tribute to his ability and wisdom, but also to the general regard which his personality inspired. He was a member of the House of Representatives of Delaware, and held other important positions, both honorary and otherwise.

His wife Emily was always deeply concerned in perpetuating amongst their descendants the memory of early Americans, both men and women, who had served a role in the Colonial period. It is due to Mrs. Banning's intimate association with these historical and genealogical matters that their residence became a landmark, in many ways. In the south parlour of their home on 809 South Broom Street, Wilmington, Mrs. Banning served as hostess on 19 May 1892 when the National Society of Colonial Dames of America was founded. Representatives of Delaware, Pennsylvania, New Jersey and the District of Columbia were present, and the Constitution adopted provided that State organisations could be formed in each of the Original Thirteen States and in the District of Columbia. Five years later an amendment allowed societies to be formed in other States. Mrs.. Banning was President of the Delaware Society of Colonial Dames from the formation until her death in 1897. During those years she was also Vice-President of the national body.

The Banning House[563], where they lived for forty-five years, was built in 1812. Henry G. Banning purchased it from the Bird family in 1861 and it is said that it seems he attached his personality to the house more strongly than any of the other owners. The house was two-stories with an attic, a five-bay stuccoed brick structure and much larger than most of the homes of that day and age. It is two full rooms deep on each side of a central hall. A railed deck between the pairs of chimneys at

---

[563] Harold Donaldson Eberlein, and Cortlandt V.D. Hubbard,, *Historic Houses and Buildings of Delaware*, Dover, Delaware, Public Archives Commission 1963, p. 207, 208

105. Willard Stewart, Banning House, residence of Henry Geddes
Banning from 1861 to 1906
Willard Stewart Photographs for the WPA and HABS Collection,
University of Delaware Library. Newark, Delaware

each end relieves the austerity of the otherwise rather severe lines. It was
an example of 'Quaker Georgian' architecture reduced to simplicity. The
Banning House is now the Rectory of St. Elizabeth's Roman Catholic
Church.

Henry Geddes Banning carefully preserved the journal written by
his grandfather Jeremiah, which is now in the possession of a museum in
Oxford, Maryland. He died in 1906 at the age of 90, in Delaware. It was
said that with his courtly manners, his passing took away from the life of
the city one of the last surviving gentlemen of the old school.

Anthony Banning *(G1.A.12)*, great-grandson of Edward, born 12 May
1768, married Sarah Murphy Pierce on 30 June 1791 at Connellsville,
Pennsylvania. They had eight children. Sarah was the widow of George
Pierce, who had married her as the result of a duel fought between Col.
Paul and himself, while standing on barrels in the river at Connellsville.
In this dramatic duel the Colonel had his thumb shot off and Miss Murphy
became the wife of his rival.

Anthony was left an orphan and went to live with his
grandparents, who apprenticed him to a tailor. He joined the Methodist
Episcopal Church at the age of ten, for which he was disowned. The
prominent preacher, Freeborn Garrettson, who was at this time confined

to jail for his religious beliefs along Methodist lines, preached from the prison windows to the crowds that gathered outside to listen. Here young Anthony often went to listen, and here received his theological training.

At the age of nineteen Anthony took up employment by the Presiding Elder as local preacher in 1789, remaining in this position for two years, after which he was ordained Deacon by Bishop Asbury. While so engaged he married and settled in Fayette County, Pennsylvania. He moved to Mount Vernon, Ohio, in 1812, where he had on previous visits bought several pieces of property in the centre of town; these later increased substantially in value. The first tannery in Connellsville, PA, was built by Anthony some time between 1791 and 1799. He also built the first house made of locally produced brick shortly after the town was started; there were many valuable deposits of fire clay, silica rock and other excellent brick-making materials in the immediate surroundings.

In 1836 he built the Banning Chapel, often preaching there, and finally deeded it to the Methodist Episcopal Church. He carried on several lines of business, his interests being large and varied. In time he became wealthy and a major influence in local affairs. He was Associate Judge in Knox County from 1827 to 1834, as well as holding many important and honorary positions, and was held in high esteem by all. On 4 Feb. 1844, Anthony Banning drowned while crossing the ice on Vernon River at Mount Vernon.

106.   Anthony Banning
The First Banning Genealogy, P.W. Banning, Chicago 1909

James Smith Banning (*G1.A.70*), son of Anthony, was born 11 Jan. or June 1800 in Connellsville, PA.. He married Eliza A. Blackstone on 12 Mar. 1822, the daughter of James Blackstone of Connellsville, born 1805 in Pennsylvania and a descendent of Sir William Blackstone. In 1812 James moved to Mount Vernon, Ohio, where he engaged in farming, milling and other mercantile business. In 1850 they were located in Knox County, where he was a miller and farmer with real estate valued at $25,000. He died 22 May 1867 in Mount Vernon.

A-70

107.   James Smith Banning
The First Banning Genealogy, P.W. Banning, Chicago 1909

Sarah Banning *(G1.A.67)* a sister to James Smith Banning, born 13 June 1792, married Daniel S. Norton of Uniontown, Pennsylvania, in 1816. They had seven children, one of whom was Anthony Banning Norton.

Anthony Banning Norton *(G1.A-452/1821-1893)* became a journalist and politician. His brother Daniel became a United States senator from Minnesota. Anthony graduated from Kenyon College in

Gambier, Ohio, in 1840 and was admitted to the bar later that year. He became active in the Ohio Whig party and edited several Whig newspapers. In 1844 he vowed never to shave or to cut his hair until Henry Clay should be elected president, and he kept his vow to his death. He moved to Texas in about 1855, where he was elected a representative in the Texas legislature from Henderson and Kaufman counties in 1857 and 1859 as a Know-Nothing. As a staunch Unionist, he strongly supported Sam Houston for governor in 1859. Houston reciprocated by appointing Anthony Banning Norton adjutant general in April 1860. He acted as chairman of the Texas delegation to the Constitutional Union party convention in May 1860, where he urged the nomination of Houston for president. In the same year he became the editor of the Austin *Southern Intelligencer*, a Unionist newspaper.

Although he had opposed secession, Anthony remained in Texas until he was forced to leave. He returned to Mount Vernon, Ohio, in November 1861. During the Civil War he helped ease the living conditions of Texas prisoners of war at Camp Chase in Columbus, Ohio. Returning to Texas in 1865, he was elected to the Constitutional Convention of 1866, where he served as chairman, as a representative of Henderson, Kaufman, and Van Zandt counties. By 1868 Banning Norton had allied himself with the Republican party. He ran unsuccessfully for governor in 1878 and 1884 and for Congress in 1866 and 1871. He was appointed judge of the Fifth Judicial District of Texas in 1868, postmaster of Dallas in 1875, and United States marshal for northern Texas in 1879. Around 1868 he settled in Dallas, where he spent the remainder of his life. Anthony established a newspaper in Dallas called *Norton's Union Intelligencer*, which he published until his death. He married three times and had five children. He died on 31 Dec. 1893, in Dallas.

(signature)

108. Henry Blackstone Banning
The First Banning Genealogy, P.W. Banning, Chicago 1909

Henry Blackstone Banning (*G1.A-481*), born 10 Nov. 1836 in Mount Vernon, Ohio, was a son of James Smith Banning. He married Julia Kirby in September 1868. They had four children. As a lawyer, he practiced in Mount Vernon for some time under the firm name of Dunbar & Kirby. He enlisted and was made Captain of Co. B. 4th OVI. He was appointed Major of the 52nd OVI, but never joined that company, being transferred and placed in command of the 87th OVI, a three months Reg. at the expiration of which time he was made Lieutenant Colonel of the 125th OVI and served as such until 1863, when he was made Colonel of the 121st OVI. In the spring of 1865, on recommendation of Generals Davis and Thomas, he was promoted for gallant service to the rank of Brev. Brig. General, during the Atlanta Campaign. In the spring of 1865 he was placed in charge of the Port of Alexandria, Virginia, where he remained until 2 Dec. 1865, when he mustered out of service with the rank of Brev. Brig. General. While in service he was elected to the Legislature of Ohio, from Knox County. In 1872 Henry defeated Ex-President Hayes for Congress and in 1874 he defeated Hon. Job E. Stephenson, and in 1876 the Hon. Stanley Mathews, in the second district of Cincinnati. He died on 10 Dec. 1881 in Cincinnati. Banning is one of 41 Union Army generals buried at Spring Grove Cemetery in Winton Place.

Anthony Rogers Banning *(G1.A.478)*, another son of James Smith Banning, was born in Mount Vernon, Ohio in 1831. He married Catherine Torrence of Connellsville, Pennsylvania. They had no children. They lived in Connellsville, where he owned much coal land, and the town of Banning, Pennsylvania, had it's origins on one of his farms. He was director of the B & O Railway Company for many years.

109.   Anthony Rogers Banning
The First Banning Genealogy, P.W. Banning, Chicago 1909

It was most likely Anthony Rogers Banning who founded the Banning Connellsville Coke Company in Uniontown, Pennsylvania, and after whom the Banning Coal Mines nr. 1, 2, 3 and 4 were named. Coal mining around the turn of the century was still an arduous process fraught with danger, and accidents were frequent. On 19 Dec. 1907, one of the worst mining disasters in history occurred in the nearby Darr Mine. A memorial stands today in Westmoreland County, Pennsylvania, commemorating 239 miners who died during a dust and gas explosion on that day[564]. Only two survived. The entry of the mine was sealed a month after the terrible disaster. By 1910 the Pittsburgh Coal Company had resumed operations at the Darr Mine, though the company dropped the name in a attempt to erase its terrible history, and simply operated the mine as another entry of the adjacent Banning No. 3 Mine.

---

[564] Darr Mine & Banning No. 3 Mine; http://patheoldminer.rootsweb.com/darr.html, accessed May 2004

By 1913 Banning No. 3 Mine employed 350 persons. That year its miners produced about 155,000 tons of coal. Situated on the 72 inch-thick Pittsburgh coal seam, the slope-entry Banning No. 3 Mine was served by the Pittsburgh & Lake Erie Railroad. There was also a tipple on the Jacobs Creek side of the Youghiogheny River, on the B & O R.R., connected to the Banning No. 3 Mine by a cable car running across the river.

In 1919 Banning No. 3 Mine employed 227 persons, though it was operated only a small part of the year. Workers at the mine produced less than 30,000 tons of coal in 1919. Soon thereafter, Pittsburgh Coal Company closed and abandoned the Banning No. 3 Mine and the old Darr Mine entry.

Pittsburgh Coal Company, a division of Consolidation Coal Company (CONSOL) after 1945, continued to Operate Banning No. 1 & Banning No. 2 Mines in nearby Fayette County through the 1940's.

110. Mine Pick-up Service, Banning No. 2 Collery, Republic Steel Corp., Jacobs Creek, Pennslyvania, 1958.
New York Central System-The Pittsburg & Lake Erie Railroad Company print from the original painting by Howard Fogg, 1958
Collection Larry and Susan Bunce

While Anthony Rogers Banning drew his income from coal and railroads, a **John Anderson Banning** *(G1.B.624)* also fared well in this field. Born in Wheeling, West Virginia, on 18 Aug. 1836, he was a farmer of Weld County, as was his father, and became actively involved in the construction of railroads for many years. He was considered a most competent and reliable individual, very conscientious in his business dealings and highly regarded by his employers. For five years John A. Banning was also involved in various parts of Colorado in a field similar

331

to two Bannings in the Netherlands – construction of ditches. His exploits involved frequent travel. He purchased a ranch of three hundred and twenty acres where he successfully devoted his time to farming and stock raising. He dealt extensively in Shorthorn and graded cattle and bred fine specimens of Cleveland Bay horses and Poland-China and Berkshire hogs, which he raised for the Denver markets.

John A. Banning moved at the age of 12 with his parents and ten brothers and sisters to Burlington, Iowa. He enjoyed an excellent reputation as a student of Mount Pleasant High School. On becoming of age, he moved to Nebraska and spent four years engaged in freighting across the plains from Nebraska City to Salt Lake, his associates in the enterprise being Messrs. Russell and Waddell.

In 1860 John settled in Lincoln City, Colorado, becoming involved in mining operations. He owned an interest in mines No. 40 and 41, in the Lincoln district, and remained there until 1864. In the succeeding two years he aided the development of coal mines in the Golden City, as a member of the firm of Wheeler & Banning. From 1866 until 1874 he was contracted for various railway and road construction projects, including the Union Pacific Railroad, Denver & Pacific Railroad, the Kansas Pacific Railroad, the Omaha Short Line and the Denver and Rio Grande road.

His next project, which was to last five years, was to construct irrigation canals all over the west, the major ones being the Eaton, Arapahoe, Welch, and the Banning and Beasley ditches. For several years he owned a half-interest in the last-named ditch, which he helped to incorporate, and was president of the same for years. In 1896 he built a private ditch, fed from the Platte River. During the years 1881, 1882 and 1883 he graded and constructed a portion of railroad on the Santa Fe and Southern Pacific lines.

In 1860 John married Susan Tompkinson, of Burlington, Iowa. The couple had two sons and three daughters.

Richard Anthony Banning (G1.A.524) descended from Jeremiah's side of the family; his grandfather being a brother to Mary Elizabeth Banning. Born in Baltimore, Maryland in 1859. By 1882 he had set up the Banning Carriage Works on 104 & 106 E. Lombard Street in Baltimore where he manufactured and sold road carts and buggies, surreys and daytons, spindle and road wagons and accessories such as harness and whips. He produced an annual Banning Horse and Carriage Trade Catalogue to promote business. An example of the catalogue from 1892, illustrated below, had 32 pages with 27 full-page pictures showing 20 different models and 7 harnesses.

111. Banning Horse & Carriage Trade Catalogue dated 1892
private collection

Benoni Banning (*G1.B.17*), is believed to have come from Ireland, sailing from Dublin and coming to Talbot County, Maryland, some time between 1740 – 1745. This has not been verified and is disputed by some, who claim that his father was born in Maryland[565]; P.W. Banning suggests that Benoni's father went to Dublin from Scotland or England some years prior to the time of his voyage to America.

The story passed down by the Chicago branch is that they descend from a line of Irish kings, but nothing is offered in proof, while the descendants of James (brother of Benoni) assert that they descend from a line of Scottish chiefs. This is also without sound basis. It is suggested that the lineage may be through the female side. The story may well be based on the lineage of William Lowber Banning's wife Mary Alice Sweeney, (1850) said to be a direct descendant of Donal of Armagh[566], 173rd monarch of Ireland, but the story could equally be a variation on the first claims that Bannings descended from Viking chiefs. Such claims are easy enough to make, since they are next to impossible to dispute, or to verify, and since many thousands of people descend from one individual in the course of over 1,000 years, such a relation would seem rather irrelevant.

---

[565] L. Banning, *The Banning Branches*, Heritage Books, Maryland, 1997
[566] P.W. Banning, *The First Banning Genealogy*, Chicago, 1909

Sarah Banning Daughter of James Banning and his Wife Angelica was born May 3 1743

Benoni Son of D° was born June 26 1744 —

James Son to D° was born November ye 17th 1746

Sarah 2 Daughter to D° was born October 10 1740

Angelica Daughter to D° was born December 17 1749

Sarah Daughter to D° was born May 25 1752

Jere: Son of Ditto was born March ye 5 1756

Alexander Son of Ditto was born September 16 1759

JAMES BANNING AND WIFE, ANGELICA, OF THE STATE OF MARYLAND

1. Sarah Banning	Born: May 2, 1743
2. Benoni Banning	Born: June 26, 1744
3. James Banning	Born: Nov. 17, 1746
4. Sarah 2 Daughter Banning	Born: Oct. 10, 1748
5. Angelica Banning	Born: Dec. 17, 1749
6. Sarah Banning	Born: May 25, 1752
7. Jere Banning	Born: March 5, 1756
8. Alexander Banning	Born: Sept. 16, 1759

2-25 1817

From Benoni Baninds Bible

112. Page from the Benoni Banning family Bible, 1729
courtesy of M. Cox

334

Ages of B Bannings Child
Clark Banning 73 December 25 1769. Elizebeth Banning march 18 1772 Angelica Banning April 26 1775 Sarah Banning May 2 1778 Frazier Banning February 1 1781 James Banning March 31 1783 Alexander Banning october 25 1785 Jeremiah Banning August 26 1788 Henry Banning march 19 1791 1813 Philadelphia Banning February 11 1794

BENONI BANNING b. June 26, 1744 d. Feb. 25, 1827		WIFE, ANN ~~FRASIER~~ *CLARK* BANNING b. Dec. 1, 1749 d. Mar. 23, 1824
	Born	Died
1. Clark Banning	Dec. 25, 1769.	
2. Elizabeth Banning	Mar. 16, 1772	Oct. 27, 1851
3. Angelica Banning	Apr. 26, 1775	Oct. 5, 1863
4. Sarah Banning	May 2, 1778	
5. Frazier Banning	Jan. 1, 1781	Aug. 6, 1844
6. James Banning	March 31, 1783	Between 1860/70
7. Alexander Banning	Oct. 25, 1785	1848
8. Jeremiah Banning	Aug. 26, 1788	May 1851
9. Henry Banning	Mar. 19, 1791	~~Between 1860/70~~ *1869*
10. Philadelphia Banning	Feb. 4, 1794	Between ~~1870/80~~ *1874*

From Benoni Banning Bible Note

From Margie Cox 164 Hoskins Co. Rd. Marion, N.C. 24752

113. Page from Benoni Banning's family Bible 1729
courtesy of M. Cox

Benoni settled on a farm in Talbot Country, Maryland, located on a point of land on the Tred Avon River, now know as 'Benoni's Point'. This he eventually owned and he became quite prosperous, holding considerable other property and many slaves.

Benoni was one of the first to enlist in Captain Campbell's Virginia Regiment when the call for troops went out over the country at the time of the American Revolution. The regiment, made up mostly of men from West Virginia, suffered heavy losses in battle. Benoni was allegedly stabbed three times by British bayonets in the charge up the slope of King's Mountain, in a battle bearing that name. Because of the courageous action of a young man named William Fullwood, who later married Benoni's daughter Elizabeth (8 Apr. 1762), he survived.

Benoni's sons moved to the Virginias and their descendants to Illinois, Iowa, Missouri, Kansas and the west, where, in 1909, most of them were located.

The Missouri branch was, at the time, probably the most populous. A number of prominent lawyers came from this line, the most well-known being Ephraim Banning of Chicago, the father of P.W. Banning, to whom he dedicated his First Banning Genealogy.

From: The History of Shelby County, established in 1827 entry for 1828:[567]

"Bannings began migrating to This area at This time. Jeremiah Banning arrived from Virginia in 1828 and settled on Section 35 Range 10 of Dry Point Township, about 12 miles south of Shelbyville. His daughter, Mary E. Banning, was the first child born in the settlement. "The Indians had just vacated their wigwams, which were on a lake, on what is now the Ferrell place, and taken their departure from happy hunting grounds before the approach of the pale face." (Eden Martin p.289)"

"Alexander Banning entered land four years later, followed by Clark M. Banning. It was not until 1860 that W. Jackson Banning opened the first post office in Dry Point. Over the years, the community's name has been changed to Hart and to Thompson's Mill. The only thing remaining of this settlement is the Thompson's Mill covered bridge, east of Cowden."

Benoni's brother James moved from Talbot Country to Edgartown, Massachusetts. Some of his descendants moved to Ohio and Indiana.

Phineas Banning is alleged to have been a brother of these two Bannings, as they all came to America at about the same time and settled in the general area, although Phineas is known of in Delaware. Although

---

[567] History of Shelby County; http://ecolitgy.com/it/LostInShelby.html; accessed May 2004

Delaware and Maryland are two states, the points at which the Bannings lived were only a few miles apart and their sibling relationship seems a reasonable assumption.

General Phineas Banning, *(G1.C.20)* born 19 Aug. 1830 in Wilmington, Delaware, was a grandson of the above-mentioned Phineas. He left home at the age of thirteen to work in the law office of his brother William in Philadelphia. By the time he was sixteen, Phineas was learning the freight business as a shipping clerk on the Philadelphia wharves.

In 1851 he travelled from Wilmington, Delaware via Panama to the south of California. He figures prominently in the history of the town of Wilmington, California, as its founder. Developing a shipping company there, he also operated the stage line from Wilmington to Yuma, Arizona through what became known as the Banning Pass.

Having started off as a junior partner in a firm hauling freight in 1853, as the business grew he bought out his partner and expanded. His network of freight and stage lines were extended to include northern California., Arizona and Utah. Recognising the importance of communications and transportation, he built the telegraph line between Los Angeles and Yuma, Arizona, as well as the first railroad link between what subsequently become Los Angeles Harbour and the downtown area.

Phineas Banning had many steam ships working up and down the Pacific coast. When a devastating explosion occurred on one these - the *Ada Hancock* - his brother-in-law and several Banning children were killed. He himself was injured, as well as his wife and mother-in-law.

Phineas was a very prominent citizen of the state. His commission as commanding Brigadier General in the California Militia was granted in exchange for his donation of a large tract of land to the federal government to be used for training Union troops. Elected California State Senator in 1865, he signed California's ratification of the 13th amendment to the U.S. Constitution abolishing slavery. Taking the initiative to petition Congress for an appropriation to begin work on a breakwater and lighthouse, Phineas worked on continual development of Los Angeles Harbour, which eventually became the busiest port in the nation.

He was a very popular, large and powerful personality, over six feet tall, with a booming voice. He loved children. He raised horses, cattle and sheep and owned considerable real estate. This included a shipyard, several saw mills and lumberyards, warehouses, a contracting firm, soap factory, and the Pioneer Oil Company, which he founded.

Behind the scenes, Phineas showed his ingenuity in developing new technical concepts to facilitate transportation, such as his design for an improvement in railroad 'car trucks and wheels'. His patent registration for this design was granted on 28 March 1876 by the United

States Patent Office. He describes his invention as "an improvement for railway carriages, by which I am enabled to lay a line of road and to operate it over a country where but little grading is necessary, so cheaply that it can be made available for the transportation of freight, lumber, and is some cases passengers, in thinly settled districts, where an ordinary line would be too expensive[568]." He described it in great detail, citing it's advantages to access outlying reaches of country. The 'road' for this simple carriage could be constructed from timber felled along the line: slabs sawed from the outside of logs and laid next to each other. Some two thousand ties would be employed per mile, providing a solid surface of twenty-four to thirty inches in width, the wheels or rollers of the carriage being specially adapted to "my peculiar road". He estimated the cost of the road at "only three to five hundred dollars per mile, exclusive of rolling stock, etc.".

P. BANNING.
CAR-TRUCKS AND WHEELS.
No. 175.266.   Patented March 28, 1876.

Fig. 1.

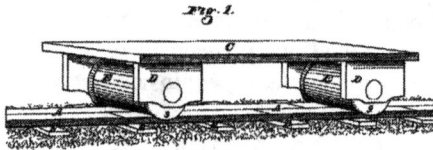

Fig. 2.

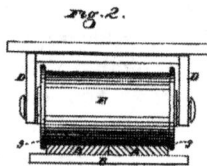

Witnesses   Inventor

114. Patent application number 175.266, signed and designed by Phineas Banning, 28 March 1876
private collection

[568] patent application filed 14 Dec. 1875 at the United States Patent Office by Phineas Banning of Wilmington, California; private collection

This kind of innovation demonstrates Phineas' insight into the practical problems encountered in the transport of provisions and building material to undeveloped areas, greatly facilitating their accessibility and development.

Phineas Banning and his family lived in a 23 room (it had some 30 rooms when originally built) Greek Revival mansion, which he had built in 1864. It is now the Banning Residence Museum, located in the 20-acre Banning Park in Wilmington.

115.   Home of General Phineas Banning,
photographed by his son Joseph Brent Banning , ca. 1880
now the Banning Residence Museum
photo courtesy of the Banning Residence Museum, Wilmington, CA.

One of the most significant monuments to Phineas T. Banning is the city of Banning in Riverside County, California, named in his honour.

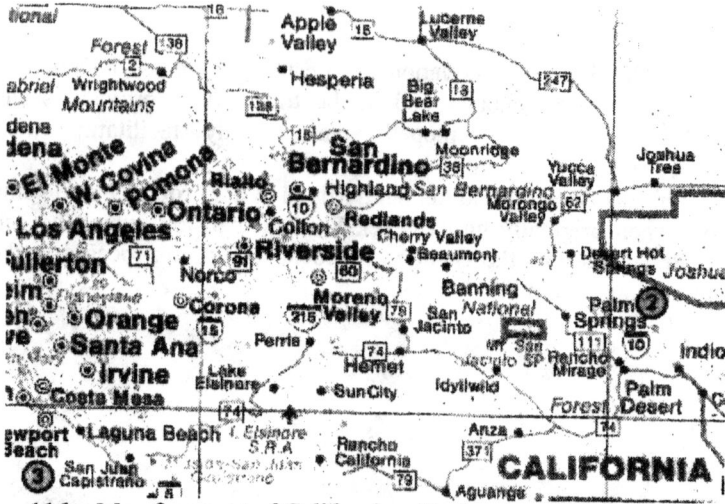

116. Map fragment of California with the city of Banning, in Riverside county

The city of Banning, at 120 km. distance from Los Angeles, lies on the eastern slope of the San Gorgonio Pass, a valley in the high mountains. It is a most beautiful and bountiful region, renowned for its ideal climate.

Memorialised in the name of a city, Phineas Banning was also honoured on an occasion less well-known. Captain Phineas Banning Blanchard was born at sea in 1879, son of a sea captain and personal acquaintance of Phineas Banning, and named after him. Phineas Banning Blanchard, a captain before he was twenty, was one of the few mariners whose wife accompanied him on his voyages. Departing from Philadelphia in the afternoon following a hasty wedding in 1906, the ensuing expedition around Cape Horn to San Francisco with a load of coal on the square-rigger Bangalore was their honeymoon. Captain Banning Blanchard's wedding gift to his wife was a sextant, so that she could help to navigate the 1,700 ton vessel.

In a letter dated November 1986[569], J.Banning of the Netherlands cites Sybren Banning from Nhill, Australia, who quotes from an extensive treatise on the life and work of Phineas T. Banning. A biographical sketch opens with:
"Phineas Banning was among those enterprising individuals who came to Southern California from the East Coast during the 19th century and envisioned Los Angeles, then an isolated pueblo, as becoming a major transportation and commercial centre. His home, built in 1864, now the Banning Residence Museum, has become known as a symbol of one of the most dynamic periods in Southern California history."

---

[569] personal communication from J. Banning, Dedgum to the author, Nov. 1986

117. Phineas T. Banning as a young man
photo courtesy of Catalina Island Museum, California

Phineas married Rebecca Sanford on in 1854. Sadly, of their eight children only three survived: William, Joseph and Hancock. Rebecca died from complications of childbirth in 1868. Phineas married Mary Hollister in 1870; they had three children. Although one of the children Mary bore him died in infancy, two daughters, Mary and Lucy, survived.

118. William, Joseph and Hancock, three sons
of Phineas T. Banning, ca. 1870
Photo courtesy of Catalina Island Museum, California

119. Mary Banning   120. Lucy Banning
Photos courtesy of the Catalina Island Museum, California

General Banning met an untimely death in 1885 of injuries received in a streetcar accident in San Francisco. He was buried beside his first wife and six children in Wilmington. Mary, his second wife, had his body re-interred several years later in Rosedale Cemetery in Los Angeles. After his death, his wife lived at her North Broadway home on top of Fort Moore Hill in downtown Los Angeles.

An article appeared in the Los Angeles Times of 1 November 1914 which was devoted to Mrs. Mary Banning's new home: "Wealthy Pioneer Woman Has Opinions of Her Own About Architecture"[570], designed by architect Irving J. Gill. Mrs. Banning was elderly when she had her dream house built, a widow of long standing. "The architect thought it was only a sick woman's whim," Mrs. Banning said when interviewed. "He humoured me by talking over the plans, and waited for me to die instead of beginning the house. My man of affairs, too, thought I would die, and so did all my friends - but you see I'm used to having my way and here I am. I have my house at last. Come and look at it."

The author, Bertha A. Smith, said: "It is a pretty way they have, those women of a certain type of the passing generation, of trying to explain the wholly inexplicable method by which they secured to themselves more rights than the most belligerent suffragette has yet succeeded in wrestling by force of law from anybody. All of which would be neither here nor there, but for the kind of house that Mrs. Banning has built. Only one used to having her own way, wholly unafraid of cutting across the opinion of others, would build as Mrs. Banning has built."

Called the "City's Most Daringly Original Dwelling", a "daring departure in architecture", in an era of gingerbread cornices and jigsaw ornament, this house featured lines of monastic severity, absolute simplicity and neutral colour. Space was created for the Banning family

---

[570] A Collection of Articles Written during the lifetime of Irvin J. Gill, http://www.irvinggill.com/biblio.html; accessed Feb. 2003

heirlooms, such as a huge black walnut sideboard which Mrs. Banning's daughter implored her to leave behind. Many of the rare plants and trees from the original Banning home were transplanted in the garden.

Bertha A. Smith refers to Mrs. Banning as "free from subservience to tradition, wholly indifferent to the opinion of others". She closes with: "Wrestling with house-building usually makes the owner feel miles nearer to his grave, but Mrs. Banning long ago abandoned her invalid's chair and counts the past year one of the happiest of her life. She stands ready to recommend the building of a house after one's own heart as a panacea for all human life."

121. General Phineas T. Banning
The First Banning Genealogy, P.W. Banning, Chicago 1909

The three surviving sons of Phineas Banning, the Banning Brothers William (*G1.C.66*), Joseph (*G1.C.67*) and Hancock (*G1.C.68, b. 1865*) were as enterprising as their father. William, the eldest, was born in 1858 in Los Angeles, living as a bachelor in Wilmington, California. One of his passions was driving a stage coach, which he did until he was well into his seventies.

Joseph was born Aug. 12, 1861 in Wilmington, California. He married his cousin, Katherine Stewart Banning of St. Paul, Minnesota in 1888. Katherine was a founder of the Los Angeles Children's Hospital. Along with his brother, Hancock, he ran the immense Banning interest in California.

122. Katherine
Stewart Banning
photo courtesy of the
Catalina Island Museum, CA.

123.   Hancock Banning   124. Anne Ophelia Smith Banning
photos courtesy of the Catalina Island Museum, California

Hancock was born 12 May 1865 in Wilmington, California, and married Anna Ophelia Smith on 12 Nov. 1890 in Los Angeles. Anna was a winsome and remarkable woman, who founded the Assistance League of Southern California (Founder Chapter) in 1919. The Assistance League pioneered several philanthropic projects in the 1920's and 1930's, emulated by other organizations. Anna Banning was named president of the National Assistance League when it was organized in 1935, serving in this capacity, and as President of Founder Chapter, until 1948. When The National Assistance League celebrated it's 50th anniversary in 1985, the organisation encompassed 72 chapters in 17 states.

The three enterprising Banning brothers bought Santa Catalina Island, off the coast of Southern California, in 1891 for $200,000 and ran the resort like a feudal kingdom. They had constables who deported anyone who misbehaved. The family already had a stake in the development of the Island as a resort destination when it was purchased. The Bannings owned and operated the Wilmington Transportation Company, which provided much of the passenger transportation to and from the Island. The Banning family had also been extremely influential in the development of Wilmington, California and the Port of Los Angeles.

125. William Banning
photo courtesy of the Catalina Island Museum, California

William, Joseph and Hancock established the Santa Catalina Island Company in 1894 and immediately improved transportation to the resort town and began construction of several new attractions. These included the first stage coach tours to the island's interior in 1894, expansion of the golf course to 9 holes (the brothers first developed a 3-hole golf course in 1892 and then expanded it to a 7-hole course in 1893) and building an aquarium. Their substantial investments in development were paying off until a devastating fire swept through the town in November of 1915, in which half of the town's buildings and homes were destroyed. In an attempt to recoup their losses, the Bannings immediately began to rebuild, constructing a large cafeteria where the Hotel Metropole formerly stood and building the Hotel Catalina and Hotel St. Catherine. However, public interest declined during World War 1 and the brothers were never able to recover financially. The island was sold in 1919 to William Wrigley of the chewing gum empire.

The Banning brothers also ran the business created by their father. William died in 1946, Joseph in 1920 and Hancock in 1925.

126.   Banning family home, Descanso, Catalina   ca. 1911
photo courtesy of M. Rojas

The Banning family home was built in 1895 in Descanso Canyon, and is reminiscent in style to the brothers' ancestral home in Wilmington which Joseph photographed around 1880. Hancock Banning, in another progressive plan, installed a solar water heating system in the house in 1921. The house became more-or-less obscured from sight when the St. Catherine Hotel was built on the property; it later served as a dormitory for hotel personnel.

William Lowber Banning (*Gl.C.13; 1814-1893*) was an older brother to Phineas T. Banning. William married (20 Jan. 1850) Mary Alice Sweeney, a direct descendant of Donal of Armagh[571] , 173rd monarch of Ireland, who died in 978 AD.

A very perseverant individual, William Lowber Banning was the founder of the Lake Superior and Mississippi Railroad, an enterprise for which he besieged congress for over ten years for funding. The Philadelphia financier Jay Cooke finally relented and in 1866, William L. Banning, president of the St. Paul and Duluth Railroad, also became president of the newly founded Lake Superior and Mississippi Railroad Company.

The significance of this railroad was the access it created to one of world's greatest grain ports, the Duluth-Superior harbour, transhipping millions of bushels of grain per annum. When Minnesota's North Shore was opened to white settlement in 1854, a stable farm economy was already developing in the southern part of the state between the Minnesota and Mississippi Rivers. William L. Banning was one of those pioneers who saw the potential for a great port for the movement of rich farm produce from warehouses to fleets of big ships docking at Duluth.

---

[571] P.W. Banning, *The First Banning Genealogy*, Chicago, 1909

The completion of the Sault Locks at the other end of Lake Superior promised to bring international shipping to Duluth's waterfront.

The Lake Superior & Mississippi Railroad was chartered at St. Paul in 1857, ostensibly to haul grain from southern Minnesota to the yet undeveloped port of Duluth and then down the Lakes. A land grant to the State of Minnesota in 1864 encouraged construction of a rail link between St. Paul and the Head of the Lakes, inspiring William L. Banning to approach financier Jay Cooke. Construction on the railroad began in 1867 at the southern end of the 160-mile line. Immense grain storage elevators were constructed in St. Paul and Duluth. The railroad was completed in August 1870.

William L. Banning was the Democratic candidate for governor of Minnesota in 1877, but was defeated.

He was, however, immortalized on another front - the town of Banning, Minnesota, being named in his honour. In the late 1800's and early 1900's over 500 stonecutters mined and cut sandstone in the quarry here, popular in building construction. In 1894 the great Hinckley forest fire swept through the area, inflicting heavy financial losses on the company and on the St. Paul and Duluth Railroad line serving it. Business resumed after the fire and by 1896 the village of Banning was starting to develop in the fields flanking the quarry. The village grew and by the turn of the century it was incorporated with a population of approximately 300. However, by 1912, frequent fires and the increasing use of structural steel in construction had put the quarry out of business, marking the end of the town. Today, the old Banning site is embodied in the breathtaking landscape of the Banning State Park, established by the legislature in 1963[572].

The park comprises 6,237 acres of tumbling rivers and rapids, hiking trails and spectacular views. Now the home of white-tailed deer, more than 180 species of birds, black bear, coyote, fox, raccoon, beaver, red and gray squirrels, snowshoe hares and ruffed grouse, the park is also marked by dilapidated stone buildings and other overgrown remnants of the mining and cutting operation which once thrived around the sandstone quarry.

James Edward Banning (*G1.B.626*) was born near Wheeling, W. Virginia, 19 Aug. 1840. His family moved to a farm in Des Moines County, Iowa, when he was quite young. At the age of fourteen James E. Banning went to Story County, Iowa, and was employed in flourmills there and in other places in that state, until he came to Otoe County in Nebraska in 1859. He spent six years engaged in farming, after which he was became involved in freighting across the plains. James came to

---

[572] Farmer, Sue: Banning State Park offers four season venue for enjoying Minnesota's great outdoors, wildlife; http://www.lpleader.com/nature/banning.html; accessed June 2004

Factoryville in 1874, where he leased and operated the flourmill up to July 1880. The mill building was torn down by Lawrence Miller and a new one erected in the same year, after which the gentlemen became joint partners of the firm Miller and Banning, proprietors of the Factoryville Flouring Mills. The mill capacity came to twenty-five barrels per day. James E. Banning left in 1887, becoming involved in the grain elevator business in Nehawka, Iowa until he died in 1899.

His wife's obituary was published in the Plattsmouth Journal, about 1907[573], as follows:

"DEATH OF MRS J. E. BANNING
Passes Away at 2 O'clock This Morning at Home in Nehawka
The sad intelligence of the death of Mrs. Parthena Banning, widow of James E. Banning, which occurred very suddenly at 2 o'clock Tues. morning at her home in Nehawka, was received at this office. The end came after three weeks illness with organic heart trouble, super induced by rheumatism. It is with much regret that the many friends throughout the county learn of her demise.

The deceased is one of the best known early settlers of Cass county and a highly esteemed women [sic] in Nehawka precinct, where she has resided so many years. Her husband, James E. Banning, who was engaged in the milling business in Nehawka for about thirty years, passed away twelve years ago last January. The children who survive the mother are Stella Banning and Jas. E. Banning, who are still at home, and the stepchildren, C. W. Banning of Pleasanton, Neb., Mrs. Frank P. Sheldon and Mrs. Henry Sturm of Nehawka."

---

[573] Obituaries of Cass County Residents; http://www.rootsweb.com/~necass/obits7.htm; accessed July 2004

Ephraim Banning (*G1.B.88*), Benoni's grandson, was born on 2 June 1811, in Rock Bridge County, Virginia. He was named in honour of Ephraim Doty who, shortly before his birth, saved the life of his father when near drowning.

Ephraim Banning
B 88

LOUISA CAROLINE WALKER BANNING
B 88

127. Ephraim Banning   128. Louisa Caroline Walker Banning
The First Banning Genealogy, P.W. Banning, Chicago 1908

Ephraim moved to Wheeling in 1824, where he remained for ten years, afterward moving to McDonough Country, Illinois, settling near the present site of Bushnell. He later returned to Wheeling and there married Mary Potter, on 26 Jan. 1836, returning again to Illinois and settling in Walnut Grove, eight miles southeast of Macomb. Two sons were born of this marriage before his wife died on 11 Oct. 1840.

On 12 May 1842 Ephraim married Louisa Caroline Walker, born 15 Jan. 1817, the daughter of Joseph Gilmer Walker and Martha Scott. She was the sister of Judge Pinkney H. Walker of the Supreme Court of Illinois. For years the Walker family was known for their legal ability and prominence in public life. Their union produced nine children.

The family moved to Kansas in 1855 and settled in Douglas County. Although Ephraim was an advocate of a free state, he most likely moved because he succumbed to the pioneer's urge to escape from neighbours who were pressing too close. Ephraim's definition of 'overcrowded' was "when the original settler could see three of four farm houses from a single hill top"[574]. (In 1850 Illinois, measuring 56,000 square miles of territory, had a population of some 850,000 – with about half living in the cities). In addition, the lure of land to be had for almost nothing ($ 1.25 an acre) was irresistible, enabling a man with several sons to provide each of them with a farm of their own.

The family prospered in Kansas. Their home was said to be of the finest, at the time the meeting place of the 'Free Soilers', during the Border warfare which took place when Kansas tried to enter the Union as a Free State. Ephraim took an active part in these affairs, and the Committee that drew up the documents later admitting Kansas as a Free State met at his home. However, a terrible drought in the summer of 1859 resulted in a prairie fire and the devastation, in a single afternoon, of all they had built up, driving them on into Missouri in 1860. After spending one year in Petis County, Missouri, they moved to Polk County in the same state. This was short-lived as they were compelled to flee before the Rebel Army on Sunday morning of 25 Nov. 1861, reaching Brookfield, Missouri in 1862. Emphraim spent the remainder of his life here and died on 8 Nov. 1878.

Emphraim Banning is said to be man of exceptional ability, a great organiser for public good, and held in the highest esteem.

One of Ephraim's sons bore his father's name. Ephraim Jr. (G1.B650) was born 21 July 1849 on a farm near the present site of Bushnell, Illinois, and later married Lucretia Pierson Lindsley. They had three children. Lucretia descended from the Buell and Pierson families of early New England stock. She died on 10 Aug. 1887. Ephraim jr. married again in 1889 to Emilie Bartlett Jenney, a descendant of John Jenney of Norwich England, who came to the United States in 1623, landing at Plymouth, Massachusetts on the ship 'Little James', of which he was part owner.

Ephraim Jr. struggled to acquire an education. After completing local schools and a private school started by Rev. J.P. Finlay (in 1909 known as Brockfield Academy), he studied law and finally entered the law office of Rosenthal & Pence in Chicago in 1871.

---

[574] P.M. Angle, (edited by), *Pioneers, Narratives of Noah Harris Letts and Thomas Allen Banning 1825-1865*, The Lakeside Press, R.R. Donnelley & Sons Co., Chicago, 1972, p. 145

129. Ephraim Banning   130. Lucretia Thalia Lindsley Banning

The First Banning Genealogy, P.W. Banning, Chicago 1908

Ephraim Jr.'s younger brother Thomas Allen soon joined him, after a year entering into a partnership specialised in patent, trademark and corporation law. The practice, known as Banning & Banning, ran for nearly forty years.[575] As an attorney, Ephraim Jr. attained the highest rank and became exceptionally well-known.

Ephraim Jr. was a Republican and very influential in his district. Although he held only honorary political office, he was often urged to accept many of the most important positions in city and state government. These he refused, although he consented to an urgent request to run for Congress just prior to his death in 1907, having been promised the nomination. He was Presidential Elector several times. He was a member of the State Board of Charities for several years, as well as a member of many representative committees in public matters, among which may be mentioned the following:

President of the Shawneetown Relief Committee, of Chicago; Chairman of the Committee on Organisation of the Congress of Patent and Trademarks, at the World Fair at Chicago in 1893, member of the Committee that represented Chicago in the 'Lakes to Gulf Deep Water Way' Convention at Memphis in 1907.

---

[575] (note: roughly a century later and an ocean away, the law firm of Banning Advocaten was founded by a Banning in the Dutch city of 's-Hertogenbosch. It has become one of the largest law firms in the Netherlands, will have existed 40 years in 2005, and also deals in legal matters very similar to those of Banning & Banning in the USA.)

Early in 1899 he was strongly encouraged to accept the position of United States District Judge in Chicago, having the support of both U.S. Senators and a majority of Congressmen of the state, as well as hundreds of endorsements from leading business and other interests. Someone else was appointed, however, apparently for personal reasons.

One of Ephraim Banning's lasting and most significant achievements was the founding of a Juvenile Court in Chicago. This required modifications to the State Laws, and as a member of the Committee on Legislation he had a hand in this process. His name is associated with that of the late Harvey B. Hurd as 'father' of the first Juvenile Court, not only in Chicago but in the world. He was one of the principal speakers at the Dedication of the New Juvenile Court Building 'The Kids Court' in Chicago in 1907 (Chicago Legal News, 9 Nov. 1907)

This was one of his last public appearances. Ephraim Banning Jr. met a sudden and untimely death less than a month later, on 2 Dec. 1907, as a result of injuries sustained when he was jerked from a Madison Streetcar on the morning of 29th November, while on his way to the office. Pierson Worrall has dedicated his genealogy to the memory of Ephraim Jr., his father.

Thomas Allen Banning (*G1.B.651*), Ephraim's brother and partner in law, was born on 16 January 1851. He married Sarah H. Hubbard; the couple had three children. The law partnership which he shared with his brother was known, appropriately, as Banning & Banning. Their briefs and arguments can be found in most of the United States Courts today, from the Supreme Court to the District Courts.

THOMAS ALLEN BANNING

131. Thomas Allen Banning
The First Banning Genealogy,
P.W. Banning, Chicago 1909

THOMAS ALLEN BANNING

132. Thomas Allen Banning
from Pioneers, Letts and Banning Narratives,
R.R. Donnelly & Sons, Chicago, 1972

When he neared the age of 80, Thomas Allen wrote a wonderful account of his first 15 years for his grandchildren, which was published in 1972 a small volume entitled *Pioneers, Letts and Banning Narratives 1825-1865*[576].

He recalls having his ears boxed by a public school teacher, because of his juvenile inability to pronounce the letter 'r'. He speaks with admiration of his mother, marvelling at her calm, serene and patient mind, a person with a cheerful and peaceful disposition who believed that time and patience and industry would bring the rewards of effort. Throughout his childhood Thomas established a reputation among the schoolboys for courage and the ability to back it, a disposition to be fair and just in his dealings. After a few boyish scraps where the boys learned that he would not yield to bullying, one more determined and equally resolute lad contested him. Thomas accepted the challenge, soon learning that there was nothing to be afraid of, and says that he learned a lesson from this boy that he carried through life. "Which was, " he writes, "that in legal battles in the court room, before judge or jury, or in business, a calm, quiet, confident manner was more impressive than noise or bluster."

He vividly recalled the 'Free Soilers' who frequently met with his father at their home, a stone house which was the largest and best in that part of the territory. It was a time of border warfare while Kansas was vying to come into the Union as a free state. The committee that started the movement, that later resulted in the admission of Kansas as a free state, met at the Banning's home and drew up resolutions to Congress. "These were exciting times, and we children, who had only the faintest idea of what it was all about, were greatly interested in seeing the rough and bearded men coming to our house from time to time."

The house was all that remained of a their proud holdings after a prairie fire swept through the fields in 1859 when Thomas was eight years old. "When the sun had risen that October morning clear and smiling on a prosperous farm, it looked on a bare and desolate waste as it went down at night, red and glowering in the thick and smoky air." In the course of one short afternoon, his father was ruined. Thomas recalled living on various rented farms, followed by an arduous journey by wagon which lasted well over a year. Together with his parents, five brothers and three sisters, the family fled from the Confederate army. In 1862 they settled on a farm in Brookfield, Missouri, where the tale of his childhood ends.

---

[576] P.M. Angle, (edited by), *Pioneers, Narratives of Noah Harris Letts and Thomas Allen Banning 1825-1865,* The Lakeside Press, R.R. Donnelley & Sons Co., Chicago, 1972

133. Map of the Banning family 'trail' from 1836-1862
private collection

Hubert Ashley Banning *(G1.B.653)* was the youngest son of the same family, and made history for other reasons. Born on 4. Jan. 1853, he is said to be the first child born in Kansas after it had been deemed a Free State Territory. This must have been a significant event for his father, who had worked so hard to achieve this political status for the state. Hubert Ashley lived in New York City, working as an attorney.

Helen Ruth Banning *(G1.B.5088)*, born 16 December 1885 in Chicago, merited mention in Pierson Worrall's genealogy because she showed exceptional literary ability at an early age, writing numerous poems which would have done credit to a person many years her senior. She died in Brussels in 1899, during a visit with the family, and is buried in La Parte, Indiana.

Arba Hanson Banning *(G1.E.271)* born around 1820 in Sussex County, Connecticut, was Judge of the Probate Court in Deep River, Connecticut, for sixteen years, up to the time of his decease. He owned the oldest shoe store in the locality, having purchased it from Joshua Moore in 1838.

Joseph Beaumont Banning, (*G1.E.1822*) the only son of Arba Hanson Banning, was mentioned in *Popular Biographies of Connecticut*[577] around 1890, as a Judge of Probate in Deep River (Saybrook), a native and resident of this town. Joseph B. Banning was born 16 Dec. 1840. He was educated in the public schools of his home town, learned the trade of shoe making, and was connected as junior partner with his father's firm, A. H. Banning & Son, until his father died in 1880, where after he conducted the business on his own. At the age of twenty-two he married Ansolette A. Smith.

Joseph was chosen to succeed his father as Probate Judge in 1880, a position he held for over 22 years, for which he enjoyed an enviable reputation. He was a member of the Connecticut Probate Assembly, as well as its secretary and treasurer since the death of Judge West of Rockville. He was also a Justice of the Peace for the town of Saybrook, Clerk of the Court and a member of the Prison Committee. As Secretary of the Connecticut Probate Assembly he held a position of great esteem. Joseph B. Banning remained in the boot and shoe trade all his life. In 1886 he erected a building on Main Street, Deep River, which served both as a store and residence. He was a member of the Congregational church, a steadfast Republican and a member of Webb Lodge, IOOF of Deep River.

Benjamin Banning, (*G1.E.50*) born some time around 1765 in Lyme, Connecticut, and his wife Theodora Bramble, had 20 children, of whom 17 survived into adulthood. **William Josiah Banning,** (*G1.E.169*) born 30 Aug. 1810 in Lyme Conneticut, was an artist and portrait painter, as well as a singing master and poet 'of no little fame'. **Nancy Banning,** (*G1.E.247*) born 26 Jan. 1907 in Hadlyme Connecticut, disappeared for many years, finally returning home, where she died unmarried around 1898. She withdrew to a retreat in Poughkeepsie NY for many years and after leaving there fell heir to a good sized fortune

Walter Edgar Banning (*G2.E.301*) was another descendant of this line, born 18 March 1833 in Leyden, New York. Very little is known of him, but Walter demonstrated inventiveness and initiative even at the age of 62, when he lived in Syracuse, in applying for a patent for a 'Bicycle-License-Number Plate on 12 Dec. 1895. He describes the dimensions and contours of his invention in detail, and the patent was subsequently granted to him on 21 July 1896. It is unknown whether the bicycles becoming popular at the time ever bore this mark of distinction or whether it served to aid their registration, nor to what purpose. However, the patent served to record Walter in a the archives of American history.

---

[577] Popular biographies of Connecticut
http://www.usgennet.org/usa/ct/county/fairfield/ctbbios.html accessed May 2004

DESIGN.

W E BANNING.
NUMBER PLATE.

No. 25,829. Patented July 21, 1896

FIG-1-

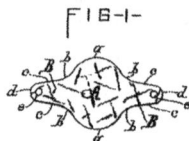

FIG-2-

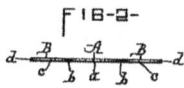

UNITED STATES PATENT OFFICE.

WALTER R. BANNING, OF SYRACUSE, NEW YORK.

DESIGN FOR A NUMBER-PLATE.

134. Patent application submitted by Walter E. Banning in 1896, for a
'Bicycle-Licence-Number Plate', with his signature
private collection

Banning of Lyme, Connecticut

John Banning was born in England around 1650 and probably came to
New Shoreham, Rhode Island, prior to 1685. He died in Lyme,
Connecticut shortly before September 1717, when his will was probated.
His son John was born around 1671 in England, from a first marriage, and
his daughter Frances in 1673. A record exists in the Register of St. Martin
in the Fields, County Middlesex, England[578], written 31 October 1673, of
the baptism of Frances, daughter of John and Elizabeth Baning, of whom
both children are named in John Banning's last will and testament.

Son John moved to Lyme with his father in 1702 and was later
recollected as being a 'strong, tall, straight, well-built Englishman[579]'.
Family legend has it that, while standing in the doorway of his house one
clear day in 1760, he was struck by a bolt of lighting from a single, small
cloud in an otherwise clear sky and killed.

A descendant of this line, **Benjamin Banning**, (*G5.F.62*) of Vernon,
Ohio, was mentioned on several occasions in *A History of Lorrain*

---

[578] Mary Banning Friedlander, The Banning Line;
http://freepages.genealogy.rootsweb.com/~mbfriedlander/banning.html; accessed July 2004
[579] P.W. Banning,, letter from Amelia Eells in *The First Banning Genealogy*, Chicago, 1909

County[580]. He was known as Captain Banning[581] because of a short service in the war of 1812. When Huntington was incorporated in 1822, Benjamin was named one of the three trustees, and one of two supervisors of the poor. It is not unlikely that Banning Avenue in Huntington was named in his honour. He was the second to be elected Justice of the Peace, and died while still in office. His death, in 1827, was the first adult death in the town and he was interred in the orchard just south of his residence.

One of Benjamin's sons, **Edmund Prior Banning**, (*G1.F.142*) was born 3 June 1810 in Canfield, Ohio. Edmund was raised by his mother's parents and married in 1834, to Lydia Humiston Peck. They had ten children. Edmund Banning was a surgeon with advanced ideas concerning the treatment of deformities. He was often held in ridicule by his profession, but at the time of publication of Pierson Worrall Banning's genealogy (1909) his ideas were considered the most advanced in that particular field. His fundamental ideas resulted in numerous new approaches to what eventually became known as Orthopaedics, although little credit is given to their originator. He was a man of exceptional character and force. He died in Mount Vernon in 1892.

Edmund was known as an extremely charismatic personality and much loved by those who knew him. His tough and practical uncle, Archibald Tanner, made this perceptive and eloquent statement concerning Edmund in his will of 1861:

"....I give and bequeath to my Nephew Dr. Edmund P. Banning, all the debts and claims which I shall have against him at the time of my decease and hereby direct my executors to discharge the same. And I hereby take the opportunity to remark that whatever may hereafter be the fortune of the said Edmund P. Banning, or his success in life, that I am satisfied he has been animated by a laudable desire to be useful in his profession and that he will eventually make his mark and show himself a useful and viable man. And as men of his stamp are often found to be deficient in their attention to their pecuniary affairs, or in the requisite skill to manage them, I request my executors that in case the said Banning shall die leaving his family in palpable need of pecuniary aid, or if such need shall exist.......that they extend to his family from time to time such limited temporary relief as they in their discretion shall deem appropriate: they taking into consideration the interest I have always taken in the welfare of my said nephew. In short, it is my will that they render such assistance to the family of said Banning if it shall be necessary as shall be

---

[580] Mary Banning Friedlander, The Banning Line;
http://freepages.genealogy.rootsweb.com/~mbfriedlander/banning; accessed March 2003
[581] Mary Banning Friedlander, The Banning Line,
http://freepages.genealogy.rootsweb.com/~mbfriedlander/banning; accessed March 2003

consistent with my own concern towards him during my life." (*Warren County Registers Docket #3*, page 449)[582]

135. Dr. Edmund Prior Banning
1811-1888
reproduced with permission by the heirs of
Mary Banning Friedlander[583]

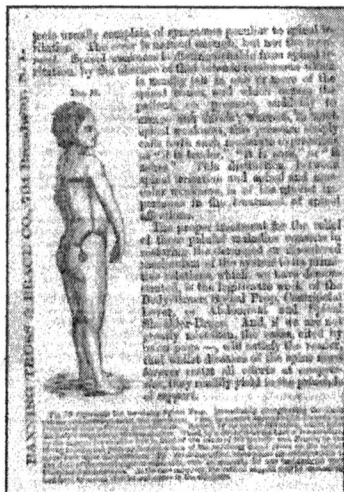

135a. Page from the essay
A Peep Into the House You Live In
published by the Banning Truss and
Brace Company in 1872
private collection

In 1838 Edmund opened the abdominal cavity of a patient to correct an intestinal obstruction, an operation never before attempted. It was successful. In 1839 he explored the mechanical nature of the human body and invented the first mechanical device ever used for the permanent cure of what later became known as enterectesis, the device being used to reposition the internal organs in their proper relation to each other. He was a writer and lecturer of great force, and devised the natural philosophy governing the erect posture and the fact that the harmonious symbiosis of all the systems composing the human body and the prevention of chronic derangements depends on observance of these laws. His philosophy was that by bringing the body into a perfect alignment in relation to gravity, diseases could be prevented, alleviated or cured.

In 1872 *The Banning Truss and Brace Company* of New York, which sold numerous of Edmund Prior's patented devices, published the essay *A Peep Into the House You Live In: causes of some of the ailments to which the flesh is heir.* The booklet sold for ten cents and included

[582] Mary Banning Friedlander, The Banning Line;
http://freepages.genealogy.rootsweb.com/~mbfriedlander/banning; accessed March 2003
[583] http://freepages.genealogy.rootsweb.com/~mbfriedlander/banning; accessed March 2003

numerous letters of acclaim from patients who had obtained relief or been cured from crippling deformities or other chronic or acute ailments .

Edmund Prior Banning's son - also named **Edmund Prior Banning** *(G1.F-607)* and born 1 Jan. 1845, followed in his father's footsteps and became a physician of considerable repute. For many years he lectured at Herring Medical College in Chicago on the subject of Orthopaedics, in which his father was a pioneer. Although this sometimes made him the subject of derision – the approach being untried - the graduating class of 1908 presented him with a loving cup and an earnest request to carry on advanced classes after hours.

Edmund Prior Jr. was educated in the public schools of New York City and the Irving Institute, Tarrytown-on-the-Hudson. When the Civil War broke out in 1861, he enlisted in the U.S. Marine Corps, serving in the fleets of Admiral Porter, Feet, Dahlgren, Yarragut, Goldsboro and Wilkes. At the request of his commanding officers, President Lincoln in 1863 broke an unwritten law of the U.S. Marine Corps by commissioning Edmund Prior Jr. as a lieutenant in this, the oldest corps in the services, apparently the first instance of the kind in the Marine Corps of a man being promoted from the ranks to a commission.

He resigned from the services in October 1869 and was granted six months leave of absence with pay, at the end of which time his resignation was accepted. For some years he was a partner in his father's practice of medicine and surgery in New York City.

Edmund's aunt, Amelia Vinning (daughter of Malinda Banning and Richard Vinning) wrote the following expansive and entertaining letter[584] on the family history in 1866:

"A letter from Amelia Vinning Eells, from Johnstown, Trumbull County, O., to her cousin,
August 3rd, 1866:

Our grandfather, Abner Banning, said in my hearing that he remembered his grandfather and spoke of him as a strong, tall, straight, well-built Englishman, and stated that there was a small cloud rose one morning and, as he was standing in the door, he was killed by a stroke of lighting. He might have died when grandfather was quite young. I never heard him speak of his progenitor further than I have stated. They lived at that time in Lyme, Conn.. I have often heard him remark that they lived seven miles from the landing where they did their trading. Lyme, it appears, is bounded North by Long Island Sound, East by the Connecticut River; therefore very near you. I learned from a lady a short time previous, residing in Lyme; spoke of one as Limner. I think they must have been

---

[584] P.W. Banning,, *The First Banning Genealogy*, Chicago, 1909

descendants of that Englishman. I have heard grandfather speak of a cousin Bibble, a batchelor in Lyme. Our great-grandfather's name was Samuel Banning. I got the information from grandfather they were all well situated in Lyme until his eldest daughters were married off. In furnishing them housekeeping, he became embarrassed with debt, about 1765. Sold out in Lyme and, with his family, removed fifty miles to East Hartland, Conn., then an almost unbroken wilderness with but few families in the township. Then their troubles and privations commenced. The girls came on a week before their mother, her health not being good, to arrange things. The night after she arrived, she reached up to take her night cap from the bed curtains, gave a groan and soon died. My grandfather was then ten years old and his youngest brother, David, four. They were at an age when they needed a mother's counsel and care. There must have been still other sisters as there appear to have been ten children in the family. In the course of time the father, Samuel, married again. For some time he was almost blind. He had furnished his oldest son with a new farm in West Hartland and a yoke of cattle. His name was Samuel Banning, Jr.. He was sixteen years older than Abner Banning (our grandfather). This left his father with no help but his two little boys to work his new farm, there being but three sons in the family. There must have been five daughters by the first wife and two by the second. I have the impression that he might have married his third wife, one had cancer; I think his second wife.

Our great-grandfather and his last wife lived to be very aged; they died in the family of David Banning, his youngest son, on the farm where they first located him. They must have died between the years 1800 and 1803. They were buried in the cemetery of East Hartland, Conn..

Samuel Banning Jr., the oldest son of our great-grandfather, married a Miss Stirling. They had two sons and three daughters and lived to become heads of families, to my knowledge. Samuel Banning Jr., must have died about 1814. His age must have been about seventy-six. His widow died a year or so afterwards. Sterling Banning lived and died in West Hartland. He raised a family but I am not informed respecting it.

John Banning married a Miss Read of West Hartland; removed to Hartford, Trumbull Country, Ohio, some forty years ago. He raised quite a numerous family, five sons and four daughters, who lived to settle in life. I believe they are all living but a Mrs. Andrews. One married Daniel Bushnell's son (second cousin) and removed to the West. The Widow Maron or Mason in Hartford. One went West, I do not know where she did marry.

The five sons, - Galord, Nelson, Abner, John and Charles. Galord Banning; two sons, three daughters. Nelson Banning: no children. Abner Banning; no children. John Banning Jr.,; two sons. Charles Banning; one son and one daughter. Mr. John Banning and wife died in the west part of

Hartford. He must have lived his three score years and ten. This closes the history of Samuel Banning Jr.'s families as far as I am acquainted.

Abner Banning, our grandfather, lived and died three-quarters of a mile N.W. of the center of East Hartland where he first located when commencing for himself. He received a present from his father of fifteen acres of ledge land. At twenty-three he became acquainted with Annah Sparrow of east Hadam, (Mass). They were subsequently married. She was an orphan girl, one of a numerous family; was put out to be brought up. She was at the time of marriage, twenty-six years old. They commenced with empty hands but with determined minds (having known the bitterness of poverty) to have a respectable living if there was one to be got by proper means. He soon commenced building for himself a frame house. He worked out by day's work and worked digging his cellar evenings. By perseverance he completed a house in which himself and wife lived and died, and when I visited the east twenty years ago his grandson was occupying it with his wife and children. It must have been standing then some seventy-eight years. In fact it stood over eighty years.

They both united with the Congregational Church, and their children baptized and endeavoured to direct them in the way they should go. Most of them became, it is hoped, Christians. Not any of them in youth, but in after life. His family consisted of one daughter and five sons, Malinda, Benjamin, Arabel, Morgan, Calvin and Samuel. They all lived to settle in life and to become heads of families.

The writer's mother, Malinda Banning, was united in marriage with Richard Vinning Jr., of Grandby. They were both tall and of slender form. After a happy connection of seven years, Richard Vinning died of Consumption, leaving his wife a widow with a daughter six years old, Amelia Vinning, and a son four years old, Albert Vinning. In about four years she was connected again with a John Robins with whom she lived nearly a year and died leaving a babe a fortnight old which was called after her, Malinda. On the death of the mother, John Robins left for parts unknown; the children were taken to their grandfather, Abner Banning, to be cared for, where the two eldest remained until of age. On the death of the grandfather, Malinda then fourteen years old, went to live with the Rev. Eells, in Johnstown, Ohio. At fifteen, commenced school teaching, which she followed until twenty-two, when she connected with Lorenzo Bushnell, a second cousin. They are now living in Wawkeon, Callichee Co., Iowa, in good circumstances. They had two sons and three daughters. Abner is a member of the Congregational Church. He enlisted for the second term of three years during the Rebellion. He was a prisoner for six months, captured at Pittsburg Landing. After the close of the war, he was employed in taking a list of Government property and in the Freeman's Bureau for a year, in Mobile, Ala.. He returned to his friends, without a scar, in good health. It is said that he was a young man, over six feet. Abner Vinning is a man full six feet in height, is now sixty years old. When twenty-two he went down into the Southern States, where he continued most of the time until he was twenty-eight. At twenty-seven, he married Miss Ellin Berter of Clinesburg, Conn., a daughter of Dr. Berter, and after settling up his business at the South, established himself as a farmer near Quincy, Ill.. The last son, John Vinning, had three daughters, all married.

Amelia Vinning was married to the Rev. Osiah Shelden Eells, pastor of the first Congregational Church of Johnstown, Ohio. He is now residing there and has been laboring in the same church for the past thirty-eight years. He is now seventy-one years old. At the commencement of the Rebellion they had three sons on whom they, like other parents, doted, but they must now be written childless.

The eldest left a widow but no children; he was a member of the 6th Iowa Cavalry; died near Davenport, Iowa. His name was Samuel Eells. His next brother, Jerome S. Eells, died in York State, three weeks after leaving home. The youngest was in Burnside's second corps before Petersburg, belonging to the 10th Company of Sharp Shooters, Ohio Volunteers. His division was brought into battle on the Wildeen Railroad, August 21st. Henry, with then of his company and sixty of his regiment, were placed in the skirmish line between the two enemies. There were all taken prisoners. It is not known what became of Henry, but it is supposed that he starved to death in Rebel hands. He was twenty when taken prisoner. When seventeen he served four months at Harpers Ferry under Col. Banning, from Mount Vernon, Ohio. They were then given up by Miles (General) to Stenswall Jackson as prisoners of war, but were paroled. Their sons have a monument erected to their memory in Johnson's cemetery, of Italian marble costing $ 175. So fades our hopes, and, as a bubble, all are dashed aside. Thus ends the history of Malinda Banning.

Benjamin Banning, the eldest son of Abner Banning, married Miss Mary Coe, daughter of Elijah Coe, one of the first families in Hartland, Conn.. She was said to be handsome and well educated for these times. In one short year she was consigned to the tomb, leaving an infant daughter but a few days old. She was called Mary Coe after her mother. The next summer there were twenty families left East Hartland for Ohio, with Ox teams. Benjamin Banning hired a woman of the company to nurse his babe and started with them. The woman was taken sick and he used often to drive his team, with the babe in his arms. They were a long time on the road, I think over forty days. These twenty families settled in Vernon and Hartford, in Trumbull Co., Ohio, and many of their descendants are peopling the northwestern states. It is sixty-two years this summer since they started for Ohio. But to return again to the history of my subject. After their arrival, the father put his little child out to nurse and married a Miss Laura Tanner of Canfield, Ohio, for his second wife. She lived to present him with three sons; one died (one that they called Elijah), one a babe when his mother died of consumption, called Edmund and given to his mother's parents in Canfield (Trial Tanner) by whom he was brought up. The father, now a widower, again takes his two remaining children Mary, seven years old, and Elijah, three years old, and with a sad heart, he commences a lonely journey back to his native state. The first summer after his return he spends with his sister, the widow Vinning, she having lost her husband the May before. He placed his little Elijah with his father and his daughter Mary with his grandfather Coe.

In a short time he became acquainted with a Miss Mary Lengar of Litchfield, aged twenty-two. He was now thirty-four at the time of his connection with her. She became a mother of the two sons and four daughters, - Laura, Cornelia, Sylvester, Granville and Maryette. After the birth of his two sons he again moved to Ohio. The two youngest daughters were native of Ohio, Benjamin Banning died of heart disease in 1827, leaving his third wife a widow and two children. His wife, a widow, married a lawyer, a Mr. Slocum. Mary, the eldest daughter, married a Mr. Granger. They had one son and one daughter. The son died with heart disease when he was about seventeen. Elijah married and had a number of children; lived in Rochester, Ohio, a new place, and was insane and was taken to an insane retreat, . His health failed and he became very anxious to be carried home. He was taken home to die. Sylvester married and had quite a family of children; one was a tailor by trade; did not succeed well in life. Laura married a Mr. Robins; was left a widow with one child. Cornelia was married. Granville and Maryette died young. The history of Benjamin Banning complete.

Arabel Banning, Abner Banning's second son, married Dr. Jeremiah Wilcox's oldest daughter, Amelia Wilcox. Soon after came to Ohio and settled in Vernon. After being married eleven years his wife died with consumption, leaving him with three children, one son, Abner Banning, and two daughters, Amelia and Malinda. Abner Banning married Malissa Brockway, of Hartford, Ohio. He died when forty years of age, leaving one son and four daughters. His son, George Banning, was living near Cleveland. Mary, his oldest daughter, was married to a Mr. Clark, of Twinbury, Summit County, and moved west. Mr. Stoddard Stevens married Arabel Banning's oldest daughter, Amelia, for his first wife, and Malinda, his second daughter, for his second wife. The first wife left one son, who married and soon died. Malinda left one daughter who was married to a Mr. Stanup. He was an officer in the Army; he died there, leaving his widow with two sons.

Arabel Banning married for his second wife Dency Crosby (soon after he lost his first wife) by whom he had five sons and two daughters.

David and Jeremiah married and removed to Cincinnati, and went into the Commission business. It is said before the war, that they were worth $ 100,000. They have since dissolved partnership, and Jeremiah has his son a partner. They each had a son, but David's son, Charles, was drowned in the Ohio River. Timothy Banning married a Miss Peabody. Mary Ann was connected with Dr. Peabody. Stoddard Banning married a Miss Clinby; has one son, may have more. Malinda was married to a Mr. Robins. They all found their companions in Gustavus._____ died when seventeen in Cincinnati.

Arabel Banning's children are all well off for this world goods and some of them are hoping for a better portion in another world. Arabel Banning died about 1839, of his skull being fractured by the fall of a stick of timber. His widow is still living; she is over seventy. This finishes the history of Arabel Banning.

Morgan Banning, the third son of Abner Banning, came to Ohio sixty-two years ago, or, in 1804. Married Laura Tanner, died 1819 or twenty, leaving a widow but no children.

Calvin, the fourth son of Abner Banning, was a man nearly six feet, the last time I saw him, well proportioned for his height, not very corpulent, naturally of an animated turn of mind and quite sociable. For a number of years he was a professor of religion, and I think enjoyed it. He marred a Miss Lucy Chase of Grandby. They had quite a family of children they lost four sons in infancy and a son and a daughter at the period of youth. Three sons and two daughters became heads of families, Edwin and Jerome. The two eldest sons married sister the nieces of Gordon Hall, one of the four first missionaries that went to India from America. Edwin had two sons. Edwin, his wife and one son died within a few years of each other. Richmond Banning, Edwin's oldest son, enlisted in the regular army in 1864. Jerome Banning removed to Illinois, settled in the eastern part of that state. He has some family; I am not particularly informed respecting them. Almon Banning, the youngest son living, is located on the homestead of Abner Banning his grandfather. He was a lieutenant in the army. At a skirmish near New Orleans he was hit by a bullet near the hip which came out near the neck in 1865, from which he has not so far recovered as to be able to labor. He had a son eleven years old and a daughter thirteen. His wife died in 1865. His father, Calvin Banning, died in 1864. He must have been over seventy-five. Almon's mother lives with him now, -- is seventy-six. Calvin Banning was the last of Abner Banning's family. Twenty-three years ago this August the writer visited him. He appeared to be almost in the prime of active life.

Samuel Banning, the fifth son of Abner Banning, married the youngest daughter of Samuel Jones of East Hartland, Conn., Miss Betsy Jones. Soon after marriage, they started for Ohio and settled at Vernon, Trumbull Co. in 1810. All of Abner Banning's five sons were in Ohio owning farms east side of Vernon Creed. Samuel Banning, after residing in Vernon a few years, exchanged his farm with his cousin, Anson Coe, for one in Hartland. In a few years sold his farm, left his family and started on a speculating trip to Ohio. He there fell in with Benjamin Banning that had started on a similar errand, took property of his and likewise of his brother Morgan's, and went to St. Louis where he was soon deranged, living but three or four days. He might have been thirty-two at the time of his death. But little of his property was ever recovered to satisfy his creditors or for the comfort of his family. He left a wife and four children, two sons and two daughters – Ruth, James, Nancy and Samuel Jr.. Abner Banning, their grandfather, furnished them with a home while living and provided for them by will after his death. Ruth married a Mr. Marcks of West Hartland. She was left a widow with one son. James and Nancy never married. They lived in the family with their mother until James died. His mother has since died and Nancy is living with her sister, Mrs. Marcks. Samuel Jr. married a Miss Case, died some years since, leaving his widow and some small children. Thus ends the history of Samuel Banning and family.

P.S. Dear cousin:
I received your letter in due time, the first I heard of you since you were at our house. It was at the commencement of haying. My time was so much taken up that I could not give it attention; since haying I have had no help in my family and in connection with my family cares I have sketched which I have. If it will be in any way acceptable, I shall be gratified. Trusting that you will make all due allowances, I submit it to your examination. Should it meet your approbation, at some future day I may extend it. If sufficient I will drop the subject here. My respects to Mrs. Banning.
Ever yours in friendship, Amelia V. Eells.

Addenda: I wish to give a little more of a descriptive account of our common grandfather, Abner Banning. He was a man over six feet, with strong muscular frame, not corpulent. He was naturally social, very stern in his family, still possessed a warm parental attachment to his family. The remark that he commenced with but little pecuniary means, likewise, his determination to have a competency. He at one time had six hundred acres of land, intending to settle each of his sons around him, three hundred of which he afterwards disposed of to enable him to purchase land in Ohio for his sons as they chose to settle there. As a patrimony to his children he gave each a bible and a psalm book, as they were all members of a choir of singers; each of his sons a horse, saddle and bridle; his daughter a saddle and bridle, and each of his children twelve hundred dollars in cash as they were often calling for help and did not

call in vain if he had the means. On regard to other families of Bannings, in the time of the War I read of a bishop Banning, - I think in the northeastern part of Virginia or Maryland. I had an Irish girl in our family; she stated that three were Bannings came from Scotland to Ireland, and that one or more of that name went to Canada, but my opinion is that all the Bannings in the United States must have originated from Samuel Banning's father, who was struck by lighting in his doorway at Lyme, Conn., about 1760.
David Banning's history I may forward at some future time.

Whether Amelia Eells Banning ever forwarded David's history is unrecorded, but it was located through other sources. The American Historical Society published a book entitled *Genealogical and Biographical Records of the Banning and Allied Families' in 1924*[585], prepared for Kate Banning, David's daughter.

136.   David Banning   137.   Asenath C. Banning
Genealogical and Biographical Records of the Banning and Allied Families, The American Historical Society, Inc., 1924

David Banning (*G1.F.153*) was the son of Ashel Banning and Dency (Crosby) Banning, born in Vernon, Ohio on 11 April 1819.

He became one of Cincinnati's foremost citizens, actively contributing to it's growth and development and known throughout the city and the larger commercial cities of Ohio as a man of the strictest

---

[585] *Genealogical and Biographical Records of the Banning and Allied Families*, The American Historical Society Inc. 1924

integrity. He was connected in executive capacities with many of the large financial and commercial enterprises of the city, and was for 32 years a member of the board of directors of the Fourth National Bank of Cincinnati, his connections with that institution dating from its founding.

David grew up on his father's large farm. He was a boy of studious tastes, an avid reader and in search of knowledge. His first employment was at a general store in his native town, in the capacity of clerk, followed by employment with the Federal Government. Shortly after his arrival in Cincinnati he entered into his first business venture, forming a partnership with his brother, Jeremiah W. Banning. This was a commission business, which they pursued very successfully. The partnership was soon dissolved and the two brothers continued their operations separately. David Banning immediately organized another business, which he directed for 25 years; it occupied a position of importance among the largest enterprises of its kind in the city of Cincinnati. He was described as a man of broad tolerance and understanding with an astute business sense, a leader who was instinctively obeyed. He inspired confidence and support, both through his integrity and through his success.

A Republican, David Banning was not actively involved in politics, although he was very active in social and fraternal affairs and his death on 8 March 1901 was widely mourned. He was married in April 1824 to Asenath C. Bradley, the daughter of one of the foremost physicians in the state. Mrs. Banning belonged to one of the old Colonial families of that region; she died in Cincinnati on 13 Nov. 1909. The couple had six children.

Jeremiah Wilcox Banning, (*G1.F.154*) another great-great grandson of Samuel, (born 17 Aug. 1820) in Vernon, Ohio, entered into the commission business in 1847 with his brother David. They were instrumental in having the first bridge built across the river in Cincinnati, Ohio. Jeremiah was a prominent and well-to-do citizen.

Archibald Tanner Banning, (*G1.F.611; b. 15 May 1854*) was a physician in Mount Vernon, New York, a publicly spirited and assertive personality. His dedication to his profession was exemplified when the Mt. Vernon Hospital, of which he was a founder – as well as President of the Mt. Vernon Medical Society – was forced to close in 1896 due to lack of funds. Dr. Banning offered the use of his home for receiving and treating emergency cases. (The hospital reopened 6 months later.) He held office as Coroner and Health Officer for many terms, often elected by a large majority. As an ardent lover of music, he played several instruments, being a particularly fine lutist. His deep bass voice could be heard in the choir of Trinity Church, and he was one of the founders of the Mozart Club. He was held in high regard.

138. Archibald Tanner Banning (1854-1924)
reproduced with permission by the heirs of Mary Banning Friedlander[586]

Of Archibald Tanner's ten children, the first son, **William Peck Banning**[587], (*G1.F. 3009*) was born in New York City 24 May 1880. He married Helen Cameron Vroom in 1916. William P. Banning received his A.B. degree from New York University in 1902. He went to China in 1911 as one of the founders of the newspaper China Press. In 1920 he joined AT&T, becoming Assistant Vice President of Public Relations in 1944. William P. Banning wrote *Commercial Broadcasting Pioneer; the WEAF experiment, 1922-1926*, which was published by the Harvard University Press in 1946. William Peck inherited his father's aptitude and passion for music: he was an excellent pianist.

Archibald Tanner Banning,(*G1.F.3011; b. 10 May 1884)* the second son, and named after his father, acquired his A.B. at Cornell University in 1904. He received his L.L.N. at Georgetown University in 1908. Becoming a lawyer, he held office as Private Secretary to the Gallatin National Bank, New York City, Private Secretary to the Honourable Andrew D. White, (former Cornell University President and U.S. Ambassador to Germany), Private Secretary to the Director of the Census, Washington, Special Agent of the Bureau of Corporations and secretary to Dept. Comm. of Corporations, Washington.

---

[586] http://freepages.genealogy.rootsweb.com/~mbfriedlander/banning; accessed March 2003
[587] Mary Banning Friedlander: The Banning Line;
http://freepages.genealogy.rootsweb.com/~mbfriedlander/banning; accessed May 2004

139.   Archibald Tanner Banning 1884-1965
reproduced with permission by the heirs of Mary Banning Friedlander[588]

Archibald T. Banning Jr. married Margaret Culkin (1891-1982) in 1914. (The couple divorced in 1934). Margaret Culkin Banning[589] was a best-selling author and early advocate of women's rights, the wealthy daughter of William E. Culkin who served two terms in the Minnesota State Senate (1895-99). With a strong sense of civic activity, she was active in politics, a delegate to one National Republican Convention and an alternate to another. Margaret Culkin Banning was the author of some forty novels and more than four hundred essays and short stories, generally focussed on civic, moral and social issues. She was a Vassar College trustee, 1936-1944, Duluth Public Library trustee, board member of the city symphony and the first woman admitted to the Duluth Hall of Fame. She was a member of the British Information Service in World War II. Following the war she worked in refugee and displaced persons camps in Austria and Germany. At the time of her death, one month before her ninety-first birthday, she was writing another novel, which was never published.

Edwin Rutherford Banning, (*G1.F.667; b.19 Sept.1842*) was also a physician, in Hartford Connecticut.

---

[588] http://freepages.genealogy.rootsweb.com/~mbfriedlander/banning; accessed March 2003
[589] American National Biography, Vol. 2, Oxford University Press, New York 1999, p. 119

Wells Tanner Banning, (*G1.F.604*) born 10. Oct. 1838 in Titusville, Pennsylvania, was raised and educated in New York City. He graduated at the age of nineteen as E.A. at the New York Free Academy, known (in 1909) as the College of New York. He had a strong literary ability and was a man of lofty ideals, deeply loved and respected. At the time of his death numerous eulogistic editorials on his life and ideals appeared in the New York City papers. He was a brilliant musician with an excellent mind, able to play seven simultaneous games of chess while blindfolded. He died in 1862 in Providence, Rhode Island.

The 'Banning Record', the local newspaper of Banning, California, carried an article on 17 June 1909, stating that the Bannings had emigrated to the Netherlands from Denmark as early as the fourth or fifth century[590].

In this respect we quote Miss Mary Banning (1820-1903) from Winchester, Virginia. She wrote the following[591] in a letter dated 19 Jan. 1897 to her nephew Richard A. Banning (1859- ?) from Baltimore, Maryland:

"We are of very ancient date, our name is in the 'Scot and Bard songs', the first ballad on record, where it says 'Becca rule the Banning'; each clan had it's ruler or hero. The Bannings were in the Crusades. Our blood was spilt in the Crusades, in the fight for the Holy Sepulchre. They were Vikings, in other words, like all the early Norwegians and Danes, Piratical Chieftains, great fighters, warlike to the very teeth and I believe with all our modern civilisation there is fight in us yet. Banning is easy enough to spell; it is found in the earliest documents on record with its three terminal letters 'ing'. It makes me mad to see our antique name fall into the hands of ignorant printers and so lose its 'ing'. Lose the 'ing' and you rouse my blood and the blood of a Dane is hard to wipe out. Thus you have doubtless heard said a Banning is a strong friend but a bitter enemy. They have the spirit of old Hero Worship in them yet and you will find them clinging to those they love with lifelong affection. Our 'ing' termination is our inheritance through all time; without it we should be as abridged as a dog without a tail. I am only giving you information about your name and your ancestors who were the bravest, boldest fighting old Danes and Anglo-Saxons that ever figured in History; if you were to read 'Beowulf', and this would be hard for you to do as it is (without study) unreadable to us moderns. Nothing disgusts me more than this brand and beast about ancestry, but there is much in it that tells upon modern generations."

---

[590] P.W. Banning, *Europeesche Geschiedenis der Banning's,* De Geldersche Bode, 8 July, 1936)
[591] P.W. Banning, *The First Banning Genealogy,* Chicago, 1909

Mary Elizabeth Banning (*G1.A.21*) was a granddaughter of Jeremiah the mariner, born in 1822, who lived in Winchester, Virginia. After a move with her older sisters and widowed mother to Baltimore shortly before 1856, her proscribed task was to tend to ailing family members. Perhaps this is where she accrued her considerable fund of knowledge on the Banning family. She was said to be a woman of remarkable mind and a great student along scientific lines, with an indomitable spirit. In a sense, her letter tells us more about Mary than about the Bannings.

Mary Elizabeth is known as a rather eccentric and gifted mycologist (one who studies fungi) and natural history illustrator who avidly studied and illustrated natural objects. She focussed on mushrooms because she found them the most challenging and mysterious. This avid pursuit is best explained in her own words: "As each day brings its pleasant little episodes, so does each collecting trip, and as time rolls on they have become bright spots which my memory loves to refer to. Thus when the dark days of winter come and we draw near the fireside, we turn our sketchbook with a feeling of delight. Each page contains a record of a day, each plant a history filled with pleasant recollections. There is often associated with it some quiet woodland nook, some undreamt of world of beauty, where wild flowers bloomed in rich profusion- where mosses, ferns, and fungi lent their varied shades and revealed that undeviating law in nature, harmony.[592]"

In 1868 Mary began to write and illustrate a book on the fungi of Maryland, a project which took over 20 years and resulted in a manuscript of scientific descriptions and amusing stories, accompanied by 174 detailed watercolours.

In 1868 there were no books of this kind. Mary Banning's consuming interest in this subject led her to the New York State Museum's Charles Peck, one of America's leading Mycologists. Although they never met in person, Peck became Mary Banning's mentor through correspondence. Letters and paintings passed regularly in the mail until she became the leading mycologist in her region. Mary undoubtedly aspired to acceptance in the fraternity of nineteenth century scientists but as a woman, she did not have easy entry into formal education, nor was she taken seriously by most of the all-male scientific establishment. It was the kindly and patient Peck who was her main supporter in her continuing mycological endeavours and it was to him that she finally dedicated and donated her illustrated manuscript. Among the fungi described in her manuscript are 23 species previously unknown to science, described and published in the *Botanical Gazette* and in Peck's *Annual Report of the New York State Botanist*.

---

[592] Personal communication from J. Haines, New York State Museum Education Dept., 28 May 2004, from the *Biography of Mary Banning*

140. Painting of the Agaricus campestris, by Mary E. Banning
Courtesy of the New York State Museum, Albany, NY

Miss Banning's relatives, several of whom lived in Baltimore, spoke of her reserve, her high ideals, her charity, and always of her delight in nature. She loved music and flowers which she pressed, and cared a great deal for animals of which she made little sketches with indelible ink on the table linen, bed linen and towels. A curious pastime was dissecting fish, and after wiring the bones, putting them together again.

Mary Banning was a regular visitor to Baltimore parks and made periodic excursions through the Maryland and Southern Virginia countryside on expeditions to gather and draw fungi. She became well known to the other Baltimore naturalists and was a regular visitor to Baltimore's Peabody Library and Institute. By 1890, failing eyesight and rheumatism made it impossible for her to continue her work. She donated her manuscript to The New York State Museum for safekeeping, where it lay in obscurity for nearly a century. Toward the end of her life, with her beloved family and most of her money gone, she moved to a boarding house in Winchester, Virginia, where she was able to pay only $5 per week. In 1890 she described it with wry humour: "This boarding-house life, even under the most pleasant of circumstances, as it is certainly here, is a constant jostle—an upheaval if I may so call it of all the elements contained in humanity. It is certainly much better adapted to the study of human nature than to the arts and sciences."

She died, unmarried and alone, in 1903. Since 1981 her paintings have been the subject of the exhibit *Each a Glory Bright* and have been exhibited at museums around the country. In 1994 Mary Banning was inducted into the Maryland Women's Hall of Fame.[593]

141. Mary Elizabeth Banning 1822-1903
Photo reprinted with the permission of The Natural History Society of Maryland

Mary Banning spent much time investigating the name Banning, especially it's very earliest history, and claimed to be an authority on etymology, as well as on many other matters. The above-mentioned letter was used as a basis for the statements concerning the name and its history. Pierson Worrall Banning wrote that Mary had compiled a manuscript on the Banning family, which she had left with a family member and which, according to her instruction, was not to be opened for 100 years (which date would now be due). Pierson Worrall expresses his doubt concerning this odd stipulation, and if Mary did leave a manuscript, its whereabouts are unfortunately unknown.

James Herman Banning (1899-1933), cannot be traced in the existing genealogies. Son of Riley and Cora Banning of Oklahoma, James Herman differs from the other Bannings in this book in that he was black. When

---

[593] Women's History in the Collections; New York State Museum; www.nysm.nysed.gov/research_collections/collections/history/womenshistory/banning.html accessed May 2004

and how coloured Bannings entered into the lineage is unknown. However, after the abolition of slavery in 1862, it was common for the freemen to take the surnames from their former masters. This would have been even more likely if they had been well treated while in bondage, and it is known that Jeremiah Banning, for example, who came to abhor slavery, not only provided for the liberty of his slaves in his will, but also for their welfare and education afterward. It is not unlikely that Riley W. Banning descended from a slave once held by a Banning and thus took this name. We know that Riley took advantage of the Homestead Act of 1862, whereby he acquired 160 acres of land in Oklahoma on 31 Dec. 1903 for the sum of $10. The Homestead Act, passed in 1862, offered 160 acres of land to anyone who would pay this fee, live on the land for five years, and cultivate and improve it. This deed of ownership, signed with the name of President Roosevelt, must have been a proud possession for Riley to pass on to his son James, who would have been a lad of four when the Bannings moved onto their new homestead.

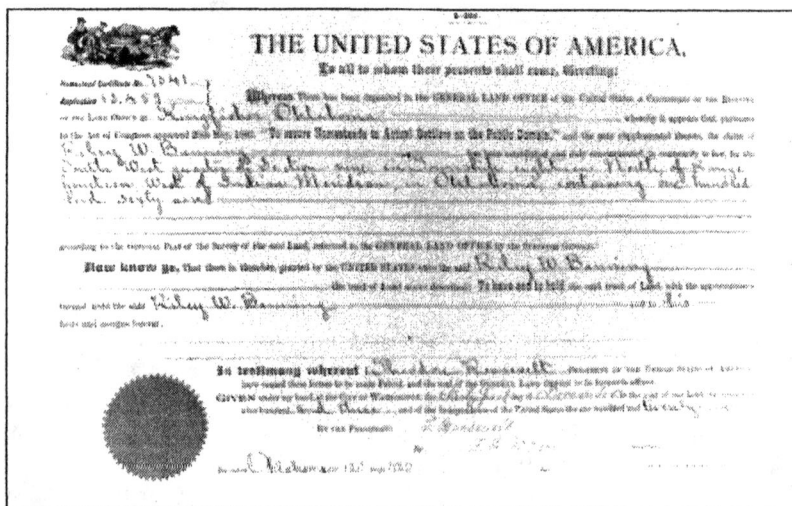

142. Deed for land granted to Riley W. Banning in 1903,
by President T. Roosevelt
courtesy of the Farwell T. Brown Photographic Archive, Ames Public Library,
Ames, Iowa

The family moved to Ames in 1919, where Herman studied electrical engineering at Iowa State College for a little more than a year, but was soon captivated by the adventure of the air. He learned to fly at Raymond Fisher's Flying Field in Des Moines and became the first black aviator to obtain a license from the U. S. Dept. of Commerce. James Banning operated the J. H. Banning Auto Repair Shop in Ames from 1922 to 1928.

He left Ames to live in Los Angeles in 1929 where he was the chief pilot for the Bessie Coleman Club, named after a pioneer black woman flyer.

143. James Herman Banning 1899-1933
courtesy of the Farwell T. Brown Photographic Archive,
Ames Public Library, Ames, Iowa

Herman, as he was commonly known, and Thomas C. Allen, another black pilot, became the first black pilots to fly coast-to-coast from Los Angeles to Long Island, NY, in 1932. In an airplane assembled from junkyard scrap, they made the 3,300 mile trip in less than 42 hours aloft. The trip actually required 21 days to complete because the pilots were compelled to raise funds each time they stopped. Banning performed in air circuses and flew politicians during their campaigns. (One of his passengers was Illinois representative Oscar Depriest, the first black person elected to serve in U. S. Congress since the Civil War.)

J.H. Banning participated in a San Diego air show in 1933 as a passenger in a biplane, sitting in the front open cockpit without controls. The Navy pilot at the controls, in an apparent bid to impress his more accomplished passenger, pulled the nose of the tiny plane up into a steep climb. The engine stalled and the plane fell into a fatal spin in front of hundreds of horrified spectators. J. Herman Banning died of a fractured skull and internal injuries an hour after he was lifted from the wreckage.

Ruth Banning, a daughter of William Marion and Elizabeth Anne Banning, is as conspicuously absent from the existing genealogies as is James Herman. She was born 11 July 1892 in Colorado. After graduating from Colorado Springs High School in 1910 and Phi Beta Kappa from

Wellesley College in 1915, she taught English for one year at Colorado College. Her father, William Marion Banning, was the owner of the Union Ice and Coal Company and the Banning Ranch. When he died in 1914, the operations of the company and the ranch were assumed by Ruth's brother, William. After William's death in 1916, Ruth Banning took over as manager of the ranch and of Union Ice and Coal. She soon organised and became president of the Consumers Ice Delivery Company and was the first woman to serve on the executive board of the Mountain States Ice Manufacturer's Association.

When her mother died in July of 1921, Ruth was left without immediate family. In September of that year she married Raymond W. Lewis, a Colorado College graduate and ranch owner from Fowler, Colorado. In January of 1922, Ruth Banning Lewis purchased ten head of registered heifers, declaring that she intended to make Colorado Springs known for purebred Herefords, and in 1924 Ruth sold her ice and coal businesses to devote more time to cattle ranching. By 1927 she and Raymond had formed the Banning-Lewis Ranches and began buying what would eventually be over 30,000 acres for their prize winning Hereford operation. Banning-Lewis Ranches had the champion bull, Prince Domino 101st, at the American Hereford Association's Golden Jubilee Show in Kansas City in 1932.

In addition to time spent raising cattle and horses, Ruth Banning Lewis was an active participant in numerous civic activities and organizations. She was one of the founding members of the Girl Scouts Council in Colorado Springs and organiser of the Pikes Peak Chapter of the American Red Cross Volunteer Nurse's Aid Corps. In 1923 she was elected to the Board of Education for District #11 and served as its president from 1927 until her resignation in 1934. Ruth Banning Lewis was the first woman elected to the Board of the National American Hereford Association and was on the Board of the Colorado Springs Fine Arts Center, the Drama League, and the Visiting Nurse's Association. From 1943 to 1947 she served on the Colorado Springs City Council. After an active and productive lifetime, she died on 19 Nov. 1962, survived by her husband. They had no children.

Ruth's brother William Banning was an accomplished portrait painter and artist.

Lt. Col. Kendall Banning[594] (*G1.E.6319*) born 20 Sept. 1879 in New York City, was a soldier, author and publisher. He came from an impressive line of pioneers, Indian fighters and prominent men. Kendall Banning received his A.B. from Dartmouth College in 1902, where he

---

[594] *Biographical Encyclopedia of the World*, 3rd Edition, Institute for Research and Biography, 1946, p. 932

was class poet and Editor of the Dartmouth Magazine. Col. Banning started his career as a advertising writer in 1902 with the Cheltenham Press; he was editor of the National Cash Register Co. house organ (1902-1903), editor of *System-The Magazine of Business* until 1917, Managing Editor of Hearst's *Cosmopolitan* (1919-1921), Editorial Director of *Popular Radio* , Leslie-Judge Co., and the New Fiction Publishing Co.(1922-1928), Editorial Director of the *Public Utilities Fortnightly* (1929-1934) and Chief of the Pictorial Division of the Committee on Public Information (Creel Committee) (1917). He began his military career in 1902 as a Private in the New York National Guard, was Lieutenant from 1907-1910, served during World War I as Major in the Signal Corps, U.S. Army, and in 1918-1919 was a member of the War Department General Staff, was Lieutenant Colonel Signal Corps Reserve from 1919-1943, attached to the office of the Chief of Ordnance, 1943-1944. Works published by Kendall Banning are: *West Point Today* (1938), *Annapolis Today* (1939), *The Fleet Today* (1940), *Our Army Today* (1943), *Submarine! The Story of the Undersea Fighters* (1942) and *Drum Beats* (1937). Between 1902 and 1937 many other volumes of his work were published, as well as three plays and some forty songs. His profile and portrait are included in *Who's Important in Literature*. Kendall Banning died 17 Dec. 1944.

Although Bannings in Chicago later became more numerous, details on the origins of the first by that name are scant. It is known only that a Banning lived in Chicago from around 1855 to 1861. After the death of his wife he left for parts unknown, placing his son Daniel in a half orphan asylum on 22nd Street and Tabash Avenue in Chicago.

Daniel was born on 24 June 1858, in Chicago. He was later adopted by a Mr. Eads, who worked in the file business in that city. Daniel never heard from his father again. He was killed in a railway accident at Lanark Junction, Illinois in 1888, while in the employ of the C.M.A. st. Ry. Co. in Chicago.

The Canadian Bannings are believed to have come from Orange County, New York, having originated from Ireland, although there is nothing to verify this supposition. In turn, the Irish Bannings likely came from Scotland or England, although nothing is recorded. The progenitor of this branch migrated from Orange County to an area near Wardsville, Ontario, from which place his descendants spread to Detroit, Chicago Nevada, San Francisco, Winnipeg, Honolulu and elsewhere. There is a possibility that they belong to one of the other lines originating from Connecticut, or are connected with the English lines through Daniel Banning, born in the United States, but this is only surmised.

The Christian name of the first Banning known to settle in Canada is unknown. He apparently came to New York State from Ireland, the family originating before that from Scotland or England and perhaps prior to that time from the Netherlands. James Banning, born December 17, 1794, was one of his nine children. James married Mary Ann Ward, the only daughter of Sir George Ward of Ireland, around 1820. They had twelve children and lived in Middlesex County, near Wardsville. He died there on 3 May 1860.

JAMES BANNING
G-1

SHELDON ARTHUR BANNING
G-20

144. James Banning 1825-1897   145. Sheldon Arthur Banning
The First Banning Genealogy, P.W. Banning, Chicago, 1908

James Banning Jr. (*G1.G.11*)was born on 11 June 1825, near Wardsville Ontario. He married Mary Fleming; they had one son. After Mary died in 1884, James married Belle Rutherford of Wardsville on 11 Feb. 1885. This union produced three children. The family lived in Chatham, Ontario. James died on 2 May 1897, and his wife in 1902.

Sheldon Arthur Banning, (*G1.G.20*) born 12 Aug. 1848, was a son of James Banning.. He married Sarah M. Campbell of Strathroy, Ontario in 1869. They had two children. Sheldon later married Jennie Roberts of Detroit (19 Aug. 1869). This marriage remained childless.

A grandson of James (1794, above) and nephew of James and Sheldon, was **Edward James Banning** (*G1.G24; b. 6 June 1873*) in San Francisco, California. He was appointed First Assistant United States District Attorney by President McKinley, for a period of six years, for the Northern District of California.
Edward died on 4 Febr. 1906.

There are now many more Bannings in Canada; some being first or second generation emigrants from Europe and others descending from earlier settlers. They were by no means as numerous as those in the United States, but some left a more-or-less permanent mark in the form of Banning Streets in Winnipeg, Manitoba and in Thunder Bay, Ontario, as well as a Banning Road in Canada's capital city of Ottawa and Banning Lake in Ontario, the center of the famous Seine Chain of Lakes and part of the Historic Boundary Waterway.

Numerous cities, towns, communities and streets, both historic and more recent, have been named after Bannings in various parts of the world. There are too many to research for this book, but a selection is listed below.

NETHERLANDS
Banningstraat, Soesterberg: This broad, tree-lined avenue was named in honour of Henricus Adrianus Banning (1818-1909) in 1924.

146. Banningstraat, Soesterberg
photo courtesy of Kees van Iwaarden   July 2003

W. Banninglaan: avenue in Driebergen. The avenue was named after the well-known Dutch socialist minister Willem Banning (1888-1971).
Van Banninglaan, avenue in Geleen. Named in honour of J.P.D. van Banning, (1906-1986) mayor of Geleen from 1951-1971 and before that to two other Dutch towns.
Jan van Banningstraat: street in the city of Zoeterwoude. named after the archpriest Joannes (Jan) van Banning (1766-1840).
E. Banning Straat, Leiden, named after Emerentia Banning (Benningh) (1585-1667) of the Amsterdam Banning family.
Banningweg, Eibergen; Bannings still live on this road.

Banninghof: a district in the township of Groenlo with 1630 residents (1999) named after the original estate Banninghof in this town. The estate was built in 1916, originally for Lady H.L. Colson Aberson and named 'Hermanshof' after her late husband. Situated on grounds of 13,500m^2, the estate passed into ownership of F.J.H. Banning (G2.A.VIII) in 1929, after which it became known as the 'Banninghof'.

147.   Banninghof, Ruurloschenweg, Groenlo, built in 1916
photo courtesy of F. Banning

Benningspad, also known as Hans Benningenpad, bearing the name of one Hans Benning (Benningh/Banning) of Amsterdam in 1609/10.
Jan Benninghstraat: Amstelveen, named after Jan Jansz. Benningh (Banning) (before 1470-after 1534), one of the most influential men of his time in Amsterdam, playing a significant role in the history of Amstelveen and Amsterdam.
Benningh, Benninghbrug: Ouderkerk a/d Amstel: a district and bridge named after Jan Benningh (Banning), above.
Jan Benninghweg: road, Ouderkerk aan de Amstel, named after Jan Benningh, above.

148. Jan Benninghweg, Ouderkerk a/d Amstel
source: http://www.verkeersveiligouderkerk.nl/kp7.htm

Bennyckstraat: a street named for the Banning family of Amsterdam magistrates in the 16th and 17th centuries, also known as the St. Olofskapelsteeg, as the St. Olof's chapel was on this street.

Kornelis Banningssteeg: street/lane in Amsterdam in the 16th century, named after the burgomaster Cornelis Banning, also known as the Kornelis Buyckensteeg.

Banninkstraat: street to the west of the city of Hengelo in the Dutch province of Hengelo

Banninkstraat: street running between the towns of Keijenborg and Zelhem.

Burgemeester Banninglaan: an avenue in Leidschendam, Netherlands, named in 1970 in honour of the mayor, H.A.C. Banning (1900-1970). Before that it was the 'Laanzichtweg'.

Burgemeester Banninglaan
1940-1943 en 1945-1965

149. Street sign on the Burgemeester Banninglaan, Leidschendam
private collection

Banninklaan, avenue in Zierikzee, named in honour of J.C.A. Bannink (1877-1938) honorary Major-General and Mayor of Zierikzee from 1929-1934.

150. Banninklaan, Zierikzee, 1982
collection: Municipal Archives of Schouwen-Duiveland, Zierikzee, Netherlands

Dr. Banningstraat, street in Nijmegen, named in honour of Dr. Franciscus Bernardus Banning. (1829-1893).

BELGIUM

Benninghsteghe, Gent, also **Bennincsteghe, Bennesteghe**. First mentioned in historical documents in 1314 and 1326 and still exists today. This alley or lane was named after the well-known Belgian Benning (Bening/Benninc) family of the Middle Ages. The family referred to was most likely that of Alexander (Sanders) Bening, a celebrated illuminist, his son Simon Bening, who excelled in the same profession, and his sister Levina Teerlinck, also a well-known artist.

Simon Benningstraat, Bruges, most likely named after the above Simon Bening (Benning)

Rue Emile Banning, Brussels, a street named in honour of Emile Banning (1836-1898), who worked closely with King Leopold of Belgium to establish the Belgian Congo, now Zaire.

151. Emiel Banningstraat, Antwerp, named after Emile Banning.
photo source: www.2747.com, courtesy of F. Beuckelaers, Antwerp

BELGIAN CONGO, NOW ZAIRE, AFRICA
Banningville:

152. Banningville, Belgian Congo   Banningstad, Belgian Congo

City near Leopoldville, shown here in the French 'Banningville' and in the Dutch 'Banningstad', from the Colonial Age. Named in honour of Emile Banning, above. The city was renamed Bandudu in 1966.

ENGLAND
Banning Street, Greenwich, London: a few block removed and running parallel to the Thames) in one of London's popular districts.

153. Banning Street, Greenwich, London

Bayning's Quay, Barking, London: Probably one of the wharves owned by Paul Bayning of London in the 16th and 17th centuries, located on the Thames River near the Tower of London and no longer in existence.

Banningham, 11th century market town in Norfolk, mentioned in the Domesday Book . Several members of the De Banningham family lived here in the 12th, 13th and 14th centuries. A Banningham Court and a very long Banningham Road also exist near here.

Bannings Vale, Saltdean, East Sussex : formerly Barndean, Barendens, refers to farm buildings and arable fields in Telscombe. Banningsdown,

Benings, Bannings, Bannings Farms and Bannings Bottom are mentioned in various archives from 1792 to 1928. Barn-dean may derive from the surname Berndon. Lower Bannings farmhouse, which survives as 38-40 Bannings Vale, dates from the mid-eighteenth century. The name is also attributed to a farmer Banning,

Banning Marsh, mentioned in the 1851 census for Worcestershire, and probably named after the Banning family living in Birmingham, Warwick.

Banning Street, Rochester, Kent
Banning Close, Birkenhead, Merseyside
Banning Street, Romsey, Hampshire

GERMANY
Banningstrasse, city of Hamm
Benninghausen; city

SWEDEN
Banninge, Floda Parish, lies in the administrative county district Oppunda, province Södermanland and is very small, originally having been just a farm. It is mentioned for the first time in the original sources on 6 July 1347, as 'Bandunge'. The name seems to have been derived not from a person, but from the geographical location, an elongated elevation - a band or belt of land – where the village is located.

Banningetorp, also in the parish of Floda, is the name of a farmstead (meaning: the Banninge (or Banning's) pastureland or enclosure).

UNITED STATES
Banning : city Riverside County, California, estimated population of 26,000 in 2002, 18.44 square miles, named in honour of General Phineas T. Banning of Wilmington. Located in the San Gorgonio Pass, between Mt. San Gorgonio on the north and Mt. San Jacinto to the south, where Phineas Banning ran a stage-coach line from Wilmington to Yuma Arizona. This route is now called the **Banning Pass.**

Banning Hill and Banning House, Catalina Island, California; after the time when the brothers William, Joseph and Hancock Banning owned Catalina Island from 1891 to 1919.

Banning Cottage, also known as 371P Banning, California, designed in 1932 by James Van Evera Bailey. Home to the well-known architect of the progressive 'Prairie Style Group' William Gray Purcell (1880-1965) from 1932-1936. He lived here during a prolonged recuperation from tuberculosis, a period from which diaries, correspondence and sketches have survived.

Banning, and **Banning Mills;** city, Carroll County, Georgia. The town originated in 1842 as Bowensville, and in 1878 had both a paper and a textile mill. In 1882 is was renamed Banning, to better differentiate it from surrounding towns with similar names. By 1895 the town saw a thriving industry, focused around two pulp mills, a paper mill, a grist mill and a saw mill. Banning was probably one of the first towns in the world to produce its own electricity; references can be found in old family diaries recounting buggy rides from Atlanta to Banning to watch the lights come on. One of the first known industrial towns of the Americas, the Pine paper pulp company also had its origins here. Today it is a serene and scenic setting for visitors and conferences.

154. No. 5 Mill in Historic Banning Mills
photo courtesy of Mike and Donna Holder, owners & operators

Banning, town, Pine County, Minnesota; also includes Banning Junction. Named for William Lowber Banning, the town flourished around the turn of the 19th century. In the late 1800's and early 1900's over 500 stonecutters mined and cut sandstone in the quarry here. In 1894 the great Hinckley forest fire swept through the area. Business resumed after the fire and by 1896 the village of Banning was starting to develop in the fields flanking the quarry. The village grew and by the turn of the century it was incorporated with a population of approximately 300. However, by 1912, frequent fires and the increasing use of structural steel in construction had put the quarry out of business, marking the end of the town. Today, the old Banning site is part of the Banning State Park.

Banning State Park, Minnesota. The Park comprises 6,237 acres, the original site of the town Banning, above, established by the legislature in 1963.

Banning, city, Fayette County, Pennsylvania. The site of the Banning and Darr Mines; most likely named for Anthony Rogers Banning (1831-?).

Banning Place, city, in the district of Colfax County, New Mexico

Banning Road, Dawson, Pennsylvania

Banning Road, Brownsville, Pennslyvania

Banning Road, Cincinnati, Ohio

Banning Road, Whitesburg, Georgia

Banning Road, Camden, Delaware

Banning Road Coleraine township, Cincinnati

Banning Avenue, Huntington, California

Banning Corner, Warren County, Indiana

Banning Creek, Goldwater Lake, Arizona
Banning Lake, Kosciusko County, Indiana
Banning Street, Marshfield, Missouri
North Banning Boulevard, Los Angeles, California
Banning Cemetery, Camden, Delaware (where no Bannings are buried)
Banning Drive, Oakland, California
Banning Drive, Crocker, Missouri
Banning Drive, Houston, Texas
Banning Boulevard, Wilmington, California
Banning Way, San Marino, California
Banning Way, Diamond Bar, California
Banning Way, Valleja, California
Banning Way, Walnut, California

PHILIPPINES
Banning Street, North Fairview, Quezon City, Manila

CANADA
Banning Street, Winnipeg, Manitoba
Banning Street, Thunder Bay, Ontario
Banning Lake, Ontario, the center of the famous Seine Chain of Lakes and part of the Historic Boundary Waterway.
Banning Road, Ottawa

17. Glass door panel from the estate of Ooijenbergh, photo courtesy of P. Dekker, from *Oude Boerderijen en Buitenverblijven langs de Zijper Grotesloot*, Pirola, Schoorl, Netherlands, 1988, p. 568

18. 'Zeenimf', photo 1986, courtesy of P. Dekker, from *Oude Boerderijen en Buitenverblijven langs de Zijper Grotesloot*, Pirola, Schoorl, Netherlands, 1988, p. 111/113

19. 'Hoop en Vlijt', photo 1986, courtesy of P. Dekker, from *Oude Boerderijen en Buitenverblijven langs de Zijper Grotesloot*, Pirola, Schoorl, Netherlands, 1988, p. 353

20. 'De Vos' , photo 1986, courtesy of P. Dekker, from *Oude Boerderijen en Buitenverblijven langs de Zijper Grotesloot*, Pirola, Schoorl, Netherlands, 1988, p. 190

21. Cromhout houses, Municipal Archives of Amsterdam, Netherlands

22. 'Sluiswijk', photo ca. 1930, courtesy of P. Dekker, from *Oude Boerderijen en Buitenverblijven langs de Zijper Grotesloot*, Pirola, Schoorl, Netherlands, 1988, p. 343

23. Detail of a map of Amstelveen showing the locations of the country estates by G. Drogenham, 18th century, J.W. Groesbeek, *Amstelveen: Acht Eeuwen Geschiedenis*, De Lange, Amsterdam, Netherlands, 1966

24. Estate Welna on the Amstel River, photo: Iconografisch Bureau/Rijksbureau voor Kunsthistorische Documentatie (Netherlands Institute for Art History), the Hague, Netherlands

25. Jan Banning Wuytiers on his deathbed, etching by Theodore Matham, 1647, photo courtesy of Th. F.M. Weyn Banningh, Netherlands

26. The Eendracht, Mauritius, Hendrick Fredrick and the Hope, source: Olivier van Noort, *Om de Wereld, 1601-1602, (Around the World)*, translation by Roeper, Vibeke and Wildeman, Diederik, SUN, Nijmegen, 1999

27. Account of a sea voyage, Rijksmuseum, Amsterdam, Netherlands

28. Account of a sea voyage, source: Olivier van Noort, *Om de Wereld, 1601-1602, (Around the World)*, translation by Roeper, Vibeke and Wildeman, Diederik, SUN, Nijmegen, 1999

29. Margriet Benningh, ca. 1610, Nicolaes Eliaszn. Pickenoy, Rijksmusum, Amsterdam, Netherlands

30. The Benninckweer, detail of a map of Amsterdam by Cornelis Anthoniszn. 1544, Municipal Archives of Amsterdam, Netherlands

31. The Dam Square in about the year 1570, seen to the north, circa 1610; artist unknown. Municipal Archives of Amsterdam, Netherlands

32. Gasthuismolensteeg 20, Amsterdam, Municipal Archives of Amsterdam, Netherlands

33. Page from a 3-volume handwritten genealogical record entitled 'Geslacht Register van Catherine van Hoogenhouck', written by Mr. Pieter Marcus et al; some time between 1700 and 1800. Photo courtesy of F. van Heijningen

34. Portrait of Emerentia Banningh, 1626, R. van Ravesteyn; Stedelijk Museum De Lakenhal, Leiden, Netherlands

35. Parade of the Civic Militia on the Dam Square in Amsterdam, during the Annual Fair of 1686, engraving by Daniel Marot, Municipal Archives of Amsterdam, Netherlands

73. The High Land of Benninghbroeck, collection:Topographical-historical atlas, Map Book of the Almshouse Poor of the City of Hoorn, Westfriese Archieven, Hoorn (ref. no. 65j.208(32))

74. Banning windmill (de Wolf), Alkmaar, Netherlands, 1890-1911, photo by M. Kater, courtesy of the Regionaal Archief Alkmaar (Regional Archives of Alkmaar), Netherlands

75. Banning windmill, Edam, Netherlands, ca. 1900, collection Zuiderzeemuseum, Enkhuizen, Netherlands

76. Benninkmolen, Doetinchem, Netherlands, photo courtesy of Hans de Kroon, Veenendaal, Netherlands

77. Banninghof, Wettringen, Germany, photo courtesy of Frans van Heijningen, Netherlands

East Frisia, Germany and Scandinavia

78. Reconstruction of a stone section of Beningaburg I Wirdum after excavation findings, image: G. Kronsweide, Ostfriesische Landschaft; *Emder Jahrbuch für historische Landeskunde Ostfrieslands* 80, 2000, S. 219; source: http://www.ostfriesischelandschaft.de/af/wirdum00.htm; accessed May 2004

79. Castle of Upleward in Grimersum, private collection

80. Entry to Beningaburg, Dornum, unsigned sketch, private collection

80a. Hermann Moritz Banning (1799-1866) from *Geschichte der Vereinigteevangelischen Gemeinde Unterbarmen vom Jahre 1822 bis zum Jahres 1922", Thümmel, Schreiner und van den Bruck, Barmen (Wuppertal), 1922*

81. Felix Heinrich Wilhelm Banning, *The First Banning Genealogy, P.W. Banning*, Chicago, USA, 1909

82. Letter from Felix Banning to his brother-in-law, Willy Peters, written on company stationary in 1885,courtesy of his grandson, Ing. J. Banning, Düren, Germany

England

83. Map of Banningham, Norfolk, year,© Crown Copyright and Landmark Information Group Ltd., Exeter, England

84. Segment of a map of London, woodcut, ca.1550; by permission of British History Online, Institute of Historical Research, University of London; from http://www.british-history.ac.uk/iframe

85. The name Anthony Bannyng on the frontspiece of a 15th century manuscript held by St. John's College, Oxford; courtesy of: The President and Scholars of Saint John Baptist College in the University of Oxford, England

86. Monument to Paul and Andrew. St. Olave's Church, London, photo courtesy of Stephen Millar, London, England

87. Paul Bayninge, detail of the monument in St. Olave's Church, London, photo courtesy of Stephen Millar, London, England

88. Andrew Bayninge, detail of the monument in St. Olave's Church, London, photo courtesy of Stephen Millar, London, England

89. Fragment of will of Sir Paul Bayning, The National Archives, Surrey, (PRO) PROB 11/156

90. Map of Essex in 1594, John Norden, 1594, private collection

91. Handwritten draft petition from Sir Paul Bayning to King Charles I, concerning a loan to the king, ref. D/DRg 2/47, Courtesy of the Essex Record Office, Chelmsford, England
92. William Villiers, Viscount Grandison, engraving by H.R. Cook, 1643, private collection
93. Fragment of the last will and testament of Mary Bayning, Lady Anglesey, dated 30th March 1671, ref. D/DL F94, courtesy of the Essex Record Office, Chelmsford,England
94. Barbara Villiers, from the UT Library Online, from http://www.lib.utexas.edu/photodraw/portraits/#top accessed 12 July 2004
95. Henry Fitzroy, 1st Duke of Grafton, ca. 1678, National Portrait Gallery, London, England
96. Barbara Villiers and son, ca. 1670, sketch after Sir Peter Lely, private collection
97. Dr. Robert Joseph Banning and his wife, Alice Cooper Banning, *The First Banning Genealogy*, P.W. Banning, Chicago, 1909
98. Letter from James Banning to George Spurrell, 11 March 1884, reproduced with permission of Llyfrgell Genedlaethol Cymru / The National Library of Wales
99. Captain A. Banning, DSO, Merchant Navy Officer, by Bernard Hailstone, 1945, © Queen's Printer and Controller of HMSO, 2003. UK Government Art Collection

United States
100. Frontspiece of *The First Banning Genealogy*, P.W. Banning, Chicago, USA, 1909
101. Pierson Worrall Banning, *The First Banning Genealogy*, P.W. Banning, Chicago, USA, 1909
102. Jeremiah Banning : drawing by John Moll, taken from a daguerreotype, published in *Jeremiah Banning, Mariner and Patriot* by Jane Foster Tucker, published under auspices of the Oxford Bicentennial Commission, Maryland, USA, 1977
103. Page from the *Log of Jeremiah Banning*, written 1733-1798, transcribed by Emily E. Banning in 1880, privately printed by W.F. Austin, New York, USA, 1932
104. Henry Geddes Banning, *The First Banning Genealogy*, P.W. Banning, Chicago, USA, 1909
105. Willard Stewart, Banning House, Willard Stewart Photographs for the WPA and HABS Collection, University of Delaware Library. Newark, Delaware, USA
106. Anthony Banning, *The First Banning Genealogy*, P.W. Banning, Chicago, USA, 1909
107. James Smith Banning, *The First Banning Genealogy*, P.W. Banning, Chicago, USA, 1909
108. Henry Blackstone Banning, *The First Banning Genealogy*, P.W. Banning, Chicago, USA, 1909
109. Anthony Rogers Banning, *The First Banning Genealogy*, P.W. Banning, Chicago, USA, 1909

110. Mine Pick-up Service, Banning No. 2 Collery, Republic Steel Corp., Jacobs Creek, Pennslyvania, 1958. New York Central System-The Pittsburg & Lake Erie Railroad Company print from the original painting by Howard Fogg, 1958, Collection Larry and Susan Bunce

111. Banning Horse & Carriage Trade Catalogue, 1892, private collection

112. Page from the Benoni Banning family bible, 1729, courtesy of M. Cox, USA

113. Page from the Benoni Banning family bible, 1729, courtesy of M. Cox, USA

114. Patent application number 175.266, signed and designed by Phineas Banning, 28 March 1876, private collection

115. Home of General Phineas T. Banning, Wilmington, California, taken by his son Joseph Brent Banning ca. 1880, now the Banning Residence Museum, courtesy of the Banning Residence Museum, Wilmington, California, USA

116. Map fragment of California, illustrating Banning in Riverside County

117. Phineas T. Banning as a young man, photo courtesy of the Catalina Island Museum, California USA

118. William, Joseph and Hancock Banning, photo courtesy of the Catalina Island Museum, California, USA

119. Mary Banning, photo courtesy of the Catalina Island Museum, California, USA

120. Lucy Banning, photo courtesy of the Catalina Island Museum, California, USA

121. General Phineas T. Banning, *The First Banning Genealogy*, P.W. Banning, Chicago, USA, 1909

122. Katherine Stewart Banning, photo courtesy of the Catalina Island Museum, California, USA

123. Hancock Banning, photo courtesy of the Catalina Island Museum, California, USA

124. Anne Ophelia Smith Banning, photo courtesy of the Catalina Island Museum, California, USA

125. William Banning, photo courtesy of the Catalina Island Museum, California, USA

126. Banning family home, Descanso California, ca. 1911, photo courtesy of M. Rojas, USA

127. Ephraim Banning, The *First Banning Genealogy*, P.W. Banning, Chicago, U.S.A., 1909

128. Louisa Caroline Walker Banning, *The First Banning Genealogy*, P.W. Banning, Chicago, USA, 1909

129. Ephraim Banning, *The First Banning Genealogy*, P.W. Banning, Chicago, U.S.A., 1909

130. Lucretia Thalia Lindsley Banning, *The First Banning Genealogy*, P.W. Banning, Chicago, USA, 1909

131. Thomas Allen Banning, from *The First Banning Genealogy*, P.W. Banning, Chicago, U.S.A., 1909

132. Thomas Allen Banning, *Pioneers, Letts and Banning Narratives*, R.R. Donnelly & Sons Company, Chicago, 1972

133. Map of the route taken by the Banning Family in Illinois, Kansas and Missouri, 1836-1862, private collection

134. Patent application submitted by Walter E. Banning in 1896, for a 'Bicycle-Licence-Number Plate', with his signature, private collection

135. Dr. Edmund Prior Banning, reproduced with permission by the heirs of Mary Banning Friedlander, http://freepages.genealogy.rootsweb.com/~mbfriedlander/banning; accessed March 2003

135a.Page 47 from the essay A Peep Into the House You Live In, published by the Banning Truss and Brace Company, New York, 1872, private collection

136. David Banning, *Genealogical and Biographical Records of the Banning and Allied Families*, The American Historical Society, Inc., 1924

137. Asenath Banning, *Genealogical and Biographical Records of the Banning and Allied Families*, The American Historical Society, Inc., 1924

138. Archibald Tanner Banning, reproduced with permission by the heirs of Mary Banning Friedlander, http://freepages.genealogy.rootsweb.com/~mbfriedlander/banning; accessed March 2003

139. Archibald Tanner Banning jr., reproduced with permission by the heirs of Mary Banning Friedlander, [1] http://freepages.genealogy.rootsweb.com/~mbfriedlander/banning; accessed March 2003

140. Agaricus campestris, by Mary E. Banning, Courtesy of the New York State Museum, Albany, NY, USA

141. Mary Elizabeth Banning, photo reprinted with the permission of The Natural History Society of Maryland, USA

142. Deed for land granted to Riley W. Banning in 1903, by President T. Roosevelt, courtesy of the Farwell T. Brown Photographic Archive, Ames Public Library, Ames, Iowa, USA

143. James Herman Banning, courtesy of the Farwell T. Brown Photographic Archive, Ames Public Library, Ames, Iowa, USA

144. James Banning, , from The First Banning Genealogy, P.W. Banning, Chicago, U.S.A., 1909

145. Sheldon Banning, , from *The First Banning Genealogy*, P.W. Banning, Chicago, U.S.A., 1909

Banning on the Map

146. Banningsstraat, Soesterberg, photo courtesy of Kees van Iwaarden, 2003

147. Banninghof, Ruurloschenweg, Groenlo, courtesy of F. Banning

148. Jan Benninghweg, Ouderkerk aan de Amstel, source: http://www.verkeersveiligouderkerk.nl/kp7.htm

149. Street sign on the Burgemeester Banninglaan, private collection

150. Banninklaan, Zierikzee; collection: Municipal Archives of Schouwen-Duiveland, Zierikzee, Netherlands

151. Emiel Banningstraat, Antwerp, photo source: www.2747.com, courtesy of F. Beuckelaers, Antwerp

152. Map of Banningville in the former Belgian Congo

153. Map of Banning Street, Greenwich, London

154. Banning Mill no. 5, photo courtesy of Mike and Donna Holder, owners & operators

BIBLIOGRAPHY

1. Aa, A.J. van der, *Aardrijkskundig Woordenboek der Nederlanden*, (*Geographical Dictionary of the Netherlands*) Jacob Noorduyn, Gorinchem, Part II, 1840
2. Aa, A.J. van der, *Biographisch Woordenboek der Nederlanden*, (*Biographical Dictionary of the Netherlands*)J.J. van Brederode, Haarlem, Part I, 1852
3. Aa, A.J. van der, *Biographisch Woordenboek der Nederlanden*, (*Biographical Dictionary of the Netherlands*) J.J. van Brederode, Haarlem, Part II, 1853
4. *Adresboek Nederlandse Drukkers en Boekverkopers*, (*Address Book of Dutch Printers and Booksellers*) Koninklijke Bibliotheek, The Hague, 1999
5. *American National Biography*, Vol. 2, Oxford University Press, New York, 1999
6. *Amstelodamum, De Bruiloftszangen van Bredero*, (*The Wedding Songs of Bredero*) Gemeente Amsterdam, 1968
7. Amsterdams Historisch Museum, *De Smaak van de Elite*, (*The Taste of the Elite*) De Bataafsche Leeuw, Amsterdam 1986
8. Angle, Paul (edited by*), Pioneers, Narratives of Noah Harris Letts and Thomas Allen Banning 1825-1865*, The Lakeside Press, R.R. Donnelley & Sons Co., Chicago, 1978
9. *Archief van de Familie Heereman van Zuydtwijck, 1360-1880*, (*Archives of the Family of Heereman van Zuydtwijck, 1360-1880*) Vol. I, Rijksarchief in Zuid-Holland, The Hague, 1987
10. Banning, J.A.W., *Genealogie van het Geslacht Banning*, (*Genealogy of the Banning Family)* Ferd. Banning & Zonen, Groenlo, 1934
11. Banning, Jeremiah, *Log and Will of Jeremiah Banning*, W.F. Austin, New York, 1932
12. Banning, J.A., *Stamboom van Maurits Arnoldus Banning, Predikant te Oudemirdum*, (*Genealogy of Maurits Arnoldus Banning, Pastor of Oudemirdum*) Dedgem, 1984
13. Banning, Leroy, *The Banning Branches*, Heritage Books, Maryland, 1997
14. Banning, Pierson Worrall, *First Banning Genealogy*, Chicago, 1908
15. Banning, Pierson Worrall, *Europeesche Geschiedenis der Bannings (European History of the Bannings)*, De Geldersche Bode, (The Gelderland Courier) 8 July 1936
16. Barnhart, Robert K., *The Barnhart Dictionary of Etymology*, The H.W. Wilson Company, New York, 1988
17. *Biographical Encyclopedia of the World, 3rd Edition*, Institute for Research and Biography, Institute for Research in Biography, New York, 1946
18. *Biografisch Lexicon van de Geschiedenis van het Nederlandse Protestantisme*, (*Biographical Lexicon of the History of Dutch Protestantism*) J.H. Kok, Kampen, 1978
19. Blomefield, Francis, Rector of Ferfield, continued by Parkin, Rev. Charles, Rector of Oxburgh, *An Essay towards a Topographical*

History of the County of Norfolk, London, 1807
20. Bloys van Treslong Prins, P.C. Mr., Belonje, J. Mr.,
    *Genealogische en Heraldische Gedenkwaardigheden in en uit de
    Kerken van N. Holland, (Genealogical and Heraldic Memorabalia
    in and from the Churches of N. Holland),* Oosthoek, Utrecht, 1928
21. *Boerderij- en Veldnamenonderzoek van Hengelo,* (G), Staring
    Instituut, Doetinchem, Netherlands, 1988
22. Bont, B.J.M. de, *De Libryen der Voormalige Amsterdamse
    **Kloosters, Bijdragen voor de Geschiedenis van het Bisdom van
    Haarlem,** (The Libryen of the former Convents of Amsterdam,
    Contributions toward the History of the Bishpric of Haarlem),*
    Amsterdam, 1903
23. Bont, B.J.M. de, *Bijdragen voor de Geschiedenis van het Bisdom
    van Haarlem; 'De oude- of St. Nicolaaskerk te Amsterdam, hare
    kapellen, altaren en fundatiën,* volume XXIV, *(Contributions
    toward the History of the Bishopric of Haarlem, The old, or St.
    Nicholas Church of Amsterdam, its chapels, altars and
    foundations),* Amsterdam, 1899
24. Bont, B.J.M. de, *Bijdragen voor de Geschiedenis van het Bisdom
    van Haarlem; De O.L. Vrouwe- of Nieuwe Kerk te Amsterdam,
    (Contributions to the Bishopric of Haarlem; The Our Sacred Lady or
    New Church in Amsterdam),* Amsterdam, 1908
25. Bontemantel, H., *De Regeering van Amsterdam, soo in 't Civiel en
    Militaire (1653-1672), (The Government of Amsterdam, both Civil
    and Military)* Dr. G.W. Kernkamp, M. Nijhoff, the Hague, 1897
26. Brenner, *Merchants and Revolution,* charter of 31 Dec. 1600,
    Encyclopedia Britannicas, 1928
27. *Briefwisseling van Hugo Grotius, Rijks Geschiedkundige
    Publicatieen, (Correspondance of Hugo Grotius, National Historical
    Publications)* The Hague, 1928-2001, Volume XII
28. Brockpähler, Wilhelm, *Geschichte einer Münsterländischen
    Gemeinde, (Accounts of a Munsterland Township),* Emsdetten, 1970
29. Bruinier, J.W., *Die Germanische Heldensage, (Germanic Heathen
    Legends),* Teubner Verlag, Leipzig/Berlin: 1915
30. Burke, J. Esq., *Genealogical and Heraldic History of the Extract of
    Dormant Baronetcies of England, Ireland and Scotland,* John
    Russell Smith, London, 2nd edition, 1844
31. Burke, J., Esq., *An Essay on the Position of the British Gentry,*
    Burke's Peerage and Gentry, 4th Edition, Part 1, 1862
32. Burnet, G., *Burnet's History of his Own Times,* Thomas Ward and
    Joseph Downing, London, 1724-1734, vol. I.
33. Caluwé, The Reverend Robert de; *Guide Notes on Heraldry of the
    Sovereign Order of Saint John of Jerusalem Knights Hospitaller ,*
    OSJ, Belgium, 2000
34. Carasso-Kok, M. edited by, *Geschiedenis van Amsterdam tot 1578,*
    SUN, Amsterdam 2004
35. Chambers, R.W., Widsith, *A Study in Old English Heroic Legend,*
    Cambridge University Press, 1912,
36. Clark, Hugh, An Introduction to Heraldry, Beel & Dandy, London 1873

37. Cockayne, G.E,, *Complete Peerage*, St. Catherine's Press, London, 1910-1959, Vol II
38. Commire, A. (editor), Klezmer, D. (Ass. Editor), *Women in World History, A Biographical Encyclopedia*, Vol. 2, Yorkin Publications, Detroit, 1999
39. *De Nederlandse Leeuw, (The Dutch Lion)*, Koninklijk Nederlandsch Genootschap voor Geslacht- en Wapenkunde, The Hague, No. 1, LIIIe, Jan. 1935
40. Dekker, *Oude Boerderijen en Buitenverblijven langs de Zijper Grotesloot, (Old Farms and Country Estates along the Zijper Grotesloot)* Parts I, II and IIa, Uitgeverij Pirola, Schoorl, 1988
41. *Deutsches Biographisches Jahrbuch, (German Biographical Yearbook)* Deutsches Verlagsanstalt, Stuttgart, 1932
42. Dillen, Dr. J.G. van, *Bronnen tot de Geschiedenis van het Bedrijfsleven en het Gildewezen van Amsterdam, (Sources to the History of Commerce and the Guilds of Amsterdam)* Part I, 1512-1611, Martinus Nijhoff, The Hague, 1929
43. Dillen, Dr. J.G. van, *Bronnen tot de Geschiedenis van het Bedrijfsleven en het Gildewezen van Amsterdam, (Sources to the History of Commerce and the Guilds of Amsterdam)* Part II, 1612-1632, Martinus Nijhoff, The Hague, 1933
44. Doorninck, Mr. J.I. van, *Catalogus der archieven van het Groote- en Voorster Gasthuis te Deventer, (Catalogue of Archives of the Groote and Voorster Hospice of Deventer)* Deventer, 1879
45. Doorninck, Mr. J.I. van, Acquoy, J. *Cameraars-rekeningen van Deventer 1348- 1360, (The Cameraar's Accounts of Deventer1348-1360)* Deventer, 1885
46. Dudok van Heel, S.C.A., Amstelodamum, *Cornelis Benningh en het Benninghweer, (Cornelis Benningh and the Benninghweer)*, Gemeente Amsterdam, 1996
47. Eberlein, Harold Donaldson, and Hubbard, Cortlandt V.D., *Historic Houses and Buildings of Delaware*, Dover, Delaware, Public Archives Commission 1963.
48. Ekwall, Eilert, *English Place-names in – ing*, Lund, Gleerop, 1962
49. Elgenstierna, Gustaf, *Den introducerade svenska adelns Ättartavlor, med tillägg och rättelser, (Introduction to the Genealogy of Swedish Nobility, with supplements and amendments)* Norstedt, 1925-1936
50. Elhorst, K., *Floris V*, J.H. Kok, Kampen, 1982
51. Elias, J.E. Dr., *Geschiedenis van het Amsterdamse Regenten-patriciaat, (History of the Amsterdam Regent's Patriciate)* Martinus Nijhoff, The Hague, 1923
52. Elias, J.E. Dr., *De Vroedschap van Amsterdam 1578-1795, (The Council of Amsterdam 1578-1795)* Part I, Vincent Loosjes, Haarlem, 1903
53. Emmison, F.G., *Elizabethan Life: Morals & The Church Courts*, Essex County Council, Chelmsford, 1973
54. Emmison, F.G., *Elizabethan Life: Wills of Essex Gentry & Merchants*, Essex County Council, Chelmsford, 1978
55. Emmison, F.G., *Elizabethan Life: Wills of Essex Gentry & Yeoman*,

Essex County Council, Chelmsford, 1980

56. Ernout, A., Meillet, A., *Dictionnaire Etymologique de la Langue Latine, (Etymological Dictionary of the Latin Language)* 4th Edition, Editions Klincksieck, Paris, 1979

57. Fortuné Koller, *Annuaire des Familles Patriciennes de Belgique,* volumes 1-6, Edelweiss, Belgium, 1940-1945

58. Fox-Davies, A.C., *Complete Guide to Heraldry,* T.C. & E.C. Jack, London/Edinburgh, 1909

59. Fraser, Antonia, *King Charles II,* Wiedenfeld and Nicolson, London, 1979

60. Friedlaender, Dr. Ernst, *Ostfriesisches Urkundebuch,* Vol.. II, 1471-1500 AD, *(East Frisian Book of Charters)* W. Haynel, Emden, 1881

61. Friedlaender, Dr. Ernst, *Ostfriesisches Urkundenbuch, (East Frisian Book of Charters)* Vol. I, 787-1470 AD, W. Haynel, Emden, 1878

62. *Frommannsche Buchhandlung,(Frommanic Guidebook)* Walter Biedermann, Jena, Germany, 1935

63. Gallée, Prof. Dr. J.H., Kern, Prof. Dr. H., Muller, Dr. J.W., Rogge, Prof. Dr. H.C., *Nomina Geographica Neerlandica (Geschiedkundig Onderzoek der Nederlandsche Aardrijkskundige Namen),(Historical Study of Dutch Geographical Names)* Part IV, E.J. Brill,

64. *Geïllustreerd Volksblad voor Nederland, (Illustrated Newspaper for the Netherlands)* 8 Dec. 1898

65. *Genealogical and Biographical Records of the Banning and Allied Families,* The American Historical Society, reprinted by the Higginson Book Company, Salem, 1924

66. *Gens Nostra, (OurPeople)* Nederlandse Genealogische Vereniging, Amsterdam, 1976,1991, 1998

67. Goudhoeven, *Chronycke, (Chronicles),* Netherlands 1636

68. Gouw, J. ter, *Geschiedenis van Amsterdam, (History of Amsterdam)* Scheltema & Holkema, Amstedam, 1880-1886

69. Groesbeek, J.W., Amstelveen; *Acht Eeuwen Geschiedenis, (Amstelveen; Eight Centuries of History),* De Lange, Amsterdam, 1966

70. Groesbeek, Mr. J.W., *Middeleeuwse Kastelen van Noord-Holland, (Medieval Castles of North-Holland)* ,Elmar, Rijswijk, 1981

71. Gutenbrunner, Siegfried, *Die Herkunft der Baininge, Beiträge zur Geschichte der Deutschen Sprache und Literatur,* Max Niemeyer Verlag, Halle (Saale) 1936, vol. 60

72. Halbertsma, H. *Frieslands Oudheid,* Matrijs, Utrecht, 2000

73. Hamilton, Elizabeth, *The Illustrious Lady,* Hamish Hamilton Ltd., Gr. Britain, 1980

74. Hapke, R., *Niederlandische Akten und Urkunden zur Geschichte der Hanse und zur Deutsche Seegeschichte, (Dutch Deeds and Charters concerning the Hansa Accounts and the German Sea Accounts)* volume III, Lubeck, 1923

75. Hasseloo-Oldenmenger, H.A. te, *Kwartierstaat Johanna Willemina Bannink, (Genealogy of Johanna Willemina Bannink),* OTGB, Gelderland, 1998

76. Hekket, B.J., *Oost-Nederlandse Familienamen (hun ontstaan en*

betekenis) (Eastern Dutch Family Names (their origins and meaning)), Twentse Uitgeverij W.G. Witkam, Enschede, 1975

77. *Historische Atlas Gelderland,* Uitgeverij Robas, Weesp, 1989
78. *Hofjes in Nederland, (Residential Courtyards in the Netherlands),* J.H. Gottmer, Haarlem, 1977
79. Hofland, P., *Delftsche Courant, (Delft News),* 1 Feb. 2003
80. Hoops, J., *Reallexikon der Germanische Altertumskunde, (Enyclopaedia of Germanic Antiquity),* Trübner, Strassburg, 1911
81. Hueck, Walter v., Adelslexikon, *Genealogisches Handbuch des Adels, (Genealogical Guide to the Nobility),* C.A. Starke Verlag, Limburg a.d.Lahn, Görlitz, 1972
82. Jonker, M., Noordegraaf, L., Wagenaar, M., (editors) *Van Stadskern tot Stadsgewest, Stedebouwkundige Geschiedenis van Amsterdam, (From City Core to Metropolis),* Verloren, Amsterdam, 1984
83. *Katholieke Illustratie, (Catholic* Illustration), (periodical) 3 Nov. 1920
84. Kok, Jacobus, *Vaderlandsch Woordenboek, (National Dictionary),* part VI, Johannes Allart, Amsterdam, 1787
85. Koopmans, S., *Het Notariaat in Friesland vóór 1811, (The Notaryship in Friesland before 1811),* Leeuwarden 1883
86. Laan, K. ter, *Van Goor's Aardrijkskundig Woordenboek van Nederland, (Van Goor's Geogrphical Dictionary of the Netherlands),* VN Goor Zonen, Den Haag, Brussels, Leiden, 1899
87. Leeuwen, J. van, Matricula Notarium, *Naamlijst van Notarissen in* **Friesland, 1606-1850; (Matricula Notarium, List of Names of** *Notaries in Friesland, 1606-1850)*
88. Lobies, Jean-Pierre, *Index Bio-Bibliographicus Notorum Hominum, (Index of Bio-Bibliography Notorum Hominum)* Biblio Verlag, Osnabrück, 1978
89. Langland, W., *Piers Plowman,* Athlone, London, 1960
90. Laveleye, Emile de, Cliffe Leslie, T.E., Marriott, G.R.L., *Primitive Property,* 1878
91 Looijenga, J.H., *Runes around the North Sea and on the Continent AD 150-700, Texts and Contexts,* SSG Uitgerverij Groningen, 1997
92. MacNeil, Barbara, *Abridged Biography and Genealogy Master Index,* Gale Research, New York, 2nd Edition, 1995
93. Malone, Kemp, *Anglistica,* Rosenkilde and Bagger, Copenhagen, 1962
94. Meijer, T. and M., *Athenaeum,* Polak and van Gennip, Amsterdam, 1999
95. Melker, B.R. de, *Metamorphose van Stad en Devotie, (Metamorphasis of City and Worship)*Thesis presented at the University of Amsterdam, Amsterdam, 2002
96. Meyer-Lübke, W., *Romanisches Etymologisches Wörtenbuch, (Roma Etymoligical Dictionary),* Carl Winters Universitätsbuchhandlung, Heidelberg, 1935
97. *Meyers Grosses Konversations-Lexikon, (Meyer's Large Conversational Lexicon),* Vol. III, Bibliographisches

Institut, Leipzig and Vienna, 1904 Encyclopedia of the Spoken Word

98. Middelkoop, Norbert (editor) *Kopstukken – Amsterdammers Geportreteerd, (Figureheads – Portraits of Amsterdam Citizens),*Uitgeverij THOTH, Amsterdam 2002

99. Molhuysen, Dr. P.C., Blok, Prof. Dr. P.J., *Nieuw Nederlandsch Biografisch Woordenboek, (New Dutch Biographical Dictionary),* Part II, A.W. Sijthoff's Uitgevers-Maatschappij, Leiden, 1912

100. Molhuysen, Dr. P.C., *Briefwisseling van Hugo Grotius, (Corrspondance of Hugo Grotius),* Martinus Nijhoff, The Hague, 1936

101. Much, Dr. Rudolf, *Deutsche Stammeskunde, (Germany Study of Tribes)* G.J. Güschen'sche Berlagshandlung, Leipzig, 1900

102. Muller, Dr. Mr. S., and Bouman, Dr. A.C., *Oorkondeboek van het Sticht Utrecht (tot 1301),(Book of Charters of the Bishopric of Utrecht (until 1301)),* Part I, A. Oosthoek, Utrecht 1920

103. *Nieuw Nederlands Biografisch Woordenboek,* N. Israel, Amsterdam, 1974

104. *Nieuwe Drentse Volksalmanak, (New People's Almanac of Drente)* 1977

105. *Nomina Geographica Neerlandica, (Geographical Names of the Netherlands),* Koninklijke Nederlandse Aardrijkskundige Genootschap, E.J. Brill, Leiden, 1899, volume V

106. Noordbeek, B. *Aus der Genealogie des Nordbecks (Jahrbuch des Heimatvereins der Grafschaft Bentheim '71) (From the Genealogy of the Nordbecks (Yearbook of Lineage of the County of Bentheim '71)),* Verlag Heimatverein der Grafschaft Bentheim, Bentheim, 1951

107. Noort, Olivier van, *Om de Wereld, 1601-1602, (Around the World),* translation by Roeper, Vibeke and Wildeman, Diederik, SUN, Nijmegen, 1999

108. Posthumus, Mr. Dr. N.W, *De Nationale Organisatie der Lakenkopers tijdens de Republiek, (The National Organisation of Cloth Merchants in the time of the Republic)*Utrecht, Kemink & Soon, 1927

109. Pott, M., *Aardrijkskundig Woordenboek van Nederland, (Geographical Dictionary of the Netherlands),* J.B. Wolters, Groningen, 1913

110. *Prisma Woordenboek, (Prisma Dictionary),* Uitgeverij het Spectrum B.V., Utrecht, 1995

111. Ptolemeus, C., *Geographia,* 150 AD; abridged, from Edward Luther Stevenson , New York Public Library, New York, 1932

112. *Revue der Sporten, (Sports Review),*periodical, Netherlands, November 1919

113. Rietstap, J.B., *Armoiries des Familles, (Family Coats of Arms),* Institutut Héraldique Universel, Paris, 1903

114. Rietstap, J.B., *Armoires des Familles, (Family Coats of Arms),* Institutut Héraldique Universel, Paris, 1873

115. Rietstap, J.B., *Wapenboek van den Nederlandse Adel,(Book of Coats of Arms of the Dutch Nobility)* J.B. Wolters, Groningen, 1883- 1887

116. Ripley, A., A Love Divine, Warner Vision Books, New York, 1996
117. Rivet A.L.F., Smith, C., The Place-Names of Roman Britain, B.T. Batsford Ltd., London, 1979
118. Roever, Mr. N. de, and Bredius, A., *Oud-Holland, Nieuwe Bijdragen v.d. Geschiedenis der Nederlandse Kunst, Letterkunde, Nijverheid, enz., (The Early Netherlands, New Contributions to the History of Dutch Art, Literature and Industry, etc.)*, Uitgevers Gebroeders Binger, Amsterdam, 1887
119. Romein, T.A.,*Naamlijst der predikanten in de Hervormde Gemeenten van Friesland, sedert de Hervorming (List of names of pastors in the Dutch Reformed townships of Friesland, since the Reformation)*,1886
120. Samson, R., *Claiming Finnish Origins for Picts, review of P. Dunbavin's Picts and Ancient Britons in British Archeaology*, April 1999, issue no. 43
121. Scheltema, Dr. P., *Aemstel's Oudheid, (Amstel's Antiquity)*, Part I, J.H. Scheltema, Amsterdam, 1855
122. Schilder, Marian, *Amsterdamse Kloosters in de Middeleeuwen,(Amsterdam Convents in the Middle Ages)*, Vossiuspers, Amsterdam, 1997
123. Schiltmeijer, J.R., *Amsterdam in 17ᵉ Eeuwse Prent*, ((A 17th Century Image of Amsterdam), Minerva Boekuitgaven, Zandvoort aan Zee, 1966
124. Schütte, Gudmund, Gotthiod und Utgard, *Altgermanische Sagengeographie, in neuer Auffassung (Gotthiod and Utgard, Geography of Old Germanic Legend, in new Perspective)*; republished under auspices of the Carlsbergfonds; Copenhagen: Aschehoug dansk forlag, G. M. Steffensen & Co. Jena:1935
125. Schütte, Gudmund, *Die Umstrittenen Baininge, Beiträge zur Geschichte der Deutschen Sprache und Literatur*, Max Niemeyer Verlag, Halle (Saale) 1936, vol. 62
126. *Schutters in Holland, (The Militia in Holland)*, Uitgeverij Waanders, Zwolle, 1988
127. Slicher van Bath, Dr. B.H., *Mensch en Land in de Middeleeuwen, (People and Property in the Middle Ages)*, Assen-Utrecht, Netherlands, Van Gorcum & Comp. N.V., 1944
128. Slive, Seymour, Hoetink, H.R., *Jacob van Ruisdael*, Meulenhoff/Landshoff,Amsterdam 1981
129. Stearne, John, *A Confirmation and Discovery of Witchcraft*, London, 1648 (Exeter 1973)
130. Stein, Walther, *Hansisches Urkundenbuch, 1471-1485, (Hanseatic Book of Charters, 1471-1485)* Leipzig, Germany, Duncker & Humblot, 1907
131. Stein, Walther, *Hansisches Urkundenbuch, 1451-1463, (Hanseatic Book of Charters, 1451-1463)*, Leipzig, Germany, Duncker & Humblot, 1899
132. Sterck, J.F.M. Dr., *Van Kloosterkerk tot Athenaeum; uit de geschiedenis der S. Agneskapel te Amsterdam, (From convent church to Athaneaeum; from the history of the St. Agnes Chapel of*

Amsterdam), Amsterdam, volume XL, 1921

133. Stoke, W. (translated by) ; *Medieval Sourcebook: The Destruction of da Derga's Hostel,* ca. 1100, The Harvard Classics, New York, P.F. Collier & Son Company, 1909-14

134. Tucker, Jane Foster, *Jeremiah Banning Mariner and Patriot,* Oxford Bicentennial Commission, Printed by Economy Printing Company, Easton, 1977

135. Veen, P.A.F., *Etymologsich Woordenboek, (Etymological Dictionary)* Van Dale Lexicografie, Utrecht/Antwerp, 1993

136. Versfelt, H.J., *De Hottinger Atlas van Noord- en Oost-Nederland (1773-1794), (The Hottinger Atlas of the North and East Netherlands (1773-1794)),* Heveskes, Groningen, 2003

137. Vondel, J., *De Werken van J. van den Vondel, (The Works of J. van den Vondel),* Mr. J. van Lennep, revised and edited by J.H.W. Unger, Leiden, A.W. Sijthoff, Part 1657-1660

138. Waller, F.G., *Biografisch Woordenboek van Noord Nederlandse Graveurs,(Biographical Dictionary of Northern Dutch Engravers)* Israel, Amsterdam, 1974

139. Weale, M. E., Weiss, D. A. Jager, R.F. , Bradman, N., Thomas, M.G., *Y chromosome evidence for Anglo-Saxon mass migration, Molecular Biology & Evolution* ,Oxford University Press, July 2002

140. *Westfälisches Urkundenbuch, die Urkunden des Bisthums Munster 1201-1300, (Book of Charter of Westphalia, the Charters of the Bishopric of Munster1201-1300),* Vol. III, Reprint of the edition of Munster 1871, H. Th. Wenner, Osnabruck, 1973Munster,

141. Wijnbeek, D., *De Nachtwacht, de Historie van een Meesterwerk, (The Nightwatch, History of a Masterwork),* N.V. Uitgeverij Holdert & Co., Amsterdam, 1944

142. *Winkler Prins Encyclopedia,* Elsevier, Amsterdam, Brussels, 1948

143. Wispelwey, Berend, *Biographical Index of the Benelux Countries,* Vol. 1, K.G. Sauer, Munich, 2003

144. *Winkler Prins, Elsevier,* Amsterdam, Brussels, 6th edition, 1948

145. Wordsworth, Charles, *Marlborough Poll Tax 1379,* WNQ, vol. 6, 1910

146. *Zierikszeesche Nieuwsbode (Zierkzee Newsbulletin),* 18 March 1938

147. *Zierikszeesche Nieuwsbode (Zierkzee Newsbulletin),* 21 May 1965

WEBSITE BIBLIOGRAPHY

1. Access to Archives; http://www.a2a.org.uk/, accessed Feb. 2003 through July 2004
2. Aldermen of the City of London; http://genealogy.patp.us/aldermen_1500.shm;accessed Mar. 2004
3. Ames Public Library; www.amespubliclibrary.org; accessed July 2004
4. Anglo-Saxon Origins, The Reality of Myth, Malcom Todd; www.intellectbooks.com/nation/html/anglos.htm; accessed Feb. 2004
5. Andreas Olai Floraeus & Margareta Gudmundsdotter; http://home.swipnet.se/~w-87123/Andreas%20Olai%20Floraeus%20&%20Margareta%20Gudmundsdotter.htm; accessed March 2004
6. archaeologie-online.de/magazin/fundpunkt/2004/04/liebersee_5.php; accessed June 2004
7. Ättlingar efter Ingelbertus Olai Helsingus född omkr. 1520 i Rogsta by i Tuna sn., Hälsingland; http://members.tripod.com/~masgen/ingelber.htm; accessed July 2004
8. Banna; Hadrian's Wall Fort & Settlement; http://www.archaeologie-online.de/magazin/fundpunkt/2004/04/liebersee_5.php; accessed July 2004
9. Banna: Hadrian's Wall Fort and Settlement: http://www.roman-britain.org/places/banna.htm; accessed Feb. 2004
10. Bannaventa, Romano-British Fortified Town; http://www.roman-britain.org/places/bannaventa.htm; accessed Feb. 2004
11. Banning Line, Mary Banning Friedlander; http://freepages.genealogy.rootsweb.com/~mbfriedlander/banning.html, accessed Feb. 2004
12. BBC, Making History, the Frisians;[1] http://www.bbc.co.uk/education/beyond/factsheets/makhist/makhist4_prog4b.shtml; accessed June 2004
13. Business of Slavery; http://1911encyclopedia.org/A/index.htm, accessed July 2004
14. Business of Slavery; http://www.danbyrnes.com.au/business/business9.html; accessed July 2004
15. Celtic Coin Index; http://www.writer2001.com/cciwriter2001/coinrecords/71/710105.htm; accessed Feb. 2004
16. Collection of Articles Written during the lifetime of Irvin J. Gill, http://www.irvinggill.com/biblio.html; accessed Feb. 2003
17. Darr Mine & Banning No. 3 Mine; http://patheoldminer.rootsweb.com/darr.html, accessed May 2004
18. Database der Nederlandse Sontregisters, National Archives, the Hague, http://www.nationaalarchief.nl/sont, accessed Feb. 2004
19. Descendants of Robert Banning of Burbage, Wiltshire; http://www.mandellstreit.com/genealogy/families/bannings/ May 2004
20. Divine Comedy, Inferno, Canto 29:125; www.worldwideschool.org/library/books/lit/poetry/TheDivineComedy1-Inferno/chap29.html; accessed Feb. 2004

21. Domesday Book, 1066; http://www.domesdaybook.co.uk/norfolk.html; accessed July 2004
22. Dornum und seine Burgen; http://www.nordwestreisemagazin.de/dornum/Burgen1.htm; accessed May 2004
23. Early Villages of the Marsh, http://www.saltfleetby.co.uk/east_lindsey_2.htm, accessed Feb. 2004
24. 1911 Edition Encyclopedia, Clevedon: http://1911encyclopedia.org/A/index.htm; accessed Feb. 2003
25. 1911 Edition Encyclopedia; http://85.1911encyclopedia.org/F/FR/FRISIANS.htm; accessed July 2004
26. English Business of Slavery, Dan Byrnes, website book, chapters 8 & 9; http://www.danbyrnes.com.au/business/, accessed Feb. 2004
27. Etymology of British Place-Names; http://www.pbenyon.plus.com/Misc/Etymology.html accessed Feb. 2004
28. Farmer, Sue: Banning State Park offers four season venue for enjoying Minnesota's great outdoors, wildlife; http://www.lpleader.com/nature/banning.html; accessed June 2004
29. Fryslâns ferline ; http://www.fryskeside.nl/mainframe_bestanden/fryslan_best/frl_main8.htm; accessed July 2004
30. Gegevens rond eigenaars/bewoners vd kavels in de Schermeer; http://de-wit.net/bronnen/kavel.txt, accessed Mar. 2003
31. Genealogical page of D.J. Oldenboom, http://home.planet.nl/~djo/home.htm, accessed March 2004
32. Genealogy of Plunkett, Balis, http://freepages.genealogy.rootsweb.com/~nplunkett/Balis/balis8.html; accessed Feb. 2004
33. Gravestones on Lundy, http://www.lundyisleofavalon.co.uk/lioa/ch11.htm, accessed Feb. 2004
34. Great Villiers; http://www.kirkbymoorside.com/LocalHistory/Kirkby/Buckingham_House/BuckinghamHouse.htm; accessed Nov. 2003
35. Hallands Historia och Beskrivning; http://www.glimten.net/hok/Knered.HTM, accessed June 2004
36. Historic Emmen: http://www.historisch-emmen.nl/f_100_historie/f_100.htm, accessed March 2004
37. History of the Maltese Cross as used by the Order of St. John of Jerusalem, Dr. Michael Foster, http://www2.prestel.co.uk/church/oosj/cross.htm; accessed Apr. 2003
38. History of Shelby County; http://ecolitgy.com/it/LostInShelby.html; accessed May 2004
39. History of Tudhoe Village, Jeremy Hutson,Dissent an Rebellion in County Durham; http://www.dur.ac.uk/j.m.hutson/tudhoe/docs.html, and http://www.dur.ac.uk/j.m.hutson/tudhoe/index.html#pre1570 accessed Feb. 2004
40. History of a Tudhoe Village; http://www.dur.ac.uk/j.m.hutson/tudhoe/; accessed

41. History: all about Bann; http://www.bann2000.de/e1-history.html, accessed Feb. 2004
42. History; Bath Baroque; http://www.bathbaroque.com/history.htm, accessed Feb. 2004
43. Holy Grail; www.newagedarkage.freeserve.co.uk/grail.htm - accessed Dec. 2002
44. Hundred of Kynworthstone; http://freepages.genealogy.rootsweb.com/~dutillieul/ZWiltsMuster/Places/Cl enche.html; accessed May 2004
45. intellectbooks.com/nation/html/anglos.htm; accessed Feb. 2004
46. International Law Forum, www.2747.com
47. Jackson-Chambers Genealogy, http://freepages.genealogy.rootsweb.com/~mgjga/Jackson/Wills/edwbanning will.html, accessed Feb. 2004
48. Jewish Virtual Library, The Cave of Machpelah, Tomb of the Patriarchs, http://www.us-israel.org/jsource/Judaism/machpelah.html, accessed Feb. 2004
49. Katholische kirche Zuckau, Kreis Karthaus, Provinz Westpreussen; http://pom-wpru.kerntopf.com/kathkirche/zuckau.htm, accessed June 2004
50. Kings and Queens of Scotland; Celtic and Celtic-Norman Kings,http://www.legenca.freeserve.co.uk/monarchs/kings2.html, accessed Feb. 2004
51. Krummhörn, Upleward; http://www.upleward.de/; accessed May 2004
52. Letters and Papers of Edward de Vere, Oxford Tin letter of 15 June 1599; http://ist-socrates.berkeley.edu/~ahnelson/TINLETTS/990600A.html; accessed July 2004
53. London Subsidy Rolls; http://ist-socrates.berkeley.edu/~ahnelson/SUBSIDY/369b.html; accessed July 2004
54. Lundy Isle of Avalanon; http://www.lundyisleofavalon.co.uk/lioa/ch11.htm, accessed Feb. 2004
55. Marikavel.net/lieux-accueil.htm, accessed Feb. 2004
56. Merchants and Bankers, 1550-1575, http://www.danbyrnes.com.au/merchants/merchants5.htm, accessed Febr. 2004
57. Minderbroeders- of Grauwmonnikenklooster; http://www.hhit.hsholland.nl/sammeta/pg181.htm
58. Monumenten en Archaeologie in Amsterdam: http://www.bma.amsterdam.nl/adam/nl/monum.html
59. Monumenten en Archeologie in Amsterdam; http://www.bmz.amsterdam.nl/adam/nl/huizen/h364.html, accessed Feb. 2004
60. Nederlandse Molendatabase, http://www.hippowebdesign.com/molens/molen.php?nummer=201, accessed March 2004
61. Norfolk Banningham, Frances Whites History; Obituaries of Cass County Residents; http://www.rootsweb.com/~necass/obits7.htm; accessed July 2004
62. Old Bailey Proceedings Online; www.oldbaileyonline.org;accessed 7 July 2004; 03 June 1767; trial of Elizabeth Banning, ref: T17670603-45

62. Old Bailey Proceedings Online; www.oldbaileyonline.org;accessed 7 July 2004; 12 Jan. 1774, trial of James Banning, ref:: T17740112-17

63. Old Bailey Proceedings Online; ; www.oldbaileyonline.org; accessed 7 July 2004; 14 Sept. 1785; Punishment summary from Old Bailey Proceedings; Richard Clark, Session VII, Parts I-XII, 943-1181; ref. s17850914-1

64. Parenteel van Benninck, Jan; http://home.planet.nl/~djo/frben3.htm, accessed Aug. 2003

65. Popular biographies of Connecticut http://www.usgennet.org/usa/ct/county/fairfield/ctbbios.html accessed May 2004

66. Publick Levy and Payments of 1678, http://www.combs-families.org/combs/records/md/1678.htm; accessed July 2004

67. Rectors at Easton Gray; Duncan and Mandy Ball; http://www.oodwooc.co.uk/ph_egrey_vics.htm, accessed June 2004

68. Roman Map of Britain; Bannatia Balnageith, Moray, http://www.romanmap.com/htm/nomina/Bannatia.htm; accessed Feb. 2004

69. Roman Map of Britain, Ptolemy's Geography,II 3.8-9; http://www.romanmap.com/htm/ptolemy/pt3_8-9.htm, accessed Feb. 2004

70 . Sacred Text Archive; III. Ibid., fol. 58, col. 1; http://www.sacred- texts.com/jud/hl/hl06.htm; accessed Mar. 2004

71. Scuren ende Diepen, BartIbelings, http://www.waterstaatsgeschiedenis.nl/ tijdschrift/tvw2001mei1/ Ibelings.htm; accessed Mar. 2003

72. Settlement: http://www.roman-britain.org/places/banna.htm; accessed Feb. 2004

73. sunsite.berkeley.edu/OMACL/Graal, accessed Feb. 2004

74. Swinburne, A.C., King Ban: A Fragment; www. camelot.celtic-twilight.com/poetry/swinburne12.htm, accessed Feb. 2004

75. Geminiano, Folgore da San, translated by Rossetti, D.G.; Early Italian Poets, Canto: www.worldwideschool.org/library/books/lit/poetry/TheDivine Comedy1-Inferno/chap29.html; accessed Feb. 2004

76. Unser Dorf Neukamperfehn; http://www.neukamperfehn.de/Schone_Ecken/_schone_ecken.html; accessed May 2004

77. Vrienden van de Amsterdamse Binnenstad; http://www.amsterdamsebinnenstad.nl/index.html; accessed July 2004

78. http://www.verkeersveiligouderkerk.nl/kp7.htm

79. Watching Brief, Great Hatfield; www.hullcc.gov.uk/archaeology/watch06.htm; accessed Feb. 2004

80. Widsith, a verse translation by Douglas B. Killings; http://www.georgetown.edu/faculty/ballc/oe/widsith-trans.html;

accessed July 2004

81. Wikipedia; Saxons: http://en.wikipedia.org/wiki/Saxons, accessed Feb. 2004

82. Will of Edward Banning Sr.; http://freepages.genealogy.rootsweb.com/~mgjga/Jackson/Wills/edwbanningwill.html; accessed Jan. 2004

83. Women's History in the Collections; New York State Museum; www.nysm.nysed.gov/research_collections/collections/history/womenshistory/banning.html accessed May 2004

84. Wirdum 2000; http://www.ostfriesischelandschaft.de/af/wirdum00.htm; accessed May 2004

85. Wie "Schutzengel" zu Kirchenräubern wurden; http://www.webarchiv-server.de/pin/archiv01/1001ob13.htm; accessed June 2004

INDEX

410

412

413

www.ingramcontent.com/pod-product-compliance
Lightning Source LLC
Chambersburg PA
CBHW071828270326
41929CB00013B/1929